ੴ ਸਤਿਗੁਰ ਪ੍ਰਸਾਦਿ ॥

Warriors of the Spirit

Sikhism and the Khalsa Legacy

Dr. Satpreet Singh

Warriors of the Spirit: Sikhism and the Khalsa Legacy

LCCN: 2024934936

ISBN   978-1-963353-02-0 (Print)

ISBN   978-1-963353-05-1 (E-book)

Printed in the USA by Sikh Reference Library USA

www.sikhreferencelibraryusa.org

DEDICATION

This book is dedicated to Sahib Sri Guru Nanak Sahib Ji, the Akal (God) itself, The timeless and boundless source of strength and wisdom. With His divine guidance and grace, all endeavors became possible. In profound reverence and gratitude, this endeavor is humbly offered, acknowledging your perpetual presence in every page, every word, and every soul inspired by the Khalsa spirit.

CONTENTS

FOREWORD

In the vast tapestry of human history, there emerge moments and movements that stand as beacons of light, guiding generations toward ideals of justice, equality, and compassion. Sikhism, with its rich tradition and profound teachings, is undeniably one such radiant thread in the fabric of civilization. Its inception, evolution, and enduring legacy echo with the resonance of spiritual fortitude and unwavering commitment to righteousness.

In "Warriors of the Spirit: Sikhism and the Khalsa Legacy," Dr. Satpreet Singh embarks on a journey through time, unraveling the intricate layers of Sikh philosophy, history, and the profound influence of the Khalsa—the community of the pure. Through meticulous research and profound insight, Dr. Satpreet Singh illuminates the transformative power of Sikhism and its enduring relevance in the modern world.

From the origins of Sikhism and the visionary teachings of its founding Gurus to the emergence of the Khalsa as a warrior community embodying timeless value, this book is a testament to the resilience and spiritual depth of the Sikh faith. Through the exploration of historical contexts, key teachings, and the saintly spirit of the Khalsa, Dr. Satpreet Singh invites us to reflect on the universal message of Sikhism—a message that transcends the boundaries of time, culture, and creed. The Khalsa Code, enshrined in the five Ks and steeped in the ethos of courage, discipline, and compassion, serves as a guiding light for seekers of truth and justice.

As we journey through the pages of this book, we encounter not only the luminous figures of Sikh history—the Gurus, saints, and warriors—but also the timeless principles they embodied. Through acts of valor, sacrifice, and unwavering devotion, the Khalsa exemplifies the union of spiritual strength and warriorhood—a union that continues to inspire generations around the globe.

In today's complex and tumultuous world, the teachings of Sikhism offer a beacon of hope—a reminder of our shared humanity and the transformative power of love, service, and unity. "Warriors of the Spirit" stands as a testament to the enduring legacy of Sikhism and the indomitable spirit of the Khalsa—a legacy that continues to resonate across the ages, inspiring all who seek truth, justice, and spiritual enlightenment.

May this profound exploration of Sikhism and the Khalsa legacy ignite the flames of understanding, compassion, and unity in the hearts of readers around the world, guiding us toward a brighter, more harmonious future for all.

Dr. Satpreet Singh's dedication to illuminating Sikhism's timeless wisdom is a gift to humanity—a reminder of our shared journey toward truth, justice, and spiritual fulfillment.

Rupinder Kaur, MBA
President
Sikh Reference Library USA

PREFACE

As I embark on the journey of writing "Warriors of the Spirit: Sikhism and the Khalsa Legacy," I am filled with a profound sense of reverence and responsibility. Sikhism, with its rich tapestry of history, philosophy, and tradition, is a subject of immense depth and complexity—one that deserves careful exploration and thoughtful reflection.

Growing up in a Sikh household, I was immersed in the teachings and stories of the Gurus from a young age. Yet, it was only as I delved deeper into the Granths and historical texts, with the help of Akal, that I respected Sikhism's profound relevance in today's world. The timeless principles of equality, justice, and compassion espoused by the Gurus resonate as strongly now as they did centuries ago.

In this book, I seek to offer readers a comprehensive understanding of Sikhism and the Khalsa legacy—a legacy that continues to inspire millions around the world. From the origins of Sikhism in the visionary teachings of Sri Guru Nanak Sahib Ji to the emergence of the Khalsa as a warrior community dedicated to righteousness, each chapter is a journey through the annals of history and spirituality.

Through meticulous research and heartfelt devotion, I have endeavored to capture the essence of Sikhism—the ethos of selfless service, spiritual enlightenment, and unwavering commitment to truth. Drawing upon a wealth of sources—from historical texts and Granths to personal anecdotes and reflections—I invite readers to embark on a voyage of discovery, guided by the luminous figures of Sikh history and the timeless principles they embodied.

In exploring the Khalsa Code, enshrined in the five Ks and imbued with the spirit of courage, discipline, and compassion, we encounter not only the warrior ethos of the Khalsa but also the saintly virtues that lie at its heart. Through acts of valor, sacrifice, and unwavering devotion, the Khalsa exemplifies the union of spiritual strength and worldly duty—a union that continues to inspire seekers of truth and justice.

As we navigate the complexities of the modern world, the teachings of Sikhism offer a beacon of hope—a reminder of our shared humanity and the transformative power of love, service, and unity. In these pages, I hope readers will find not only knowledge and insight but also inspiration and guidance for their own spiritual journey.

I am deeply grateful for the opportunity to share this exploration of Sikhism and the Khalsa legacy with readers around the world. May the wisdom and compassion of the Gurus continue to illuminate our path and guide us toward a future of peace, harmony, and understanding.

Dr. Satpreet Singh

INTRODUCTION

In the chronicles of human history, there is a unique story that is captivating and inspiring, which is Sikhism and the Khalsa legacy. Born out of the fertile soil of the Punjab region in the 15th century, Sikhism emerged as a beacon of hope and enlightenment in a world plagued by darkness and injustice. From its humble beginnings to its evolution into a global faith community, Sikhism has remained steadfast in its commitment to truth, equality, and compassion.

In "Warriors of the Spirit: Sikhism and the Khalsa Legacy," we embark on a journey through the corridors of time, tracing the origins, evolution, and enduring impact of Sikhism on the world stage. Drawing upon a wealth of historical texts, Granths, and personal narratives, we unravel the intricate tapestry of Sikh history, philosophy, and tradition—a tapestry woven with the threads of courage, sacrifice, and unwavering faith.

At the heart of Sikhism lies the revolutionary vision of Sri Guru Nanak Sahib Ji, whose divine call to "Naam Japna, Kirat Karni, Vand Chhakna" (meditate on the Divine Name, earn an honest living, and share with others) laid the foundation for a new spiritual ethos—one grounded in social justice, equality, and service to humanity. From the visionary teachings of Sri Guru Nanak to the warrior spirit of the Khalsa, Sikhism embodies a unique synthesis of the saint and the soldier, the mystic and the warrior.

As we delve deeper into the historical context surrounding Sikhism's birth, we encounter a world in flux—a world torn apart by religious strife, social hierarchies, and political upheaval. Against this backdrop of turmoil and uncertainty, the Sikh Gurus emerged as beacons of light, guiding their followers on a path of righteousness and self-realization.

Through the lives and teachings of the ten Gurus, we witness the evolution of Sikhism from a nascent religious movement to a vibrant faith community—a community bound together by a common creed, a shared heritage, and a profound sense of duty to humanity. From Sri Guru Nanak Sahib Ji's message of universal love and compassion to Sri Guru Gobind Singh Ji's revelation of the Khalsa, each Guru contributed to the rich tapestry of Sikh spirituality and identity.

At the heart of the Khalsa lies the Khalsa Code—a code of conduct that embodies the virtues of courage, discipline, and selflessness. Through the observance of the five Ks—Kesh, Kara, Kirpan, Kanga, and Kachera—the Khalsa seeks to cultivate a sense of spiritual strength and moral integrity while also serving as a beacon of hope and inspiration for humanity.

In the pages that follow, we will explore the enduring legacy of Sikhism and the Khalsa—a legacy that continues to inspire millions around the world to lead lives of courage, compassion, and service. From the saintly virtues of the Khalsa to the warrior spirit that animates its members, Sikhism offers a timeless message of hope, resilience, and unity in a world too often divided by hatred and ignorance.

As we embark on this journey of discovery and enlightenment, may we be guided by the wisdom and compassion of the Sikh Gurus, whose teachings continue to illuminate our path and inspire us to strive for a better world—a world where justice, equality, and peace reign supreme.

Dr. Satpreet Singh

SIKHISM AND THE KHALSA LEGACY

SIKHISM AND THE KHALSA LEGACY

Sikhism, founded in the 15th century by Guru Nanak, stands as a testament to spiritual depth and inclusivity. At its core is the belief in the oneness of God, encapsulated in the phrase "Ek Onkar," fostering a sense of unity among all of creation. Guru Nanak's teachings emphasized the practice of Naam Japna, meditating on God's name, as a means of spiritual awakening. These foundational principles laid the groundwork for the ethical framework of Sikhism, embodied in the "Three Pillars" — Naam Japna, Kirat Karni, and Vand Chhakna.

The journey of Sikhism continued through the ten successive Gurus, each contributing unique insights and expanding Sikh philosophy. The Sri Guru Granth Sahib, compiled from their hymns, became the eternal Guru, guiding Sikhs in their spiritual quests. The evolution of Sikhism incorporated values such as humility, devotion, and community service, reinforcing the interconnectedness of spiritual and ethical dimensions.

As we look into the past and the events that led to the formation of the Khalsa, we can see that the times in Panjab during the Mughal Empire were full of turmoil and chaos which paved the way for a significant chapter in Sikh history. The persecution faced by the Sikhs and their fundamental freedoms being challenged pushed them to seek a separate identity. Sri Guru Gobind Singh saw the need for a community

9

that could stand up for Sikh values, and thus the idea of Khalsa was born. In 1699, a landmark moment occurred when Sri Guru Gobind Singh Amritdhari the first group into the Khalsa, marking the birth of a unique community that was committed to justice, fearlessness, and righteousness. Besides being a defensive force against tyranny, the Khalsa became a spiritual brotherhood that transcended societal divisions.

The Khalsa legacy endures through its core values and symbols, collectively known as the "Five Ks": Kesh (Kesh), Kara (iron bracelet), Kanga (wooden comb), Kachera (cotton undergarments), and Kirpan (ceremonial sword). Each symbol holds profound significance, representing the Khalsa's commitment to spirituality, discipline, and readiness to defend the oppressed. Beyond its role as defenders, the Khalsa played a crucial unifying role within the Sikh community, embracing individuals from diverse backgrounds who pledged to uphold its principles. The Khalsa became a unifying force, fostering a collective identity grounded in Sikh values.

The essence of Sikhism and the Khalsa Legacy lies in the harmonious integration of spiritual principles, ethical values, and a commitment to justice. Sikhs, guided by the teachings of the Sri Guru Granth Sahib and inspired by the courage of the Khalsa, navigate the complexities of the modern world while staying rooted in timeless wisdom. The impact of Sikhism and the Khalsa Legacy extends beyond the boundaries of religion, influencing diverse fields such as art, literature, and social justice. It is with great admiration that we recognize the timeless relevance of Sikh philosophy and the unwavering determination of the Khalsa in shaping a more compassionate and just world.

Origins of Sikhism

Sikhism, a dynamic and inclusive faith, traces its origins to the fertile spiritual landscape of the 15th century, where Sri Guru Nanak Sahib Ji, a visionary spiritual leader, laid the foundation for a unique and transformative religious tradition. Sri Guru Nanak Sahib's teachings, permeated with a profound vision of oneness, equality, and selfless service, form the bedrock upon which Sikhism stands today.

Sri Guru Nanak Sahib Ji's Visionary Teachings

Sri Guru Nanak Sahib, born in 1469 in the village of Talwandi (now Nankana Sahib), embarked on a spiritual journey that would redefine the contours of religious thought in South Asia. From an early age, Sri Guru Nanak Sahib Ji displayed a deep sense of introspection and a questioning spirit, challenging prevailing religious norms and seeking a path that transcended divisive practices.

The cornerstone of Sri Guru Nanak Sahib's teachings lies in the concept of "Ek Onkar" — the belief in the oneness of God. This profound idea underscored the unity of the divine, emphasizing that there is only one Creator who manifests in myriad forms. It laid the groundwork for dismantling barriers between different religious communities and establishing a universal understanding of God that transcended sectarian boundaries.

Equality of All Humanity

Central to Sri Guru Nanak Sahib's vision was the principle of equality. In a society marked by caste divisions and social hierarchies, Sri Guru Nanak Sahib preached the inherent equality of all humans. He unequivocally asserted that irrespective of one's caste, creed, or gender, all individuals share an equal and direct connection with the divine. This radical idea challenged the prevailing societal norms and laid the foundation for a community that would later be known as the Sikhs.

Sri Guru Nanak Sahib's egalitarian philosophy found expression in his interactions with people from diverse backgrounds. He undertook extensive journeys, or Udasis, spreading his message of equality, compassion, and devotion to the divine. These journeys took him to various parts of Asia and even beyond, fostering a community of followers who began to see themselves not as adherents of a new religion, but as seekers of truth and champions of human equality.

Importance of Selfless Service

Another pivotal aspect of Sri Guru Nanak Sahib's teachings was the emphasis on selfless service or "seva." Sri Guru Nanak Sahib believed that true spirituality is not confined to rituals alone but extends to serving others with compassion and humility. This concept of seva became ingrained in the Sikh ethos, later evolving into a fundamental practice within the Sikh community.

Sri Guru Nanak Sahib's life itself was a testament to this principle. He worked as a farmer and later as an accountant, engaging in manual labor and contributing to societal well-being. The idea of combining honest labor with devotion to God, known as "Kirat Karni," became one of the foundational tenets of Sikhism.

The Emergence of the Sikh Community

As Sri Guru Nanak Sahib's teachings gained followers, a community of disciples, known as Sikhs, began to coalesce around him. This community was not defined by rigid religious rituals or exclusive practices but by a shared commitment to Sri Guru Nanak Sahib's vision of spirituality, equality, and service.

Sri Guru Nanak Sahib's successor, Sri Guru Angad Sahib, continued to propagate these foundational principles. The transmission of spiritual authority from one Guru to the next, known as Guruship, became a distinctive feature of Sikhism. Sri Guru Nanak Sahib's hymns, along with those of subsequent Gurus, were compiled into the Sri Guru Granth Sahib Ji, the current living Guru of Sikhism, ensuring that the teachings remained a guiding force for generations to come.

The origins of Sikhism can be traced to Sri Guru Nanak Sahib's visionary teachings that challenged the social, religious, and philosophical norms of his time. His emphasis on the oneness of God, equality of all humanity, and the importance of selfless service laid the foundation for a dynamic and inclusive faith that would evolve into Sikhism. The subsequent Gurus continued to build upon these principles, fostering a unique religious tradition that transcended the boundaries of its historical and cultural origins.

Evolution through the Ten Gurus

The journey of Sikhism is a dynamic and evolving narrative, intricately woven through the lives and teachings of ten successive Gurus. Each Guru played a pivotal role in shaping Sikh philosophy, expanding its spiritual dimensions, and addressing the ethical and social challenges of their time. This continuous lineage, marked by spiritual succession, is a unique feature that distinguishes Sikhism from other religious traditions.

Sri Guru Nanak Dev Ji (1469-1539)

Parkash Place: Rai Bhoi Di Talwandi, Sri Nankana Sahib Ki

Parkash Diwas: 1526 Bikrami Katak Sudhi Puranmasi (Wednesday, November 29, 1469).

Parents: Sri Mehta Kalu Ji and Mata Tripta Ji

The odyssey commenced with Sri Guru Nanak Dev Ji, born in 1469 in the village of Talwandi, now Nankana Sahib. His teachings, emphasizing the oneness of God, equality, and selfless service, laid the foundation for Sikhism. Guru Nanak undertook extensive travels, spreading his message and building a community of followers who became the bedrock of Sikhism.

Sri Guru Angad Dev Ji (1504-1552)

Parkash Place: Matte Di Sra (Naghe di Sra), Muktsar, Panjab

Parkash Date: 1561 Bikrami, Vaisakh Sudhi Ekam (Saturday, 23 April, 1504).

Parents: Bhai Pheru Mal Ji and Mata Sabhirai Ji

Guru Angad Dev Ji, the second Guru, continued Sri Guru Nanak Sahib's work, solidifying the foundation of the Sikh community. He introduced the Gurmukhi script and emphasized physical fitness, contributing to the holistic development of the Sikh way of life.

Sri Guru Amar Das Ji (1479-1574)

Parkash Place: Basarke (Sri Sun Sahib), Amritsar, Panjab

Parkash Date: 1526 Bikrami Vaisakh Sudhi Chaudas (Friday, May 5, 1479).

Parents: Sri Tej Bhan Ji and Mata Lachmi Ji

Guru Amar Das Ji, the third Guru, implemented social reforms and institutionalized the practice of langar (community kitchen). His teachings emphasized equality, humility, and devotion to God.

Sri Guru Ram Das Ji (1534-1581)

Parkash Place: Chuna Mandi, Lahore

Parkash Date: 1531 Bikrami Katak Vadi Duj
(Thursday, 2 November 1534).

Parents: Sri Hari Das Ji and Mata Daya Vati Ji

      Guru Ram Das Ji, the fourth Guru, established the city of Amritsar and Amritdhari, the construction of the Sri Harmandir Sahib (Golden Temple). His hymns focused on the divine relationship and the importance of meditation.

Sri Guru Arjan Dev Ji (1563-1606)

Parkash Place: Sri Goindval Sahib Ji

Parkash Date: 1620 Bikrami Vaisakh Vadi
Saptami (14 April 1563).

Parents: Sri Guru Ram Das and Bibi Bhani Ji

      Guru Arjan Dev Ji, the fifth Guru, compiled the Sri Adi Granth Sahib Ji, the precursor to the Guru Granth Sahib. He emphasized devotion to God and laid the foundation for the Sikh concept of martyrdom.

Sri Guru Har Gobind Sahib Ji (1595-1644)

Parkash Place: Guru Ki Wadali (Sri Wadali Sahib),
Amritsar, Panjab

Parkash Date: 1652 Bikrami Harrh Vadi Ekam (Sunday, 6 June 1596), Sangradi 21 Harrh.

Parents: Sri Guru Arjan Sahib Ji and Mata Ganga Ji

Sri Guru Har Gobind Ji, the sixth Guru, introduced the concept of Miri-Piri, combining spiritual and martial pursuits. He fortified the Sikh community against external threats while promoting self-defense.

Sri Guru Har Rai Sahib Ji (1630-1661)

Parkash Place: Sri Kiratpur Sahib Ji

Parkash Date: 1687 Bikrami Magh Sudhi Chaudas (05 February 1630).

Parents: Baba Gurdita Ji and Mata Nihal Kaur Ji

Sri Guru Har Rai Ji, the seventh Guru, focused on compassion, nature, and the preservation of life. He expanded the medical facilities in Kiratpur Sahib, emphasizing the importance of healthcare.

Sri Guru Har Krishan Ji (1656-1664)

Parkash Place: Sri Kiratpur Sahib Ji

Parkash Date: 1713 Bikrami Sawan Vadi Noauvi (Thursday, 14 July 1656).

Parents: Sri Guru Har Rai Sahib Ji and
                  Mata Krishan Kaur Ji

Sri Guru Har Krishan Ji, the eighth Guru, became the youngest Guru at the age of five. Despite his short earthly life, he emphasized the importance of spirituality and selfless service.

Sri Guru Tegh Bahadur Ji (1621-1675)

Parkash Place: Sri Amritsar Sahib Ji

Parkash Date: 1678 Bikrami Vaisakh Vadi
                  Panchami (Tuesday, 12 April
                  1621).

Parents: Guru Hargobind and Mata Nanki

Sri Guru Tegh Bahadur Ji, the ninth Guru, is known for his supreme sacrifice to protect the freedom of religion. He defended the rights of Kashmiri Pandits against religious persecution.

Sri Guru Gobind Singh Ji (1666-1708)

Parkash Place: Sri Patna Sahib Ji

Parkash Date: 1723 Bikrami Poh Sudhi Saptami
                  (Sunday, 01 January 1666),
                  Sankranti 23 Poh.

Parents: Sri Guru Tegh Bahadur Sahib Ji
                  and Mata Gujri Ji

Sri Guru Gobind Singh Ji, the tenth Guru, transformed the Sikh community by establishing the Khalsa in 1699. He institutionalized the Sri Guru Granth Sahib Ji as the eternal Guru and introduced the concept of Singh and Kaur, emphasizing equality and courage.

Sri Guru Granth Sahib Ji: The Eternal and Living Guru

The teachings of the ten Gurus were compiled into the Sri Guru Granth Sahib, the eternal and final living Guru of Sikhism. In 1775 Bikrami, Katak Sudhi Duj (20 October 1708), Guru Gobind Singh Ji declared that there would be no more living Gurus, and Sikhs were to turn to the final living Guru Sahib, Sri Guru Granth Sahib Ji as their eternal, final living and spiritual Guru. The Sri Guru Granth Sahib Ji encompasses hymns not only from the Sikh Gurus but also from saints and poets of various traditions, emphasizing the universality of spiritual wisdom.

The journey through the ten Gurus illustrates Sikhism's dynamic evolution. Each Guru contributes unique insights and shapes the spiritual, ethical, and social dimensions of the faith. The Sri Guru Granth Sahib Ji, as the eternal Guru, continues to guide Sikhs on their spiritual journey, ensuring that the essence of Sikhism transcends time and remains a beacon for generations to come.

Core Tenets of Sikhism

Sikhism, a faith founded on the principles of equality, oneness of God, and service to humanity, is characterized by its distinct set of ethical guidelines. At the heart of Sikh life are the "Three Pillars," three fundamental principles that encapsulate the essence of Sikh philosophy. These pillars — Naam Japna (meditating on God's name), Kirat Karni (earning an honest living), and Vand Chhakna (sharing with others) — serve as the guiding force shaping the lives of Sikhs and fostering a deep connection between spiritual practice and daily conduct.

Naam Japna

The first pillar, Naam Japna, is a foundational aspect of Sikh spirituality. It involves the meditative repetition of the name of God, commonly referred to as "Simran." The practice of Naam Japna is not confined to a specific time or place; instead, it is a continuous, mindful remembrance of the divine throughout one's daily life. Sikhs believe that by immersing themselves in the divine name, they cultivate a sense of spiritual awareness and foster a direct connection with the divine.

Meditation as a Path to Spiritual Awakening

Naam Japna is more than a ritualistic practice; it is a transformative journey towards spiritual awakening. The repetitive recitation of God's name is viewed as a means to transcend the ego, dissolve the illusion of separateness, and attain a state of oneness with the divine. This pillar encourages Sikhs to integrate mindfulness and contemplation into their daily routine, recognizing that spirituality is not confined to religious rituals but extends to every facet of life.

Naam Simran in Sikh Devotional Practices

In Sikh devotional practices, congregational singing of hymns and prayers, known as "Kirtan," becomes a communal form of Naam Japna. The collective recitation of hymns from the Sri Guru Granth Sahib Ji amplifies the spiritual energy, creating an environment conducive to meditation and reflection. Naam Japna, as exemplified through Naam Simran, is a unifying force that binds the Sikh community in a shared commitment to spiritual growth and devotion.

Kirat Karni

The second pillar, Kirat Karni, underscores the importance of honest labor and ethical conduct in Sikh life. Sikhs are encouraged to engage in productive and dignified work to sustain themselves and their families. The concept of Kirat Karni rejects the notion of idleness and emphasizes the inherent value of labor, irrespective of its nature.

Integration of Spirituality and Work

Kirat Karni embodies the idea that spirituality is not divorced from the practical realities of life; rather, it is an integral part of one's daily endeavors. Sikhs are encouraged to approach their work with dedication, integrity, and a sense of responsibility. By doing so, they contribute positively to society while maintaining a sense of humility and gratitude for the blessings received.

Ethics in Business and Professional Life

The principle of Kirat Karni extends beyond the realm of manual labor to encompass all professions and occupations. Sikhs are urged to uphold ethical standards in business, professional dealings, and interpersonal relationships. This pillar challenges individuals to navigate the complexities of the modern world with a moral compass, ensuring that their actions align with the principles of Sikhism.

Vand Chhakna

Vand Chhakna, the third pillar, revolves around the spirit of selfless service and sharing with others. Sikhs are encouraged to actively engage in acts of charity, compassion, and community service. The concept of Vand Chhakna is deeply rooted in the Sikh belief that the fruits of one's labor are to be shared with those in need.

Langar (Community Kitchen) as a Manifestation of Vand Chhakna

The practice of Langar, a community kitchen where free meals are served to all, exemplifies the principle of Vand Chhakna. Regardless of caste, creed, or social status, individuals from diverse backgrounds come together to share a common meal, breaking down barriers and fostering a sense of equality and community.

Charity and Compassion in Sikh Tradition

Beyond the institution of Langar, Sikhs are encouraged to engage in charitable acts, contribute to philanthropic endeavors, and extend a helping hand to those facing adversity. Vand Chhakna is not limited to material wealth; it encompasses sharing one's time, skills, and resources for the greater good. Through acts of kindness and compassion, Sikhs embody the selfless spirit of Vand Chhakna in their interactions with the world.

The Interconnectedness of the Three Pillars

While Naam Japna, Kirat Karni, and Vand Chhakna are distinct pillars, they are interconnected, forming a comprehensive framework for Sikh living. Naam Japna nurtures the spiritual consciousness, providing the inner strength and clarity needed to engage in honest labor (Kirat Karni). The ethical conduct and sense of responsibility cultivated through Kirat Karni, in turn, create a conducive environment for the practice of Vand Chhakna, fostering a community centered on compassion and shared well-being.

Challenges and Growth through the Three Pillars

The adherence to the Three Pillars is not without its challenges. Navigating the demands of the modern world while upholding spiritual principles requires a conscious effort and a steadfast commitment to Sikh values. Sikhs are called to reflect on the dynamic interplay between Naam Japna, Kirat Karni, and Vand Chhakna, recognizing that the pursuit of spiritual growth is intricately woven into the fabric of daily life.

Sikh Life with Wisdom and Compassion

The core tenets of Sikhism, encapsulated in the Three Pillars, serve as a compass guiding Sikhs on their spiritual journey. Naam Japna instills a deep connection with the divine, Kirat Karni promotes ethical living and responsible engagement with the world, and Vand Chhakna fosters a spirit of selfless service and compassion. Together, these principles form a harmonious framework that empowers Sikhs to navigate the complexities of the modern world while staying grounded in timeless wisdom and compassion for all of humanity.

Historical Context Leading to the Formation of the Khalsa

During the Mughal Empire's dominance, the socio-political conditions in Panjab played a crucial role in shaping Sikhism. This period was marked by religious persecution, challenges to fundamental freedoms, and the need for the Sikh community to assert its distinct identity. The external pressures that the Sikh community faced during this period had a transformative impact on their psyche, which prompted a collective response to preserve their faith and values. This era was significant in the emergence of the Khalsa, a unique and resilient community envisioned by Sri Guru Gobind Singh Ji, the tenth Guru. The formation of the Khalsa marked a significant turning point in Sikh history, as it was a strategic vision that emerged from the dynamic interplay of external adversities and Sikh resilience.

Turbulent Times in Panjab

In the heart of the Asian subcontinent, Panjab witnessed a tumultuous era marked by the dominance of the Mughal Empire. This period of socio-political turbulence became a crucible for the Sikh community, compelling them to navigate a landscape fraught with religious persecution, challenges to fundamental freedoms, and the imperative to carve out a distinct identity. This historical context laid the foundation for a transformative chapter in Sikh history, shaping the emergence of the Khalsa as a response to the adversities faced by the communities.

Mughal Dominance and Religious Persecution

During the Mughal rule in Panjab, all communities encountered religious persecution that stemmed from their rejection of certain aspects of the prevailing socio-religious order. The Mughal emperors posed a threat to religious pluralism in all areas and viewed the Sikh faith as a challenge to their existing power structures.

Challenges to Fundamental Freedoms

Sikhs faced significant challenges to their fundamental freedoms, including the freedom to practice their faith without fear of persecution. The imposition of discriminatory policies and harsh measures aimed at suppressing Sikh religious practices fueled a sense of urgency within the community to protect their identity and beliefs.

The Need for a Distinct Identity

The socio-political turbulence in Panjab propelled the Sikhs to seek a distinct identity that would serve as a bulwark against the encroachments on their religious freedoms. The challenges they faced were not merely external; they extended to the very core of Sikh values, emphasizing the oneness of God, equality, and the right to practice their faith without fear.

Religious Identity and Resistance

In response to the religious persecution and suppression, the Sikh community underwent a process of self-reflection and consolidation. The principles laid down by Sri Guru Nanak Sahib Ji and subsequent Gurus became not just spiritual tenets but a rallying point for resistance against oppression. The Sikh identity became a beacon of resilience, with the community steadfastly holding onto their distinct religious practices, including the recitation of hymns, congregational worship, and adherence to the principles of equality.

Transformation into a Warrior Community

The turbulence in Panjab acted as a crucible, forging the Sikh community into a resilient force. It became increasingly evident that mere adherence to spiritual principles was not sufficient in the face of external threats. Sri Guru Gobind Singh Ji, the tenth Guru, recognized the need for a paradigm shift — the transformation of the Sikhs into a community that could not only withstand external pressures but actively defend their faith and values.

Strategic Vision of Sri Guru Gobind Singh Ji

Guru Gobind Singh, in response to the turbulent times, envisioned the Khalsa not solely as warriors on the battlefield but as spiritual guardians committed to upholding justice, equality, and the Sikh way of life. The Khalsa was not merely a military force; it was a fraternity bound by a shared commitment to the principles laid down by the Gurus. This vision was not only a response to external threats but also a strategic move to preserve the essence of Sikhism in the face of adversity.

The Khalsa as a Transformative Response

The formation of the Khalsa in 1699, through the Amrit Sanchar (the initiation ceremony), marked a turning point in Sikh history. Sri Guru Gobind Singh infused the Khalsa with a spirit of fearlessness, selflessness, and a deep sense of duty. The Khalsa was not just a defensive force; it was a proactive community dedicated to standing against injustice and upholding the principles of Sikhism.

Legacy of Sikh Resilience

The turbulent times in Panjab, under the dominance of the Mughal Empire, became the crucible in which the Sikh community forged its resilience. The challenges posed by religious persecution and the suppression of fundamental freedoms prompted Sikhs to seek a distinct identity, setting the stage for the transformative chapter of the Khalsa. Sri Guru Gobind Singh Sahib Ji's strategic vision recognized the need for a community that could withstand external pressures while embodying the core principles of Sikhism. The Khalsa, emerging from this historical context, became a living testament to Sikh resilience, fearlessness, and an unwavering commitment to justice and equality. The legacy of this transformative period continues to shape the Sikh ethos, serving as a source of inspiration for generations to come.

The Need for a Warrior Community

Against the backdrop of a turbulent socio-political landscape dominated by the Mughal Empire, Sri Guru Gobind Singh Sahib Ji, the tenth Guru of Sikhism, astutely recognized the imperative for a transformative response to the challenges faced by the Sikh community. In the face of religious persecution and encroachments on fundamental freedoms, Sri Guru Gobind Singh Sahib Ji envisioned the creation of a community that could not only defend the principles of Sikhism but also stand as a formidable force against tyranny. This vision led to the establishment of the Khalsa, a community that transcended the conventional definition of warriors on the battlefield. Sri Guru Gobind Singh Sahib Ji conceptualized the Khalsa as more than mere soldiers; they were spiritual guardians, unwavering in their commitment to upholding justice, equality, and the Sikh way of life.

Strategic Recognition of External Threats

Sri Guru Gobind Singh Sahib Ji's leadership was based on a deep understanding of the external threats that the communities faced. The Mughal rulers, feeling threatened by the rejection of certain socio-religious norms, persecuted the population and aimed to suppress their unique identity. In response, Sri Guru Gobind Singh Sahib Ji strategically recognized that a paradigm shift was required. This shift went beyond the realm of spiritual teachings to address the immediate challenges that threatened the very survival of truth.

The Khalsa as a Defensive and Spiritual Force

The Khalsa, instituted by Sri Guru Gobind Singh Sahib Ji in 1699 through the Amrit Sanchar initiation ceremony, was not merely a military force created for self-defense. It was a spiritual brotherhood, an embodiment of fearlessness, selflessness, and an unwavering commitment to justice. Sri Guru Gobind Singh Sahib Ji infused the Khalsa with a dual identity – warriors on the battlefield and spiritual guardians of Sikh principles. This dual role was adopted strategically to address the multifaceted challenges faced by the communities.

Upholding Justice and Equality

The Khalsa, in Sri Guru Gobind Singh Sahib Ji's vision, was entrusted with the sacred duty of upholding justice and equality. Beyond the physical battles, the Khalsa was to stand as a symbol of resistance against oppression and injustice. Sri Guru Gobind Singh Ji emphasized the importance of fighting not for personal gain or power but for the greater ideals of justice and equality. The Khalsa, as spiritual guardians, became the vanguards of Sikh values, standing firm against any force that sought to suppress the principles of the faith.

Commitment to the Sikh Way of Life

At the core of Sri Guru Gobind Singh Sahib Ji's vision was the preservation of the true way of life. The Khalsa was not just a response to external threats; it was a proactive measure to ensure that the essence of Sikhism endured through generations. The commitment to the Sikh way of life encompassed not only religious practices but also ethical conduct, humility, and a sense of community. The Khalsa, as envisioned by Sri Guru Gobind Singh Ji, became the living embodiment of Sikh principles in action.

Legacy of Sri Guru Gobind Singh Sahib Ji's Vision

Sri Guru Gobind Singh Sahib Ji's vision for the Khalsa left an indelible mark on Sikh history and consciousness. The Khalsa, as a warrior community and spiritual guardians, played a pivotal role in shaping the destiny of the Sikh community. The legacy of Sri Guru Gobind Singh Sahib Ji's vision continues to resonate, inspiring Sikhs to stand against injustice, uphold the principles of equality, and embrace the Sikh way of life. The Khalsa remains a beacon of resilience and unwavering commitment to Sikh values, symbolizing the enduring spirit of Sri Guru Gobind Singh Sahib's transformative vision.

Significance of The Khalsa Legacy

The significance of the Khalsa legacy reverberates through Sikh history as a testament to resilience, sacrifice, and unwavering commitment to Sikh principles. The Khalsa is more than a military or martial tradition; it embodies the spirit of fearlessness, justice, and equality. The Khalsa legacy is a symbol of defiance against religious persecution and tyranny, standing as a testament to the Sikh community's determination to preserve its distinct identity. The five Ks—Kesh (Kesh), Kara (iron bracelet), Kanga (wooden comb), Kachera (cotton undergarments), and Kirpan (ceremonial sword)—adorned by Khalsa members, are not just symbols but reflections of a profound commitment to Sikh values. The Khalsa's role extends beyond the battlefield; it serves as a spiritual and ethical compass for Sikhs, guiding them to live in accordance with the teachings of the Gurus. The legacy of the Khalsa is etched in the annals of Sikhism, inspiring generations to stand against injustice, uphold justice and equality, and embrace the rich tapestry of the Sikh way of life. As custodians of this legacy, Sikhs continue to draw strength and inspiration from the Khalsa, ensuring that its significance endures as a guiding light for the Sikh community and beyond.

The Pioneering Spirit of the Khalsa

The Khalsa, which was revealed by the visionary leadership of Sri Guru Gobind Singh Ji in 1699, embodies a pioneering spirit that has been a catalyst for transformative change within the Sikh community and beyond. It is more than just a military force, as it represents a dynamic and revolutionary approach to spirituality, resilience, and the pursuit of justice. There are various facets to the Khalsa's pioneering spirit, each contributing to its unique identity and enduring legacy.

Fearlessness in the Face of Adversity

The Khalsa's pioneering spirit is perhaps most evident in its fearlessness, a quality instilled by Sri Guru Gobind Singh. Members of the Khalsa are taught to face adversity with unwavering courage, confronting challenges head-on. This fearlessness is not confined to the battlefield but extends to the realm of spiritual and social challenges, embodying a spirit that refuses to be subdued by external pressures.

Revolutionizing the Concept of Warriorhood

Sri Guru Gobind Singh Sahib Ji's vision transformed the traditional concept of warriors. The Khalsa was not merely an army; it was a community of spiritual warriors, dedicated to upholding justice, equality, and the Sikh way of life. The revolutionary idea of integrating spirituality with martial prowess set the Khalsa apart, challenging conventional norms and establishing a new paradigm for what it meant to be a warrior.

Distinct Identity Through the Five Ks

The adoption of the five Ks—Kesh (Kesh), Kara (iron bracelet), Kanga (wooden comb), Kachera (cotton undergarments), and Kirpan (ceremonial sword)—was a revolutionary move that solidified the distinct identity of the Khalsa. These symbols were not just physical adornments; they became markers of a profound commitment to Sikh values and a visual representation of the Khalsa's pioneering spirit in preserving its unique identity against external pressures.

Community and Equality

The Khalsa's pioneering spirit is deeply rooted in its commitment to community and equality. Sri Guru Gobind Singh Sahib Ji, through the initiation ceremony of Amrit Sanchar, broke down barriers of caste and creed, forging a united community dedicated to the pursuit of justice and spirituality. The egalitarian principles embedded in the Khalsa ethos challenged societal norms, offering a pioneering model of a community where all individuals, irrespective of background, stood as equals.

Empowerment of Women in the Khalsa

Another revolutionary aspect of the Khalsa's spirit is the empowerment of women. Sri Guru Gobind Singh Sahib Ji, in an unprecedented move for his time, included women in the initiation ceremony, making them equal members of the Khalsa. This pioneering approach challenged gender norms, emphasizing the equality of men and women in the pursuit of spirituality and justice.

Legacy of Compassion and Service

The pioneering spirit of the Khalsa is not only about resistance but also about compassion and service. The institution of Langar, the community kitchen providing free meals to all, exemplifies the Khalsa's commitment to selfless service. This legacy continues to inspire Sikhs to actively contribute to the well-being of society, fostering a spirit of compassion and community engagement.

Contemporary Relevance and Global Impact

The pioneering spirit of the Khalsa remains relevant in the contemporary world, transcending borders and cultures. Sikhs, imbued with the values instilled by Sri Guru Gobind Singh Sahib Ji, continue to be trailblazers in various fields, from academia and technology to social justice and humanitarian efforts. The Khalsa's spirit of fearlessness, equality, and service has a global impact, resonating with individuals and communities seeking a model of empowerment rooted in spiritual values.

The pioneering spirit of the Khalsa is a living testament to the transformative power of visionary leadership. It continues to inspire generations, urging individuals to navigate challenges with courage, uphold justice and equality, and embrace a profound sense of community and service. As the Khalsa's legacy persists, its pioneering spirit acts as a guiding force, shaping the Sikh community's identity and influencing a broader global narrative of resilience, compassion, and visionary leadership.

Enduring Values and Symbols

At the heart of the Khalsa's legacy lie enduring values and symbols that transcend time, shaping the identity of Sikhs and serving as a guiding light for generations. The Khalsa is not just a historical entity but a living embodiment of timeless principles that continue to resonate with Sikhs worldwide. The enduring values and symbols of the Khalsa encapsulate the essence of Sikhism, fostering a profound connection to spirituality, justice, and community.

1. **The Five Ks:** Immutable Symbols of Identity, Central to the Khalsa's identity are the five Ks— Kesh (Kesh), Kara (iron bracelet), Kanga (wooden comb), Kachera (cotton undergarments), and Kirpan (ceremonial sword). These symbols, mandated by Sri Guru Gobind Singh Sahib Ji during the Amrit Sanchar, are not mere external markers; they embody a commitment to Sikh values and a visible representation of the Khalsa's distinct identity. The unshorn hair signifies a natural

acceptance of the body as created, while the steel bracelet, comb, and undergarments symbolize discipline, hygiene, and modesty. The Kirpan, a ceremonial sword, embodies the responsibility to defend the truth and protect the vulnerable.

2. **Fearlessness (Nishkamta):** The Bedrock of Courage, Fearlessness is a cornerstone value instilled by Sri Guru Gobind Singh Sahib in the Khalsa. This virtue encourages Sikhs to confront challenges with unwavering courage, transcending fear and adversity. The Khalsa's commitment to fearlessness extends beyond physical courage on the battlefield; it encompasses a spiritual fortitude that empowers individuals to stand up against injustice, discrimination, and social inequities. The enduring value of fearlessness is a source of inspiration, motivating Sikhs to navigate life's complexities with resilience and unwavering conviction.

3. **Equality and Community (Sangat and Pangat):** Pillars of Unity, The Khalsa places a premium on the values of equality and community. The concepts of Sangat (spiritual congregation) and Pangat (communal kitchen) emphasize the importance of communal living and equality among Sikhs. In the Gurdwara, Sikhs gather as a united Sangat to engage in collective worship and contemplation. The institution of Langar, a Pangat where free meals are served to all, exemplifies the principle of equality, breaking down social barriers and

fostering a sense of community. These enduring values promote inclusivity, harmony, and a shared responsibility for the welfare of all.

4. **Service (Seva):** Selfless Devotion to Others, Service, or Seva, is a fundamental value deeply ingrained in the Khalsa tradition. Sikhs are encouraged to engage in acts of selfless service for the betterment of society, regardless of caste, creed, or background. The spirit of Seva extends to various forms of community service, humanitarian efforts, and contributions to social welfare. Through Seva, the Khalsa embodies selfless devotion to the well-being of others, reflecting the broader Sikh ethos of compassion and community engagement.

5. **Sri Guru Granth Sahib Ji:** Eternal Spiritual and Final Living Guru, At the core of Khalsa values is the Sri Guru Granth Sahib Ji, the eternal Guru for Sikhs. Comprising the teachings of the Sikh Gurus and other spiritual leaders, the Sri Guru Granth Sahib Ji serves as a timeless guide and direction for the Khalsa, providing spiritual wisdom and ethical principles. Sikhs turn to the Guru Granth Sahib for guidance in moments of joy and sorrow, seeking solace and direction in their spiritual journey.

6. **Ek Onkar:** The Concept of Oneness, The symbol "Ek Onkar," meaning "One God," encapsulates the Sikh belief in the oneness of the divine. This principle, highlighted in the Guru Granth Sahib, underscores the unity of all creation and the interconnectedness of humanity. The enduring value of Ek Onkar

guides the Khalsa in recognizing the divine spark within every individual, fostering a sense of equality, humility, and reverence for all life.

The enduring values and symbols of the Khalsa form a rich tapestry that weaves together spirituality, justice, and community. These principles, instilled by Sri Guru Gobind Singh Sahib Ji, continue to guide Sikhs in their daily lives, fostering a deep connection to their faith and a commitment to timeless values that transcend the boundaries of time and space. The Khalsa's legacy is not just a historical relic; it is a living testament to the enduring essence of Sikhism, resonating through the hearts and actions of Sikhs around the world.

Unifying the Sikh Community

The unification of the Sikh community stands as an enduring testament to the visionary principles set forth by Sikh Gurus, particularly in the establishment of the Khalsa by Sri Guru Gobind Singh Sahib Ji. This cohesive force, deeply rooted in the values of faith, equality, and service, not only defines the Sikh identity but also fosters a sense of solidarity among Sikhs worldwide. The unification process, intricately woven into the fabric of Sikh ethos, manifests in various aspects that transcend geographical and cultural boundaries.

1. **Forging a Spiritual Brotherhood**: At the heart of Sikh unification is the transformative ceremony of Amrit Sanchar. Instituted by Sri Guru Gobind Singh Ji, this sacred initiation involves the preparation and consumption of

Amrit, a sweetened elixir stirred with a double-edged sword (Khanda). Those who undergo this ceremony commit themselves to the Khalsa principles, symbolizing a profound dedication to live by the values of courage, equality, and service. Amrit Sanchar transcends individual identity, forging a spiritual bond that unites Sikhs as members of a broader brotherhood.

2. **Unity in Spiritual Congregation and Communal Kitchen:** Sangat and Pangat exemplify the ideals of unity and equality that characterize the Sikh community. Sangat refers to the congregation of individuals gathering for collective worship, reflection, and prayer. In the presence of the Sri Guru Granth Sahib Ji, Sikhs come together as one, transcending differences and fostering a sense of community. Pangat, the communal kitchen where free meals are served to all, epitomizes equality. Sikhs, regardless of social status, sit side by side, partaking in the same nourishment. These practices erase distinctions, nurturing a sense of unity that extends beyond the physical boundaries of the Gurdwara.

3. **The Eternal Unifying Force:** The Sri Guru Granth Sahib Ji, the central religious current living Guru for Sikhs, serves as an eternal unifier. Comprising the teachings of Sikh Gurus and spiritual leaders, it transcends individual interpretations, providing a common spiritual ground for the entire Sikh community. It is revered as the living Guru, and its presence in

the Gurdwara reinforces the unity of purpose and faith among Sikhs.

4. **Fostering the Principle of Oneness**: The foundational principle of Ek Onkar, emphasizing the oneness of God, resonates through Sikh consciousness, fostering a deep sense of unity. This concept transcends religious dogmas, underscoring the interconnectedness of all creation. Sikhs, guided by the belief in Ek Onkar, recognize the divine spark within every individual, breaking down barriers and promoting a sense of kinship that unifies the Sikh community.

5. **Binding Through Selfless Service**: The practice of Seva, or selfless service, serves as a unifying force that binds the Sikh community together. Sikhs are encouraged to engage in acts of service for the well-being of others, irrespective of caste, creed, or background. From participating in community kitchens (Langar) to contributing to humanitarian initiatives, the spirit of Seva transcends individual interests, reinforcing a collective commitment to fostering the welfare of society.

6. **Strengthening Communal Bonds**: Festivals and celebrations play a crucial role in strengthening the unity of the Sikh community. Events such as Vaisakhi, commemorating the formation of the Khalsa, and Sri Guru Nanak Sahib Ji Parkash Gurpurb, celebrating the birth of Sri Guru Nanak Sahib Ji, bring Sikhs together in joyous observance. These occasions provide an opportunity for the community to unite, share

in collective prayers, and reinforce a sense of shared history and purpose.

7. **A Unified Presence Worldwide**: The Sikh diaspora, dispersed across the globe, stands as a testament to the global unification of the Sikh community. Despite geographical distances, Sikhs maintain a strong connection to their faith and cultural heritage. Gurdwaras worldwide act as focal points for the Sikh community, providing spaces for worship, community engagement, and cultural preservation. The global Sikh diaspora stands as a unified presence, contributing to social, economic, and cultural landscapes while upholding the core values of Sikhism.

The unification of the Sikh community is a multifaceted and dynamic process, interwoven with spiritual, cultural, and social dimensions. From the initiation ceremony to the principles of equality, service, and shared celebrations, the Sikh community finds strength in its cohesive identity. Whether within the precincts of the Gurdwara or in the broader global context, the unifying force of Sikhism remains resilient, fostering a sense of oneness that transcends boundaries and empowers Sikhs to navigate the complexities of the modern world with a collective spirit of faith, equality, and service.

*****

PANJAB

BEFORE

THE BIRTH

OF SIKHISM

PANJAB BEFORE THE BIRTH OF SIKHISM

The Sikh faith, with its vibrant history and profound teachings, stands as a testament to the enduring spirit of humanity's quest for spiritual truth. Rooted in the socio-religious landscape of 15th-century India, Sikhism emerged as a distinct and transformative force, challenging prevailing norms and fostering a unique community bound by principles of equality, justice, and devotion.

Sikhism

At its core, Sikhism is a monotheistic religion founded on the teachings of Guru Nanak, the first of the ten Sikh Gurus. Born in 1469 in the town of Talwandi (now Nankana Sahib, Pakistan), Guru Nanak's life experiences and divine revelations laid the foundation for a new spiritual path. The Sikh scripture, Guru Granth Sahib, encapsulates the wisdom of the ten Gurus, providing guidance on ethical living, devotion to the One Creator, and a commitment to social justice.

The Sikhs, known for their distinctive appearance and unwavering principles, form a global community united by shared beliefs and practices. The Five Ks – Kesh (Kesh), Kara (iron bracelet), Kanga (wooden comb), Kachera (cotton undergarments), and Kirpan (ceremonial sword) – symbolize the Sikh identity and commitment to the faith's principles.

Importance and Relevance of Understanding the Birth of Sikhism

To comprehend the essence of Sikhism, delving into its historical origins is essential. The 15th-century Asia subcontinent was marked by social stratification, religious orthodoxy, and political upheaval. Sri Guru Nanak Sahib Ji's teachings challenged existing norms in this context, emphasizing equality, compassion, and a direct connection with the Divine.

Understanding the birth of Sikhism is not merely an exploration of historical events; it is a journey into the philosophical underpinnings that continue to shape Sikh identity today. The Gurus' teachings laid the groundwork for a unique blend of spiritual enlightenment and active engagement in societal affairs. The formation of the Khalsa Panth by Sri Guru Gobind Singh Ji marked a pivotal moment, transforming Sikhs into a community devoted to justice, fearlessness, and selfless service.

The relevance of Sikhism extends beyond its historical roots. In an era marked by diversity, social challenges, and the pursuit of individual and collective well-being, the principles of Sikhism offer a timeless guide. The Sikh emphasis on selfless service (seva), equality of all humans, and the pursuit of justice holds universal significance, providing valuable insights for navigating the complexities of contemporary life.

15th-century: Political, Social, and Religious Landscape

The Asian subcontinent during the 15th century was a diverse and dynamic mix of cultures, political entities, and religious traditions. This period saw significant changes, both in terms of power structures and societal norms, which paved the way for the emergence of Sikhism. To truly comprehend the environment in which Guru Nanak, the founder of Sikhism, lived and began spreading his revolutionary spiritual insights, it is essential to understand the perspective of 15th-century Panjab.

Political Landscape

During the 15th century, the political landscape of Panjab underwent a profound transformation characterized by the fragmentation of power. The Delhi Sultanate, once a centralizing force, faced internal challenges, including court intrigues, succession disputes, and political instability. These internal conflicts weakened the authority of the sultans, contributing to the decline of the Delhi Sultanate as a dominant political entity.

Simultaneously, external invasions, most notably the incursions led by Central Asian conquerors like Timur, dealt severe blows to the stability of the Delhi Sultanate. Timur's invasion in the early 15th century not only resulted in widespread destruction and upheaval but also left a lasting impact on the geopolitical landscape. The aftermath of these invasions created a power vacuum, allowing various regional kingdoms and sultanates to assert their autonomy.

As the centralized authority of the Delhi Sultanate waned, regional powers rose to prominence. Different territories witnessed the emergence of distinct power centers, each with its own ruling elite and political structures. This fragmentation of political power led to a complex web of relationships, alliances, and conflicts among the various regional entities.

The decline of centralized authority had significant consequences for governance and administration. Now, local rulers and chieftains, with greater autonomy, governed their territories independently. This shift from a centralized to a more decentralized system reshaped the political map of Asia, fostering the development of diverse regional identities.

The social and economic ramifications of this political fragmentation were profound. Local communities adapted to the changing political landscape by becoming more self-reliant. Economic systems, trade routes, and cultural interactions were influenced by the shifting power dynamics. The decentralization of political control contributed to the formation of unique and dynamic societies across different regions of Asia.

This intricate political milieu created the backdrop for the emergence of Sikhism in Panjab. In this environment of political uncertainty and social transformation, Guru Nanak's spiritual teachings offered a profound response, emphasizing principles of equality, justice, and devotion that resonated with those seeking solace and guidance amid the complex political dynamics of 15th-century India.

Rise of Regional Powers

The 15th century in the world witnessed a transformative period where the decline of the centralized authority of the Delhi Sultanate led to the rise of regional powers, each carving out its own destiny and influencing the complex socio-political fabric of the subcontinent. Two prominent regional powers that gained prominence during this era were the Vijayanagara Empire in the south and the Bahmani Sultanate in the South. Concurrently, in the northern part, the Lodi dynasty faced challenges from emerging regional rulers, setting the stage for a nuanced interplay of political dynamics.

Vijayanagara Empire

The Vijayanagara Empire emerged as a beacon of cultural richness and military might in the southern part. Established in 1336 by Harihara I and Bukka Raya I, the Vijayanagara Empire grew to become one of the most significant powers in the region during the 15th century. The empire was strategically located on the South Plateau, with its capital, Hampi, serving as a cultural and economic hub.

Founding and Early Expansion

The founding of the Vijayanagara Empire marked a response to the political vacuum created by the weakening Delhi Sultanate. Harihara I and Bukka Raya I, initially serving as governors under the Hoysala Empire, established an independent kingdom. Their rapid expansion, coupled with diplomatic acumen, led to the establishment of the Vijayanagara Empire.

Cultural Flourishing and Architecture

Under the reign of the Sangama Dynasty, particularly during the rule of Deva Raya I, the Vijayanagara Empire witnessed a cultural renaissance. The empire became a patron of art, literature, and architecture. The city of Hampi, adorned with splendid temples and monuments, reflected the cultural and artistic achievements of the Vijayanagara rulers.

Military Might and Conflict

The Vijayanagara Empire's military prowess was evident in its conflicts with various neighboring powers, including the Bahmani Sultanate. The Battle of Raichur in 1520, under the reign of Krishnadevaraya, demonstrated the empire's military strength, solidifying its position as a dominant force in the South.

Bahmani Sultanate

Contemporaneous with the rise of the Vijayanagara Empire, the South witnessed the emergence of the Bahmani Sultanate, a dynamic political entity that shaped the South region during the 15th century.

Establishment and Expansion

Founded in 1347 by Ala-ud-Din Bahman Shah, the Bahmani Sultanate was established with its capital at Gulbarga. Initially, the Sultanate aimed to counter the growing influence of the Vijayanagara Empire. However, internal divisions among the Bahmani rulers eventually led to the fragmentation of the Sultanate into five South sultanates—Bijapur, Golconda, Ahmadnagar, Bidar, and Berar.

Cultural Synthesis and Legacy

The Bahmani Sultanate was marked by a unique blend of Persian and indigenous South influences. The sultans were patrons of art, literature, and architecture, fostering a cultural synthesis. The legacy of the Bahmani Sultanate continued in the individual sultanates that emerged from its dissolution, each contributing to the diverse cultural tapestry of the South.

Conflicts with Vijayanagara and Internal Strife

The Bahmani Sultanate engaged in persistent conflicts with the Vijayanagara Empire for regional dominance. Internal strife among the Bahmani rulers, coupled with external pressures, contributed to the eventual disintegration of the Sultanate. This dissolution led to the establishment of the five independent South sultanates, each asserting its authority over a specific territory.

Lodi Dynasty

In the northern part, the Lodi dynasty succeeded the Delhi Sultanate, facing challenges from emerging regional rulers and setting the stage for a dynamic interplay of political forces.

Succession and Ascension

The Lodi dynasty, led by Bahlul Lodi, ascended to power in 1451. Bahlul Lodi's reign marked a continuation of the political decline that had befallen the Delhi Sultanate. His successor, Sikandar Lodi, faced internal challenges and conflicts with regional powers.

Emerging Regional Rulers

During the Lodi dynasty's rule, regional rulers and chieftains emerged as formidable contenders for power. The weakening centralized authority in Delhi allowed these local leaders to assert their autonomy and challenge the dominance of the Lodi rulers. The stage was set for a transition from the Lodis to the Mughals.

Regional Dynamics and Political Flux

The northern political landscape during the 15th century was characterized by shifting alliances, conflicts, and a fluid geopolitical scenario. The Lodi rulers, grappling with internal challenges, witnessed the rise of influential regional rulers who sought to establish their own spheres of influence. This period of political flux played a crucial role in shaping the subsequent course of Asian history.

Impact on Socio-Cultural Landscape

The rise of regional powers during the 15th century had a profound impact on the socio-cultural landscape. Each power center, be it the Vijayanagara Empire in the south, the Bahmani Sultanate in the South, or the regional rulers challenging the Lodi dynasty in the north, contributed to the diverse and dynamic tapestry of Indian society.

Art and Architecture

The patronage of art and architecture by the Vijayanagara rulers and the Bahmani Sultanate left an indelible mark on the cultural heritage of the South. Temples, forts, and palaces built during this period reflected the unique artistic styles and cultural syntheses that defined the regional powers.

Cultural Synthesis and Trade

The cultural synthesis promoted by the Bahmani Sultanate and the Vijayanagara Empire fostered an environment where diverse traditions and influences coexisted. Trade flourished, connecting different regions and facilitating the exchange of ideas, goods, and technologies. This cultural cross-pollination contributed to the rich tapestry of Indian civilization.

Religious Diversity

The religious landscape also underwent transformations. While the Vijayanagara Empire was a stronghold of Hindu culture, the Bahmani Sultanate, with its Persian and Southi influences, exemplified religious diversity. The patronage of Sufi saints and scholars in the South added to the cultural and religious pluralism of the region.

Legacy and Transition

The legacy of the rise of regional powers during the 15th century endured through subsequent centuries, shaping the course of history. The Vijayanagara Empire, despite its eventual decline, left an indelible mark on South culture. The South sultanates, born out of the Bahmani Sultanate's fragmentation, continued to play significant roles in regional politics. Meanwhile, the challenges faced by the Lodi dynasty in the north set the stage for the transition to the Mughal Empire.

Vijayanagara's Enduring Legacy

The Vijayanagara Empire's enduring legacy is evident in the cultural, artistic, and architectural achievements that continue to define the South. Despite its decline after the Battle of Talikota in 1565, the empire's impact on the region's cultural identity remained resilient.

South Sultanates and Regional Dynamics

The South sultanates, emerging from the remnants of the Bahmani Sultanate, played pivotal roles in regional politics. Each sultanate developed its own unique identity, contributing to the diverse mosaic of the South region. The Qutb Shahi dynasty in Golconda, the Adil Shahi dynasty in Bijapur, and the Nizam Shahi dynasty in Ahmadnagar were among those that rose to prominence.

Transition to the Mughal Empire

In the north, the challenges faced by the Lodi dynasty paved the way for the rise of Babur, the founder of the Mughal Empire. The First Battle of Panipat in 1526 saw the decisive victory of Babur over Ibrahim Lodi, marking the establishment of the Mughal Empire. This transition marked a new chapter in Panjab history, where the Mughals would go on to shape the socio-political landscape for centuries.

A Tapestry of Diversity

The 15th century unfolded as a period of intricate political dynamics, with the rise of regional powers creating a diverse and dynamic tapestry. The Vijayanagara Empire, the Bahmani Sultanate, and the challenges faced by the Lodi dynasty in the north contributed to the complex socio-political landscape of the time. The enduring legacy of these regional powers is evident in the cultural, artistic, and architectural heritage that continues to shape the identity of different regions. The transitions and interactions during this period set the stage for the subsequent epochs of history, illustrating the resilience and adaptability of the Asian subcontinent's diverse civilization.

Turbulence and Invasions

The 15th century was marked by a tumultuous period of invasions, with Timur's campaign standing out as a significant event that reshaped the political landscape of the subcontinent. Timur, a Central Asian conqueror, launched a devastating invasion in 1398, leaving cities in ruins, cultural treasures destroyed, and countless lives lost. Delhi, then under Sultan Mahmud Tughlaq, faced unprecedented destruction. The aftermath of Timur's invasion weakened the already declining Delhi Sultanate, creating a power vacuum that allowed regional powers to assert greater autonomy. This decentralization of political power led to the emergence of regional entities such as the Vijayanagara Empire in the south and the Bahmani Sultanate in the South. The invasions not only contributed to political instability but also resulted in the realignment of territories and cultural shifts. The destruction wrought by Timur's forces led to a period of rebuilding and cultural synthesis, showcasing the resilience and adaptability of societies. While the legacy of this turbulence included the loss of cultural artifacts and architectural wonders, it also laid the groundwork for the subsequent emergence of regional powers and the shaping of a diverse and dynamic subcontinent. As the 15th century drew to a close, the impact of these invasions continued to reverberate, influencing the course of history in the centuries to come.

Caste System and Social Hierarchies

The caste system, an ancient social structure deeply ingrained in the fabric of Indian society, exerted a profound influence on the socio-cultural landscape, defining social hierarchies and imposing stringent restrictions on social mobility. Rooted in ancient Hindu scriptures, the caste system divided society into distinct groups, or castes, each assigned specific roles, duties, and privileges. This hierarchical social order became a defining feature of life, impacting individuals' lives, opportunities, and interactions for centuries.

The Four-Fold Varna System

The caste system evolved from the Varna system outlined in ancient Hindu scriptures, particularly the Rigveda. According to this system, society was divided into four varnas or classes: Brahmins (priests and scholars), Kshatriyas (warriors and rulers), Vaishyas (merchants and farmers), and Shudras (laborers and service providers). Each varna had its prescribed duties and responsibilities, forming the basis of a hierarchical social structure.

Rigidity and Hierarchy

Over time, the Varna system metamorphosed into a more rigid and complex caste system, incorporating numerous jatis or sub-castes. This intricate hierarchy was not only based on one's birth but also determined by occupation, creating a complex network of social divisions. The Brahmins occupied the highest rung, followed by the Kshatriyas, Vaishyas, and Shudras. Beyond these four main varnas, individuals were further categorized into numerous jatis, each associated with specific occupations and social roles.

Birth-based Discrimination

A fundamental characteristic of the caste system was its basis on birth. An individual's caste was predetermined by their family lineage, and this birth-based discrimination perpetuated a system where social status and opportunities were inherited rather than earned. The concept of purity and pollution associated with different castes further reinforced these divisions, restricting social interactions and marriages.

Occupational Rigidity

Caste determined not only an individual's social status but also their occupation. Occupational roles were hereditary, passed down from one generation to the next. The rigidity of the caste-based occupational system restricted individuals to specific professions, perpetuating economic disparities and limiting opportunities for social and economic advancement.

Social Exclusion and Untouchability

At the lowest rung of the caste hierarchy were the Dalits or Scheduled Castes, historically referred to as "untouchables." These communities faced severe social ostracism, discrimination, and were often relegated to performing menial and degrading tasks.

Restrictions on Social Mobility

The caste system significantly curtailed social mobility, making it challenging for individuals to transcend their predetermined social status. The concept of varna dharma emphasized adherence to one's assigned duties, discouraging individuals from aspiring to roles outside their designated caste. Social interactions, education, and economic opportunities were often dictated by one's caste, limiting the upward mobility of individuals.

Discrimination and Marginalization

Discrimination based on caste permeated various aspects of life, including access to education, employment, and public spaces. Many professions were traditionally closed off to individuals from certain castes, leading to the exclusion of talented individuals from diverse fields. The marginalization of certain caste groups perpetuated socio-economic disparities and hindered the overall progress of society.

Bhakti and Sufi Movements

The medieval period in Asia witnessed a profound spiritual renaissance marked by the Bhakti and Sufi movements. These transformative movements, originating in different religious traditions, converged in their emphasis on a more direct, personal connection with the divine. Challenging ritualistic practices and hierarchical norms, the Bhakti and Sufi movements not only shaped the religious landscape but also influenced the socio-cultural fabric of the subcontinent. Prominent figures like Bhagat Kabir, Bhagat Ravidas, and Sufi mystics left an indelible mark on the spiritual consciousness of the time, fostering a sense of unity and transcending religious boundaries.

Bhakti Movement

The Bhakti movement, rooted in the devotional traditions of religion, emerged around the 7th century but gained momentum during the medieval period. It sought to foster a more personal and immediate relationship between the individual and the divine, transcending the rigidities of ritualistic practices. The movement was characterized by a fervent devotion (bhakti) to a chosen deity, often seen as a manifestation of the ultimate reality.

Bhagat Kabir: A Weaver of Spiritual Wisdom

Among the prominent Bhakti saints, Bhagat Kabir stands as an icon of spiritual wisdom. Born in the 15th century, Kabir's verses, known as "Dohas," emphasized the universality of divine love and the futility of sectarian divisions. His teachings transcended the boundaries of Hinduism and Islam, reflecting a vision of spirituality that united rather than divided. Kabir challenged orthodoxies and rituals, advocating for a direct communion with the formless, transcendent God.

Bhagat Ravidas: The Saint of Equality

Bhagat Ravidas, another luminary of the Bhakti movement, hailed from the marginalized community of leatherworkers. His verses, infused with devotion and social consciousness, advocated for the equality of all individuals before God. Rejecting the caste-based hierarchy prevalent in society, Bhagat Ravidas emphasized the universality of spiritual experience and the idea that devotion surpassed social distinctions.

Sufi Movement

Parallel to the Bhakti movement, the Sufi movement emerged within Islam, emphasizing mystical experiences and a direct connection with God. Sufism sought to go beyond the legalistic and ritualistic aspects of Islam, encouraging practitioners, known as Sufis or mystics, to delve into the depths of spiritual consciousness through practices such as dhikr (remembrance of God), meditation, and ecstatic dance.

Sufi Orders and Khanqahs

Sufism gave rise to various Sufi orders, each with its unique practices and teachings. The establishment of Khanqahs, Sufi hospices, or monasteries became centers for spiritual learning and communal gatherings. Sufi saints aimed to guide individuals on the path of spiritual awakening, emphasizing the importance of love, humility, and renunciation of worldly attachments.

Rumi: The Poet of Divine Love

Jalaluddin Rumi, a 13th-century Sufi mystic and poet, transcended the boundaries of cultural and religious distinctions. His poetry, compiled in works like the "Masnavi" and the "Diwan-e-Kabir," delved into the realms of divine love, self-realization, and the unity of all existence. Rumi's teachings, characterized by inclusivity and spiritual ecstasy, continue to resonate globally.

Al-Hallaj: The Martyr of Divine Union

Mansur Al-Hallaj, a Sufi mystic from the 9th century, became infamous for his controversial utterance, "Ana al-Haqq" (I am the Truth), symbolizing the mystical union of the self with the divine. His unorthodox expressions of divine love led to his persecution and eventual execution. Al-Hallaj's life became a testament to the challenges faced by those who sought to express the ineffable dimensions of Sufi experiences.

Unity in Diversity

Both the Bhakti and Sufi movements rejected the rigidities of ritualistic practices prevalent in their respective religious traditions. The emphasis shifted from external observances to inner devotion and the cultivation of a personal connection with the divine. This rejection of ritualism fostered a more inclusive and direct approach to spirituality.

Universalism and Inclusivity

The Bhakti and Sufi movements embraced universalism, transcending religious boundaries and challenging sectarian divisions. The poetry and teachings of saints like Bhagat Kabir, Bhagat Ravidas, and Rumi emphasized the unity of all existence, portraying a vision where love for the divine surpassed the constraints of religious affiliations.

Social Consciousness

Both movements exhibited a keen social consciousness, challenging societal norms and advocating for equality. Bhagat Ravidas, from the low-caste community, exemplified how the transformative power of devotion could bridge social divides. Sufi saints often engaged in charitable activities, contributing to the welfare of their communities.

Mystical Love

Central to both movements was the theme of mystical love. Bhakti saints expressed profound love for their chosen deities, often using metaphors of human love to convey their devotion. Sufi poets like Rumi employed similar imagery, portraying divine love as the ultimate force that unites humanity and the divine.

Impact on Society

The Bhakti and Sufi movements played crucial roles in the cultural synthesis of medieval Asia. The intermingling of diverse cultural elements, influenced by the teachings of saints and mystics, resulted in a rich tapestry of art, music, and literature. The Bhakti and Sufi poetry became mediums for expressing the ineffable dimensions of spiritual experiences, fostering a unique syncretic culture.

The poetry of Bhakti saints and Sufi mystics not only contributed to the spiritual realm but also left an indelible mark on Asian arts and literature. Bhakti poetry, composed in regional languages, inspired devotional music and dance forms. Similarly, Sufi poetry influenced Panjabi, and Persian literature, creating a shared cultural heritage that transcended religious boundaries.

The teachings of Bhakti saints and Sufi mystics advocated for social reforms and harmony. Rejecting caste-based discrimination, these movements fostered a sense of equality and fraternity. The influence of these movements contributed to the gradual breakdown of rigid social hierarchies, creating spaces for dialogue and understanding among diverse communities.

Panjab Before the Advent of Sikhism

Before the emergence of Sikhism and the advent of Sri Guru Nanak Dev Ji in the 15th century, Panjab, situated in the northwest of the Indian subcontinent, bore witness to a diverse and dynamic historical tapestry shaped by various civilizations, empires, and cultural influences. The region's history, marked by the confluence of rivers, fertile plains, and strategic location, set the stage for the socio-political and cultural milieu that would ultimately give birth to Sikhism.

Ancient and Early Medieval Period

Indus Valley Civilization

The roots of Panjab's history delve into the ancient Indus Valley Civilization, one of the world's oldest urban cultures. The archaeological sites of Harappa and Mohenjo-Daro, situated in the western part of present-day Panjab, provide glimpses into the advanced urban planning, trade networks, and sophisticated lifestyle of the Harappan people.

Achaemenid Empire and Persian Influence

Under the rule of Persian kings like Darius and Xerxes, the Achaemenid Empire extended its influence into the northwestern regions, including Panjab. Persian cultural and administrative practices left an imprint on the local socio-political structures, contributing to the region's historical complexity.

Mauryan and Gupta Empires

In the ancient and early medieval periods, Panjab witnessed the rise and fall of empires, with the Mauryan and Gupta dynasties playing significant roles. The Mauryan Empire, under the rule of Emperor Ashoka, extended its influence into the region, spreading Buddhist teachings and contributing to the cultural mosaic. The Gupta Empire, known as the "Golden Age" of Indian history, saw the flourishing of art, science, and literature.

Islamic Invasions and the Delhi Sultanate

Arrival of Islam

The Islamic influence in Panjab began with the arrival of Muslim traders and Sufi mystics in the early medieval period. The region became a crossroads for cultural interactions between the indigenous Hindu-Buddhist traditions and the emerging Islamic civilization.

Ghaznavid and Ghuri Invasions

The 11th and 12th centuries witnessed invasions by Mahmud of Ghazni and Muhammad Gaur, marking the entry of Islam into the political landscape of Panjab. These invasions had a significant impact on the region, leading to cultural interactions, religious transformations, and the establishment of Muslim rule.

Delhi Sultanate

The establishment of the Delhi Sultanate in the 13th century further transformed the socio-political dynamics of Panjab. The sultans, including Qutb-ud-din Aibak and Alauddin Khilji, expanded their territorial control into the region, introducing Islamic governance and administrative structures.

Political Fragmentation and Mongol Invasions

Tughlaq and Sayyid Dynasties

The 14th century saw the rise of the Tughlaq and Sayyid dynasties within the Delhi Sultanate. However, this period was marked by political instability, administrative challenges, and the fragmentation of central authority, leading to the emergence of regional powers.

Mongol Invasions

The 14th century also witnessed invasions by the Mongols, particularly under the leadership of Timur (Tamerlane). The invasion of Timur in 1398 resulted in widespread devastation, including the sacking of Delhi and its impact on the political and cultural landscape of Panjab.

Socio-Cultural Fabric

Religious Pluralism

Before the advent of Sikhism, Panjab was characterized by religious pluralism, with Hinduism, Buddhism, and indigenous folk traditions coexisting alongside the emerging Islamic influences. The syncretic nature of the region allowed for cultural exchanges and interactions, shaping a diverse socio-religious fabric.

Sufi Influence

Sufi mystics played a crucial role in shaping the spiritual and cultural dynamics of Panjab. The teachings of Sufi saints, emphasizing love, tolerance, and direct communion with the divine, resonated with the local population and contributed to the synthesis of diverse religious traditions.

Economic Prosperity

Agrarian Economy

Panjab's fertile plains and the network of rivers, including the Indus and its tributaries, facilitated a flourishing agrarian economy. The region was known for its abundant harvests of wheat, barley, and other crops, contributing to its economic prosperity.

Trade Routes

The strategic location of Panjab made it a vital hub for trade and commerce. The Grand Trunk Road, connecting Central Asia with the Indian subcontinent, passed through Panjab, fostering trade networks and cultural exchanges. The region's economic vitality attracted merchants and travelers, further enriching its cultural milieu.

Emergence of Bhakti and Sufi Movements

Bhakti Movement

As the 15th century dawned, the socio-religious landscape witnessed the emergence of the Bhakti movement. Bhakti saints like Bhagat Kabir, Bhagat Ravidas, and others challenged established norms, emphasizing a direct, personal connection with the divine and transcending sectarian divisions.

Sufi Influence Continues

Simultaneously, the Sufi influence persisted, with Sufi mystics continuing to play a significant role in shaping the spiritual consciousness of the region. Their emphasis on love, inclusivity, and direct experiential knowledge of the divine resonated with a diverse population.

Before the Birth of Sri Guru Nanak Dev Ji

Before the birth of Sri Guru Nanak Dev Ji in the 15th century, the Asian subcontinent, including the region of Panjab, experienced a complex socio-political landscape characterized by various forms of oppression and cruelties on the common people. The prevailing power structures, including the ruling elites and religious authorities, often suppressed the voices of the common folk, leading to widespread exploitation, discrimination, and social injustice.

Feudal Exploitation and Economic Oppression

One of the significant forms of cruelty to the common people was rooted in the feudal system. Landownership was concentrated in the hands of a few powerful landlords and aristocrats, while the majority of the population worked the land as peasants. These peasants, often landless or with minimal landholdings, were subject to economic exploitation. The feudal lords imposed heavy taxes, arbitrary levies, and forced labor, extracting a significant portion of the agricultural produce. The economic oppression was a glaring injustice that contributed to the impoverishment of the common people.

Caste-based Discrimination and Social Injustice

Caste-based discrimination was deeply entrenched in the social fabric of the pre-15th century. The caste system, a hierarchical social structure, divided people into rigid categories, determining their social status, occupations, and rights. The upper castes, especially the Brahmins and Kshatriyas, enjoyed privileges and held positions of power, while the lower castes, including Shudras and Dalits, faced systemic discrimination and exploitation. Social mobility was severely restricted, and the common people, especially those from lower castes, endured cruelty in the form of untouchability, segregation, and denial of basic human rights.

Religious Intolerance and Oppression

Religious intolerance was another aspect of cruelty that affected the common people. The medieval period witnessed the rise of different religious empires, including the Delhi Sultanate, where the rulers belonged to the Islamic faith. The interactions between various religious communities were often marked by tension, leading to instances of persecution and oppression. The common people, who adhered to diverse religious beliefs and practices, faced discrimination based on their faith. Forced conversions, destruction of religious sites, and the imposition of religious taxes were some of the means through which the voices of the common people were suppressed.

Exploitative Practices of the Clergy

The clergy, both in Hindu and Islamic traditions, played a significant role in shaping the socio-religious landscape. However, in many instances, the clergy became a tool for exploitation rather than a source of spiritual guidance. In Hinduism, the Brahminical class exercised considerable influence, exploiting their religious authority to maintain social hierarchies. In Islam, the ulema (religious scholars) sometimes collaborated with the ruling elite to consolidate power, contributing to the oppression of the common people. The clergy often reinforced discriminatory practices and suppressed dissenting voices.

Unjust Taxation and Administrative Oppression

The common people were burdened with heavy taxation imposed by the ruling authorities. Land revenue, arbitrary taxes, and tributes took a substantial toll on the economic well-being of the populace. The administrative machinery often lacked transparency and accountability, enabling corrupt practices that further oppressed the common people. Unjust taxation became a tool of coercion, contributing to social inequalities and economic hardships.

Lack of Legal Protections

The absence of effective legal protections for the common people exacerbated their vulnerability. The legal systems of the time were often biased in favor of the ruling elite and lacked mechanisms to address the grievances of the common folk. The absence of a fair and impartial judiciary meant that instances of cruelty and injustice went unchecked, perpetuating a culture of impunity.

Ignored Voices and Suppression of Dissent

The voices of the common people were systematically ignored and suppressed by the ruling authorities. Attempts to voice dissent or challenge oppressive practices were met with severe consequences. Those who dared to question the established norms faced persecution, social ostracization, or even violence. The lack of avenues for expressing grievances and seeking redressal meant that the common people were silenced and subjugated.

Cultural and Spiritual Stagnation

The prevailing social and political conditions contributed to a sense of cultural and spiritual stagnation. Innovation and intellectual pursuits were often stifled, and the common people were denied the opportunity for holistic development. The oppressive structures in place hindered the growth of a society where individual expression, creativity, and spiritual exploration could flourish.

Lack of Impartiality

The justice system lacked impartiality, with the ruling elite often enjoying preferential treatment. The authorities, influenced by political considerations, social hierarchies, and religious biases, were prone to delivering judgments that favored those in positions of power. This lack of impartiality contributed to a culture of inequality and injustice.

Influence of Clergy on Legal Decisions

The clergy, both in Hindu and Islamic traditions, exerted significant influence on legal decisions. Religious leaders often interfered in legal matters, shaping the outcomes based on religious dogmas and hierarchical norms. This interference compromised the objectivity of the justice system and reinforced social divisions.

Discrimination Based on Caste and Social Status

Caste-based discrimination extended into the justice system, where individuals from lower castes faced systemic biases. The higher castes, including Brahmins and the ruling elite, often received preferential treatment in legal matters, while individuals from lower castes struggled to find justice. The caste system's grip on societal structures permeated the justice system, perpetuating inequality.

Arbitrary Nature of Punishments

Punishments meted out by the justice system were often arbitrary and disproportionately severe. The lack of standardized legal procedures allowed for subjective interpretations of laws, leading to inconsistent and unfair judgments. The powerful could escape with lenient sentences, while the common people faced harsh penalties for similar offenses.

Limited Access to Legal Representation

Access to legal representation was limited, especially for the common people. The absence of a robust legal framework meant that individuals often had to navigate the complexities of the justice system without adequate support. This lack of legal representation further marginalized those who sought justice, leaving them vulnerable to exploitation.

Absence of a Centralized Legal Code

The absence of a centralized and comprehensive legal code contributed to legal ambiguity. Different regions and rulers had their own set of laws, leading to confusion and inconsistency in legal proceedings. The lack of a unified legal framework undermined the principles of justice, creating a fragmented and unreliable system.

Corruption and Bribery

Corruption was rampant within the justice system. Bribery and nepotism influenced legal decisions, allowing the affluent to manipulate the system for their benefit. The common people, lacking resources and connections, faced challenges in navigating a system that prioritized personal interests over justice.

Ineffective Enforcement of Laws

Even when laws were in place, their enforcement was often ineffective. The authorities were sometimes complicit in allowing injustices to persist, especially when the powerful were involved. This lack of enforcement further eroded public trust in the justice system.

Repression of Dissent

The justice system was often used as a tool to repress dissent and stifle opposition. Those who questioned the established norms or sought to challenge the status quo were subjected to legal persecution, leading to a climate of fear and silencing of voices that called for social justice.

In this milieu of systemic oppression, Sri Guru Nanak Dev Ji emerged as a beacon of light, advocating for the rights and dignity of the common people. His teachings emphasized equality, social justice, and a direct connection with the divine, challenging the oppressive systems of his time. Sri Guru Nanak Sahib's message laid the foundation for the Sikh faith, which would continue to champion the cause of the marginalized and oppressed, providing a voice to those who had long been silenced by the cruelty of power structures.

Before the birth of Sri Guru Nanak Dev Ji in the 15th century, Panjab found itself ensnared in a complex web of socio-political challenges that cast a shadow over the lives of its inhabitants. Politically, the region grappled with frequent invasions, internal strife, and shifting power dynamics among various rulers, leading to a state of perpetual instability. Economic oppression was rampant as the feudal system entrenched itself, subjecting the majority of the population to exploitation by a privileged few who imposed heavy taxes and forced labor. Socially, the caste system dictated the lives of individuals, perpetuating discrimination and inequality, with the lower castes experiencing systemic oppression and untouchability. The religious landscape was marked by tensions as different religious communities navigated conflicts and occasional persecutions. The clergy, both in Hinduism and Islam, wielded considerable influence, often contributing to the suppression of dissent and the imposition of dogmas.

The justice system of Panjab was marred by a lack of impartiality, with the ruling elite enjoying preferential treatment and the clergy influencing legal decisions based on religious biases. Discrimination based on caste and social status permeated the justice system, resulting in systemic biases that favored the higher castes. Punishments were often arbitrary and disproportionately severe, and the common people faced challenges in accessing legal representation. The absence of a centralized legal code led to confusion and inconsistency in legal proceedings, while corruption and bribery further compromised the integrity of the system. The enforcement of laws was ineffective, allowing injustices to persist, and dissent was repressed through legal persecution, creating a climate of fear. Economic disparities and poverty were widespread, exacerbating social inequalities and hindering intellectual and cultural development. In this landscape of divisiveness and cruelty, the birth of Sri Guru Nanak Dev Ji brought a transformative message of justice, equality, and spiritual enlightenment, challenging the prevailing norms and laying the foundation for a more inclusive and compassionate society within the world tradition.

*****

THE BIRTH
OF
SIKHISM

THE BIRTH OF SIKHISM

Sikhism, one of the major world religions, originated in the Asian subcontinent during the 15th century. The founder of Sikhism, Sri Guru Nanak Sahib Ji, was born in 1469 in the village of Talwandi, now known as Nankana Sahib, in present-day east Panjab. Sri Guru Nanak Sahib Ji's teachings formed the basis of Sikhism, which sought to bridge the gap between Hinduism, Islam, and other world religions emphasizing the oneness of God and the equality of all human beings.

Sri Guru Nanak Sahib Ji declared, "There is no Hindu, there is no Muslim." This statement laid the foundation for Sikhism's core principles of equality, justice, and devotion to one God. Sri Guru Nanak Dev Ji traveled extensively, spreading his message and gaining followers known as Sikhs, meaning disciples or learners.

The ten successive Gurus played crucial roles in shaping Sikhism during its early stages. Sri Guru Nanak Sahib Ji was succeeded by Sri Guru Angad Dev Ji, Sri Guru Amar Das Ji, Sri Guru Ram Das Ji, Sri Guru Arjun Dev Ji, Sri Guru Hargobind Sahib Ji, Sri Guru Har Rai Ji, Sri Guru Har Krishan Sahib Ji, Sri Guru Teg Bahadur Sahib Ji, Sri Guru Gobind Singh Ji and the final eternal Guru Sri Guru Granth Sahib Ji. Sri Guru Arjan Dev Ji, the fifth Guru, compiled the Adi Sri Guru Granth Sahib Ji and established the foundation of the Sri Harmandir Sahib in Amritsar, Panjab, as the central place of worship.

The early Sikh community faced challenges and persecution, particularly under the Mughal rulers. The ninth Guru, Guru Tegh Bahadur Ji, sacrificed his life in defense of religious freedom, standing against the forced conversion of non-Muslims. This event further solidified Sikhism's commitment to the principles of justice and freedom.

The tenth Guru, Sri Guru Gobind Singh Ji, played a pivotal role in the institutionalization of Sikhism. He established the Khalsa, a community of Amritdhari Sikhs, on April 13, 1699, during the Vaisakhi festival. Guru Gobind Singh introduced the five articles of faith, known as the Five Ks (Kesh, Kara, Kanga, Kachera, and Kirpan), which Sikhs still observe today.

Sikhism's birthplace is often associated with the Panjab region, which spans parts of present-day India and Pakistan. The historical events and teachings of the Sikh Gurus laid the groundwork for the development of Sikhism as a distinct and vibrant religious tradition. The community's commitment to social justice, equality, and the remembrance of God continues to guide Sikh practices and values to this day.

Sri Guru Nanak Dev Ji

Sri Guru Nanak Dev Ji, the founder of Sikhism, was born on 1526 Bikrami Katak Sudhi Puranmasi (Wednesday, November 29, 1469), in the village of Rai Bhoi Di Talwandi, which is now known as Sri Nankana Sahib Ji and is located in present-day east Panjab. His parents, Sri Mehta Kalu Ji and Mata Tripta Ji, were devout lovers of God, and Sri Guru Nanak Sahib Ji grew up in a humble household.

From an early age, Sri Guru Nanak Sahib ji displayed a deep spiritual inclination and a compassionate nature. His innate curiosity and spiritual awareness set him apart from his peers. Legend has it that even as a child, he questioned prevailing religious practices and societal norms, showing signs of a profound understanding of the divine.

At the age of seven, Sri Guru Nanak Sahib Ji began his formal education and soon surpassed his teachers in wisdom and knowledge. Despite his early display of spiritual awareness, he also carried out his familial duties by assisting his father in agricultural work. Sri Guru Nanak Sahib's teachings of life often emphasized the importance of honest labor and living a truthful life.

One pivotal incident from Sri Guru Nanak Sahib's childhood, known as the "Sacha Sauda" or "True Bargain," exemplifies his extraordinary nature. Sent by his father to buy and sell goods in the market, young Sri Guru Nanak Sahib used the money not to engage in a profitable trade but to feed a group of hungry ascetics. When asked to account for the money, he explained that he had made a "true bargain" by providing nourishment for those in need.

As Sri Guru Nanak Sahib Ji physically matured, his inclination toward solitude and meditation became more apparent. He would often retreat to nature, engaging in contemplative practices. Legend has it that during one such occasion, he disappeared into the Kali Bei River for three days. Upon his reappearance, he declared, "There is no Hindu, there is no Muslim," emphasizing the fundamental unity of all humankind.

Sri Guru Nanak Sahib Ji had a transformative meeting during a divine communion, which marked the beginning of Udasis for his public mission on earthly realm. He emerged with a message of love, equality, and devotion to the one formless God. His teachings emphasized the futility of rituals and rituals that were devoid of genuine love and compassion.

Throughout his life, Sri Guru Nanak Sahib Ji undertook extensive journeys, traveling far and wide to spread his spiritual message. He engaged in dialogues with religious leaders of various traditions, aiming to bridge the gaps between different communities and Akal (God). Sri Guru Nanak Sahib's teachings laid the foundation for Sikhism, emphasizing the oneness of God, equality of all, and the importance of selfless service. His teachings continue to inspire millions of Sikhs and others worldwide and have left an indelible mark on the spiritual landscape of South Asia.

The divine call and spiritual experiences

Sri Guru Nanak Sahib Ji, the esteemed founder of Sikhism, experienced a profound divine calling that became the cornerstone for common public spiritual journey. This pivotal moment occurred when Sri Guru Nanak Sahib ji embarked on a meditative retreat into the Kali Bei River. After three days of deep contemplation, he emerged with a transcendent proclamation asserting the unity of God and the universal brotherhood of humanity, encapsulated in the profound statement, "There is no Hindu, there is no Muslim." This proclamation marked the commencement of Sri Guru Nanak Sahib's sacred mission to disseminate the principles of love, equality, and unwavering devotion to the formless Supreme Being.

Integral to Sri Guru Nanak Sahib's spiritual narrative is his profound experiences of divine realms, particularly his visitation to Sach Khand, the realm of truth. These mystical encounters bestowed upon him revelations and insights that he earnestly shared with his disciples. Sri Guru Nanak Sahib's hymns within the Sri Guru Granth Sahib Ji reflect his intimate connection with the divine, recounting dialogues with the Almighty and depicting celestial encounters that significantly shaped his spiritual teachings. His compositions, notably the Sidh Gosht, capture dialogues between Guru Nanak and Siddhas, exemplifying the depth of his spiritual experiences.

Sri Guru Nanak Sahib's spiritual odyssey also featured dialogues with celestial beings and divine entities, from which he tells profound wisdom and insights into the nature of God and the universe. The divine revelations he told throughout his life became the bedrock of Sikhism's ethical and spiritual doctrine. His hymns, known as Shabads, were composed during moments of divine inspiration, imparting universal truths, ethical principles, and the path to spiritual enlightenment.

The enduring significance of Sri Guru Nanak Sahib's divine call and spiritual experiences resonates in the foundational tenets of Sikhism. Emphasizing the oneness of God, equality among all human beings, and the imperative of leading a truthful and compassionate life, these experiences continue to serve as guiding principles for millions of Sikhs globally. Sri Guru Nanak Sahib's profound teachings, forged in the crucible of his direct communion with the divine, endure as a beacon of spiritual enlightenment, shaping the ethical and spiritual fabric of Sikh identity across generations.

Udasis (Travels)

Sri Guru Nanak Sahib's travels, known as Udasis, took him to various parts of South Asia and the Middle East, including regions that are now part of India, Pakistan, Bangladesh, Saudi Arabia, Iraq, and Sri Lanka. His journeys, spanning from the early 16th century, were not merely geographical expeditions but transformative voyages aimed at imparting spiritual wisdom and promoting a message of universal love and brotherhood.

First Udasi (1500-1506)

Sri Guru Nanak Sahib Ji's First Udasi, spanning from 1500 to 1506, marked the initiation of his transformative journeys aimed at spreading the message of oneness, compassion, and spiritual enlightenment. This first odyssey took Sri Guru Nanak Sahib Ji southeast towards the vibrant and culturally diverse regions of eastern India, notably Bengal and Assam. The journey was not merely a geographical exploration but a profound spiritual quest, during which Guru Nanak engaged with diverse communities, including Hindus and Buddhists, with the overarching theme of emphasizing the oneness of God and promoting ethical living.

Geographical Exploration

Sri Guru Nanak Sahib's decision to embark on his first Udasi was rooted in a profound calling to disseminate spiritual wisdom and foster a deeper understanding of the divine. The journey covered a vast expanse, with the Guru traversing through regions that are now part of modern-day India and Bangladesh. The geographical diversity of eastern India provided Sri Guru Nanak Sahib with a unique opportunity to interact with people from various cultural, linguistic, and religious backgrounds.

Interactions with Hindus

During his journey through eastern India, Sri Guru Nanak Sahib Ji engaged in meaningful dialogues with the Hindu community. His interactions were characterized by a profound emphasis on the oneness of God, transcending the boundaries of religious distinctions. Sri Guru Nanak Sahib challenged certain ritualistic practices prevalent in Hinduism, encouraging individuals to focus on the essence of true devotion and ethical living rather than external observances.

Sri Guru Nanak Sahib's conversations with Hindu priests, scholars, and ordinary individuals revolved around the fundamental unity of all existence. The Guru's teachings transcended sectarian divisions, urging people to recognize the divine thread that unites humanity. This approach aligned with his broader mission of promoting a universal spirituality that transcends religious boundaries.

Engaging with Buddhists

In the first Udasi, Sri Guru Nanak Sahib Ji interacted with the Buddhist community in the region. Buddhism emphasizes compassion and enlightenment. Buddhism learned common ground with Guru Nanak Sahib's teachings. The Guru's dialogues with Buddhists centered around ethical living, mindfulness, and the pursuit of spiritual enlightenment.

Sri Guru Nanak has engaged in discussions with Buddhists regarding the impermanence of life, the nature of suffering, and the path to liberation. While Buddhism and Sikhism have theological differences, Sri Guru Nanak Sahib's teachings emphasize ethical conduct, meditation, and the pursuit of a virtuous life.

Emphasizing the Oneness of God

Central to Guru Nanak's interactions during the First Udasi was the recurring theme of the oneness of God. His teachings echoed the profound spiritual insight during his divine communion, where he declared, "There is no Hindu, there is no Muslim." This proclamation encapsulated the essence of Guru Nanak's message – the recognition of a singular, formless God that transcends religious labels and affiliations.

The Guru's emphasis on monotheism was revolutionary in an era marked by religious diversity and sectarian conflicts. By transcending religious boundaries and emphasizing the universal nature of God, Sri Guru Nanak Sahib sought to establish a foundation for interfaith harmony and understanding.

Promoting Ethical Living

Alongside the theological aspects of his teachings, Guru Nanak consistently advocated for ethical living. His interactions with diverse communities included discussions on the importance of compassion, truthfulness, and selfless service. The Guru's emphasis on ethical conduct was aimed at transforming individuals and societies, fostering a culture of righteousness and justice.

Sri Guru Nanak Sahib's teachings on ethical living were not prescriptive; instead, they were rooted in the idea of self-realization and personal transformation. By engaging with people from various backgrounds, he addressed the practical aspects of leading a virtuous life in the context of different cultural and religious frameworks.

Legacy of the First Udasi

The First Udasi laid the foundation for Sri Guru Nanak Sahib's subsequent journeys and the overarching mission of Sikhism. The engagements with Hindus and Buddhists in eastern India provided valuable insights into the diverse tapestry of religious and cultural practices. The Guru's teachings during this period set the tone for the inclusivity and universality that would define Sikhism as a distinct spiritual path.

The legacy of the First Udasi is imprinted in the Sri Guru Granth Sahib Ji, the living Guru of Sikhism, where Sri Guru Nanak Sahib's hymns capture the essence of his interactions and teachings. The Guru's emphasis on the oneness of God and ethical living continues to resonate as a timeless message, guiding

Sikhs and seekers on the path of spiritual enlightenment.

Second Udasi (1506-1509)

Sri Guru Nanak Sahib Ji's Second Udasi, spanning from 1506 to 1509, marked another significant phase in his transformative journeys. During this period, Sri Guru Nanak Sahib traveled towards southern India, covering regions such as Andhra Pradesh, Karnataka, and Tamil Nadu. The Second Udasi presented an opportunity for the Guru Sahib to engage with the cultural and religious diversity of the southern part of the Indian subcontinent, fostering dialogues on spiritual principles and promoting the message of equality.

Geographical Exploration

The Second Udasi's geographical trajectory took Sri Guru Nanak Sahib Ji to the vibrant landscapes of southern India. His travels encompassed a wide range of terrains, from the fertile plains of Andhra Pradesh to the culturally rich regions of Karnataka and the ancient temples of Tamil Nadu. The Guru's interactions with the diverse cultural and linguistic milieu of southern India provided unique guidance and direction to the southern part of the country.

Engaging with Diverse Religious and Cultural Groups

One of the defining features of Sri Guru Nanak Sahib's Second Udasi was his engagement with diverse religious and cultural groups. With its rich tapestry of traditions, Second Udasi offered Southern

India the opportunity to talk with Guru with people from various backgrounds, including Hindus, Jains, and individuals adhering to indigenous spiritual practices.

1. **Dialogues with Hindus:** Sri Guru Nanak Sahib's interactions with the Hindu community in southern India were marked by discussions on spiritual principles and the universal nature of God. He continued to emphasize the oneness of God, encouraging individuals to move beyond ritualistic practices and embrace a deeper, more personal connection with the divine.

2. **Encounters with Jains:** The southern regions of India have a significant Jain presence, and Sri Guru Nanak Sahib's journey involved interactions with prominent members of the Jain community.

3. **Indigenous Spiritual Practices:** The southern part of India is known for its rich tapestry of indigenous spiritual practices and local traditions. Sri Guru Nanak Sahib's engagements have included dialogues with practitioners of various folk and tribal traditions, contributing to a broader understanding of the cultural and spiritual diversity prevalent in the region.

Fostering a Dialogue on Spiritual Principles

The Second Udasi was characterized by Sri Guru Nanak Sahib's commitment to fostering a dialogue on spiritual principles. His discourses went beyond theological differences, focusing on the common threads that unite humanity. The Guru's teachings emphasized the universal truths found in various religious traditions, fostering a sense of shared spirituality.

1. **Equality of All:** A recurring theme in Sri Guru Nanak Sahib's interactions during the Second Udasi was the promotion of equality. The Guru emphasized the inherent worth and dignity of all individuals, irrespective of their background. His teachings challenged societal hierarchies and discrimination, advocating for a society based on justice and equality.

2. **Oneness of God:** Continuing the theme from the First Udasi, Sri Guru Nanak Sahib reiterated the concept of the oneness of God. His discussions on this topic sought to transcend religious boundaries, encouraging people to recognize the divine unity that underlies diverse spiritual paths.

3. **Ethical Living:** The Guru's dialogues extended to discussions on ethical living. He encouraged individuals to lead virtuous lives, emphasizing the importance of compassion, truthfulness, and selfless service. The practical aspects of spirituality were integral to Guru Nanak's teachings, transcending theoretical doctrines.

Legacy of the Second Udasi

The legacy of Guru Nanak's Second Udasi is embedded in the teachings preserved in the Sri Guru Granth Sahib Ji. The hymns composed during this period reflect the Guru's engagement with the southern

Indian cultural landscape and his efforts to promote spiritual understanding and equality.

The Guru's emphasis on the oneness of God and the promotion of equality resonates as a timeless message that transcends geographical and temporal boundaries. The interactions during the Second Udasi contributed to the foundation of Sikhism as a path that recognizes and embraces the diversity of human experiences while emphasizing the commonality of our spiritual essence.

Third Udasi (1514-1518)

Sri Guru Nanak Sahib Ji's Third Udasi, spanning from 1514 to 1518, represents a significant phase in his journeys as he traveled northwest through present-day Pakistan, Afghanistan, and parts of the Middle East. This Udasi was distinguished by the Guru's exploration of historical and religious sites, including iconic destinations such as Mecca and Baghdad. The interactions with people of the Islamic faith during this journey played a pivotal role in promoting interfaith understanding and dialogue.

Geographical Exploration

The Third Udasi's geographical trajectory took Sri Guru Nanak Sahib through regions of great historical and cultural significance. The Guru traversed the northwestern expanses of the Indian subcontinent, covering present-day Pakistan and Afghanistan, before extending his journey into parts of the Middle East. This route allowed him to engage with diverse communities and visit renowned religious and historical sites.

Visits to Mecca and Baghdad

One of the notable aspects of the Third Udasi was Sri Guru Nanak Sahib's visits to Mecca and Baghdad. Mecca, the holiest city in Islam, holds profound significance for Muslims worldwide, being the birthplace of Prophet Muhammad and the site of the Kaaba. Sri Guru Nanak Sahib's presence in Mecca marked a unique moment of interfaith interaction with Islam by providing them with the right direction in spirituality and humanity. Sri Guru Nanak Sahib ji taught Islamic people the importance of loving humanity and embracing brotherhood and sisterhood to foster prosperity and bring peace to the world.

The journey also took Sri Guru Nanak Sahib Ji to Baghdad, a city steeped in history and known for its cultural and intellectual contributions. The Guru's visit to these iconic locations served as a bridge between Islam and Islamic thought, fostering an environment for dialogue and mutual understanding.

Interactions with People of Islamic Faith

Sri Guru Nanak Sahib's interactions with people of the Islamic faith during the Third Udasi played a significant role in promoting interfaith understanding. The Guru engaged in conversations with Muslims, scholars, and leaders, transcending religious boundaries to emphasize the common spiritual thread that unites all of humanity.

1. **Dialogue on Monotheism:** Sri Guru Nanak Sahib's discussions with people of Islamic faith centered around the shared belief in the oneness of God. The Guru's teachings

mentor and provide the right direction to the monotheistic principles of Islam, emphasizing the idea that there is only one formless and omnipresent God, irrespective of religious affiliations.

2. **Interfaith Harmony:** The Guru's journey through regions with a predominantly Islamic population provided an opportunity to cultivate interfaith harmony. Sri Guru Nanak Sahib's emphasis on the universality of spiritual truths aimed at fostering mutual respect and appreciation for the diverse paths that lead to the divine.

3. **Engaging with Islamic Scholars:** Sri Guru Nanak Sahib's travels involved interactions with Islamic scholars and leaders, contributing to an exchange of ideas and insights. The Guru's dialogues with intellectuals of the time went beyond theological differences, focusing on the core principles that unite various religious traditions.

Promoting a Message of Unity

The interactions during the Third Udasi Sri Guru Nanak Sahib Ji's commitment to promoting a message of unity among diverse communities. By engaging with people of the Islamic faith in their sacred spaces, the Guru sought to bridge cultural and religious divides, fostering an environment of mutual understanding and respect.

Sri Guru Nanak Sahib's teachings emphasized that the divine is beyond the confines of religious labels, and his interactions with the Islamic community exemplified Sikhism's universal nature. The Guru's message transcended regional and religious boundaries, advocating for a holistic understanding of spirituality that embraces the diversity of human experiences.

Legacy of the Third Udasi

The legacy of Sri Guru Nanak Sahib's Third Udasi is evident in the teachings preserved in the Sri Guru Granth Sahib Ji. The hymns during this journey reflect the Guru's engagement with the Islamic world and his efforts to promote understanding of interfaith. The emphasis on the oneness of God and the universal principle of spirituality resonates as a timeless message that transcends religious and cultural boundaries.

The Guru's journey through Mecca and Baghdad and his interactions with people of the Islamic faith remains an example of the potential for interfaith harmony. Sri Guru Nanak Sahib's vision of a world where diverse communities coexist in peace and understanding continues to inspire individuals seeking a path of unity and compassion.

Fourth Udasi (1519-1521)

Sri Guru Nanak Sahib Ji's Fourth Udasi, spanning from 1519 to 1521, marks another significant phase in his transformative journey. During this period, the Guru Sahib traveled to the Himalayan regions, including places like Kashmir and Nepal. The Fourth

Udasi was characterized by Sri Guru Nanak Sahib's engagement with ascetics and seekers, fostering discussions on spiritual truths and the path to enlightenment.

Geographical Exploration

The Fourth Udasi took Sri Guru Nanak Sahib to the majestic Himalayan regions, known for their awe-inspiring landscapes and spiritual significance. The Guru's journey included visits to places like Kashmir and Nepal, where the serene natural surroundings provided contemplation for his interactions with ascetics and seekers.

Engaging with Ascetics and Seekers

One of the distinctive features of the Fourth Udasi was Sri Guru Nanak Sahib's intentional engagement with ascetics and seekers. The Himalayan regions have long been associated with ascetic practices, meditation, and spiritual seeking. Sri Guru Nanak Sahib's interactions during this journey were characterized by dialogues with those who had chosen a life of renunciation and contemplation in pursuit of higher truths.

1. **Discourses on Spiritual Truths:** Sri Guru Nanak engaged in profound discussions with ascetics and seekers on matters of spiritual significance. The dialogues delved into the nature of reality, the purpose of life, and the essence of true enlightenment. The Guru's teachings emphasized the importance of a balanced and purposeful life, transcending the extremes of asceticism.

2. **Paths to Enlightenment:** The Fourth Udasi provided Guru Nanak with the opportunity to share insights on the various paths to enlightenment. While engaging with ascetics who followed rigorous practices, the Guru emphasized the holistic approach to spirituality advocated in Sikhism. His teachings underscored the integration of spiritual principles into everyday life, embracing both contemplation and active participation in society.

Emphasizing the Unity of Paths

Sri Guru Nanak Sahib's interactions during the Fourth Udasi reinforced his commitment to emphasizing the unity of spiritual paths. The Guru mentored the sincerity and dedication of ascetics and seekers while imparting the message that enlightenment could be attained through a variety of approaches. The common thread in these dialogues was the universal essence that transcends the diversity of spiritual practices.

1. **Unity in Diversity:** The Guru's teachings emphasized the unity found within the diversity of spiritual paths. Sri Guru Nanak Sahib recognized the value of various approaches to seeking the divine, encouraging individuals to find common ground in their shared pursuit of spiritual truths.

2. **Holistic Spirituality:** While engaging with ascetics and seekers, Sri Guru Nanak Sahib

Ji highlighted the concept of holistic spirituality. His teachings advocated for the integration of spiritual principles into every facet of life, emphasizing the importance of living with mindfulness, compassion, and ethical conduct.

Legacy of the Fourth Udasi

The legacy of Guru Nanak's Fourth Udasi is reflected in the teachings preserved in the Sri Guru Granth Sahib Ji. The hymns composed during this journey capture the essence of the Guru's interactions with ascetics and seekers, emphasizing the universal principles that underlie diverse spiritual paths.

The Guru's commitment to promoting a message of holistic spirituality, unity among diverse paths, and the integration of spiritual truths into everyday life continues to resonate within Sikhism. The Fourth Udasi serves as a testament to the Guru's vision of a spiritually enlightened and harmonious existence that encompasses the diversity of human experiences.

Interactions with People of Various Backgrounds

Sri Guru Nanak Sahib Ji's interactions with people of various backgrounds stand as a testament to his commitment to fostering unity, understanding, and spiritual enlightenment among diverse communities. The founder of Sikhism, Sri Guru Nanak Sahib Ji, embarked on extensive journeys spanning over two decades, covering a vast geographical expanse and engaging with individuals from different religious, cultural, and social backgrounds.

Dialogues with Hindus

Sri Guru Nanak Sahib Ji's dialogues with the Hindu community stand as a significant aspect of his teachings during his journeys. The Guru engaged extensively with Hindus, challenging certain ritualistic practices prevalent during his time and emphasizing the essence of true devotion. His interactions with Hindu priests and scholars were characterized by a profound focus on inner spirituality over external rituals.

In the course of his dialogues, Sri Guru Nanak Sahib Ji questioned certain ritualistic practices that had become prevalent within the Hindu religious framework. He advocated for a deeper understanding of the spiritual essence beyond mere adherence to external rituals. The Guru's teachings emphasized the importance of aligning one's actions with a genuine and heartfelt devotion to the divine.

Encounters with Hindu priests and scholars were often centered on the core principles of spirituality. Sri Guru Nanak Sahib Ji sought to redirect the focus from outward rituals to the inner transformation of the individual. His teachings underscored that true devotion goes beyond performing rites and ceremonies, emphasizing the cultivation of a sincere and loving connection with the divine.

The dialogues also addressed issues related to social justice and equality within the Hindu community. Sri Guru Nanak Sahib Ji challenged societal hierarchies and discrimination prevalent in his time, advocating for a more inclusive and compassionate society. His teachings mentor individuals to move beyond superficial distinctions and recognize the oneness of humanity, fostering a sense of unity and equality.

A spirit of dialogue and mutual understanding characterized Sri Guru Nanak Sahib's engagement with the Hindu community. Rather than rejecting Hindu practices outright, the Guru sought to redirect the focus towards the core spiritual principles that underlie various religious traditions. His teachings, captured in hymns within the Sri Guru Granth Sahib Ji, continue to resonate, emphasizing the universal and timeless aspects of true devotion and inner spirituality that transcend specific religious affiliations.

Interfaith Conversation

Sri Guru Nanak Sahib Ji imparted profound spiritual wisdom that transcended the boundaries of religious affiliations through his teachings. In his interfaith conversations, particularly with people of different faiths, such as Islam, Sri Guru Nanak Sahib Ji emphasized universal principles that could resonate across religious traditions. His teachings aimed to inspire individuals to cultivate a deep understanding of the divine, fostering unity and promoting a harmonious coexistence among diverse religious communities.

Sri Guru Nanak Sahib Ji stressed the oneness of God, underscoring that the ultimate reality is singular and formless. He encouraged followers of different faiths, including Islam, to recognize the commonality of their beliefs in a singular, omnipresent Creator. The

Guru's message was rooted in the notion that despite the diverse ways people may express their devotion, the essence of spirituality lies in acknowledging the shared humanity and the universal truth that binds all believers.

The teachings of Sri Guru Nanak Sahib Ji emphasized the importance of inner spirituality over external rituals. He encouraged individuals to go beyond the surface-level practices and delve into the depths of their hearts, fostering a sincere and loving connection with the divine. This emphasis on inner devotion and personal transformation sought to unite people of different faiths under a common understanding of the core principles that guide a spiritual life.

Furthermore, Sri Guru Nanak Sahib Ji mentored for social justice, equality, and compassion, values to the teachings of Islam, Hindus, Buddhism, Jainism, and other religious traditions. His vision extended beyond theological discussions to address the practical aspects of living a virtuous and compassionate life. The Guru's teachings on ethical conduct and the pursuit of a righteous existence provided a shared ethical foundation for followers of various faiths.

Sri Guru Nanak Sahib Ji's teachings encouraged an inclusive approach to spirituality, mentored individuals to rise above sectarian divisions, and recognized the divine unity that underlies diverse religious paths. His message sought to create a space where people of different faiths could come together in mutual respect and understanding, fostering a sense of unity and brotherhood. The legacy of Sri Guru Nanak

Sahib Ji's teachings in interfaith dialogue continues to inspire individuals to embrace a broader, inclusive vision of spirituality that transcends religious boundaries.

Encounters with Siddha and Yogis

Sri Guru Nanak Sahib Ji's encounters with Siddhas (enlightened beings) and Yogis during his transformative journeys added another dimension to his spiritual discourse. These encounters, as captured in the Sidh Gosht, a composition in the Sri Guru Granth Sahib Ji, reveal profound conversations with those who had delved deeply into mystical and ascetic practices. The dialogues emphasize the importance of humility, selflessness, and devotion on the spiritual path.

Central to Sri Guru Nanak Sahib Ji's discussions with the Siddhas and Yogis was the emphasis on humility and selflessness. The Guru challenged any sense of spiritual arrogance or ego that might arise from advanced mystical experiences. He advocated for a humble approach to the divine, recognizing the importance of egolessness on the journey to true spiritual realization.

The Sidh Gosht, a poetic dialogue within the Sri Guru Granth Sahib Ji, serves as a timeless guide for seekers. It emphasizes the importance of a humble, selfless, and devoted approach to the spiritual path. Sri Guru Nanak Sahib's teachings during these encounters encouraged a heart-centered connection with the divine, transcending mere ritualistic or intellectual pursuits.

The dialogues also underscored the significance of devotion on the spiritual path. Sri Guru Nanak Sahib Ji emphasized that irrespective of one's spiritual attainments or practices, true devotion to the divine is essential. The Guru's messages resonated with the timeless principles of humility, selflessness, and devotion, fostering a shared understanding of the spiritual journey that transcends specific religious or ascetic practices.

Furthermore, Sri Guru Nanak Sahib's discussions with the Siddhas and Yogis delved into the nature of illusion (Maya) and the path to transcending it. The Guru guided the Siddhas to recognize the impermanence of the material world and the importance of anchoring oneself in the eternal truth, stressing that true liberation comes from understanding and transcending the illusions that bind the soul.

The Sidh Gosht reflects Sri Guru Nanak Sahib Ji's ability to integrate diverse spiritual perspectives. While engaging with Siddhas and Yogis, the Guru seamlessly wove Sikh principles into the conversation, emphasizing the universality of spiritual truths and the common essence that underlies various paths. These encounters showcase the universal wisdom embedded in Sikh teachings, inspiring seekers to embrace a holistic and heart-centered approach to the divine. The legacy of Sri Guru Nanak Sahibs's encounters with Siddhas and Yogis endures as an integral part of Sikh spirituality, offering valuable insights into the essence of the spiritual journey.

Social and Economic Justice

Sri Guru Nanak Sahib Ji's transformative journey went beyond religious dialogues as he actively engaged with social and economic issues, advocating for justice, equality, and compassion. The Guru's commitment to addressing societal concerns is a prominent aspect of his teachings, emphasizing the interconnectedness of spiritual and worldly affairs.

Sri Guru Nanak Sahib's focus on social justice was evident in his critique of prevailing societal norms that perpetuated discrimination and inequality. He challenged the caste system and other forms of social hierarchy, advocating for a society where every individual is treated with dignity and respect regardless of their background. The Guru's teachings aimed to dismantle the barriers that separated communities and fostered a vision of a just and inclusive society.

Equality was a cornerstone of Sri Guru Nanak Sahib's message, and he confronted societal disparities that marginalized certain groups. The Guru emphasized the inherent worth and dignity of all individuals, irrespective of their caste, creed, or social status. His teachings sought to uplift the downtrodden, encouraging a society that valued each person's contributions without prejudice.

Compassion played a crucial role in Sri Guru Nanak Sahib's vision for social harmony. He urged individuals to cultivate empathy and kindness towards one another, fostering a spirit of brotherhood and unity. The Guru's teachings on compassion extended beyond mere sentiment to practical actions that aimed at alleviating the suffering of the less fortunate.

Economic justice was another dimension of Sri Guru Nanak's advocacy for a just society. He critiqued exploitative economic practices and encouraged ethical conduct in business and trade. The Guru promoted the concept of "kirat karo," emphasizing the importance of honest labor and fair dealings to sustain oneself and contribute to the welfare of the community.

Sri Guru Nanak Sahib's engagement with social and economic issues was not confined to theoretical discourse. He led by example, establishing the principles of the "langar" system, where people from all walks of life could sit together and share a communal meal. This practice underscored the Guru's commitment to breaking down social barriers and promoting equality through shared sustenance.

The legacy of Sri Guru Nanak Sahib's advocacy for social and economic justice endures in Sikh teachings and practices. The Guru's teachings laid the foundation for Sikh principles of seva (selfless service) and the pursuit of justice. The Sri Guru Granth Sahib Ji, the living Guru of Sikhism, contains hymns that reflect Sri Guru Nanak Sahib's vision for a just and compassionate society, inspiring generations to come to strive for social equality and economic fairness. The Guru's teachings on social justice remain a guiding light, encouraging individuals to actively contribute to creating a world where all people are treated with fairness, dignity, and compassion.

Advocacy for Women's Rights

Sri Guru Nanak Sahib Ji's transformative journey and teachings extended to include advocacy for women's rights and equality. The Guru's interactions reflected a commitment to challenging societal norms that marginalized women, emphasizing the dignity and equal spiritual potential of women in a time when prevailing norms often subordinated them.

Sri Guru Nanak Sahib's advocacy for women's rights was grounded in the principle of equality. He challenged the discriminatory practices of the time that limited women's social and spiritual participation. The Guru's teachings underscored the inherent worth and spiritual potential of women, urging society to recognize and respect their contributions on an equal footing with men.

In a society where women faced various forms of inequality, Sri Guru Nanak Sahib's teachings sought to dismantle these barriers. He emphasized the importance of recognizing women's agency and their right to actively participate in both spiritual and worldly affairs. The Guru's message rejected the notion of women as inferior or subordinate, encouraging a paradigm shift toward a more inclusive and egalitarian society.

Sri Guru Nanak Sahib's engagement with women went beyond theoretical discourse. He actively promoted the involvement of women in religious practices and community affairs. The Guru challenged gender-based restrictions, advocating for women's participation in congregational worship, spiritual discussions, and the overall development of their spiritual potential. This inclusive approach aimed at breaking down the barriers that limited women's access to education and spiritual growth.

The Guru's teachings on women's rights were integrated into the broader framework of Sikh principles. Sri Guru Nanak Sahibs's successors, the Sikh Gurus, continued this advocacy for women's equality. The institution of langar, where individuals sit together regardless of gender or social status, exemplified the Guru's commitment to fostering equality and inclusivity.

Sri Guru Nanak Sahib's legacy in advocating for women's rights remains influential in Sikhism. The Sri Guru Granth Sahib Ji, the living Guru of Sikhism, includes hymns that emphasize the equal spiritual potential of men and women. Sikh women, known as "Kaur," carry the title bestowed by Sri Guru Gobind Singh Ji, emphasizing their sovereign and equal status. Sikhism's emphasis on equality, justice, and respect for all individuals, irrespective of gender, reflects Sri Guru Nanak Sahib's revolutionary stance on women's rights during his time and serves as an inspiration for promoting gender equality in contemporary societies.

Key Teaching and Philosophy

Sri Guru Nanak Sahib Ji, the founder of Sikhism, imparted a profound and transformative set of teachings that form the bedrock of Sikh philosophy. His key teachings encompass a holistic approach to life, emphasizing the oneness of God, equality of all humans, selfless service, and a commitment to social justice. These teachings are enshrined in the Guru Granth Sahib, the holy scripture of Sikhism.

1. **Ek Onkar (Oneness of God):** Central to Sri Guru Nanak Sahib's philosophy is the concept of "Ek Onkar," affirming the oneness of God. The Guru emphasized that there is only one formless, omnipresent, and eternal Creator who transcends religious and cultural boundaries. This principle lays the foundation for Sikh monotheism, emphasizing a universal and inclusive understanding of the divine.

2. **Equality and Oneness of Humanity:** Sri Guru Nanak Sahib Ji vehemently advocated for the equality of all human beings, irrespective of caste, creed, gender, or social status. The Guru rejected societal hierarchies and discrimination, proclaiming that all individuals share the same divine spark within. The teachings promote a sense of oneness, recognizing the entire human race as one family.

3. **Naam Simran (Meditation on God's Name):** Sri Guru Nanak Sahib Ji emphasized the significance of connecting with the divine through constant remembrance and meditation on God's name, known as "Naam Simran." This practice is central to Sikh spirituality, fostering a continuous awareness of the divine presence in everyday life.

4. **Kirat Karo (Honest Livelihood):** The Guru emphasized the importance of engaging in honest labor and ethical conduct to sustain

oneself and contribute to the welfare of the community. "Kirat Karo" encourages Sikhs to earn their livelihood through hard work and integrity, avoiding exploitation and dishonest practices.

5. **Vand Chhakna (Sharing with Others):** Sri Guru Nanak Sahib Ji's teachings include the principle of "Vand Chhakna," advocating selfless service and sharing with those in need. This concept is reflected in the Sikh tradition of langar, a community kitchen where free meals are provided to all, regardless of background. It promotes the idea of collective well-being and compassion for others.

6. **Rejecting Ritualism:** Sri Guru Nanak Sahib Ji rejected ritualistic practices that were devoid of true devotion and spiritual understanding. He emphasized the importance of sincere devotion and ethical living over empty rituals.

7. **Humility and Humbleness:** The Guru placed a significant emphasis on humility, encouraging individuals to remain modest and recognize the divine within themselves and others. The Sikh greeting "Sat Sri Akaal" translates to "True is the timeless one," reinforcing the acknowledgment of the divine in every interaction.

8. **Social Justice and Activism:** Sri Guru Nanak Sahib Ji actively engaged with issues of social justice, challenging discrimination, and advocating for equality. His teachings laid the

groundwork for Sikh activism in various social and political arenas.

Sri Guru Nanak Sahib Ji's teachings transcend the boundaries of time and remain relevant in guiding Sikh thought and practice. The philosophy emphasizes the integration of spirituality into everyday life, fostering a sense of unity, equality, and service to humanity. These teachings continue to inspire millions of Sikhs and other communities worldwide, guiding them on a path of righteousness, compassion, and devotion to the divine.

Sri Guru Angad Sahib Ji

Sri Guru Angad Sahib Ji, the second Guru of Sikhism, played a crucial role in the development and dissemination of the Sikh faith. Born on 1561 Bikrami, Vaisakh Sudhi Ekam (Saturday, 23 April 1504), in the village of Matte-di-Sarai in Ferozepur, Panjab, Guru Angad Dev Ji's early life was marked by humility, devotion, and a deep spiritual inclination.

Early Life

Guru Angad Sahib Ji was originally named Lehna. His parents were Bhai Pheru Mal Ji and Mata Sabhirai Ji. From a young age, Bhai Lehna Ji displayed qualities of kindness and compassion. He married Bibi Khivi Ji, and they had two sons, Bhai Dasu Ji and Bhai Datu Ji. Bahi Lehna Ji was known for his hard work and dedication to Guru Nanak Sahib Ji and Sikhism.

Guru Angad Sahib Ji's life took a transformative turn when he encountered Guru Nanak Sahib Ji, the founder of Sikhism. Impressed by Bhai Lehna Ji's sincerity and dedication, Guru Nanak Sahib Ji recognized his spiritual potential and appointed him as a disciple. Guru Angad Sahib Ji served Guru Nanak Dev Ji with unwavering devotion and humility.

Becoming the Guru

Before Guru Nanak Sahib Ji left his physical form, he tested the faith and commitment of his followers. Sri Guru Angad Sahib Ji emerged successful in these tests, and on 1596 Bikrami Asu Vadi Panchami (6 October 1539), Guru Nanak Sahib Ji formally bestowed Guruship upon him, renaming him Angad, meaning "one's limb" or "part of oneself." This symbolized the continuity of the divine spirit passing from one Guru to the next.

Sri Guru Angad Sahib Ji continued and expanded the work Amritdhari by Sri Guru Nanak Sahib Ji. He contributed significantly to the compilation of the Sri Guru Granth Sahib Ji, the living Guru of Sikhism. Sri Guru Angad Sahib Ji is credited with introducing the Gurmukhi script and encouraging education and literacy among the Sikh community and world communities.

Philosophy

Sri Guru Angad Sahib Ji's teachings emphasized the importance of devotion, humility, selfless service, and living a truthful life. He stressed the significance of Nam Simran (meditation on the Divine Name) and the practice of honest labor. Sri Guru Angad Sahib Ji also laid the foundation for the langar system, a community kitchen that provides free meals to all, irrespective of caste, creed, or background.

His philosophy centered around the idea of selfless service, devotion to God, and the importance of community. Sri Guru Angad Sahib Ji played a vital role in shaping the Sikh community and preparing it for the challenges ahead.

Sri Guru Angad Sahib Ji's early life was characterized by humility and devotion. His journey to becoming the Guru was marked by dedicated service to Sri Guru Nanak Sahib Ji, and his philosophy revolved around the values of selfless service, devotion, and living a truthful life. His contributions to Sikhism, including the introduction of the Gurmukhi script and the langar system, continue to shape the Sikh community to this day.

Key Principles

1. **Nam Simran (Meditation on the Divine Name):** Sri Guru Angad Dev Ji emphasized the importance of constant remembrance and meditation on the Nam Simran (Divine Name). This practice is central to Sikh spirituality and helps individuals develop a strong connection with the divine.

2. **Seva (Selfless Service):** The principle of seva, or selfless service, is a cornerstone of Sikhism. Sri Guru Angad Sahib Ji promoted the idea of serving others without any expectation of reward. This concept is reflected in the langar system, where free meals are provided to all, fostering equality and humility.

3. **Sach Da Marg Living a Truthful Life (Living a Truthful Life):** Sri Guru Angad Sahib Ji taught

the importance of leading a truthful and honest life. Sikhs are encouraged to practice truthfulness in their thoughts, words, and actions, aligning themselves with the divine truth.

Key Initiatives

1. **Introduction of Gurmukhi Script:** Sri Guru Angad Sahib Ji is credited with formalizing and popularizing the Gurmukhi script. This script was instrumental in recording the teachings of the Gurus and served as a unifying factor for the Sikh community.

2. **Educational Reforms:** Recognizing the importance of education, Guru Angad Dev Ji Amritdhari educational reforms within the Sikh community and world communities. He established schools to promote literacy and encouraged learning the Gurmukhi script to enable individuals to read and understand the Gurbani.

3. **Mal Akhara (Physical fitness):** In addition to emphasizing spiritual and moral values, Sri Guru Angad Sahib Ji recognized the importance of physical well-being and self-defense. The Mal Akhara served as a place for Sikhs to engage in physical exercises, martial arts, and training in the use of weapons. This was done not only for self-defense but also to instill discipline and a sense of responsibility among the Sikh community.

4. **Langar System:** Sri Guru Angad Sahib Ji expanded the langar system, which was Amritdhari by Guru Nanak Sahib Ji. The langar is a community kitchen that serves free meals to all, irrespective of caste, creed, or social status. This practice promotes equality, community, and selfless service.

Key Teachings

1. **Nimrata (Humility):** Sri Guru Angad Sahib Ji exemplified humility in his life. He taught Sikhs to be humble and to recognize the divine essence within all beings, irrespective of their social status.

2. **Devotion to the Guru and Akal (God):** Sri Guru Angad Sahib Ji emphasized unwavering devotion to the Guru and Akal (God). Sikhs are encouraged to cultivate a deep love for the divine and to surrender themselves to the teachings of the Sri Guru Granth Sahib Ji.

3. **Family Values:** Sri Guru Angad Sahib Ji, in his own life, demonstrated the importance of familial responsibilities. Sikhs are taught to fulfill their family obligations while maintaining a strong connection with Akal (God) and living by the principles of Sikhism.

4. **Community Service:** The concept of selfless service, or seva, is a recurring theme in Sri Guru Angad Dev Ji's teachings. Sikhs are encouraged to engage in acts of kindness and service to the community, fostering a sense of unity and compassion.

Sri Guru Angad Sahib Ji's key principles include Nam Simran, seva, living a truthful life, and recognizing the Guru Granth Sahib as the eternal Guru. His key initiatives include the introduction of the Gurmukhi script, educational reforms, Mal Akhara, and the expansion of the langar system. His teachings encompass humility, devotion, family values, and community service, providing a comprehensive guide for the Sikh way of life.

Sri Guru Amar Das Sahib Ji

Sri Guru Amar Das Sahib Ji was the third Guru of Sikhism, born on 1526 Bikrami Vaisakh Sudhi Chaudas (Friday, May 5, 1479), in Basarke village, near Amritsar, Panjab.

Early Life

Amar Das Ji was born to Bhai Tej Bhan Bhalla and Mata Lachmi Ji. His original name was Bhai Amar Das. He spent much of his early life as a devout Sikh, practicing meditation and serving the community. He worked as a successful trader in crops and livestock.

Becoming a Guru

Sri Guru Amar Das Ji's journey to becoming the third Guru of Sikhism is significant. At the age of 61, after hearing the hymns of Sri Guru Angad Sahib Ji (the second Guru), he felt a deep spiritual awakening. He traveled to Khandur Sahib, where Guru Angad Sahib Ji recognized his spiritual qualities and appointed him as a disciple. Sri Guru Amar Das Ji devotedly served Guru Angad Dev Ji for several years. Sri Guru Amar Das Ji was chosen as the third Guru by the Sri Guru Angad Sahib Ji, following the principle of Guru Nanak's divine succession.

Philosophy

Sri Guru Amar Das Ji made substantial contributions to Sikh philosophy and institutional practices. He emphasized the principle of equality, rejecting caste-based discrimination. Sri Guru Amar Das Ji established the concept of the "Piri-Miri" system, appointing Sikh spiritual leaders (Piris) and administrators (Miris) without any consideration of their social background.

Sri Guru Amar Das Ji highlighted the importance of devotion to God and selfless service (Seva) to humanity. He institutionalized the practice of Langar (community kitchen), where people from all walks of life could sit together and share a meal, promoting equality and unity.

Sri Guru Amar Das Ji composed several hymns that are included in the Sri Guru Granth Sahib Ji, the living Guru of Sikhism. His hymns reflect spiritual wisdom, devotion, and a deep understanding of the divine. Sri Guru Amar Das Ji's contributions played a crucial role in shaping Sikhism into a distinct and compassionate path, emphasizing equality, service, and devotion to the divine.

key principle of Sri Guru Amar Das Ji

The principles of Sri Guru Amar Das ji collectively shaped the Sikh way of life, creating a community that values equality, service, humility, and devotion to the divine. The teachings of Guru Amar Das Ji continue to inspire Sikhs worldwide to lead lives guided by these profound principles.

1. **Sarbat da Bhala (Equality):** Sri Guru Amar Das Ji rejected the hierarchical caste system prevalent in society during his time. He firmly believed that all individuals, regardless of their social background, were equal in the eyes of the divine. Sri Guru Amar Das Ji introduced the concept of "Manas Ki Jaat Sabhe Eke Pehchanbo," which translates to "recognize all of mankind as a single caste of humanity." This idea aimed to eliminate social divisions and foster a sense of unity among all people.

2. **Sewa (Service to Humanity):** Sri Guru Amar Das Ji institutionalized the practice of selfless service (sewa) as a fundamental aspect of Sikhism. This involved helping those in need, providing for the less fortunate, and engaging in acts of kindness without any expectation of personal gain. The concept of "Langar" exemplifies this principle, where a free community kitchen was established to serve food to all, regardless of their background. This practice continues in Sikh Gurdwaras worldwide today.

3. **Guru Ka Langar (Community Living):** Sri Guru Amar Das Ji established the tradition of "Guru Ka Langar," a communal kitchen where everyone, irrespective of their social status, could sit together and share a common meal.

This practice aimed to break down barriers and promote a sense of equality and community.

4. **Women's Empowerment:** Sri Guru Amar Das Ji actively worked towards empowering women and challenging societal norms that oppressed them. He condemned practices like Sati (widow immolation) and advocated for the rights and dignity of women. Sri Guru Amar Das Ji appointed women as leaders and preachers, recognizing their spiritual potential and promoting gender equality within the Sikh community.

5. **Devotion and Meditation (Naam Simran):** Sri Guru Amar Das Ji emphasized the importance of connecting with the divine through devotion and meditation. The practice of "Naam Simran," or remembrance of God's name, became central to Sikh spirituality. Sri Guru Amar Das Ji taught that true spiritual enlightenment could be achieved through a sincere and dedicated focus on meditation, leading to a closer relationship with the divine.

6. **Nimrata (Humility):** Sri Guru Amar Das Ji stressed the virtue of humility as a cornerstone of spiritual life. He taught that humility was essential for personal growth and spiritual progress. Sri Guru Amar Das Ji himself exemplified humility by leading a simple life and practicing what he preached. He believed that ego and pride hindered one's spiritual journey.

7. **Family Values:** Sri Guru Amar Das Ji emphasized the importance of ethical conduct within familial relationships. He advocated for compassion, love, and mutual respect within the family unit. Sri Guru Amar Das Ji recognized the family as a crucial institution and encouraged individuals to fulfill their familial duties while maintaining a connection with the divine through spiritual practices.

Sri Guru Ramdas Sahib Ji

Sri Guru Ram Das Ji, born in 1531 Bikrami Katak Vadi Duj (Thursday, 2 November 1534), was the fourth Sikh Guru and served as the spiritual leader of the Sikhs from 1574 until 1581. He is known for his pivotal role in shaping Sikhism, particularly in the areas of religious practices and community building. Under his leadership, Amritsar, which is now considered the spiritual capital of the Sikhs, was founded, and the Sri Harmandir Sahib Ji was constructed. Sri Guru Ramdas Sahib Ji also composed hymns, which are included in the Sikh's living Guru, Sri Guru Granth Sahib Ji. His teachings emphasized the importance of service, humility, and devotion to God. Today, he is revered as a saint, and his legacy continues to inspire millions of Sikhs and others around the world.

Early Life

Sri Guru Ram Das Ji was born in Lahore, present-day east Panjab on 1531 Bikrami Katak Vadi Duj (Thursday, 2 November 1534),. Guru Ji birth name was Bhai Jetha. He belonged to the Sodhi Khatri family, and his parents were Bhai Hari Das and Mata Anup Devi. Bhai Jetha grew up in a devout Sikh family, and from an early age, he displayed spiritual inclinations.

Becoming a Guru

Bhai Jetha became a disciple of Sri Guru Amar Das Ji, the third Sikh Guru. He dedicated himself to serving the Guru and the Sikh community. Over time, his humility and devotion earned the Guru's trust and respect. Sri Guru Amar Das recognized Bhai Jetha's spiritual qualities and appointed him his successor, giving him the name Sri Guru Ramdas Sahib Ji.

Philosophy

Sri Guru Ram Das Ji emphasized the importance of seva (selfless service), devotion to God, and the equality of all individuals. He continued the work of his predecessors in spreading the message of Sikhism. He established the city of Amritsar and began the construction of the Sri Harmandir Sahib, famously known as the Sri Darbar Sahib. The Sri Harmandir Sahib Ji became the central place of worship for Sikhs and Khalsa Panth and a symbol of the community's unity.

Sri Guru Ramdas Sahib Ji's teachings focused on the idea of surrendering to the divine will, practicing humility, and treating all people with equality and respect. His spiritual hymns, included in the Sri Guru Granth Sahib Ji, reflect these principles and continue to guide Sikhs in their spiritual journey.

Sri Guru Ramdas Sahib Ji's early life, the process of becoming a Guru, and his philosophy centered around humility, selfless service, devotion to God, and the promotion of equality among all individuals. His contributions played a crucial role in shaping Sikhism as a distinct and vibrant religious tradition.

Key Principles of Sri Guru Ramdas Ji

Sikhism is based on certain key principles that have been the foundation of this religion. The teachings of Sikhism emphasize spiritual and ethical values and promote a way of life that seeks union with the divine. Sri Guru Ramdas Sahib Ji gives several key principles that are important to this religion.

1. **Nimrata (Humility):** Guru Ram Das Ji stressed the importance of humility as a fundamental virtue. Sikhs are encouraged to cultivate a sense of modesty, acknowledging the greatness of the divine and recognizing the equality of all individuals. The Guru himself exemplified humility in his life and teachings.

2. **Bhakti (Devotion to God):** Central to Sri Guru Ramdas Ji's philosophy is the concept of Bhakti or devotion to God. Sikhs are encouraged to develop a deep, loving relationship with the divine through prayer, meditation, and selfless service. The Guru emphasized the importance of connecting with the divine through sincere and heartfelt devotion.

3. **Seva (Selfless Service):** The principle of selfless service is integral to Sikhism. Sri Guru Ramdas Ji highlighted the significance of seva, where individuals serve others without any

expectation of reward. This service can take various forms, including community service, helping those in need, and contributing to the well-being of society.

4. **Samanta (Equality):** Sri Guru Ramdas Ji strongly advocated for the equality of all human beings. He emphasized that regardless of caste, creed, gender, or social status, everyone is equal in the eyes of the divine. Sri Guru Ramdas Ji worked towards breaking down social barriers and promoting a society based on justice and fairness.

5. **Hukam (Divine Will):** Sri Guru Ramdas Ji taught the acceptance of the Hukam (divine will). Sikhs are encouraged to surrender to the will of God, understanding that everything happens as per divine plan. This principle emphasizes the importance of contentment, patience, and trust in the divine order.

6. **Sangat (Community Living):** The Guru emphasized the concept of Sangat, referring to the community of believers who gather for worship, prayer, and mutual support. Community living fosters a sense of unity, shared values, and collective spiritual growth.

Sri Guru Arjan Dev Sahib Ji

Sri Guru Arjan Dev Ji, the fifth Guru of Sikhism, was born on 1620 Bikrami Vaisakh Vadi Saptami (14 April 1563) in Goindwal, Panjab. He was the youngest son of Guru Ramdas Sahib Ji, the fourth Sikh Guru, and Mata Bhani Ji. Sri Guru Arjan Dev Ji's early life was marked by a deep sense of spirituality, and he grew up in an environment influenced by the teachings of truth.

Early Life

Sri Guru Arjan Dev Ji spent his formative years in Goindwal, where his father, Sri Guru Ramdas Sahib Ji, established the Guru Ka Chak, a center for religious activities. His mother, Mata Bhani Ji, played a crucial role in shaping his spiritual consciousness. From a young age, Sri Guru Arjan Dev Ji displayed qualities of humility, compassion, and a keen interest in the spiritual path.

Becoming a Guru

Sri Guru Arjan Dev Ji ascended to the position of Guru in 1638 Bikrami Bhadro Sudhi Duj (15 September 1581),. He became the fifth Sikh Guru at the age of 18. Sri Guru Arjan Dev Ji's appointment as Guru marked a significant moment in Sikh history. His selection was not based on heredity but on merit and divine guidance, emphasizing the Sikh principle of choosing spiritual leaders based on their qualities rather than familial lineage.

Compilation of Guru Granth Sahib

One of Sri Guru Arjan Dev Ji's most notable contributions was compiling the Adi Sri Guru Granth Sahib Ji. He collected and compiled the hymns of the first four Gurus, along with those of other saints and poets, including Hindus and Muslims. This compilation, completed in 1604, established the Adi Sri Guru Granth Sahib Ji as the eternal director for Sikhs, emphasizing the universality of spiritual teachings.

Philosophy

Sri Guru Arjan Dev Ji's philosophy was centered on the principles of equality, selfless service, and devotion to God. He emphasized the importance of living a truthful and honest life and discouraged rituals that lacked true spiritual significance. Due to his refusal to compromise on true principles, Sri Guru Arjan Dev Ji faced challenges and persecution, particularly from the Mughal Emperor Jahangir.

Sri Guru Arjan Dev Ji's martyrdom in 1606, as he endured extreme torture and ultimately gave his life for the principles of truth and religious freedom, remains a significant event in world history. His teachings and sacrifices continue to inspire Sikhs and others worldwide, shaping the core tenets of Sikhism.

Key Principle of Sri Guru Arjan Dev Sahib Ji

Sri Guru Arjan Dev Ji gives several key principles that form the foundation of Sikh philosophy. These principles guide the way Sikhs lead their lives and connect with the divine. Some of the key principles of Sri Guru Arjan Dev Ji are:

1. **Ek Onkar (Oneness of God):** Sri Guru Arjan Dev Ji emphasized the concept of "Ek Onkar," which means there is only one God. This monotheistic principle underscores the unity of the divine and rejects any form of idol worship or polytheism.

2. **Sarbat da Bhala (Equality):** Sri Guru Arjan Dev Ji advocated the idea of equality among all human beings. Regardless of caste, creed,

gender, or social status, Sikhs are taught to treat everyone with respect and dignity. The Sikh Gurus condemned discrimination and emphasized the inherent equality of all.

3. **Sat (Truthfulness):** Truth (Sat) is a central theme in Sikhism, and Sri Guru Arjan Dev Ji stressed the importance of living a truthful and honest life. Sikhs are encouraged to uphold the principles of truthfulness in all aspects of their existence, both in word and deed.

4. **Bhakti (Devotion and Surrender):** Sri Guru Arjan Dev Ji emphasized the path of devotion to God. Sikhs are encouraged to surrender themselves to the divine will and cultivate a deep sense of devotion through prayer, meditation, and seva (selfless service).

5. **Nimrata (Humility):** Sri Guru Arjan Dev Ji extolled humility. Sikhs are encouraged to practice humility in their interactions with others and in their approach to life. This principle is embodied in the concept of "Nishkam Seva," which is selfless service without expecting anything in return.

6. **Santokh (Contentment):** Sri Guru Arjan Dev Ji taught the importance of contentment and being satisfied with what one has. Sikhs are encouraged to practice contentment while simultaneously engaging in honest labor and sharing with those in need.

7. **Seva (Community Service):** The principle of selfless service, known as seva, is a

cornerstone of Sikhism. Sikhs are encouraged to engage in acts of service that benefit the community and humanity at large. This can include serving in community kitchens (langar), helping those in need, and contributing to charitable causes.

8. **Simran and Naam Japna (Meditation and Prayer):** Sri Guru Arjan Dev Ji advocated the practice of meditation and constant remembrance of God. Sikhs are encouraged to engage in Simran (meditative remembrance) and Naam Japna (recitation of God's name) to maintain a spiritual connection.

9. **Chardi Kala (Resilience and Endurance):** Sri Guru Arjan Dev Ji exemplified resilience in the face of adversity. Sikhs are encouraged to maintain a positive and optimistic attitude, even in challenging circumstances. This principle is expressed through the concept of "Chardi Kala," or the spirit of high morale.

10. **Rejecting Rituals and Superstitions:** Sri Guru Arjan Dev Ji discouraged empty rituals and superstitions that lacked true spiritual significance. Sikhs are taught to focus on the essence of spirituality and avoid practices that are devoid of genuine devotion.

These key principles, as taught by Sri Guru Arjan Dev Ji, continue to guide Sikh individuals in their spiritual journey and daily lives, shaping the ethos of the Sikh community.

Sri Guru Hargobind Sahib Ji

Guru Hargobind Sahib Ji, known as the sixth Guru of the Sikhs, was born on 1652 Bikrami Harrh Vadi Ekam (Sunday, 6 June 1596), Sangradi 21 Harrh, and was the son of Sri Guru Arjan Dev Ji, the fifth Guru of the Sikhs. He took over the spiritual leadership of the Sikhs in 1663 Bikrami Jeth Vadi Ashtami (15 May 1605) at the young age of 11. Sri Guru Hargobind Ji played a significant role in shaping Sikhism during the early 17th century. He was the first to militarize the Sikhs and led them to fight against the Evils, which was notorious for its persecution of non-Muslims. He built the Akal Takht, the highest temporal seat of authority for the Sikhs, next to the Sri Harmandir Sahib Ji in Sr Amritsar Sahib Ji.

Sri Guru Hargobind Ji also introduced the concept of Miri-Piri, which means the integration of spiritual and temporal power. He wore two swords, one symbolizing spiritual power and the other temporal power, to represent his idea of Miri-Piri. He emphasized the importance of physical fitness and encouraged Sikhs to learn martial arts and horse riding.

Under Sri Guru Hargobind Ji's leadership, Sikhism evolved from a peaceful and spiritual movement to a dynamic and powerful community that could defend itself and others against external threats.

Early Life

Sri Guru Hargobind Sahib Ji was born on 1652 Bikrami Harrh Vadi Ekam (Sunday, 6 June 1596), Sangradi 21 Harrh, in Wadali, a village in Amritsar,

Panjab. He was the only son of Sri Guru Arjan Dev Ji, the fifth Sikh Guru, and Mata Ganga Ji. From an early age, Sri Guru Hargobind Sahib Ji displayed spiritual inclinations and received guidance from his father.

Becoming a Guru

After Sri Guru Arjan Dev Ji's martyrdom in 1606, Sri Guru Hargobind Sahib Ji became the Guru at the age of 11. His accession marked a shift in the role of the Sikh Guru from a purely spiritual leader to one who would also engage in temporal affairs to protect the Sikh and other communities.

Philosophy

1. **Miri and Piri Concept:** Sri Guru Hargobind Sahib Ji introduced the "Miri and Piri" concept, symbolizing the dual nature of temporal and spiritual authority. He emphasized the need for Sikhs to be spiritually enlightened while being capable of defending themselves against oppression.

2. **Construction of Sri Akal Takht Sahib Ji:** Sri Guru Hargobind Sahib Ji constructed the Sri Akal Takht Sahib Ji, the Throne of the Almighty, at the Harmandir Sahib complex in Amritsar. This institution represented the temporal authority of the Sikhs and became a center for resolving both spiritual and worldly matters.

3. **Military Leadership:** Sri Guru Hargobind Sahib Ji was the first Sikh Guru to engage in military activities. He maintained a well-trained armed force to protect the minorities from external

threats. He emphasized that the use of force should be guided by principles of justice and righteousness.

4. **Advocacy for Religious Freedom:** Sri Guru Hargobind Sahib Ji actively opposed religious persecution and advocated for the freedom of worship. He sought to create a society where individuals could practice their faith without fear of oppression.

Sri Guru Hargobind Sahib Ji's early life was marked by spiritual upbringing, and his Guruship brought about significant changes in Sikh philosophy, introducing the concept of Miri and Piri. His contributions to the military and the construction of the Sri Akal Takht Sahib Ji have had a lasting impact on Sikhism, emphasizing the integration of spiritual and temporal aspects in the pursuit of a just and righteous life.

Key Principle of Sri Guru Hargobind Sahib Ji

Guru Hargobind Sahib Ji laid down several key principles that shaped Sikhism during his Guruship. Some of the key principles associated with Guru Hargobind Sahib Ji are:

1. **Miri and Piri:** Sri Guru Hargobind Sahib Ji introduced the concept of "Miri and Piri," symbolizing the dual nature of spiritual and temporal authority. The principle emphasized the need for Sikhs to be spiritually enlightened (Piri) while also being capable of defending themselves against oppression and injustice (Miri).

2. **Akal Takht and the Sikh Temporal Authority:** Sri Guru Hargobind Sahib Ji constructed the Akal Takht, the Throne of the Almighty, at the Harmandir Sahib complex in Amritsar. This institution represented the temporal authority of the Sikhs and became a platform for addressing both spiritual and worldly matters. The Akal Takht symbolized the sovereignty of the Sikh community in temporal affairs.

3. **Religious Freedom and Tolerance:** Sri Guru Hargobind Sahib Ji advocated for religious freedom and tolerance. He actively opposed religious persecution and believed in the coexistence of different faiths. The Guru emphasized that individuals should have the freedom to practice their religion without fear of oppression.

4. **Warrior-Saint Concept:** Sri Guru Hargobind Sahib Ji embodied the concept of a "Warrior-Saint." While promoting a life of spirituality and devotion, he also recognized the necessity of self-defense and protection of the community. This principle led to the establishment of a well-trained Sikh armed force.

5. **Equanimity in Success and Failure:** Sri Guru Hargobind Sahib Ji taught the importance of maintaining equanimity in both success and failure. He demonstrated resilience and composure in the face of challenges, setting an example for Sikhs to remain steadfast in their commitment to righteousness regardless of circumstances.

6. **Community Service and Justice:** Sri Guru Hargobind Sahib Ji emphasized the principles of community service and justice. He encouraged Sikhs to engage in selfless service (seva) and uphold justice in their interactions with others. The Guru aimed to create a society where fairness and compassion prevailed.

7. **Promotion of Industry and Hard Work:** Sri Guru Hargobind Sahib Ji promoted the values of industry and hard work. He encouraged Sikhs to engage in honest labor and contribute positively to society. The Guru believed in the dignity of labor and the importance of earning an honest living.

8. **Inclusivity and Equality:** Sri Guru Hargobind Sahib Ji advocated for inclusivity and equality within the Sikh community. He welcomed people from all walks of life, irrespective of their social or economic background. The Guru rejected discrimination and promoted a sense of brotherhood among Sikhs.

These principles collectively reflect Sri Guru Hargobind Sahib Ji's vision for Sikhism, emphasizing the integration of spiritual and worldly responsibilities, the pursuit of justice, and the promotion of a harmonious and inclusive society.

Sri Guru Har Rai Sahib Ji

Sri Guru Har Rai Sahib Ji was the seventh Guru of Sikhism, succeeding his grandfather, Sri Guru Har Gobind Sahib Ji.

Early Life

Sri Guru Har Rai Sahib Ji was born on 1687 Bikrami Magh Sudhi Chaudas (05 February 1630), in Kiratpur Sahib, Panjab, to Baba Gurdita Ji and Mata Nihal Kaur Ji. His upbringing was deeply rooted in spirituality and martial training under the guidance of his grandfather, Sri Guru Har Gobind Sahib Ji. Guru Har Rai Ji also received education in various fields, including literature, philosophy, and languages.

Becoming a Guru

Sri Guru Har Rai Sahib Ji became the seventh Guru of the Sikhs on 1694 Bikrami Chetar Sudhi Tarausdi (22 March 1638), following the Sri Guru Har Gobind Ji. His selection as the Guru was not based on familial ties but on his spiritual and moral qualities. Sri Guru Har Rai Sahib Ji demonstrated compassion, humility, and a commitment to social welfare.

Philosophy

1. **Compassion and Non-violence:** Sri Guru Har Rai Sahib Ji was known for his compassion and love for all living beings. He emphasized non-violence and discouraged the use of force except in self-defense and to protect needy ones. He extended his compassion even to animals and advocated for their welfare.

2. **Environment and Nature:** Sri Guru Har Rai Sahib Ji was an early environmentalist, encouraging his followers to live in harmony with nature. He maintained a beautiful garden known as the "Guru Ka Bagh" (Guru's Garden) and promoted the preservation of trees and plants.

3. **Service to Humanity:** The Guru stressed selfless service (seva) and humanitarian efforts. He established hospitals to provide medical care and assistance to the needy, regardless of their background.

4. **Promotion of Education:** Sri Guru Har Rai Sahib Ji continued the tradition of promoting education. He supported the establishment of schools and educational institutions to impart knowledge and wisdom.

5. **Interfaith Harmony:** Sri Guru Har Rai Sahib Ji engaged in dialogue with people of different faiths and believed in the universal teachings that transcended religious boundaries. He promoted interfaith harmony and understanding.

Sri Guru Har Rai Sahib Ji's legacy is one of compassion, humility, and service. His teachings continue to inspire Sikhs to lead a life of righteousness, compassion, and devotion to the well-being of all creation.

Key Principles

Sri Guru Har Rai Sahib Ji, the seventh Guru of Sikhism, imparted several key principles to guide his followers on the path of righteousness and spirituality. Some of the prominent principles associated with Guru Har Rai Sahib Ji are:

1. **Compassion and Mercy:** Sri Guru Har Rai Ji emphasized the importance of compassion and mercy. He believed in the compassionate treatment of all living beings, promoting a lifestyle rooted in empathy and kindness.

2. **Non-Violence:** Non-violence was a central principle in Sri Guru Har Rai Ji's teachings. He advocated for peaceful coexistence and discouraged the use of force except in cases of self-defense or to protect the needy. The Guru promoted resolving conflicts through dialogue and understanding.

3. **Seva (Service to Humanity):** Sri Guru Har Rai Sahib Ji strongly emphasized selfless service to humanity. He encouraged his followers to engage in acts of seva, serving others without any expectation of reward. This service is extended to all, regardless of their background or beliefs.

4. **Environmental Stewardship:** Sri Guru Har Rai Sahib Ji was an early advocate for environmental conservation. He believed in the sacredness of nature and discouraged activities that harmed the environment. The Guru maintained a garden, Guru Ka Bagh, and encouraged the planting of trees.

5. **Interfaith Harmony:** Sri Guru Har Rai Sahib Ji promoted interfaith harmony and dialogue. He

engaged in discussions with people from different religious backgrounds, fostering mutual understanding and respect. The Guru believed in the underlying unity of all spiritual teachings.

6. **Educational Excellence:** The Guru was a proponent of education and knowledge. Guru Ji supported the establishment of schools and educational institutions to impart both spiritual and worldly wisdom. Guru Har Rai Ji believed in the transformative power of education.

7. **Detachment and Humility:** Sri Guru Har Rai Sahib Ji advocated for detachment from materialism and worldly desires. He emphasized humility as a virtue, teaching his followers to remain humble in the face of success and to treat everyone with respect.

8. **Equality and Social Justice:** The Guru stood for the principles of equality and social justice. Guru Ji rejected discrimination based on caste, creed, or gender, promoting a society where all individuals were treated with dignity and fairness.

9. **Devotion to the Divine:** Sri Guru Har Rai Ji encouraged a life of devotion to the divine. His teachings emphasized the importance of maintaining a spiritual connection through prayer, meditation, and righteous living.

These principles collectively form the ethical and spiritual foundation Guru Har Rai Sahib Ji laid down, guiding Sikhs on the path of righteous living, compassion, and devotion to the divine.

Sri Guru Har Krishan Sahib Ji

Sri Guru Har Krishan Sahib Ji, the eighth Guru of Sikhism, was born on 1713 Bikrami Sawan Vadi Noauvi (Thursday, 14 July 1656) in Kiratpur Sahib, Panjab. His father was Sri Guru Har Rai Ji, the seventh Sikh Guru, and his mother was Mata Sulakhani Ji. Sri Guru Har Krishan Ji's early life was marked by spiritual awareness and compassion.

Early Life

Sri Guru Har Krishan Ji displayed signs of spiritual wisdom from a young age. He engaged in meditation and showed a deep understanding of spiritual concepts. Despite his tender age, he demonstrated an innate connection with the divine.

Becoming a Guru

Sri Guru Har Krishan Ji's appointment as the eighth Guru of the Sikhs occurred in 1718 Bikrami Katak Vadi Naumi (8 November 1661) when he was just five years old. This decision was made by his father, Sri Guru Har Rai Ji. Sri Guru Har Krishan Ji's nomination was a testament to his spiritual maturity and divine qualities.

The process of becoming a Guru in Sikhism involves passing Guruship from one Guru to the next in a lineage that began with Sri Guru Nanak Sahib Ji. The Guru is considered the spiritual guide and leader of the Sikh community. Selection is based on qualities such as spiritual enlightenment, compassion, and the ability to guide others on the path of righteousness.

Philosophy

Sri Guru Har Krishan Sahib Ji's brief time as Guru was marked by profound teachings and compassionate service. One notable event in his life was his response to an outbreak of smallpox in Delhi. Despite the risk, Sri Guru Har Krishan Ji selflessly served the affected, providing solace and healing.

The essence of Sri Guru Har Krishan Ji's philosophy lies in the teachings of Sikhism, emphasizing devotion to one God, selfless service (seva), equality, and compassion for all beings. His life exemplified the ideals of humility and service to humanity. Sri Guru Har Krishan Ji is honored as one of the Gurus who played a crucial role in shaping the Sikh faith.

Key Principles

Sri Guru Har Krishan Sahib Ji, despite his short physical life, imparted key principles that continue to guide Sikhism. The principles associated with Guru Har Krishan Ji's teachings include:

1. **Devotion to God:** Sri Guru Har Krishan Sahib Ji emphasized the importance of unwavering devotion to the one Supreme Being, recognizing God as the ultimate source of guidance, solace, and purpose in life. Sikhism teaches the oneness of God and the importance of cultivating a deep, loving connection with the divine.

2. **Seva (Selfless Service):** Sri Guru Har Krishan Sahib Ji exemplified the principle of selfless

service. His compassionate response to the smallpox outbreak in Delhi, where he provided care and comfort to the affected, underscores the Sikh concept of seva. Sikhs are encouraged to engage in acts of kindness and service to humanity without any expectation of personal gain.

3. **Equality and Social Justice:** Sri Guru Har Krishan Sahib Ji, like other Sikh Gurus, advocated for the equality of all human beings regardless of caste, creed, or social status. Sikhism rejects discrimination and encourages a society where everyone is treated with dignity and respect. Sri Guru Har Krishan Sahib Ji's teachings emphasized the importance of eradicating social inequalities.

4. **Humility:** Humility is a core principle in Sikhism, and Sri Guru Har Krishan Ji embodied this virtue. Despite his divine status as a Guru, he displayed humility in his interactions with others. Sikhs are encouraged to cultivate humility and recognize the divine presence in all beings.

5. **Compassion and Empathy:** Sri Guru Har Krishan Sahib Ji's compassionate response to the suffering during the smallpox epidemic highlights the importance of empathy and compassion in Sikh teachings. Sikhs are encouraged to empathize with the pain and struggles of others and actively contribute to alleviating suffering.

6. **Spiritual Awareness:** Even at a young age, Sri Guru Har Krishan Sahib Ji displayed profound spiritual awareness. Sikhs are encouraged to cultivate spiritual consciousness through meditation, prayer, and a life dedicated to righteous living. Sri Guru Har Krishan Sahib Ji's life inspires seekers on the spiritual path.

7. **Scriptural Knowledge:** Sri Guru Har Krishan Ji deeply understood Sikh scriptures and spiritual texts. Sikhs are encouraged to study and reflect on the teachings of Sri Guru Granth Sahib Ji, and other central religious scripture. Knowledge of scriptures is seen as a means to deepen one's spiritual understanding.

While Sri Guru Har Krishan Sahib Ji's physical life was short, his teachings and principles continue to guide Sikhs on their spiritual journey. The principles he imparted are integral to the broader Sikh philosophy that emphasizes devotion, service, equality, humility, and compassion.

Sri Guru Teg Bahadur Sahib Ji

Sri Guru Tegh Bahadur Sahib Ji, the ninth Guru of Sikhism, played a significant role in shaping the Sikh faith.

Early Life

Sri Guru Tegh Bahadur Sahib Ji was born on 1678 Bikrami, Vaisakh Vadi Panchami (Tuesday, 12 April 1621), in Amritsar, Panjab. His father was Sri Guru Hargobind Sahib Ji, the sixth Sikh Guru, and his mother was Mata Krishan Kaur Ji. From an early age, Guru Tegh Bahadur Ji displayed a spiritual inclination and spent time in meditation and contemplation.

Becoming a Guru

Sri Guru Tegh Bahadur Sahib Ji became the ninth Guru of the Sikhs following Sri Guru Har Krishan Sahib Ji. Guruship was passed down to him in 1721 Bikrami, Chater Sudhi Chaudas (06 April 1664). The process of becoming a Guru in Sikhism involves divine selection by the preceding Guru. It is based on the individual's spiritual qualities, commitment to the principles of truth and Sikhism, and ability to guide and inspire the Sikh and other communities.

Philosophy and Key Principles

Sri Guru Tegh Bahadur Ji's philosophy is deeply rooted in the core principles of Sikhism. Some key aspects include:

1. **Devotion to God:** Sri Guru Tegh Bahadur Sahib Ji emphasized the importance of devotion to the one Almighty, recognizing God as the ultimate truth. His teachings reinforced the central Sikh tenet of worshiping and meditating on the divine name.

2. **Seva (Selfless Service):** Sri Guru Tegh Bahadur Sahib Ji advocated for selfless service to humanity. Sikhs are encouraged to engage in acts of seva, helping those in need without any expectation of personal gain.

3. **Equality and Justice:** Sri Guru Tegh Bahadur Ji stood against oppression and injustice. He

defended the rights of people, irrespective of their religion, and spoke out against forced conversions. His ultimate sacrifice for the protection of the Hindu community in the face of religious persecution is a testament to his commitment to justice and religious freedom.

4. **Humility and Humbleness:** Sri Guru Tegh Bahadur Sahib Ji exemplified humility and humbleness. Despite his spiritual stature, he led a simple life and interacted with people from all walks of life with grace and humility. Sikhs are encouraged to cultivate these virtues in their own lives.

5. **Spiritual Wisdom:** Sri Guru Tegh Bahadur Sahib Ji was a repository of spiritual wisdom. His compositions, included in the Sri Guru Granth Sahib Ji, reflect deep insights into the nature of God, the human condition, and the path to spiritual realization. Sikhs are encouraged to study and reflect on these teachings for spiritual guidance.

6. **Martyrdom and Sacrifice:** Sri Guru Tegh Bahadur Ji's ultimate sacrifice for the protection of religious freedom is a central aspect of his philosophy.

Sri Guru Tegh Bahadur Sahib Ji's legacy is marked by his commitment to Sikhism's principles, his stand for justice and religious freedom, and his contributions to Sikhism. His teachings continue to inspire and guide Sikhs on their spiritual journey.

Sri Guru Gobind Singh Sahib Ji

Sri Guru Gobind Singh Ji, the tenth Guru of Sikhism, was born in 1723 Bikrami Poh Sudhi Saptami (Sunday, January 1, 1665), Sankranti 23 Poh, Patna, Bihar. He was the son of Sri Guru Tegh Bahadur Ji, the ninth Guru, and Mata Gujri Ji. Sri Guru Gobind Singh Ji's early life was marked by a profound spiritual upbringing and exposure to Sikhism's teachings.

Early Life

Sri Guru Gobind Singh Ji spent his early years in Sri Patna Sahib Ji and Sri Anandpur Sahib Ji. He received education in various subjects, including religious scriptures, martial arts, and languages. His early exposure to martial arts and spiritual teachings laid the foundation for a common person to become a warrior-saint.

Sri Guru Tegh Bahadur Sahib Ji's martyrdom in defense of religious freedom deeply shaped young Sri Gobind Singh Ji and strengthened his resolve to stand against injustice and tyranny.

Becoming a Guru

Sri Guru Gobind Singh Sahib Ji became the tenth Sikh Guru at the age of nine, following the martyrdom of his father, Sri Guru Tegh Bahadur Sahib Ji. This transition was not only a spiritual one but also marked a shift towards a more militant aspect of Sikhism due to the prevailing political and social circumstances.

In 1699, Sri Guru Gobind Singh Sahib Ji revealed the Khalsa Panth, a community of Amritdhari

Sikhs committed to upholding the principles of Sikhism. The revelation ceremony involved the "Amrit Sanchar," where the Guru prepared the Panj Pyare (Five Beloved Ones) and then received "Amrit" from them. This event is known as the Vaisakhi of 1699.

Philosophy and Key Principles

1. **Ek Onkar (Oneness of God):** Sri Guru Gobind Singh Sahib Ji emphasized the concept of "Ek Onkar" – the belief in the oneness of God. Sikhism rejects idol worship and promotes the worship of the formless and omnipresent creator.

2. **Warrior-Saint Ethos:** Sri Guru Gobind Singh Sahib Ji reinforced the martial spirit within Sikhism. He advocated self-defense and the protection of the oppressed. The Sikhs were encouraged to be both spiritual and warriors, ready to defend righteousness.

3. **Equality and Social Justice:** Sri Guru Gobind Singh Sahib Ji upheld the principles of equality and social justice. He actively opposed caste-based discrimination and advocated for the dignity and rights of all individuals, regardless of their background.

4. **Sacrifice and Martyrdom:** The Guru's life was characterized by sacrifice and martyrdom. He willingly sent his loved ones, including his sons, to martyrdom to teach the world how to remain steadfast in their commitment to the principles of truthfulness.

Sri Guru Gobind Singh Ji's early life was shaped by a unique blend of spiritual and martial influences. His journey to becoming a Guru marked a pivotal moment in Sikh history, and his philosophy emphasized the oneness of God, warrior-saint ethos, social justice, and sacrifice.

Sri Guru Granth Sahib Ji

The Sri Guru Granth Sahib Ji, often referred to simply as the living Guru of Sikhism and Khalsa Panth, is the central to the Sikhism. Sikhs consider it the eternal Guru and the living embodiment of the Sikh Gurus. The Sri Guru Granth Sahib Ji is revered and treated with the utmost respect in Sikh tradition.

The Sri Guru Granth Sahib Ji is a compilation of hymns of omnipresent God writings by Sikh Gurus, as well as contributions from other spiritual leaders (Bhaktas) from different backgrounds. It is written primarily in Gurmukhi script and Ragas.

1. **Adi Sri Guru Granth Sahib Ji:** The "Adi Sri Guru Granth Sahib Ji" refers to the original, timeless Sri Guru Granth Sahib Ji compiled by Sri Guru Arjan Sahib Ji.

2. **Living Guru:** Sikhs consider the Sri Guru Granth Sahib Ji the eternal Guru and address it with great reverence. The Sri Guru Granth Sahib Ji is considered a spiritual guide who provides insights into leading a righteous and meaningful life.

3. **Philosophy:** The Guru Granth Sahib Ji encompasses a rich philosophical and spiritual discourse. It addresses the oneness of God, the importance of selfless service, the equality of all human beings, and the pursuit of a life dedicated to God's love.

Become a Guru

The Sri Guru Granth Sahib Ji became the Guru of Sikhism through a historical process that involved the compilation of sacred writings by the Sikh Gurus, the recognition of its significance by Sri Guru Gobind Singh Ji, and the formal declaration of its eternal Guru status. The Sri Guru Granth Sahib Ji continues to be the spiritual, warrior, and worldly guide for Sikhs, embodying the teachings and principles of Sikhism.

1. **Compilation:** The Sikh Gurus laid the foundation for Sri Guru Granth Sahib Ji as the Guru of Sikhism. Sri Guru Nanak, the founder of Sikhism, and the subsequent Gurus composed hymns and teachings. The Gurus compiled these writings, along with contributions from other spiritual leaders (Bhagats).

2. **Sri Guru Arjan Dev Ji:** Sri Guru Arjan Dev Ji, the fifth Sikh Guru, played a crucial role in compiling and organizing the hymns of the Gurus into the Adi Sri Guru Granth Sahib Ji. He compiled the Adi Granth, which later evolved into the Sri Guru Granth Sahib Ji. Sri Guru Arjan Dev Ji included hymns not only from Sikh Gurus but also from spiritual leaders (Bhagats) of

different backgrounds, emphasizing the universality of divine wisdom.

3. **Ceremony:** Sri Guru Gobind Singh Sahib Ji, the tenth Sikh Guru, recognized the significance of the scripture and declared the Sri Guru Granth Sahib Ji as the eternal living Guru. In 1708, Sri Guru Gobind Singh Ji organized a formal ceremony where he placed the Adi Granth on a throne and declared it the eternal living Guru of the Sikhs and Khalsa Panth. He also gave it the status of the final and everlasting Guru.

4. **Sri Guru Granth Sahib Ji as Living Guru:** Sikhs consider the Sri Guru Granth Sahib Ji as the living Guru. Sikhs turn to its teachings for guidance in matters of spirituality, morality, and daily life. The Sri Guru Granth Sahib Ji is central to Sikh worship and is present in Sikh Gurdwaras (places of worship).

5. **Eternal Guidance:** Sikhs believe that the wisdom contained in the Sri Guru Granth Sahib Ji is timeless and universal. It provides guidance for Sikhs on how to live a righteous and meaningful life, emphasizing principles such as devotion to God, equality, humility, and selfless service.

Key Principles

The Sri Guru Granth Sahib Ji, being the central religious Guru of Sikhism, contains a vast array of principles and teachings that guide Sikhs and others on how to lead a righteous and meaningful life. Some key principles from the Sri Guru Granth Sahib Ji, though it's important to note that the Sri Guru Granth Sahib Ji encompasses a much broader set of teachings.

1. **Ek Onkar (Oneness of God):** The Sri Guru Granth Sahib Ji emphasizes the concept of Ek Onkar, the oneness of God, which is the core principle of Sikhism.

2. **Samanta (Equality):** Sikhs are taught to treat all human beings with equality, regardless of caste, creed, or social status.

3. **Seva (Selfless Service):** The importance of selfless service to humanity is highlighted as a fundamental principle in Sikhism.

4. **Nimrata (Humility):** Sikhs are encouraged to practice humility and avoid ego and pride.

5. **Devotion to God (Bhakti):** The Guru Granth Sahib Ji stresses the importance of a deep and sincere devotion to God.

6. **Truthfulness (Sach):** Sikhs are guided to live a truthful and honest life, following the path of Sach (truth).

7. **Contentment (Santokh):** The principle of contentment is emphasized, encouraging Sikhs to find peace and satisfaction in their current circumstances.

8. **Compassion (Daya):** Sikhs are urged to cultivate compassion and empathy for all living beings.

9. **Justice (Insaf):** Justice and fairness in dealing with others are key principles in Sikh ethics.

10. **Fearlessness (Nirbhau):** Sikhs are encouraged to live fearlessly and face challenges with courage.

11. **Equality of Women (Nari Shakti):** The Guru Granth Sahib Ji advocates for equal status and respect for women.

12. **Detachment (Vairag):** Sikhs are advised to remain detached from material possessions and focus on spiritual pursuits.

13. **Eradication of Ego (Ahankar):** The scripture teaches the need to eliminate ego and pride from one's character.

14. **Purity of Heart (Shudh Hirda):** Sikhs are encouraged to maintain purity of heart and intentions.

15. **Patience (Sabr):** The importance of patience in dealing with challenges and adversity is highlighted.

16. **Honest Livelihood (Kirat Karni):** Sikhs are encouraged to earn a living through honest and hard work.

17. **Meditation (Simran):** The practice of meditation and remembrance of God (Naam Simran) is emphasized.

18. **Conquer Five Thieves (Panj Chor):** Sikhs are advised to overcome the vices of lust, anger, greed, attachment, and ego.

19. **Acceptance of God's Will (Bhana Manana):** Sikhs are taught to accept and surrender to the will of God.

20. **Detoxification of Mind (Man Nu Sodhna):** The need to purify and detoxify the mind from negative influences is emphasized.

21. **Courage (Himat):** Sikhs are encouraged to be courageous in standing up for justice and righteousness.

22. **Equality of Religions (Sarbat Da Bhala):** The scripture promotes the well-being of all humanity, irrespective of religious beliefs.

23. **Avoidance of Hypocrisy (Pakhandvadh Chhadna):** Sikhs are advised to avoid hypocrisy and be true to their beliefs.

24. **Inner Transformation (Andar da Parakh):** The Guru Granth Sahib Ji guides individuals to focus on inner spiritual transformation.

25. **Forgiveness (Bakhshna):** Sikhs are encouraged to forgive and let go of grudges.

26. **Moderation (Mittar Pyare Nu Haal Muridan Da Kehna):** Sikhs are advised to live a life of moderation in all aspects.

27. **Elimination of Prejudice (Manas Ki Jaat Sabhe Ek Pechanbo):** The Sri Guru Granth Sahib Ji advocates for the elimination of caste-based distinctions.

28. **Contribution to the Community (Sangat and Pangat):** Sikhs are encouraged to contribute to

the community through participation in congregational prayers (Sangat) and communal meals (Pangat).

29. **Faith and Devotion (Sharda and Bhakti):** The scripture emphasizes the importance of unwavering faith and devotion in one's spiritual journey.

30. **Simplicity:** Sikhs are encouraged to lead a simple and humble lifestyle, avoiding ostentation.

31. **Love for Nature (Pavan Guru Pani Pita Mata Dharat Mahat):** The Sri Guru Granth Sahib Ji acknowledges the divine presence in nature, promoting love and respect for the environment.

32. **Renunciation of Dualism (Dooja Bhaav):** Sikhs are guided to transcend dualistic thinking and recognize the divine unity in all.

33. **Service to Humanity (Mankind is One, Recognize the Whole Human Race as One):** The Sri Guru Granth Sahib Ji emphasizes service to humanity as a way to connect with the divine.

34. **Gurmukh and Manmukh:** The Sri Guru Granth Sahib Ji distinguishes between those who follow the Guru's teachings (Gurmukh) and those who do not (Manmukh).

35. **Reflection and Self-Introspection:** Sikhs are encouraged to engage in self-reflection and introspection to understand their true nature.

36. **Constant Remembrance of God:** Sikhs are encouraged to engage in constant remembrance of God through meditation and prayer.

37. **Balancing Material and Spiritual Life:** The scripture guides individuals on finding a balance between material responsibilities and spiritual pursuits.

38. **Celibacy and Family Life (Grihasth Jeevan):** The Sri Guru Granth Sahib Ji recognizes the legitimacy of family life and emphasizes spiritual growth within the context of family responsibilities.

39. **Endurance and Perseverance (Chardi Kala):** Sikhs are encouraged to maintain a spirit of optimism, even in the face of challenges.

40. **Respect for Elders:** Sikhs are taught to respect and honor their parents and elders.

41. **Discipline and Control of Mind:** The Sri Guru Granth Sahib Ji advocates for discipline and control over the mind to recognize one's true divine nature.

42. **Detachment from Material Desires (Maya Moh):** Sikhs are advised to overcome attachments to material desires and possessions.

43. **Unconditional Love:** Sikhs are encouraged to cultivate unconditional love for the formless and infinite God.

44. **Abstinence from Intoxicants:** The Sri Guru Granth Sahib Ji advises against the consumption of intoxicants for spiritual clarity.

These are some principles of Sri Guru Granth Sahib ji that provide a comprehensive framework for leading a virtuous and meaningful life based on the tenets of Sikhism. They emphasize the importance of treating all human beings as equals and living with integrity and honesty. Additionally, they encourage Sikhs to cultivate a deep devotion to God through prayer, meditation, and service to others. Overall, these principles are an essential component of the Sikh faith, guiding practitioners on the path of righteousness and spiritual growth.

*****

THE

KHALSA

CODE

THE KHALSA CODE

Sikhism, a vibrant and inclusive faith founded by Guru Nanak in the 15th century, blossomed into a unique religious tradition under the guidance of the ten successive Sikh Gurus. The culmination of this evolution occurred in 1699 when the tenth Guru, Sri Guru Gobind Singh, established the Khalsa, a community of Amritdhari Sikhs committed to living by a sacred code – "The Khalsa Code."

Historical Roots

The roots of the Khalsa Code trace back to a momentous event in Sikh history. In 1699, Sri Guru Gobind Singh called upon Sikhs from all walks of life to gather at Anandpur Sahib. On the auspicious day of Vaisakhi, the Guru Amritdhari the first five members of the Khalsa Panth, infusing them with a spirit of fearlessness, devotion, and commitment to righteousness. This marked the formal establishment of the Khalsa and the inception of "The Khalsa Code."

The Five Ks: A Sacred Covenant

Central to "The Khalsa Code" are the Five Ks – five articles of faith that every Amritdhari Sikh, or Khalsa, is mandated to wear. These sacred symbols are not merely external markers but embody profound spiritual and ethical principles. The Five Ks are Kesh (Uncut hair), Kara (Iron bracelet), Kanga (wooden comb), Kachera (cotton undergarments), and Kirpan (ceremonial sword). Together, they constitute a visible declaration of a Sikh's commitment to living a life of discipline, courage, and compassion.

Spiritual Essence

At the core of "The Khalsa Code" is a deep spiritual essence that permeates every aspect of a Sikh's life. The Khalsa is not merely a set of practices; it is a sacred covenant, a commitment to living in accordance with the teachings of Sri Guru Nanak Sahib Ji and subsequent Gurus. The Five Ks, as symbols of this commitment, serve as a constant reminder of the divine connection, humility, and the pursuit of selfless service.

Guiding Principles

"The Khalsa Code" serves as a set of guiding principles for Sikhs, offering a moral compass for navigating the complexities of life. It emphasizes the values of equality, justice, and service to humanity. By adhering to the Khalsa Code, Sikhs strive to live a life that reflects the divine virtues encapsulated in Sri Guru Granth Sahib Ji, the central religious living Guru of Sikhism.

Identity and Unity

One of the profound aspects of the Khalsa Code is its role in shaping Sikh identity. The Five Ks distinguish the Khalsa from the wider world, fostering a sense of unity and solidarity among Sikhs. The external markers of the code become a visible representation of the inner commitment to Sikh ideals, creating a community bound by shared values and a collective sense of purpose.

Legacy and Continuity

"The Khalsa Code" is not a static set of rules but a living tradition that has been passed down through generations. Sikhs view the code as a sacred legacy, an inheritance from their forebears, and a responsibility to uphold for the benefit of future generations. The continuity of the Khalsa Code ensures the perpetuation of Sikh identity and values across time and space.

"The Khalsa Code" stands as a testament to the enduring spirit of Sikhism. It is a living embodiment of the teachings of the Gurus and a source of inspiration for Sikhs around the world.

Kesh

In the spiritual tapestry of Sikhism, the first of the Five Ks, Kesh, stands as the foundational thread, weaving a narrative of devotion, identity, and unwavering commitment to Sikh principles. As the external manifestation of an internal covenant, Kesh encapsulates the essence of the Khalsa Code, signifying a journey deeply rooted in spirituality and an unbreakable bond with the divine.

A Covenant Beyond Appearance

Kesh is not merely about the external appearance; it is a living covenant, a sacred commitment that extends far beyond the realm of physicality. At its core, Kesh represents an acceptance of the divine order, acknowledging the human body as a creation of the Supreme Being. This practice is a conscious decision to maintain a natural state, fostering humility and embodying the Sikh understanding of the inherent beauty in God's creation.

Distinctive Identity Rooted in Spirituality

Embedded within the strands of Kesh is the DNA of Sikh identity. Kesh serves as a distinctive marker, visibly differentiating Sikhs from the wider community. However, this distinctiveness is not for mere recognition; it is a symbol of spiritual resilience and commitment. By embracing Kesh, Sikhs stand out as ambassadors of a unique spiritual identity that transcends societal norms, emphasizing inner virtues over external appearances.

A Journey of Discipline and Virtue

Keeping Kesh is a daily practice that requires discipline and personal commitment. Beyond the physical act, it becomes a spiritual discipline, a conscious effort to align one's life with the teachings of the Sikh Gurus. It is a commitment to live virtuously, to cultivate humility, and to practice self-discipline. Through this commitment, Sikhs strive to embody the virtues encapsulated in the Sri Guru Granth Sahib Ji, fostering a life of righteousness and selfless service.

Living History and Courageous Narratives

The historical narratives of Sikh warriors, their Kesh flowing in the face of adversity, add layers of courage and resilience to the significance of Kesh. These stories become living testimonials to the enduring spirit of the Khalsa, illustrating how adherence to this practice has been a source of strength, courage, and unwavering commitment throughout Sikh history.

Contemporary Challenges and Resilience

In the contemporary landscape, Sikhs who maintain Kesh may face challenges – misconceptions, stereotypes, or even discrimination. Despite these hurdles, the Sikh community remains resilient. The commitment to Kesh becomes an act of defiance against societal norms that may prioritize conformity over individuality. It becomes a statement of strength and a celebration of diversity within the broader fabric of humanity.

A Symbolic Thread in the Spiritual Tapestry

At the heart of the Khalsa Code, Kesh stands as a symbolic thread intricately woven into the spiritual tapestry of Sikhism. It symbolizes more than an external appearance; it is a commitment to a way of life, a dedication to the principles of Sikhism, and a testament to the enduring spirit of the Khalsa.

Kesh Before Sri Guru Gobind Singh Sahib Ji

Long before the transformative events of Vaisakhi in 1699, Sikhism was gradually taking shape under the guidance of the ten preceding Gurus. The early Sikh Gurus, starting from Sri Guru Nanak Sahib Ji, laid the spiritual foundation for the community, emphasizing devotion, equality, and service.

In the pre-Guru Gobind Singh Ji era, Sikhs were devoted to the teachings of their Gurus, but the distinct external markers of the Khalsa Code, excluding Kesh, had not yet been formalized. Devotees followed the spiritual teachings of the Gurus, focusing on meditation, ethical conduct, and selfless service.

The Transformational Vaisakhi of 1699

The historical landscape shifted truthfully during the Vaisakhi of 1699, under the leadership of the tenth Guru, Sri Guru Gobind Singh Sahib Ji. Recognizing the need for a visible and united Sikh identity to withstand religious persecution and political tyranny, Sri Guru Gobind Singh Ji, established the Five Ks, with Kesh being the foundational element.

The Amrit Sanchar ceremony conducted during Vaisakhi marked the induction of Sikhs into the Khalsa, and the command to maintain Kesh became a symbol of the Sikh's commitment to the Guru's path. Sri Guru Gobind Singh Sahib Ji's declaration transformed Sikhs from a spiritual community to a martial order, ready to defend the principles of righteousness and justice.

Sikh Warriors and Kesh

In the post-1699 era, Sikh warriors, known as the Khalsa, donned the external symbols of the Khalsa Code, prominently featuring Kesh. The Kesh, now an essential aspect of Sikh identity, became a visible symbol on the battlefield, signifying fearlessness, commitment, and an unwavering dedication to principles of justice.

Sikh warriors like Bhai Bachittar Singh, Bhai Mani Singh Ji, Baba Deep Singh Ji, and Bhai Taru Singh showcased the valor and resilience that were deeply embedded in their commitment to Kesh. Even in the face of brutal persecution during times of religious intolerance, Sikhs save to their hair, symbolizing a connection to the divine and an unyielding commitment to their spiritual principles.

The Diaspora and Contemporary Times

As Sikhs migrated to different parts of the world, the practice of keeping Kesh became a symbol of Sikh identity beyond the borders of Panjab. Sikhs in the diaspora faced new challenges, including the need to navigate cultural pluralism while maintaining their distinct identity.

In contemporary times, Kesh continues to be a central aspect of Sikh identity. The challenges Sikhs face in the modern world, including misconceptions, stereotypes, and discrimination, highlight the resilience and determination of the Sikh community in upholding the historical legacy associated with Kesh.

A Continuum of Devotion and Resilience

The historical aspect of Kesh forms a continuum that stretches from the early days of Sikhism to the challenges faced by Sikhs in contemporary times. From the spiritual teachings of Sri Guru Nanak Sahib Ji to the transformative events of Vaisakhi in 1699 and beyond, Kesh remains a symbol of unwavering commitment, resilience, and a connection to the rich historical tapestry of Sikhism.

Embracing God's Creation

At its core, the spiritual aspect of Kesh lies in the acceptance of God's creation in its natural form. Sikhs believe that every individual is a creation of the divine, and maintaining Kesh becomes a symbolic act of acknowledging and embracing this sacred creation. By refraining from altering the natural state of their hair,

Sikhs express humility and reverence towards the Creator's design.

Symbol of Humility

The Kesh becomes a symbol of humility, a virtue deeply valued in Sikhism. The Kesh reminds the Sikh practitioner that they are but a humble part in the grand tapestry of creation. By allowing their hair to flow unaltered, Sikhs cultivate a spirit of humility, acknowledging their place in the cosmos with gratitude and surrendering to the divine order.

Connection to the Divine

Kesh establishes and nurtures a tangible connection to the divine. The Kesh is seen as a natural antenna, a conduit that facilitates a direct communion between the individual and the divine energy that permeates the universe. Sikhs believe that by maintaining Kesh, they remain receptive to the divine presence, fostering a continuous awareness of the spiritual realm in their daily lives.

A Commitment to Naturalness

The spiritual aspect of Kesh lies in its commitment to naturalness. Sikhism emphasizes simplicity and authenticity in spiritual practices, and the practice of keeping Kesh aligns with this principle. The unaltered state of Kesh reflects a commitment to authenticity, encouraging Sikhs to lead a life that is true to their innermost nature and connected to the natural rhythms of existence.

Discipline and Focus

Maintaining Kesh is a form of spiritual discipline. It requires commitment and focus and serves as a constant reminder of one's dedication to the path of righteousness. The discipline associated with Kesh extends beyond the physical act of not cutting hair; it permeates the Sikh's entire way of life, fostering a disciplined mind and spirit.

Symbol of Spiritual Sovereignty

Kesh serves as a symbol of spiritual sovereignty. By embracing Kesh, Sikhs declare their allegiance to a higher spiritual authority, prioritizing divine guidance over societal norms or personal preferences. This symbolic act represents a conscious choice to follow the path laid out by the Gurus and to uphold the principles of Sikh spirituality.

A Sacred Journey of Spiritual Expression

The spiritual aspect of Kesh embarks on a sacred journey of expression, connection, and devotion within Sikhism. Beyond being a physical observance, Kesh becomes a transformative practice, guiding Sikhs to a deeper understanding of humility, connection to the divine, and the disciplined pursuit of spiritual authenticity.

Cultural Identity and Recognition

Kesh plays a pivotal role in shaping the cultural identity of Sikhs. The Kesh becomes a recognizable symbol, visually setting Sikhs apart in diverse societies around the world. In the cultural context, Kesh is not just a personal choice but a collective identity marker that facilitates recognition and solidarity within the Sikh community.

Distinctive Appearance

The external manifestation of Kesh, combined with other elements of the Khalsa Code, creates a distinctive appearance that reflects the unique cultural identity of Sikhs. Turbans, uncut beards, and flowing hair collectively contribute to a visual identity that resonates with Sikh heritage. This distinctiveness fosters a sense of pride and unity among Sikhs, reinforcing a shared cultural heritage.

Cultural Continuity and Heritage

Kesh serves as a thread connecting Sikhs to their cultural heritage and historical legacy. The continuation of the practice from generation to generation becomes a symbolic act of preserving and passing down cultural traditions. Kesh becomes a living testament to the rich cultural history of Sikhism, reinforcing a sense of continuity and connection to ancestral roots.

Ceremonial and Ritual Significance

Kesh holds ceremonial and ritual significance in Sikh culture. From birth ceremonies (Naam Karan) to marriage ceremonies (Anand Karaj), the Kesh becomes an integral part of these rites. The presence of Kesh during such pivotal life events emphasizes the cultural importance of maintaining one's natural state in alignment with Sikh values and traditions.

Expression of Equality

In Sikh culture, the practice of keeping Kesh is an equalizer. Regardless of societal distinctions or economic status, Sikhs from all walks of life maintain Kesh as a symbol of their shared commitment to Sikh principles. This cultural equality becomes a unifying force, fostering a sense of community that transcends social hierarchies.

A Cultural Beacon in a Global Landscape

Kesh emerges as a cultural beacon within Sikhism's global landscape. It signifies cultural identity and serves as a testament to cultural continuity, resilience, and the preservation of Sikh heritage.

Scientific Benefits of Kesh

Protection of the Scalp

1. **Physical Barrier:** The practice of maintaining Kesh, known as Kesh, within Sikhism, unveils a multifaceted shield, offering a natural and dynamic defense mechanism for the scalp.

2. **Shielding from External Elements:** Kesh acts as an inherent physical barrier, standing guard against external elements that could potentially compromise the health of the scalp. Dust particles, pollutants lingering in the air, and harmful ultraviolet (UV) rays from the sun are intercepted by the cascade of Kesh.

3. **Prevention of Skin Damage:** This natural shield plays a pivotal role in the prevention of skin damage. The constant exposure to

environmental pollutants and UV rays can otherwise lead to oxidative stress, premature aging, and potential damage to the skin cells on the scalp. The protective layer of Kesh acts as a buffer, mitigating these external stressors.

4. **Mitigation of Scalp Irritation:** Kesh acts as a gentle shield, mitigating scalp irritation that may arise from direct contact with external pollutants or allergens. By acting as a buffer zone, Kesh minimizes the direct impact of potentially irritating substances, reducing the likelihood of discomfort and itchiness.

5. **Defensive Measure Against Dermatological Conditions:** The physical barrier provided by Kesh contributes to a line of defense against various dermatological conditions. Conditions such as eczema, psoriasis, or contact dermatitis can be exacerbated by external irritants. The presence of Kesh acts as a preventative measure, reducing the risk of these conditions taking root.

6. **Preservation of Scalp Health:** The physical barrier created by Kesh serves as a guardian, preserving the overall health of the scalp. By shielding against external aggressors, Kesh becomes an integral component in the maintenance of a healthy, nourished, and undisturbed scalp environment.

7. **Cultural and Spiritual Significance:** Beyond the physiological benefits, the practice of keeping Kesh carries cultural and spiritual

significance within Sikhism. The act of maintaining Kesh is not only a physical practice but a holistic commitment to a way of life, encompassing both physical and spiritual well-being.

Temperature Regulation

1. **Insulation:** The practice of maintaining Kesh, in Sikhism, introduces a remarkable dimension to the intricate process of temperature regulation within the human body.

2. **Natural Insulation Properties:** Kesh serves as a natural insulator, participating in the regulation of body temperature. The intricate structure of hair strands, with their layers and cuticles, creates a barrier that traps and retains air close to the scalp. This trapped air acts as an insulating layer, helping to modulate the impact of external temperatures.

3. **Protection Against Cold Temperatures:** In colder climates, the insulating effect of Kesh is particularly significant. The layer of trapped air acts as a buffer against the chill, reducing the rate of heat loss from the body. This natural insulation contributes to maintaining a warmer microclimate around the head, offering protection against discomfort associated with cold temperatures.

4. **Mitigation of Heat in Warm Climates:** Interestingly, the insulation provided by Kesh is not limited to cold weather. In warmer climates, the insulating layer helps regulate the impact of

heat by preventing excessive heat absorption from the surroundings. This can contribute to maintaining a more stable and comfortable temperature around the head, mitigating the effects of overheating.

5. **Microclimate Stability:** Kesh's insulation properties play a crucial role in maintaining a stable microclimate around the head. Regardless of external temperature extremes, the layer of trapped air helps create a balanced environment close to the scalp. This microclimate stability enhances comfort and allows the body to adapt more effectively to varying temperature conditions.

6. **Holistic Temperature Regulation:** The natural insulation provided by Kesh is a holistic aspect of temperature regulation. It complements the body's internal thermoregulatory mechanisms by offering an additional layer of protection. This is particularly relevant for the scalp, an area highly susceptible to temperature fluctuations due to its direct exposure to the environment.

Maintenance of Moisture

1. **Sebum Retention:** The practice of keeping Kesh, or Kesh, within Sikhism, introduces a unique aspect of the dynamic balance of moisture on the scalp.

2. **Natural Sebum Production:** The sebaceous glands on the scalp produce sebum, a natural oil that serves to moisturize and protect the hair and skin. Kesh provides a crucial environment

for this process to unfold naturally. Unlike cut hair, which may have exposed ends and altered structures, Kesh retains its natural integrity, facilitating the distribution of sebum along the entire hair shaft.

3. **Absorption and Retention:** Kesh is known to absorb and retain sebum effectively. The intricate structure of hair strands, with its cuticles and layers, allows for the absorption of sebum produced at the scalp. The retained sebum contributes to the maintenance of optimal moisture levels on both the hair and the scalp, creating a natural reservoir of hydration.

4. **Prevention of Dryness:** The retention of sebum by Kesh becomes a proactive measure against dryness. The continuous presence of sebum along the hair shaft helps prevent the excessive evaporation of moisture from the hair and scalp. This natural moisture retention is particularly significant in arid or dry climates, where it aids in safeguarding against dehydration and associated issues like brittle hair.

5. **Reducing the Likelihood of Dandruff:** Dryness of the scalp is often linked to dandruff, a common dermatological concern. The sebum retained by Kesh acts as a protective layer, reducing the likelihood of the scalp becoming excessively dry. This, in turn, contributes to the prevention of conditions like dandruff, fostering a healthier scalp environment.

6. **Holistic Scalp Health:** The practice of maintaining Kesh supports holistic scalp health by contributing to the preservation of moisture. This is not only relevant for the aesthetic quality of the hair but also for the overall well-being of the scalp, minimizing the risk of dryness-related discomfort and potential skin issues.

Reduction of Friction

1. **Friction Minimization:** Within the practice of maintaining Kesh, in Sikhism, lies a key element in the preservation of the physical integrity of each strand.

2. **Long, Kesh as a Buffer:** The length and uncut nature of hair act as a natural buffer, minimizing the friction between individual hair strands. In contrast to trimmed or shorter hair, which may have uneven ends, Kesh maintains a continuous surface, reducing the potential for inter-strand abrasion.

3. **Protecting Against Clothing Friction:** Long, Kesh also plays a crucial role in minimizing friction against clothing. The constant movement of hair against fabric can contribute to mechanical damage, including breakage and split ends. Kesh, by virtue of its length and undisturbed structure, decreases the likelihood of such friction-related damage.

4. **Contribution to Overall Hair Health:** The reduction of friction associated with Kesh contributes significantly to overall hair health. By minimizing the wear and tear caused by friction,

Kesh supports the integrity of each strand, promoting resilience and preventing common issues such as split ends.

5. **Preventing Mechanical Damage:** Friction-induced mechanical damage is a common concern, particularly in the context of hair care. The smooth, uncut surface of each hair strand reduces the likelihood of entanglement and friction-related stress, preventing breakage and other mechanical damage that can compromise the hair's health and appearance.

6. **Longevity of Hair Strands:** The reduction of friction offered by Kesh contributes to the longevity of each hair strand. Hair that experiences less friction is less prone to damage, ensuring that the overall length and quality of the hair are preserved over time.

Sensory Functions

1. **Enhanced Sensory Perception:** The practice of keeping Kesh, in Sikhism, introduces a captivating dimension to the sensory experiences associated with the scalp.

2. **Intricate Connection between Hair Follicles and Nerve Endings:** Hair follicles are not merely strands emerging from the scalp; they are intricately connected to nerve endings. This connection forms a sensory network that enhances the perception of tactile stimuli on the scalp. The uncut nature of hair preserves this intricate connection, allowing for a more nuanced sensory experience.

3. **Tactile Sensitivity of Kesh:** Kesh, with its undisturbed strands and preserved nerve endings, contributes to heightened tactile sensitivity. This heightened sensitivity is a result of the unaltered structure of the hair, which allows for a more direct and refined connection between the hair follicles and the surrounding nerve endings.

4. **Contribution to Heightened Awareness:** The tactile sensitivity provided by Kesh may contribute to a heightened awareness of environmental stimuli. Changes in temperature, air currents, or even subtle touches become more perceptible due to the preserved connection between hair and nerve endings. This heightened awareness can foster a deeper connection with one's surroundings.

5. **Potential Influence on Sensory Experiences:** The tactile experiences associated with Kesh have the potential to influence broader sensory experiences. The constant interplay between hair and nerve endings creates a sensory symphony, enriching the overall perception of touch and contributing to a more profound connection with the physical world.

Psychological Well-being

1. **Positive Self-Image:** The practice of maintaining Kesh, in Sikhism, unfolds as a powerful catalyst in the intricate landscape of psychological well-being.

2. **Embracing the Natural Appearance:** One of the profound psychological benefits associated with Kesh is its positive impact on self-image. The decision to embrace Kesh's natural appearance aligns with the authenticity of self-expression. Individuals who adhere to this practice often find a sense of liberation and pride in embracing their natural selves.

3. **Comfort and Contentment:** The natural and unaltered state of Kesh allows individuals to authentically represent their identity. This authenticity fosters a sense of comfort and contentment with one's appearance. The alignment between one's inner self and external presentation contributes to an enhanced sense of well-being.

4. **Cultural and Spiritual Connection:** Kesh's positive psychological impact extends beyond individual self-image to encompass a cultural and spiritual connection. Adhering to a practice deeply rooted in Sikh tradition fosters a sense of belonging and purpose, contributing to a positive psychological framework.

5. **Empowerment through Authenticity:** Choosing to maintain Kesh represents an act of empowerment through authenticity. The decision to defy societal norms and embrace one's natural state becomes a source of strength and resilience. This empowerment contributes to a positive mindset and a sense of agency over one's identity.

6. **Fostering Resilience:** In the face of societal pressures or stereotypes, individuals practicing Kesh often display resilience. The ability to navigate challenges while staying true to one's cultural and spiritual principles enhances psychological well-being. This resilience becomes a source of strength, enabling individuals to navigate life's complexities with a positive mindset.

Stress Reduction

1. **Sensory Calming Effect:** Within the practice of keeping Kesh in Sikhism lies a therapeutic aspect that intertwines with stress reduction through sensory experiences.

2. **Tactile Sensations and Stress Reduction:** Kesh, with its undisturbed strands and tactile sensitivity, introduces a unique avenue for stress reduction. The act of touching or combing Kesh provides sensory stimuli that can induce a calming effect. The gentle, repetitive motions associated with these actions create a soothing and comforting experience.

3. **Promoting Relaxation:** The tactile sensations linked with Kesh have the potential to promote relaxation. The simple act of running fingers through the hair or using a comb can engage the senses in a calming ritual. This physical interaction with one's hair becomes a mindful practice, diverting attention from stressors and fostering a tranquil state of mind.

4. **Enhancing Overall Well-being:** The sensory calming effect associated with Kesh contributes to enhanced overall well-being. Stress reduction is not only about managing immediate stressors but cultivating practices that promote long-term mental and emotional balance. Kesh becomes a tangible and accessible tool in this holistic approach to well-being.

5. **Integration of Mindfulness Practices:** The tactile experiences associated with Kesh can be integrated into mindfulness practices. Whether it's a moment of self-care, a brief pause for reflection, or a deliberate act of soothing the senses, practice becomes a mindful ritual that contributes to stress reduction and mental clarity.

Immune System Support

1. **Barrier Function:** In Sikhism, the practice of maintaining Kesh emerges as having a subtle yet potentially impactful role in supporting the body's immune defenses.

2. **Protective Role of Hair in Bodily Openings:** Hair, particularly in bodily openings like nasal passages, serves as a natural barrier against the entry of pathogens. The intricate network of hair acts as a physical obstacle, preventing the ingress of harmful microorganisms into the body. The uncut nature of hair ensures the preservation of this protective function.

3. **Prevention of Pathogen Entry:** While the impact may be subtle, Kesh may play a role in

supporting the body's immune defenses by preventing the entry of harmful microorganisms. This is especially relevant in areas where the body is more susceptible to external invaders, such as the nasal passages. The Kesh creates a barrier, acting as a first line of defense against potential pathogens.

4. **Maintaining the Integrity of the Barrier:** Hair's uncut nature contributes to maintaining the integrity of the barrier function. Trimmed or altered hair may not provide the same level of protection, as the natural structure of the hair, with its cuticles and layers, plays a crucial role in creating an effective shield against external threats.

5. **Subtle Impact on Immune Health:** While Kesh's impact on immune system support may be subtle, it adds to the overall resilience of the body's defense mechanisms. The preservation of the natural barrier function ensures that the body's immune system can operate in an environment that minimizes potential challenges from external pathogens.

Expression of Individuality

1. **Positive Self-Expression:** In Sikhism, the practice of maintaining Kesh unfolds a profound avenue for expressing individuality, intertwining personal and cultural choices.

2. **Personal and Cultural Choice:** The decision to keep Kesh is both a personal and cultural choice. It transcends the realm of mere

appearance, representing a commitment to cultural and spiritual values within Sikhism. This dual nature of the choice allows individuals to express their identity in a way that aligns with both personal beliefs and broader cultural traditions.

3. **Aesthetic Individuality:** Kesh becomes a canvas for aesthetic individuality. Each individual's hair is unique, and the decision to maintain its natural state allows for a diverse range of expressions. Whether it's the texture, length, or styling choices, Kesh becomes a medium through which individuals can celebrate their unique aesthetic preferences.

4. **Enhanced Self-Esteem:** The act of keeping Kesh is associated with enhanced self-esteem. Embracing one's natural appearance and adhering to personal and cultural values fosters a positive self-image. This boost in self-esteem is not solely rooted in physical appearance but extends to the alignment between personal choices and deeper beliefs.

5. **Autonomy and Empowerment:** The decision to maintain Kesh represents autonomy and empowerment. It signifies the autonomy to make choices that resonate with personal beliefs and values rather than conforming to societal norms. This sense of empowerment contributes to a positive impact on overall mental health, fostering a strong sense of self.

6. **Cultural Connection and Pride:** Beyond personal expression, keeping Kesh fosters a cultural connection and pride. It becomes a visual representation of cultural identity, reinforcing a sense of belonging to a rich tradition. This cultural connection adds depth to individual expression, creating a harmonious balance between personal choices and cultural heritage.

In the profound tapestry of Sikhism, the practice of keeping Kesh, known as Kesh, stands as a symbolic representation of the spiritual warrior's crown within the Khalsa legacy. As Sikhism espouses principles rooted in the teachings of Guru Nanak, adherence to Kesh becomes a visual and spiritual commitment to discipline, righteousness, and courage. Within Sikh tradition, Kesh is not merely a physical expression but a sacred identity marker, affirming a commitment to the disciplined path in the Sri Guru Granth Sahib Ji. It transcends personal choice to become a spiritual journey, symbolizing the crown worn by warriors in their pursuit of justice and righteousness. The Khalsa Code, encompassing the Five Ks, places Kesh at the forefront as a transformative element shaping the identity of the Khalsa. Historical narratives underscore the formidable role of the Khalsa, adorned with Kesh, in defending justice and religious freedom. It becomes clear that Kesh holds great significance beyond the physical realm. It is a symbol of spiritual strength, resilience, and an unwavering connection to the divine. As the warrior's crown, Kesh embodies defiance against societal norms, echoing the spirit of resistance that has characterized Sikh warriors throughout history. Kesh is more than just a cultural practice; it is a profound commitment to being a spiritual warrior within the rich tapestry of Sikhism and the enduring legacy of the Khalsa.

Kara

The Kara, an iron bracelet worn by Sikhs, transcends its physical form to embody profound spiritual and cultural significance. Crafted from pure iron-based materials, the Kara is characterized by its simple circular design, which represents the eternal nature of the connection between the individual and the divine. It serves as a constant and tangible reminder of the Sikh commitment to the core principles of the faith. The Kara is not merely a piece of jewelry; it encapsulates a spiritual journey, symbolizing the unbroken bond between the wearer and the divine realm. The act of wearing the Kara becomes a conscious and sacred choice, fostering a deep sense of identity and unity within the Sikh community. Beyond its individual symbolism, the Kara plays a pivotal role in social practices, accompanying Sikhs in ceremonies, celebrations, and rites of passage. Its iron composition reflects strength, resilience, and an unwavering commitment to the Sikh way of life. The Kara is not just an accessory; it is a timeless emblem of faith, unity, and the enduring connection between the Sikh and the divine.

1. **Embodying Infinity:** Crafted with simplicity, its circular design embodies the concept of infinity, underscoring the eternal nature of the bond between the individual and the divine. Beyond its material form, the Kara becomes a tangible

reminder of the unbreakable connection that exists throughout the Sikh's spiritual journey.

2. **A Wearable Commitment:** Wearing the Kara is not a casual accessory choice; it is a visible commitment to Sikh principles in the Sri Guru Granth Sahib Ji. This Kara serves as a physical manifestation of the Sikh's devotion, emphasizing the spiritual dimensions associated with the act. It becomes a wearable affirmation of one's dedication to the teachings of Sikh gurus and an outward expression of inner faith.

3. **Strength and Resilience:** The significance of the Kara extends to its material composition, typically crafted from iron. This choice of material holds profound symbolism, representing strength, endurance, and an unyielding commitment to Sikh values. As Sikhs wear the Kara, they carry with them a tangible emblem of resilience, reminding them of their spiritual grounding and the enduring strength found within the Sikh way of life.

4. **Unity and Identity:** Beyond individual symbolism, the Kara plays a pivotal role in fostering unity within the Sikh community. Its circular form represents a sense of collective identity, reinforcing a shared commitment to Sikh principles. The Kara is not confined to individual practice; it is present in social and religious ceremonies, celebrations, and rites of passage, emphasizing its centrality in Sikh culture and tradition.

5. **Conscious Choice:** The act of wearing the Kara is a conscious choice, reflecting the Sikh's dedication to principles of equality, humility, and service. It is not just a physical accessory; it is a sacred emblem that resonates with the spiritual vibrations of Sikhism. As Sikhs go about their daily lives, the Kara encircling their wrists becomes a constant proclamation of faith, a visible representation of their unwavering commitment to the divine within the rich tapestry of Sikh tradition.

Significance of Kara in Sikhism

The Kara transcends its physical form to become a symbol of spiritual identity, devotion, and resilience. At its essence, the Kara represents a tangible connection between the individual soul and the divine, embodying the eternal nature of the Sikh's spiritual journey. Its circular shape symbolizes infinity, underscoring the unbreakable bond between the wearer and the divine realm. Wearing the Kara is not merely a matter of personal adornment but a conscious choice that signifies the Sikh's commitment to the core principles and values espoused in Sikh scripture.

Embedded within the circular embrace of the Kara lies a deep sense of spiritual identity. As Sikhs don the Kara, they affirm their allegiance to the teachings of the Sikh Gurus and their adherence to the path of righteousness outlined in the Sri Guru Granth Sahib Ji. It becomes a visible proclamation of one's faith, serving as a constant reminder of the Sikh's spiritual journey and their unwavering commitment to Sikh principles. The Kara acts as a sacred emblem that resonates with the spiritual vibrations of Sikhism, fostering a deep sense of connection between the individual soul and the divine presence.

Moreover, the Kara serves as a tangible expression of Sikh values and ethics. The Kara symbolizes strength, resilience, and an unwavering commitment to Sikh ideals. It serves as a reminder to stand firm in the face of adversity and to uphold the principles of justice, equality, and service to humanity. The act of wearing the Kara is imbued with spiritual significance, as Sikhs strive to embody these values in their daily lives. It becomes a tangible manifestation of Sikh ethics, reinforcing the Sikh's commitment to live a life of righteousness and compassion.

Throughout Sikh history, the Kara has stood as a symbol of resistance and resilience in the face of oppression and persecution. Despite attempts to suppress Sikh identity, Sikhs have proudly worn the Kara as a defiant statement of their faith and as a testament to their unwavering commitment to Sikh principles. In times of hardship, the Kara serves as a source of strength and courage, empowering Sikhs to persevere in their spiritual journey and to stand firm in their convictions. It becomes a symbol of hope and resilience, inspiring Sikhs to overcome adversity and to uphold the values of Sikhism.

Historical Origin and Evolution

Before the emergence of Sikhism, the wearing of Karas did not hold specific importance or symbolism as it does within Sikh tradition. However, iron has historically held significance in various cultures and civilizations due to its practical and symbolic properties.

In ancient times, iron was valued for its strength, durability, and practical utility. It was used in weaponry, tools, and armor, symbolizing power, protection, and resilience. Iron artifacts have been found in archaeological sites dating back thousands of years, indicating its widespread use and cultural significance across different civilizations.

In some cultures, iron was associated with spiritual or supernatural beliefs. For example, in ancient Greece, iron was believed to have protective qualities against evil spirits, leading to the practice of placing iron objects on doorways or wearing iron jewelry for warding off malevolent forces.

Similarly, in Hinduism, iron is considered sacred and is associated with various deities and rituals. Iron objects are used in Hindu religious ceremonies and rituals as symbols of strength, protection, and purity.

While the specific practice of wearing iron Karas may not have existed before the origin of Sikhism, the use of iron in jewelry and adornments was not uncommon in ancient times. However, within the context of Sikhism, the significance of the iron Kara goes beyond its material properties. It has become a central symbol of Sikh identity, spirituality, and commitment to Sikh principles, as mandated by Sri Guru Gobind Singh Ji during the formation of the Khalsa in the late 17th century.

The Kara, a quintessential symbol of Sikh identity, boasts a rich historical lineage deeply intertwined with the evolution of Sikhism itself. Its origins can be traced back to the time of Sri Guru Nanak Sahib Ji, the founder of Sikhism, in the 15th century. Initially, the Kara served practical purposes, acting as a form of armor worn by Sikh warriors as they defended their faith and fought against oppression. However, over time, the Kara underwent a profound transformation, transcending its utilitarian origins to become a timeless symbol within Sikh tradition.

As Sikhism progressed through subsequent Guru periods, particularly under the leadership of Sri Guru Angad Sahib Ji and Sri Guru Amar Das Ji, the Kara began to assume symbolic significance. It evolved from a mere piece of armor to a sacred emblem representing the unbreakable bond between the Sikh and the divine. Sri Guru Gobind Singh Ji, the tenth Guru, institutionalized the Kara as one of the Five Ks, which are integral aspects of Sikh identity and spirituality. This formal recognition solidified Kara's status as an enduring symbol within Sikh tradition, symbolizing the eternal connection between the individual soul and the divine presence.

Description of the Kara

The description of the Kara, with its emphasis on material, shape, and significance, unveils a profound emblem within Sikhism. Crafted from iron, the Kara symbolizes resilience, humility, and unwavering commitment to Sikh values, while its circular form represents infinity, embodying the eternal connection between the individual soul and the divine. Through its minimalist design, devoid of ornate decoration, the Kara underscores Sikh principles of humility and modesty, emphasizing the importance of inner spiritual qualities over external appearances. As a tangible manifestation of Sikh identity, the Kara serves as a universal symbol of inclusivity, unity, and the timeless wisdom of Sikh scripture. Wearing the Kara is a visible proclamation of one's dedication to the teachings of the Sikh Gurus and a pledge to live a life of compassion, service, and righteousness, echoing centuries of Sikh history and tradition.

Material Composition

Kara is traditionally crafted from iron, a metal renowned for its strength and durability. This choice of material holds profound significance within Sikh tradition, symbolizing resilience, humility, and unwavering commitment to Sikh values.

1. **Symbol of Strength and Durability:** The Kara, a significant emblem within Sikh tradition, is traditionally forged from iron, a metal celebrated for its robustness and resilience. This material choice underscores the Sikh ethos of confronting life's challenges with strength and steadfastness, mirroring the enduring qualities required to navigate spiritual journeys amidst worldly complexities.

2. **Profound Significance within Sikh Tradition:** Within the fabric of Sikh tradition, the selection of iron for the Kara holds deep symbolic meaning. It goes beyond mere physical attributes, embodying spiritual and cultural values central to Sikh identity. The use of iron signifies resilience, humility, and an unwavering

commitment to Sikh principles, serving as a tangible reminder of the enduring spirit that permeates Sikh communities worldwide.

3. **Symbolizing Resilience and Fortitude:** Iron's inherent strength and durability symbolize the resilience of Sikhs in the face of adversity. Just as iron withstands the trials of forging and shaping, Sikhs endure life's challenges with fortitude and resolve, remaining steadfast in their pursuit of spiritual growth and adherence to Sikh values. The iron Kara serves as a powerful emblem of this unwavering resilience, inspiring Sikhs to navigate life's complexities with courage and determination.

4. **Embodying Humility in Material Form:** Despite its strength, iron remains a humble material, undergoing transformation through shaping and forging. This humility is deeply ingrained in Sikh teachings, emphasizing the importance of modesty and humility in one's interactions with the world. Through the choice of iron for the Kara, Sikhs are reminded of the value of humility in their spiritual journey, encouraging them to approach life with grace and humility.

5. **Manifestation of Unwavering Commitment:** The selection of iron for the Kara reflects the unwavering commitment of Sikhs to their values and principles. Iron's stability and steadfastness parallel the Sikh dedication to living lives of integrity and ethical conduct. By wearing the iron Kara, Sikhs symbolically express their

allegiance to Sikh values and their resolve to uphold these principles in all facets of life, reaffirming their commitment to Sikh identity and spirituality.

Shape and Design

The Kara typically takes the form of a simple, circular bracelet devoid of any intricate adornments or embellishments. This circular shape symbolizes infinity, representing the eternal nature of the connection between the individual soul and the divine presence.

1. **A Symbol of Simplicity and Infinity:** The Kara, a revered emblem within Sikh tradition, is characterized by its simple yet profound design—a circular bracelet devoid of ornate adornments. This circular shape holds deep symbolism, representing both the simplicity of Sikh teachings and the infinite connection between the individual soul and the divine presence. The absence of intricate embellishments underscores the purity and clarity of Sikh spirituality, emphasizing the essence of Sikh values and principles.

2. **Signifying the Divine Bond:** At the heart of the Kara's circular form lies a profound metaphor for the eternal nature of the relationship between the individual soul and the divine. The unbroken circle represents infinity, symbolizing the timeless bond that transcends temporal boundaries. Through the Kara, Sikhs are reminded of their inherent connection to the

divine, anchoring them in a sense of spiritual continuity and purpose. The circular shape serves as a visual reminder of the eternal journey of the soul, guiding Sikhs on their quest for spiritual enlightenment and fulfillment.

3. **Reflecting Spiritual Essence:** The simplicity of Kara's circular design reflects the minimalist ethos of Sikhism, emphasizing the essence of Sikh teachings over superficial embellishments. By eschewing elaborate ornamentation, the Kara underscores the importance of inner spiritual qualities such as humility, compassion, and service. In embracing this minimalist aesthetic, Sikhs are encouraged to cultivate a deep sense of inner peace and contentment, free from the distractions of worldly desires and attachments.

4. **Inclusive Symbolism:** The circular form of the Kara embodies the inclusive ethos of Sikhism, transcending cultural, social, and geographical boundaries. Regardless of background or identity, all Sikhs are united by the universal symbolism of the Kara's circular shape. It serves as a unifying emblem that fosters a sense of belonging and community within the global Sikh diaspora, reinforcing the interconnectedness of all beings and the universal pursuit of spiritual truth.

5. **A Profound Symbol of Spiritual Connection:** The circular form of the Kara embodies profound symbolism within Sikh tradition, representing the eternal bond between the

individual soul and the divine presence. Its simplicity and purity underscore the essence of Sikh spirituality, while its inclusive symbolism fosters unity and community among Sikhs worldwide. Through Kara's circular design, Sikhs are reminded of their eternal journey toward spiritual enlightenment and their inherent connection to the divine, guiding them on a path of inner transformation and fulfillment.

Significance of Design

The simplicity of Kara's design reflects Sikh principles of humility and modesty. Unlike other forms of jewelry, the Kara eschews ornate decoration, emphasizing the importance of inner spiritual qualities over external appearances. The circular shape of the Kara is universal and has no beginning or end, signifying the inclusivity of Sikhism and the eternal nature of Sikh teachings. It serves as a reminder of the interconnectedness of all creation and the timeless wisdom of Sikh scripture.

1. **A Testament to Humility and Modesty:** The simplicity of Kara's design serves as a powerful reflection of Sikh principles of humility and modesty. Unlike other forms of jewelry that may be adorned with elaborate embellishments, the Kara eschews such ornamentation, emphasizing instead the importance of inner spiritual qualities over external appearances. This minimalist approach underscores the essence of Sikh teachings, encouraging Sikhs to cultivate humility and modesty in their interactions with the world. By wearing the

unadorned Kara, Sikhs are reminded of the importance of inner virtues and the pursuit of spiritual growth over materialistic pursuits.

2. **Reflecting Inclusivity and Eternal Wisdom:** The circular shape of the Kara holds profound symbolism, representing the universality of Sikhism and the eternal nature of Sikh teachings. With no beginning or end, the circular form signifies inclusivity, embracing individuals from all backgrounds and walks of life within the fold of Sikhism. It serves as a potent reminder of the interconnectedness of all creation and the timeless wisdom enshrined in Sikh scripture. Regardless of cultural or geographical differences, all Sikhs are united by the universal symbolism of the Kara's circular shape, fostering a sense of unity and community within the global Sikh diaspora. Through the Kara's design, Sikhs are encouraged to embrace the universal values of compassion, equality, and service to humanity, transcending barriers and divisions to embody the timeless wisdom of Sikh teachings.

3. **A Symbol of Spiritual Essence and Unity:** The design of the Kara holds deep significance within Sikh tradition, embodying Sikh values and universal principles. Its minimalist aesthetic reflects the virtues of humility and modesty, reminding Sikhs to prioritize inner spiritual qualities over external adornments. Meanwhile, the circular shape of the Kara symbolizes inclusivity and eternal wisdom, serving as a

unifying emblem that transcends cultural and geographical boundaries. Through Kara's design, Sikhs are encouraged to embrace the essence of Sikh teachings and embody the universal values of compassion, equality, and unity, fostering a sense of spiritual connection and community within the global Sikh community.

Scientific Benefits of Wearing a Kara

While the significance of wearing a Kara within Sikhism is primarily rooted in spirituality and cultural tradition, some scientific benefits can also be associated with this practice:

Stress Reduction

Wearing a Kara can serve as a transformative tool for stress reduction through mindfulness practice. By serving as a physical reminder to cultivate mindfulness in daily life, the Kara empowers individuals to reclaim moments of calm amidst the hustle and bustle of modern living, promoting overall mental well-being and enhancing resilience against stressors.

1. **Utilizing Mindfulness Practice:** Wearing a Kara extends beyond its physical presence, as it can serve as a powerful tool for stress reduction through mindfulness practice. Much like a reminder bracelet, the constant presence of the Kara on the wrist acts as a gentle cue to cultivate mindfulness in daily life. By directing attention to the sensations of the Kara against the skin, individuals are prompted to anchor themselves in the present moment, fostering a

sense of calm and inner peace amidst the chaos of daily life.

2. **Physical Reminder for Mindfulness:** The tactile sensation of the Kara serves as a tangible reminder to practice mindfulness, encouraging individuals to pause and reconnect with their inner selves amidst the busyness of daily routines. As individuals become attuned to the presence of the Kara on their wrist, they are prompted to engage in mindful breathing, body scans, or other grounding techniques, effectively reducing stress levels and promoting overall mental well-being.

3. **Promoting Mental Well-Being:** Through its role as a physical reminder for mindfulness, Kara contributes to the reduction of stress levels and the cultivation of mental well-being. By integrating mindfulness practice into daily life, individuals develop resilience against stressors, enhancing their ability to navigate challenges with greater ease and equanimity. Over time, the consistent practice of mindfulness facilitated by Kara fosters a deeper sense of inner peace, contentment, and emotional balance.

Acupressure Points

Wearing a Kara offers subtle therapeutic benefits by stimulating acupressure points on the wrists, as recognized in traditional Chinese medicine and Ayurveda. By fostering improved circulation, relaxation, and overall well-being, the Kara becomes a holistic emblem of wellness and balance, supporting

190

individuals on their journey toward optimal health and vitality.

1. **Ancient Wisdom of Traditional Medicine:** Drawing upon the rich traditions of traditional Chinese medicine and Ayurveda, the significance of acupressure points on the wrists is deeply rooted in ancient wisdom. According to these holistic healing systems, specific points on the wrists correspond to vital energy channels, or meridians, within the body. Stimulating these points through gentle pressure or massage is believed to promote holistic well-being and balance energy flow throughout the body.

2. **Stimulating Acupressure Points with the Kara:** Wearing a Kara holds therapeutic potential by indirectly stimulating acupressure points on the wrists. Positioned strategically on the wrist, the Kara applies gentle pressure to these points as individuals move their arms and hands throughout the day. This subtle stimulation may activate the flow of energy, or qi, within the body, promoting improved circulation, relaxation, and overall well-being.

3. **Potential Therapeutic Benefits:** The stimulation of acupressure points through wearing a Kara offers a range of subtle therapeutic benefits. Improved circulation can enhance the delivery of oxygen and nutrients to tissues throughout the body, supporting optimal cellular function and vitality. Additionally, relaxation induced by acupressure may help

alleviate tension and stress, fostering a greater sense of calm and tranquility amidst the demands of daily life.

EMF Radiation

Some proponents suggest that wearing a Kara made from iron may offer protection against electromagnetic field (EMF) radiation emitted by electronic devices, scientific evidence supporting this claim remains inconclusive. As individuals navigate concerns about EMF exposure in an increasingly digital world, it is essential to balance awareness of potential risks with evidence-based practices. Whether worn for symbolic or practical reasons, the decision to wear a Kara for EMF protection ultimately reflects personal beliefs and choices regarding health and well-being.

1. **Understanding Electromagnetic Fields (EMF):** In our modern digital age, electronic devices emit electromagnetic fields (EMF), which are forms of radiation that can potentially affect the human body. While the extent of their impact remains debated, some individuals express concerns about prolonged exposure to EMF and its potential health implications.

2. **Iron as a Shielding Material:** Proponents suggest that iron, the material commonly used to make Karas, may possess properties that act as a shield against EMF. Iron is known for its magnetic properties and conductivity, leading some to believe that it could potentially deflect or absorb electromagnetic radiation emitted by electronic devices. As such, wearing a Kara

crafted from iron may be viewed as a proactive measure to mitigate the potentially harmful effects of EMF exposure.

3. **Limited Scientific Evidence:** While anecdotal reports and personal testimonies abound, scientific evidence supporting the efficacy of iron-based Karas in shielding against EMF remains limited. The complex nature of EMF and its interaction with materials makes it challenging to definitively conclude whether wearing a Kara offers significant protection against EMF radiation. Further research and empirical studies are needed to ascertain the extent to which iron-based Karas can effectively shield against EMF and whether they provide tangible health benefits in this regard.

4. **Individual Beliefs and Practices:** Despite the lack of conclusive scientific evidence, some individuals choose to wear iron-based Karas as a precautionary measure against EMF exposure, reflecting a broader trend towards holistic wellness and the adoption of protective practices in the digital age. Whether viewed as a symbolic gesture or a practical safeguard, the decision to wear a Kara for EMF protection is deeply personal and rooted in individual beliefs and practices surrounding health and well-being.

Positive Psychological Effects

Wearing a Kara can have profound positive psychological effects, enriching individuals' lives by enhancing self-esteem, fostering cultural and spiritual connection, and promoting overall well-being. As wearers embrace the significance of the Kara in their lives, they embark on a journey of self-discovery and empowerment grounded in the rich tapestry of their cultural and spiritual heritage. The Kara serves as more than just a piece of jewelry—it is a potent symbol of identity, belonging, and self-expression, empowering wearers to navigate life with confidence, authenticity, and grace.

1. **Boosting Self-Esteem and Identity:** Wearing a Kara can have profound psychological effects akin to other forms of jewelry or accessories. The presence of the Kara on the wrist can enhance self-esteem by serving as a symbol of personal identity and cultural affiliation. For many wearers, the Kara is not merely an adornment but a tangible expression of their spiritual beliefs and cultural heritage, instilling a sense of pride and confidence in one's identity.

2. **Fostering Cultural and Spiritual Connection:** The Kara serves as a potent reminder of cultural and spiritual values, fostering a deep connection to one's heritage and traditions. By wearing the Kara, individuals reaffirm their commitment to their cultural roots and spiritual beliefs, creating a sense of continuity and belonging within their community. This connection to one's cultural and spiritual heritage can provide a source of strength and resilience, particularly in times of adversity or uncertainty.

3. **Promoting Overall Well-Being:** The psychological benefits of wearing a Kara extend beyond mere aesthetics, contributing to overall well-being and self-confidence. As wearers embrace the significance of the Kara in their lives, they experience a sense of empowerment and purpose grounded in the rich tapestry of their cultural and spiritual identity. This sense of belonging and self-assurance can positively impact mental health, fostering resilience and emotional well-being in the face of life's challenges.

4. **Cultivating Self-Expression and Individuality:** The Kara serves as a vehicle for self-expression and individuality, allowing wearers to outwardly manifest their inner beliefs and values. Whether worn as a statement of faith, a symbol of cultural pride, or a personal emblem of identity, the Kara embodies the unique essence of each wearer. This celebration of individuality fosters a sense of authenticity and self-awareness, encouraging wearers to embrace their true selves and navigate life with confidence and conviction.

Reminder of Healthy Habits

Wearing a Kara serves as a powerful reminder to maintain healthy habits and embody positive values in daily life. By prompting acts of kindness and service, the Kara fosters social connection, emotional well-being, and personal growth. As individuals embrace the values associated with the Kara, they experience a deeper sense of connection to others and a greater sense of fulfillment and purpose in life, ultimately enriching their overall well-being and quality of life.

1. **Prompting Acts of Kindness and Service:** Wearing a Kara serves as more than a mere accessory; it acts as a tangible reminder of the values and principles individuals hold dear. For example, if the Kara is associated with Sikh principles of compassion and service, its presence on the wrist can serve as a gentle nudge to engage in acts of kindness and service to others. Whether through volunteer work, charitable donations, or simple acts of empathy and compassion, wearing the Kara prompts individuals to embody these values in their daily lives, fostering a deeper sense of connection to their community and promoting emotional well-being.

2. **Cultivating Social Connection:** Engaging in acts of kindness and service not only benefits others but also nurtures social connection and emotional well-being. By wearing the Kara, individuals become more attuned to opportunities for meaningful interactions with others, strengthening bonds within their community and fostering a sense of belonging. Whether through small gestures of kindness or larger acts of service, wearing the Kara encourages individuals to cultivate meaningful connections with others, enhancing their sense of fulfillment and purpose in life.

3. **Promoting Emotional Well-Being:** Acts of kindness and service have been shown to have

profound effects on emotional well-being, promoting feelings of happiness, gratitude, and fulfillment. By serving as a reminder to maintain healthy habits, such as engaging in acts of kindness and service, the Kara contributes to overall emotional well-being and psychological resilience. As individuals integrate these practices into their daily lives, they experience a deeper sense of connection to others and a greater sense of purpose, enhancing their overall quality of life.

4. **Encouraging Personal Growth and Fulfillment:** Wearing the Kara serves as a catalyst for personal growth and fulfillment, prompting individuals to strive for excellence in all aspects of their lives. By embodying the values associated with the Kara, such as compassion, service, and empathy, individuals not only contribute to the well-being of others but also experience personal growth and fulfillment. The Kara becomes a symbol of personal empowerment, inspiring individuals to live with intention and purpose, and to make a positive impact in the world.

Kanga

The word "Kanga" refers to a wooden comb that holds significance in Sikhism, particularly within the context of the Khalsa Panth. It is one of the Five Ks, or articles of faith, that Sikhs are required to wear as symbols of their commitment to their faith and community.

The Kanga is not merely a grooming tool but holds symbolic and practical importance within Sikh tradition. It represents discipline, cleanliness, and self-respect. Sikhs are expected to carry the Kanga with them at all times, and it is used to keep the hair tidy and clean, which aligns with the practice of keeping Kesh as mandated by Sikhism.

The Kanga embodies the Sikh values of hygiene, discipline, and adherence to the tenets of their faith. It serves as a tangible reminder for Sikhs to maintain their spiritual and physical cleanliness while also symbolizing their commitment to their religious identity as members of the Khalsa Panth.

Significance of Kanga in Sikhism

The Kanga holds multifaceted importance in Sikhism, serving as a practical grooming tool, a symbol of discipline and self-respect, a representation of spiritual purity, an emblem of Sikh identity, and a connection to Sikh history and tradition. Its significance extends beyond its physical form, embodying the core values and principles of the Sikh faith.

Practical Grooming

- The Kanga, a small wooden comb, is used to keep the hair tidy and neat.

- For Sikhs, who maintain Kesh as a symbol of their commitment to their faith, the Kanga is an essential tool for daily hair care.

- It helps prevent tangling, keeps the hair clean, and maintains hygiene, which is particularly important as Kesh is an integral aspect of Sikh identity.

Symbol of Discipline and Self-Respect

- The Kanga symbolizes discipline and self-respect. Its regular use demonstrates a commitment to personal grooming and hygiene, reflecting an individual's dedication to living a disciplined life according to Sikh principles.

- By carrying the Kanga at all times, Sikhs are reminded to maintain their physical appearance in a respectful manner, reflecting the inner discipline and self-awareness that are central tenets of Sikhism.

Spiritual Significance

- The Kanga holds deeper spiritual significance within Sikhism. It is one of the Five Ks, or articles of faith, that Guru Gobind Singh, the tenth Sikh Guru, mandated for all Sikhs who are Amritdhari into the Khalsa Panth.

- Each of the Five Ks represents a distinct aspect of Sikh identity and spirituality. The Kanga specifically embodies the value of cleanliness and purity, both externally and internally.

- The act of using the Kanga to keep the hair clean and groomed serves as a reminder of the importance of maintaining purity of mind and body, as cleanliness is closely associated with spiritual purity in Sikh tradition.

Symbol of Sikh Identity

- Wearing the Kanga is a visible sign of Sikh identity and allegiance to the Khalsa Panth. It distinguishes Sikhs from members of other communities and serves as a marker of their commitment to Sikh principles and values.

- The Kanga, along with the other Four Ks, helps foster a sense of unity and solidarity among Sikhs, reinforcing a shared identity and a sense of belonging within the community.

Connection to Sikh History and Tradition

- The Kanga has a rich historical significance within Sikhism, dating back to the time of Guru Gobind Singh, who instituted the Five Ks as symbols of Sikh identity and sovereignty.

- By carrying the Kanga, Sikhs honor the legacy of their Gurus and affirm their allegiance to the teachings and traditions passed down through generations.

Historical Background

The Kanga, a wooden comb, was instituted by Sri Guru Gobind Singh Ji, the tenth Sikh Guru, as part of the Khalsa identity in 1699. This occurred during the Vaisakhi festival in Sri Anandpur Sahib, Panjab. Sri Guru Gobind Singh Ji revealed the Khalsa Panth, a community of Sikhs who were Amritdhari, into a distinct order characterized by its adherence to a strict code of conduct.

As part of the Amritdhari ceremony, Sri Guru Gobind Singh Ji introduced the Five Ks, which became the outward symbols of Khalsa identity. The Kanga symbolizes discipline, cleanliness, and self-respect. It serves as a reminder of the importance of maintaining physical appearance in a respectful manner, reflecting the inner discipline and self-awareness that are central tenets of Sikhism.

The institution of the Kanga by Guru Gobind Singh underscores its significance as a foundational element of Sikh identity and spirituality within the context of the Khalsa Panth. It is a tangible manifestation of Sikh values and serves as a reminder of the commitment to Sikh principles and traditions passed down through generations.

Early Human History

The history of comb practices can be traced back to early human societies, where the maintenance of personal hygiene played a crucial role in health and social interactions. Archaeological evidence suggests that ancient humans used a variety of tools and techniques for combing, including the use of rudimentary combs made from natural materials such as wood, bone, and plant fibers.

Early combs were likely simple in design, consisting of a handle and teeth, and were used for untangling hair, removing debris, and distributing oils. These combing practices served not only practical purposes but also held cultural significance, as grooming was often associated with cleanliness, health, and social status.

As human societies evolved, so did combing practices and the tools used for combing. Combs became more refined in design and were crafted from a wider range of materials, reflecting advancements in technology and craftsmanship.

Materials and Techniques

Throughout history, combs have been crafted from various materials, each offering unique properties and aesthetic qualities. In ancient times, combs were commonly made from organic materials such as wood, bone, horn, and ivory. These materials were readily available and could be easily shaped and carved into comb-like structures.

1. **Wood:** Wood was one of the earliest materials used for making combs due to its abundance and ease of carving. Different types of wood were utilized depending on availability and local preferences. Wooden combs were often handcrafted using simple tools and techniques, with designs ranging from basic to intricately carved patterns.

2. **Bone and Horn:** Combs made from animal bones and horns were also prevalent in ancient societies. These materials were durable and could be finely polished to create smooth, functional combs. Bone and horn combs were often decorated with carvings or embellishments, adding to their aesthetic appeal.

3. **Ivory:** In some cultures, combs were crafted from ivory, particularly in regions where

elephants were native or where ivory was traded. Ivory combs were prized for their durability and luxurious appearance, making them status symbols among the elite.

Techniques for crafting combs varied depending on the materials used and the technological advancements of the time. Early combs were typically shaped and smoothed using simple tools such as knives, chisels, and abrasive materials like sandstone. As civilizations developed more sophisticated metalworking techniques, metal combs also became popular, offering durability and precision in design.

The ancient origins of combs highlight the importance of combing practices in early human societies and the evolution of grooming tools over time. From humble beginnings as simple implements for maintaining personal hygiene to finely crafted symbols of status and craftsmanship, combs have played a significant role in shaping human culture and identity.

Archaeological Evidence

Archaeological excavations in the Asian continent, particularly in sites like the Indus Valley Civilization (circa 3300–1300 BCE), have provided valuable evidence of the region's longstanding use of combs. Artifacts recovered from these sites include various types of combs made from bone, ivory, and wood.

In the ancient city of Mohenjo-Daro, located in present-day east Panjab, archaeologists have unearthed numerous examples of combs, indicating their widespread use among the inhabitants of the

Indus Valley Civilization. These combs vary in size, shape, and material, suggesting that they serve a variety of purposes.

The discovery of combs in Indus Valley sites underscores their significance as essential combing tools in ancient society. The presence of combs in archaeological contexts provides insights into the combing practices, personal hygiene, and cultural traditions of pre-Sikh Asian communities.

Cultural Practices

In pre-Sikh society, combs were vital in daily hygiene practices and rituals. Combs were used for untangling hair, removing debris, distributing oils, and promoting cleanliness and personal well-being. They were essential tools for both men and women, regardless of social status or occupation.

Combs also held cultural and symbolic significance in pre-Sikh society, often featuring in rituals, ceremonies, and religious observances. For example, in Hinduism, combs are associated with purity and cleanliness and are used in various rituals and rites of passage, such as weddings, childbirth ceremonies, and coming-of-age rituals.

In addition to their practical use, combs were sometimes adorned with decorative motifs or symbols, reflecting cultural aesthetics and religious beliefs. Elaborately carved combs made from precious materials may have been worn as adornments or status symbols by elites and royalty, highlighting the social significance of grooming and personal appearance in ancient society.

Spiritual Significance of the Kanga

The Kanga, a wooden comb worn by Sikhs as one of the Five Ks, holds profound spiritual significance within Sikhism. It symbolizes discipline, cleanliness, and self-respect. It serves as a tangible reminder for Sikhs to embody these values in their daily lives and spiritual practices, reinforcing their commitment to living a life of righteousness and devotion to the teachings of Sikh Gurus. It symbolizes several core values and principles that are central to Sikh spirituality and way of life:

1. **Discipline:** The Kanga represents discipline and self-control. By carrying and using the Kanga daily to maintain their hair, Sikhs demonstrate their commitment to leading a disciplined life in accordance with Sikh teachings. This discipline extends beyond mere physical grooming to encompass moral and spiritual discipline, reflecting the Sikh belief in living a life of righteousness and integrity.

2. **Cleanliness:** The Kanga symbolizes cleanliness and personal hygiene. Sikhs must keep their hair clean and tidy to show respect for the body, which is considered a divine gift. By using the Kanga to comb their hair regularly, Sikhs uphold the principle of cleanliness as a form of spiritual purity and reverence for the body as a sacred vessel for the divine light.

3. **Self-Respect:** Wearing the Kanga signifies self-respect and pride in one's identity as a Sikh. It serves as a reminder for Sikhs to take care of

themselves both physically and spiritually, reflecting a sense of self-worth and dignity that comes from living in alignment with Sikh principles. By maintaining their appearance with the Kanga, Sikhs honor their religious identity and uphold the values of self-respect and dignity instilled by Sikh teachings.

Practical Purpose of the Kanga

The practical purpose of the Kanga aligns with the core tenets of Sikhism, emphasizing cleanliness, tidiness, and the preservation of kesh. By using the Kanga regularly, Sikhs uphold their commitment to maintaining physical and spiritual purity while honoring the sacredness of their Kesh as a symbol of their faith and identity. The Kanga serves a crucial practical purpose in maintaining hair hygiene and adherence to the central tenet of kesh in Sikhism:

1. **Tidiness:** One of the primary functions of the Kanga is to keep the hair tidy and well-groomed. Sikhs are required to refrain from cutting or trimming their hair as a symbol of their commitment to Sikh values and their spiritual journey. The Kanga helps in untangling and arranging the hair, preventing it from becoming unkempt or tangled.

2. **Cleanliness:** In Sikhism, cleanliness is emphasized as a virtue and a form of reverence for the body, which is considered a divine gift. The Kanga aids in maintaining clean and hygienic hair by removing dirt, debris, and dead skin cells from the scalp. Regular combing with

the Kanga helps in distributing natural oils produced by the scalp, keeping the hair healthy and clean.

3. **Preservation of Kesh:** Kesh holds significant spiritual importance in Sikhism, symbolizing the acceptance of the natural state of being and the rejection of worldly vanity. The Kanga is instrumental in preserving the integrity of the hair by preventing breakage and damage. Its gentle teeth help detangle the hair without causing harm, allowing Sikhs to maintain their Kesh according to Sikh principles.

Incorporation of Kanga in Sikhism

The Kanga is an integral aspect of Sikh daily life and religious practice, serving both practical and symbolic purposes. Its use reflects the core values and principles of Sikhism, emphasizing discipline, cleanliness, and devotion to the Sikh way of life.

1. **Daily Grooming Routine:** Sikhs always carry a Kanga with them, usually kept under their kesh. In the morning and evening, Sikhs use the Kanga to comb their kesh to keep them clean, tidy, and free from tangles. This daily combing ritual is often accompanied by the recitation of prayers or Gurbani (verses from Sikh scriptures), making it a spiritual practice.

2. **Personal Hygiene:** The Kanga is a tool used for personal hygiene, which can help remove dirt, debris, and dead skin cells from the scalp. Regular combing with the Kanga can help distribute the natural oils produced by the scalp,

thereby keeping the hair healthy and clean. Additionally, Sikhs may use the Kanga to massage the scalp, which can promote blood circulation and overall hair health.

3. **Symbolic Significance:** The Kanga is a tool that holds significant importance for Sikhs. It represents values such as discipline, cleanliness, and self-respect. By including the Kanga in their daily grooming routine, Sikhs demonstrate their commitment to preserving their kesh and seeking spiritual purity, which are essential Sikh principles.

4. **Religious Observances:** During religious ceremonies, such as Gurdwara services, weddings, and festivals, Sikhs often wear the Kanga as part of their attire. The Kanga serves as a visible reminder of Sikh identity and devotion to the teachings of the Gurus. Moreover, the Kanga can also be used as part of the ceremonial items in Sikh rituals, symbolizing the importance of personal cleanliness and spiritual purity in worship.

5. **Community and Social Identity:** The Kanga is a small wooden comb that is worn by Sikhs to distinguish themselves from members of other communities. It serves as a unifying symbol among Sikhs, fostering a sense of solidarity and shared identity within the community. By wearing the Kanga, Sikhs reinforce their sense of belonging within the Sikh faith.

Humility, Equality, and Discipline

The Kanga serves as a tangible embodiment of Sikh values of humility, equality, and discipline. Through its use and symbolism, Sikhs are reminded to remain humble in appearance, embrace the equality of all individuals, and uphold principles of self-discipline and devotion to their faith.

1. **Humility:** The Kanga symbolizes humility by emphasizing the importance of maintaining personal hygiene and grooming without indulging in vanity or excessive adornment. Sikhs carry the Kanga as a reminder to remain humble and modest in their appearance, regardless of social status or material wealth. By prioritizing cleanliness and grooming as acts of self-care rather than self-aggrandizement, Sikhs demonstrate humility in their daily lives.

2. **Equality:** The requirement for all Amritdhari Sikhs, regardless of gender, age, or social background, to wear the Kanga reflects the Sikh principle of equality. The Kanga serves as a unifying symbol that transcends distinctions of caste, class, and gender, emphasizing the equality of all individuals within the Sikh community. Through the shared practice of carrying the Kanga, Sikhs reaffirm their commitment to the egalitarian ideals espoused by Sikhism, where all are considered equal in the eyes of the Divine.

3. **Discipline:** The Kanga represents discipline by encouraging Sikhs to adhere to a daily grooming

routine and maintain personal cleanliness. Carrying and using the Kanga requires self-discipline and dedication, as it is an outward expression of one's commitment to Sikh principles and values. By incorporating the Kanga into their daily lives, Sikhs cultivate habits of discipline and self-control, reflecting their devotion to living a disciplined life in accordance with Sikh teachings.

Scientific Benefits of Kanga

While the primary significance of the Kanga in Sikhism is cultural and spiritual, there are indeed some potential scientific benefits to using a wooden comb like the Kanga in daily hair care routines.

Reduces Static Electricity

Wooden combs, including the Kanga, are less likely to generate static electricity than plastic combs. Combing with a wooden comb can help minimize frizz and flyaways, leading to smoother and more manageable hair.

1. **Static Reduction.:** Wooden combs, including the Kanga, have a lower tendency to generate static electricity compared to plastic combs. This is because wood is a poor conductor of electricity, whereas plastic can build up static charge when used on dry hair. The reduced static charge means less frizz and flyaways, leading to smoother and more manageable hair.

2. **Minimizes Frizz and Flyaways:** Static electricity can cause individual hair strands to

repel each other, resulting in frizz and flyaways. Combining it with a wooden comb helps minimize static buildup, reducing the occurrence of frizz and flyaways. As a result, hair appears smoother and more controlled.

3. **Gentle on Hair:** Wooden combs, such as the Kanga, typically have smooth and rounded teeth. This design reduces friction and snagging, making combing gentler on the hair. Reduced pulling and tugging minimize the risk of hair breakage and damage.

4. **Enhances Hair Health:** The gentle action of combing with a wooden comb helps distribute natural oils from the scalp along the hair shaft. This provides additional moisture and nourishment to the hair, enhancing its overall health and appearance. Healthier, well-moisturized hair is less prone to frizz and looks smoother and shinier.

5. **Promotes Manageability:** By reducing frizz and flyaways and improving hair health, combing with a wooden comb promotes hair manageability. Hair becomes easier to style and maintain, requiring less effort to achieve desired looks. Overall, using a wooden comb like the Kanga contributes to smoother, more manageable hair.

Scalp Health

The gentle design of wooden combs like the Kanga makes them ideal for individuals looking to minimize scalp irritation and discomfort during hair care routines. By providing a smoother and more comfortable combing experience, wooden combs contribute to healthier and happier scalps.

1. **Gentle on the Scalp:** The smooth and rounded teeth of a wooden comb, such as the Kanga, are designed to be gentle on the scalp. In contrast, metal or plastic combs may have sharper edges, which can potentially cause irritation or damage to the scalp. The gentle design of the wooden comb reduces the risk of scalp irritation or discomfort during combing.

2. **Reduces Scalp Irritation:** Wooden combs are less likely to scratch or scrape the scalp compared to combs with sharper edges. This reduces the likelihood of causing irritation, redness, or discomfort on the scalp. Individuals with sensitive scalps may find wooden combs more comfortable to use, as they provide a smoother and gentler combing experience.

3. **Minimizes Risk of Damage:** The smooth and rounded teeth of the wooden comb glide more easily through the hair without snagging or pulling. This reduces the risk of hair breakage and damage, as well as potential damage to the scalp. By minimizing pulling and tugging on the hair and scalp, wooden combs help maintain the integrity of both hair and skin.

4. **Suitable for Sensitive Scalps:** Due to their gentle design, wooden combs like the Kanga are suitable for individuals with sensitive scalps or conditions such as scalp psoriasis or eczema.

The reduced risk of irritation makes wooden combs a preferred choice for those seeking a more comfortable and soothing combing experience. Additionally, the natural materials used in wooden combs are hypoallergenic, further reducing the risk of adverse reactions on sensitive skin.

Natural Conditioning

Wooden combs, especially those made from woods like sandalwood, offer natural conditioning benefits for the hair. By transferring natural oils to the hair strands during combing, wooden combs moisturize, nourish, and soften the hair, resulting in healthier and more lustrous locks over time.

1. **Natural Conditioning:** Wooden combs, particularly those made from certain types of wood like sandalwood, contain natural oils within their fibers. During combing, these natural oils are transferred from the wooden comb to the hair strands. The oils act as a natural conditioner, helping to moisturize and nourish the hair, resulting in softer and healthier-looking hair over time.

2. **Moisturizes Hair Strands:** The natural oils present in wooden combs penetrate the hair shaft, providing moisture and hydration to dry or damaged hair. This helps to replenish lost moisture, making the hair softer, smoother, and more manageable.

3. **Nourishes the Hair:** In addition to moisturizing, the natural oils from wooden combs also provide

nourishment to the hair strands. These oils contain essential fatty acids, vitamins, and antioxidants that help strengthen the hair and improve its overall health and appearance.

4. **Reduces Frizz and Static:** By moisturizing and nourishing the hair, wooden combs help reduce frizz and static electricity. Hydrated hair is less prone to frizz and flyaways, resulting in smoother and more controlled hair.

5. **Long-term Benefits:** With regular use, wooden combs can help improve the condition of the hair over time. Continued moisturization and nourishment from the natural oils contribute to healthier, shinier, and more resilient hair strands.

6. **Preference for Sandalwood:** Sandalwood is a particularly favored wood for combs due to its aromatic properties and unique benefits. Sandalwood oil has natural conditioning properties and a pleasant fragrance, making it an excellent choice for enhancing hair health and providing a relaxing aromatherapy experience during combing.

Blood Circulation

Combing with a wooden comb like the Kanga promotes blood circulation to the scalp, which in turn supports hair growth, strengthens the roots, and maintains scalp health. By incorporating regular combing with a wooden comb into their hair care routine, individuals can enjoy healthier, thicker, and more resilient hair over time.

1. **Promotes Blood Circulation:** Combing with a wooden comb, such as the Kanga, stimulates blood circulation to the scalp. The gentle pressure and motion of combing help to increase blood flow to the hair follicles and surrounding scalp tissue.

2. **Enhanced Nutrient Delivery:** Improved blood circulation means better delivery of oxygen and essential nutrients to the hair follicles. Nutrient-rich blood nourishes the hair follicles, promoting healthy hair growth and strengthening the roots.

3. **Supports Hair Growth:** The increased blood flow to the scalp can promote hair growth by encouraging the hair follicles to enter the active growth phase of the hair growth cycle. This can lead to thicker, fuller hair over time, as well as improved hair density and coverage.

4. **Strengthens Hair Roots:** Stronger blood circulation helps strengthen the hair roots, anchoring the hair firmly in the scalp. This reduces the risk of hair shedding and hair loss, leading to healthier and more resilient hair.

5. **Encourages Scalp Health:** Improved blood circulation supports overall scalp health by flushing away toxins and waste products. A healthy scalp environment is essential for maintaining optimal hair growth and preventing scalp conditions that can inhibit hair growth.

6. **Relaxation Benefits:** Besides its physiological effects, combing with a wooden comb can also provide relaxation benefits. The rhythmic motion

of combing can help reduce stress and tension, promoting a sense of calm and well-being.

Sustainable Environment

Opting for a wooden comb like the Kanga is an environmentally friendly choice that helps reduce plastic waste, minimize environmental impact, and support sustainable resource management practices. By making conscious decisions to prioritize eco-friendly alternatives, individuals can contribute to a cleaner, healthier planet for future generations.

1. **Environmental Friendliness:** Wooden combs, like the Kanga, are made from natural, biodegradable materials such as wood. Unlike plastic combs, which are made from synthetic materials derived from fossil fuels, wooden combs have a lower environmental impact throughout their lifecycle.

2. **Biodegradability:** Wooden combs are biodegradable, meaning they can naturally decompose over time without causing harm to the environment. When disposed of properly, wooden combs break down into organic matter, returning nutrients to the soil and reducing landfill waste.

3. **Reduction of Plastic Waste:** Choosing a wooden comb over a plastic one helps reduce plastic waste and pollution. Plastic combs contribute to the accumulation of non-biodegradable plastic waste in landfills and

oceans, where they can persist for hundreds of years and harm wildlife.

4. **Sustainable Sourcing:** Many wooden combs, including the Kanga, are crafted from sustainably sourced wood. Sustainable forestry practices ensure that trees are harvested in a responsible manner, preserving forest ecosystems and maintaining biodiversity.

5. **Renewable Resource:** Wood is a renewable resource that can be harvested sustainably and replenished through forest management practices. By choosing wooden combs, consumers support the use of renewable materials and reduce reliance on finite fossil fuel resources.

6. **Minimal Environmental Impact:** The production process for wooden combs typically has a lower environmental impact compared to plastic comb manufacturing. Wooden combs require fewer energy-intensive processes and generate fewer greenhouse gas emissions, contributing to overall environmental sustainability.

Aromatherapy

Wooden combs, particularly those made from aromatic woods like sandalwood, offer aromatherapy benefits that enhance the hair care experience. By providing a subtle and natural fragrance, wooden combs promote relaxation, well-being, and a sense of indulgence during grooming routines.

1. **Aromatherapy Benefits:** Wooden combs, especially those made from aromatic woods like sandalwood, can impart a pleasant fragrance to the hair during combing. The natural aroma released from the wooden comb adds a sensory element to the hair care routine, enhancing the overall experience.

2. **Sandalwood and Aromatherapy:** Sandalwood is known for its distinct and soothing fragrance, often used in aromatherapy for its calming and relaxing properties. Combs made from sandalwood release the characteristic scent of sandalwood when in contact with the hair and scalp.

3. **Promotes Relaxation:** The pleasant fragrance emitted by the wooden comb can promote relaxation and a sense of well-being during hair care routines. Aromatherapy with sandalwood has been shown to reduce stress and anxiety, inducing a feeling of calmness and tranquility.

4. **Enhances Hair Care Experience:** The subtle aroma from the wooden comb adds an element of luxury and indulgence to the hair care routine, transforming it into a sensory experience. The act of combing with a fragrant wooden comb can be uplifting and rejuvenating, providing a moment of self-care and pampering.

5. **Natural and Chemical-Free:** Unlike synthetic fragrances found in many hair care products, the scent from a wooden comb is natural and chemical-free. Individuals who prefer natural

beauty products may appreciate the aromatic benefits of wooden combs without exposure to artificial fragrances.

6. **Mind-Body Connection:** Aromatherapy with wooden combs taps into the mind-body connection, where sensory experiences can influence mood and emotions. The calming fragrance of sandalwood during hair care rituals can create a positive association with self-care and grooming practices.

Kachera

The term "Kachera" holds significant meaning within Sikhism, representing both a practical garment and a symbolic commitment to Sikh principles. At its most basic level, the Kachera refers to a specific type of undergarment typically made of cotton. This undergarment is loose-fitting and worn beneath outer clothing for comfort and modesty. Its design allows for ease of movement, making it practical for daily wear. However, the significance of the Kachera extends far beyond its physical form.

Symbolically, the Kachera embodies virtues central to Sikh ethics. It represents modesty, chastity, and sexual restraint, reflecting the importance of leading a disciplined and morally upright life. By wearing the Kachera, Sikhs symbolically commit to upholding these values in their actions and interactions with others. It serves as a constant reminder of the moral standards expected of them as followers of Sikhism.

As an identity marker, the Kachera plays a crucial role in fostering a sense of unity and solidarity among Sikhs. By wearing the Kachera, Sikhs publicly affirm their commitment to Sikh teachings and their membership in the Khalsa community. It serves as a visual representation of Sikh identity, signaling to others their adherence to Sikh principles and values.

The Kachera is more than just a piece of clothing; it is a symbol of Sikh identity, moral values, and commitment to the teachings of Sikhism. Through its practical use and symbolic significance, the Kachera serves as a constant reminder for Sikhs to uphold the virtues of modesty, chastity, and righteousness in their lives.

Significance of Kachera

The Kachera holds multifaceted significance within Sikhism, representing both symbolic and practical aspects of Sikh identity and ethics. As one of the Five Ks, it embodies values of modesty, chastity, equality, and unity, while also serving as a practical garment for daily wear. Through its use and symbolism, the Kachera reinforces the principles and ideals that define Sikh belief and practice within the Khalsa Panth.

1. **Modesty and Chastity:** The Kachera symbolizes the virtues of modesty and chastity. Its loose-fitting design reflects an emphasis on covering oneself modestly, while its use of simple cotton material underscores the Sikh commitment to humility and simplicity. By wearing the Kachera, Sikhs affirm their

dedication to leading a life of moral integrity and modesty in thought, speech, and action.

2. **Sexual Restraint:** In addition to modesty, the Kachera also symbolizes sexual restraint. Sikhs believe in the sanctity of marriage and the importance of maintaining fidelity and purity in relationships. By wearing the Kachera, Sikhs pledge to uphold these values and resist temptation, thereby fostering healthy and respectful interactions within society.

3. **Identity Marker of the Khalsa:** The Kachera serves as a visible marker of Sikh identity and membership in the Khalsa Panth. Alongside the other Four Ks, it distinguishes Amritdhari Sikhs from others and signifies their commitment to Sikh principles and values.

4. **Unity and Brotherhood:** By wearing the Kachera, Sikhs demonstrate their solidarity with fellow members of the Khalsa Panth. It fosters a sense of unity and brotherhood among Sikhs, regardless of their backgrounds or social status. The shared adherence to wearing the Kachera reinforces the bond of kinship and mutual support within the Sikh community.

5. **Equal Status:** The requirement for all Amritdhari Sikhs to wear the Kachera emphasizes the equality of all individuals within Sikhism. Regardless of gender, caste, or ethnicity, every baptized Sikh is expected to wear the Kachera, highlighting the egalitarian principles at the heart of Sikh teachings.

6. **Comfort and Utility:** The loose-fitting design of the Kachera allows for freedom of movement, making it practical for various activities, including work, exercise, and martial arts training. Its comfort and functionality contribute to its popularity as a garment worn by Amritdhari Sikhs on a daily basis.

7. **Hygiene and Cleanliness:** Sikhs are encouraged to maintain cleanliness and hygiene by wearing clean undergarments, including the Kachera. This emphasis on physical purity mirrors the spiritual purity that Sikhs strive to uphold in their lives.

Origin of Kachera in Sikhism

The origins of the Kachera within Sikh tradition can be traced back to the time of Sri Guru Gobind Singh Ji, the tenth Sikh Guru, who revealed the Khalsa Panth in 1699. Guru Gobind Singh introduced the concept of the Five Ks (Panj Kakar) as articles of faith for Sikhs, which included the Kachera along with the Kesh, Kangha, Kara, and Kirpan.

The introduction of the Kachera was part of Sri Guru Gobind Singh Ji's efforts to strengthen the identity and unity of the Sikh community. Each of the Five Ks was intended to serve as a visible marker of Sikh identity and a reminder of the principles and values that Sikhs were expected to uphold.

Historically, the Kachera also has roots in the practical necessities of the time. During the period of Sri Guru Gobind Singh Ji, Sikhs often faced persecution and were frequently engaged in battles against oppression. The loose-fitting design of the Kachera allowed for ease of movement, making it practical for Sikhs engaged in physical activities, including combat and agricultural work.

Additionally, the Kachera symbolized the Guru's call for Sikhs to renounce the luxuries and extravagances of the Mughal society prevalent at the time. By wearing simple cotton undergarments, Sikhs demonstrated their commitment to humility, simplicity, and detachment from materialism.

Over time, the Kachera became firmly established as an integral aspect of Sikh identity and practice. It continues to be worn by Amritdhari Sikhs today as a symbol of their membership in the Khalsa Panth and their dedication to the principles of Sikhism. Through its origins and continued significance, the Kachera serves as a reminder of the historical struggles and spiritual ideals that define Sikh tradition.

Historical Anecdotes and References

These historical anecdotes and references underscore the significance of wearing the Kachera within Sikh tradition. From battles for religious freedom to acts of resistance against tyranny, the Kachera has served as a potent symbol of Sikh identity, courage, and resilience throughout history. Several historical anecdotes and references highlight the importance of wearing the Kachera within Sikh tradition:

1. **Battle of Anandpur Sahib**: During the Battle of Anandpur Sahib in 1704, which was a significant conflict between the forces of Sri Guru Gobind Singh Ji and the Mughal army, the Kachera

played a crucial role. Sikh warriors, known as the Khalsa, wore their Kachera with pride and courage as they fought against overwhelming odds. The Kachera symbolized their commitment to Sikh principles, including bravery, righteousness, and selflessness in the face of adversity.

2. **Bhai Bachittar Singh**: Bhai Bachittar Singh, a prominent Sikh warrior during the early 18th century, exemplified the importance of the Kachera in the Sikh martial tradition. Known for his bravery and unwavering commitment to Sikh ideals, Bhai Bachittar Singh wore his Kachera with distinction as he fought alongside Guru Gobind Singh's forces in various battles. His steadfast adherence to the Khalsa code, including wearing the Kachera, earned him respect and admiration among Sikhs and served as an inspiration for future generations.

3. **Persecution and Resistance**: Throughout Sikh history, Sikhs faced persecution and oppression under various rulers who sought to suppress their religious identity. Despite facing immense challenges, Sikhs remained steadfast in their faith and wore their Kachera proudly as a symbol of resistance against tyranny. The Kachera became a tangible expression of Sikh defiance and resilience in the face of adversity, inspiring Sikhs to uphold their principles and fight for their rights.

4. **Baba Banda Singh Bahadur**: Baba Banda Singh Bahadur, a prominent Sikh military leader

in the early 18th century, emphasized the importance of the Kachera in Sikh martial tradition. Banda Singh Bahadur and his followers wore their Kachera as they waged a successful military campaign against the oppressive Mughal regime. The Kachera symbolized their commitment to Sikh values of justice, equality, and freedom, motivating them to challenge injustice and oppression wherever they encountered it.

Description of the Kachera

The Kachera is a simple yet significant garment in Sikh tradition, designed for comfort, modesty, and practicality. Its construction, fabric, and symbolic meaning reflect the values and principles that define Sikh identity and practice within the Khalsa Panth. Through its design and usage, the Kachera serves as a tangible expression of Sikh beliefs and a reminder of the spiritual discipline expected of Sikhs.

1. **Fabric and Material**: The Kachera is typically made of cotton fabric, although variations may exist. Cotton is preferred for its breathability, softness, and comfort, making it suitable for daily wear in various climates and conditions. The use of natural materials aligns with Sikh principles of simplicity and environmental stewardship.

2. **Construction and Fit**: The Kachera is characterized by its loose-fitting design, providing ample room for movement and comfort. It is often constructed with a simple

rectangular or square-shaped cloth, with ties or drawstrings at the waist for adjustment. Some Kacheras may feature an elasticized waistband for added convenience.

3. **Length and Coverage**: Traditionally, the Kachera extends to just above the knees, offering sufficient coverage while allowing for freedom of movement. However, variations in length may exist based on personal preference or cultural practices. The Kachera is intended to be modest and decent, providing adequate coverage without being restrictive.

4. **Design Features**: The simplicity of Kachera's design is a hallmark of its practicality and functionality. It is devoid of embellishments or unnecessary adornments, reflecting Sikh values of humility and austerity. The focus is on comfort and utility, with minimalistic detailing to ensure ease of wear and maintenance.

5. **Versatility and Adaptability**: The Kachera's versatile design makes it suitable for a wide range of activities and occasions. Whether worn under traditional Sikh attire, such as a Kurta and Pajama, or as everyday underwear beneath Western clothing, the Kachera provides comfort and coverage while remaining discreet and unobtrusive.

6. **Symbolic Significance**: Beyond its practical attributes, the Kachera holds deep symbolic significance within Sikhism. It symbolizes virtues such as modesty, chastity, and sexual

restraint, reflecting the moral principles expected of Amritdhari Sikhs. By wearing the Kachera, Sikhs affirm their commitment to Sikh values and identity, both in their outward appearance and inner conduct.

Spiritual Significance of Kachera

Wearing the Kachera is not only a physical practice but also a spiritual discipline that holds profound significance within Sikh tradition. It is believed to bestow spiritual benefits upon the wearer, guiding them on their journey towards spiritual fulfillment and union with the divine. Within Sikh tradition, wearing the Kachera is believed to bring about various spiritual benefits and blessings for those who adhere to its practice. Some of the spiritual benefits associated with wearing the Kachera are:

1. **Enhanced Spiritual Awareness:** Wearing the Kachera is seen as a constant reminder of one's commitment to Sikh principles and values. It fosters a heightened awareness of one's spiritual journey and the importance of living in alignment with Sikh teachings.

2. **Cultivation of Virtues**: The Kachera symbolizes virtues such as modesty, humility, and self-discipline. By wearing it, Sikhs strive to cultivate these virtues in their daily lives, leading to personal growth and spiritual development.

3. **Protection and Strength**: Sikhs believe that wearing the Kachera grants them spiritual protection and strength. It is seen as a form of spiritual armor that shields the wearer from

negative influences and temptations, enabling them to navigate life's challenges with resilience and fortitude.

4. **Connection to Sikh Tradition**: Wearing the Kachera connects Sikhs to their rich spiritual heritage and the legacy of the Khalsa Panth. It serves as a tangible link to the sacrifices and teachings of the Sikh Gurus, inspiring Sikhs to uphold their legacy and continue their spiritual journey.

5. **Unity and Brotherhood**: The practice of wearing the Kachera fosters a sense of unity and brotherhood among Sikhs. It symbolizes their shared commitment to Sikh values and their membership in the Khalsa Panth, creating a supportive community bound by a common spiritual identity.

6. **Merit and Blessings**: Sikh tradition holds that the act of wearing the Kachera accumulates spiritual merit and blessings for the wearer. It is believed to earn the favor of Waheguru (God) and attract divine grace, leading to spiritual upliftment and inner peace.

7. **Alignment with Sikh Principles**: By wearing the Kachera, Sikhs demonstrate their obedience to the commands of the Sikh Gurus and their dedication to living a life of righteousness and piety. It signifies their willingness to submit to the will of Waheguru and follow the path of Sikhism with sincerity and devotion.

Scientific Benefits of Wearing Kachera

The scientific benefits may enhance the wearing experience of the Kachera in terms of hygiene, comfort, and sustainability, it's important to note that the primary significance of the Kachera lies in its spiritual and cultural importance within Sikh tradition.

Hygiene and Skin Health

Using cotton fabric in the Kachera offers several hygiene and skin health benefits, including breathability, moisture management, reduction of bacterial growth, and comfort. These qualities contribute to maintaining healthy skin and minimizing the risk of skin-related issues, supporting the overall well-being of individuals who wear the Kachera.

1. **Breathability**: Cotton fabric allows for better air circulation than synthetic materials. This prevents moisture buildup and creates a more comfortable environment for the skin. By reducing moisture, the risk of skin irritation, fungal infections, and unpleasant odors is minimized.

2. **Moisture Management**: Cotton is highly absorbent, effectively wicking away sweat from the body. This helps to keep the skin dry and prevents the accumulation of moisture, which can contribute to bacterial growth and skin problems. By maintaining dryness, cotton fabric supports better hygiene and reduces the risk of skin infections.

3. **Reduction of Bacterial Growth**: The absorbent nature of cotton fabric not only helps to manage moisture but also limits the growth of bacteria on the skin. By keeping the skin dry and less hospitable to bacteria, cotton fabric promotes overall skin health and reduces the likelihood of bacterial infections.

4. **Gentle on the Skin**: Cotton is a soft and gentle fabric that is less likely to cause irritation or abrasions compared to synthetic materials. For individuals with sensitive skin or conditions such as eczema, wearing cotton undergarments like the Kachera can help minimize irritation and discomfort, supporting healthier skin.

5. **Improved Comfort**: The combination of breathability, moisture management, and gentle texture makes cotton fabric inherently comfortable to wear. This contributes to a more pleasant wearing experience and encourages individuals to maintain good hygiene practices by wearing their undergarments regularly.

Comfort and Mobility

The loose-fitting design of the Kachera provides wearers with comfort, freedom of movement, and airflow, making it a practical and versatile choice for daily wear. Its relaxed fit promotes mobility and ensures unrestricted blood flow, enhancing overall comfort and well-being for individuals who choose to wear the Kachera.

1. **Ample Room for Movement**: The loose fit of the Kachera provides freedom of movement,

allowing wearers to move comfortably without feeling constrained. This is particularly advantageous during physical activities, such as exercise, work, or recreational pursuits, where flexibility and agility are essential.

2. **Enhanced Airflow**: The generous cut of the Kachera promotes airflow around the body, preventing overheating and ensuring ventilation. This helps to regulate body temperature and reduce the risk of discomfort or perspiration buildup, enhancing overall comfort throughout the day.

3. **Reduced Chafing and Irritation**: Unlike tight-fitting undergarments, which may rub against the skin and cause chafing or irritation, the loose fit of the Kachera minimizes friction and abrasion. This reduces the likelihood of discomfort and allows for prolonged wear without discomfort or skin irritation.

4. **Unrestricted Blood Flow**: Tight-fitting undergarments can restrict blood circulation, leading to discomfort, numbness, or tingling sensations. The relaxed fit of the Kachera ensures unrestricted blood flow, promoting optimal circulation and maintaining comfort, particularly during long periods of wear.

5. **Adaptability to Various Activities**: The loose-fitting design of the Kachera makes it suitable for a wide range of activities and lifestyles. Whether worn during daily routines, leisure activities, or physical exertion, the Kachera

offers comfort and mobility without compromising on style or functionality.

Temperature Regulation

The thermoregulatory properties of cotton fabric make the Kachera an excellent choice for maintaining comfort and well-being in varying weather conditions. Its ability to keep the body cool in hot weather and warm in cold weather contributes to overall comfort and ensures that wearers can remain comfortable and protected throughout the day.

1. **Natural Thermoregulation**: Cotton fabric possesses inherent thermoregulatory properties, meaning it can help regulate body temperature by trapping heat when it's cold and allowing heat to escape when it's warm. This natural mechanism helps to keep the body comfortable and maintain a stable internal temperature, regardless of external conditions. In colder weather, cotton fabric helps to insulate the body by trapping air between its fibers, providing warmth and protection against the cold. Conversely, in warmer weather, cotton fabric allows for heat to escape, preventing overheating and promoting cooling.

2. **Cooling Effect in Hot Weather**: The breathable nature of cotton fabric allows air to circulate freely through the garment, facilitating heat dissipation and promoting a cooling effect on the skin. This helps to prevent overheating and excessive sweating, which can lead to discomfort, skin irritation, and moisture-related

issues. By wicking away moisture from the body and promoting evaporation, cotton fabric helps to keep the skin dry and comfortable, even in hot and humid conditions. This contributes to overall well-being and enhances comfort during periods of high heat or physical activity.

3. **Warmth Retention in Cold Weather**: Cotton fabric provides a layer of insulation that helps to retain body heat in colder weather conditions. The natural fibers trap air close to the skin, creating a barrier against the cold and providing warmth and comfort. Unlike synthetic materials, which may feel cold and clammy when exposed to low temperatures, cotton fabric remains comfortable and soft against the skin, ensuring a cozy and snug fit that promotes warmth and comfort.

Allergen Reduction

The hypoallergenic nature of cotton fabric makes the Kachera a suitable choice for individuals with sensitive skin or allergies. Its gentle, breathable, and moisture-wicking properties contribute to overall skin health and comfort, reducing the risk of irritation and discomfort associated with allergens or synthetic materials.

1. **Hypoallergenic Properties**: Cotton is naturally hypoallergenic, meaning it is less likely to cause allergic reactions or skin sensitivities compared to synthetic materials. This is particularly beneficial for individuals with sensitive skin or allergies, as it reduces the risk of irritation,

itching, and discomfort. The absence of harsh chemicals or synthetic additives in cotton fabric further minimizes the likelihood of allergic reactions, making it a safe and gentle choice for those with sensitivities or skin conditions.

2. **Gentle on the Skin**: Cotton fabric is soft, breathable, and gentle against the skin, making it suitable for prolonged wear without causing irritation or abrasions. Its smooth texture and natural fibers create a comfortable and soothing sensation against the skin, reducing the risk of friction-related irritation. Unlike synthetic materials, which may feel rough or abrasive, cotton fabric provides a gentle and comforting layer of protection that promotes skin health and comfort.

3. **Moisture Management**: Cotton fabric's absorbent properties help to wick away moisture from the skin, keeping it dry and reducing the risk of irritation or discomfort associated with sweat buildup. By maintaining dryness, cotton fabric minimizes the conditions that can exacerbate allergic reactions or skin sensitivities. For individuals prone to allergic reactions triggered by sweat or moisture, wearing cotton undergarments like the Kachera can help alleviate discomfort and promote skin health by effectively managing moisture and preventing skin irritation.

Environmental Sustainability

The use of cotton fabric in the Kachera reflects a commitment to environmental sustainability by leveraging biodegradability, renewability, and reduced environmental impact of natural fibers. Choosing cotton undergarments supports sustainable fashion practices and reduces the environmental footprint of textile production, contributing to the preservation of natural resources and ecosystem health.

1. **Biodegradability**: Cotton is a natural fiber derived from the cotton plant, making it biodegradable. When discarded, cotton fabric decomposes over time, returning to the environment without leaving behind harmful residues or contributing to pollution. This reduces the environmental burden associated with textile waste and supports ecosystem health.

2. **Renewable Resource**: Cotton is a renewable resource that can be cultivated through sustainable agricultural practices. Unlike synthetic materials, which are derived from non-renewable fossil fuels, cotton can be grown and harvested annually, minimizing reliance on finite resources and reducing the environmental footprint of textile production.

3. **Reduction of Pollution**: Cotton cultivation typically involves fewer chemical inputs compared to the production of synthetic fibers. By choosing cotton undergarments like the Kachera, consumers support agricultural

practices that minimize the use of pesticides, fertilizers, and other harmful chemicals, reducing the pollution associated with conventional farming methods. Additionally, the biodegradability of cotton fabric means that it does not contribute to microplastic pollution, which can occur when synthetic fabrics shed tiny plastic particles during washing and wear.

4. **Support for Sustainable Fashion**: Choosing cotton undergarments like the Kachera promotes sustainable fashion practices by prioritizing natural, eco-friendly materials over synthetic alternatives. By opting for garments made from renewable, biodegradable fibers, consumers contribute to reducing waste and environmental impact associated with the fashion industry. Supporting brands and manufacturers prioritizing sustainability in their production processes encourages adopting environmentally responsible practices across the textile industry, fostering positive change towards a more sustainable future.

Kirpan

The kirpan is a ceremonial sword carried by Amritdhari Sikhs, which is one of the Five Ks, or five articles of faith, and symbolizes the Sikh's identity and commitment to their faith. The term "kirpan" is derived from Panjabi, with "Kirpa" meaning "mercy" or "grace" and "an" denoting "the essence of."

The kirpan holds deep symbolic and practical significance within Sikhism. It represents courage, self-defense, and the commitment to protect the innocent and uphold righteousness. Historically, it served as both a defensive weapon and a tool for preserving justice and religious freedom.

Beyond its physical form, the kirpan embodies spiritual qualities such as righteousness, compassion, and the readiness to stand up against injustice. It is a reminder to Sikhs always to be prepared to defend the oppressed and uphold the principles of their faith.

In contemporary Sikh practice, wearing the kirpan is a visible expression of Sikh identity and a reminder of the responsibility to stand against tyranny and injustice. While primarily symbolic today, the kirpan remains a potent emblem of Sikh values and a representation of the Sikh commitment to justice, equality, and righteousness.

The Concept of Miri and Piri

The principle of Miri and Piri holds great significance in Sikhism, especially as highlighted by Sri Guru Hargobind Sahib Ji, the sixth Sikh Guru. According to this principle of Sri Guru Hargobind Sahib Ji, Miri signifies temporal or worldly power, whereas Piri represents spiritual authority. Sri Guru Hargobind Sahib Ji's explanation of this concept emphasizes that Sikhs have a dual responsibility that encompasses both the temporal and spiritual realms. They should wield worldly power with integrity and righteousness while also staying deeply connected to spiritual principles and divine guidance.

Miri

1. **Temporal Power**: Miri refers to the temporal or worldly authority. It encompasses the governance of worldly affairs, including political, social, and economic matters.

2. **Responsibility and Leadership**: Those who hold Miri are entrusted with the responsibility to ensure justice, protect the oppressed, and promote the well-being of society.

3. **Courage and Strength**: Miri involves the use of strength and courage to defend the weak, uphold righteousness, and confront injustice in the temporal realm.

4. **Embrace of Miri**: Sri Guru Hargobind Singh Ji embodied the concept of Miri by donning two swords, symbolizing his readiness to wield temporal authority alongside spiritual leadership. He established the Sri Akal Takht Sahib Ji (Throne of the Almighty) as a center of temporal authority for the Sikh community.

Piri

1. **Spiritual Authority**: Piri signifies spiritual authority and sovereignty. It pertains to matters of spirituality, moral guidance, and religious leadership.

2. **Connection with the Divine**: Piri involves a deep connection with the divine and adherence to spiritual principles such as compassion, humility, and devotion.

3. **Guidance and Enlightenment**: Those who hold Piri are entrusted with the task of providing spiritual guidance, nurturing the soul, and leading individuals towards enlightenment and union with the Divine.

4. **Embrace of Piri**: Alongside his embrace of Miri, Sri Guru Hargobind Sahib Ji emphasized the importance of spiritual sovereignty. He emphasized the significance of spiritual practice, meditation, and devotion to attain spiritual liberation.

Integration of Miri and Piri

1. **Balance and Harmony**: Sri Guru Hargobind Sahib Ji taught the integration of Miri and Piri, emphasizing the importance of maintaining a balance between worldly responsibilities and spiritual pursuits.

2. **Sikh Identity and Mission**: The integration of Miri and Piri is foundational to the Sikh identity and mission. Sikhs are called to engage actively in worldly affairs while remaining spiritually grounded and guided by ethical principles.

Importance of Wearing Kirpan in Khalsa Panth

The kirpan holds significant importance within the Khalsa Panth, the community of Amritdhari Sikhs. The kirpan holds immense importance within the Khalsa Panth as a symbol of Sikh identity, a reminder of spiritual values, and a commitment to the defense of truth, justice, and the Sikh community. Its significance stems from various aspects of Sikh belief and practice:

1. **Symbol of Sikh Identity**: The kirpan is one of the Five Ks, or five articles of faith, that Amritdhari Sikhs are mandated to wear at all times. Alongside other articles like the kesh, kara, kanga, and kachera, the kirpan serves as a visible marker of Sikh identity and commitment to the Sikh faith.

2. **Defense of Truth and Justice**: The kirpan symbolizes the Sikh commitment to stand up against injustice, defend the weak, and uphold the principles of truth and righteousness. It represents the readiness of Sikhs to protect themselves and others from oppression and tyranny.

3. **Spiritual Significance**: Beyond its physical form, the kirpan holds spiritual significance within Sikhism. It serves as a reminder of the importance of courage, compassion, and selflessness in the pursuit of spiritual growth and the realization of divine truth.

4. **Historical Context**: The kirpan has a rich historical significance in Sikh tradition. It was historically used as a defensive weapon by Sikhs during times of persecution and oppression. Guru Hargobind Singh Ji, the sixth Sikh Guru, initiated the tradition of carrying a kirpan as a means of self-defense and protection of the Sikh community.

5. **Commitment to Service and Protection**: Wearing the kirpan signifies a commitment to service and protection not only of oneself but

also of others. It embodies the Sikh principle of seva (selfless service) and the responsibility to serve humanity and defend the oppressed.

6. **Legal and Social Considerations**: In many countries, Sikhs have fought for and secured legal exemptions allowing them to wear the kirpan in public spaces, even in contexts where carrying weapons might otherwise be prohibited. This legal recognition reflects the acknowledgment of the kirpan's religious significance and the rights of Sikhs to freely practice their faith.

Religious Significance

The Kirpan is a ceremonial sword worn by Sikhs as a symbol of their faith and commitment to protect the weak and oppressed.

1. **Protection and Defense**: The Guru Granth Sahib contains numerous references to protection and defense. For instance, Sri Guru Nanak Sahib Ji, the founder of Sikhism, often speaks of divine protection and refuge in the Divine's Name. Sikhs interpret these references as a call to be protectors of truth and righteousness, which is symbolized by the kirpan.

2. **Warrior Spirit and Courage**: The Sri Dasam Granth Sahib Ji contains compositions that speak more directly to themes of martial spirit and defense. The famous composition "Chandi Di Vaar" depicts the warrior aspect of the Divine and the valor of the Khalsa in battle.

3. **Spiritual Warfare**: Sikh Granth often speaks metaphorically about spiritual warfare, the battle against ego, and the triumph of righteousness. While these references are not specific to the physical kirpan, they emphasize the importance of spiritual preparedness and the courage to stand up for truth in the face of adversity, which are qualities embodied by the kirpan.

Sikh Philosophy and Theology

The kirpan's role in Sikh philosophy and theology encompasses courage, defense of truth, sovereignty, equality, justice, spiritual preparedness, and the integration of Miri and Piri. It serves as a tangible symbol of Sikh values and principles, reminding the Sikhs of their duty to stand up for righteousness and uphold the dignity and rights of all beings. The kirpan holds a significant role in Sikh philosophy and theology, embodying several core principles and values of the Sikh tradition:

1. **Courage and Defense of Truth**: In Sikh philosophy, courage and the defense of truth are paramount. The kirpan symbolizes the readiness to stand up against injustice and oppression, even at personal risk. It represents the Sikh commitment to uphold righteousness and protect the weak and oppressed.

2. **Sovereignty and Self-defense**: Sikh theology emphasizes the sovereignty of the individual and the community. The kirpan embodies the principle of self-defense and the assertion of sovereignty against tyranny and oppression. It

serves as a tangible reminder of the Sikh's right and duty to defend themselves and others from harm.

3. **Equality and Justice**: Sikhism teaches the fundamental equality of all human beings and the pursuit of justice for all. The kirpan represents the Sikh's commitment to fight against discrimination, inequality, and injustice. It symbolizes the Sikh's role as a protector and advocate for the marginalized and oppressed.

4. **Spiritual Preparedness**: Beyond its physical function, the kirpan holds spiritual significance in Sikh theology. It symbolizes the Sikh's spiritual preparedness to confront internal and external challenges on the path of righteousness. Just as the physical kirpan serves as a tool for defense, Sikhs are called to cultivate inner strength and courage to overcome spiritual obstacles and uphold moral principles.

5. **Unity of Miri and Piri**: The kirpan embodies the integration of Miri (temporal power) and Piri (spiritual authority) within Sikhism. It signifies the harmonious balance between worldly responsibilities and spiritual pursuits. The Sikh is called to embody both aspects, wielding temporal authority with integrity and remaining spiritually grounded in divine principles.

Sanskar (Rituals)

The kirpan is woven into various Sikh rituals and ceremonies, symbolizing the core values of courage, righteousness, and spiritual preparedness that are central to Sikh beliefs. Its presence serves as a tangible reminder of the Sikh's commitment to upholding these values in all aspects of life. Some of these ceremonies are:

1. **Birth Sanskar**: In the Sikh tradition, the birth of a child is celebrated with a ceremony called the Gurti (first bite), which involves giving the child an Amrit as the first byte in the world with a sword. It symbolizes the Sikh commitment to protect and defend the newborn and uphold the values of righteousness and justice throughout their life.

2. **Amrit Sanchar with Khanda**: The Amrit Sanchar ceremony involves the administration of Amrit (sacred nectar) to individuals seeking to become Amritdhari Sikhs, known as Khalsa. The kirpan and Khanda play a significant role in this ceremony:

   - The kirpan represents the readiness to defend truth and righteousness, and the initiates bless and wear it as a symbol of their commitment to Sikh principles.

   - The Khanda, a double-edged sword, is a central symbol of the Sikh faith. It represents the oneness of God, the authority of the Guru, and the unity of the Sikh community. It is often displayed during the ceremony as a sign of spiritual empowerment and divine grace.

3. **Marriage Sanskar**: In Sikh weddings, known as Anand Karaj, the kirpan holds symbolic importance as a representation of the groom's responsibility to protect and defend his family and uphold the principles of Sikhism. Its presence serves as a reminder of the commitment to righteousness and the defense of truth within the marital union.

4. **Antim Sanskar**: During Sikh funeral rites, known as Antam Sanskar, the kirpan is present as a symbol of the deceased's lifelong commitment to Sikh values, including courage, defense of truth, and spiritual preparedness. Its inclusion serves as a reminder of the deceased's adherence to Sikh principles.

Design and Construction of Kirpan

The design and construction of the kirpan have evolved over time, blending traditional features with modern adaptations to meet practical and legal requirements.:

Traditional Features

- Before 1849, during the period of Khalsa Raj (Sikh rule), the kirpan was traditionally a longer weapon, with a minimum length of at least three feet. This length was determined by the order of Sri Guru Gobind Singh Ji, the martial nature of Sikh society, and the need for a formidable defensive weapon.

- Traditional kirpans featured a curved, single-edged blade made of high-quality iron or steel.

The blade often had intricate engravings or etchings depicting religious symbols, prayers, or designs reflecting Sikh heritage.

- The handle of the traditional kirpan was typically made of wood, ivory, or metal, with ornate embellishments such as carvings or inlays. It provided a secure grip for the wielder during combat.

Changes post-1849

- After the loss of Khalsa Raj in 1849, the length of the kirpan was significantly reduced due to legal restrictions. It was determined that the blade should be no longer than six inches, with a handle length of three inches. The total length was determined to be 9 inches.

- This reduction in size was aimed at conforming to legal regulations governing the carrying of weapons and ensuring that the kirpan could be worn discreetly under clothing, reflecting its primarily symbolic rather than practical role in contemporary Sikh society.

- Despite the reduction in size, efforts were made to preserve the traditional aesthetic and symbolic significance of the kirpan, maintaining its curved blade and ornate handle designs.

Modern Adaptations

- In modern times, kirpans are often crafted with a focus on both tradition and practicality. While some Sikhs still opt for traditional, handcrafted kirpans with elaborate designs and materials, others may choose more streamlined and functional designs.

- Modern kirpans may feature iron, stainless steel, or other durable materials for the blade and handle, ensuring longevity and ease of maintenance.

- The design of the modern kirpan may also incorporate safety features such as rounded edges and blunt tips to minimize the risk of accidental injury while maintaining the symbolic integrity of the weapon.

The design and construction of the kirpan have adapted to reflect changing legal requirements and societal norms while preserving its traditional significance within Sikh culture. From traditional long blades to modern compact versions, the kirpan continues to symbolize the Sikh commitment to courage, defense of truth, and spiritual readiness.

Necessary article for Sikhs

The kirpan is considered an essential and inseparable aspect of Sikh identity and faith. It embodies the core principles and values of Sikhism and serves as a constant reminder of the Sikh's commitment to truth, justice, and spiritual preparedness. The kirpan is considered necessary for every Sikh to wear.

1. **Religious Obligation**: The kirpan is one of the Five Ks, or five articles of faith, mandated for every Amritdhari Sikh to wear at all times. The

Five Ks are central to Sikh identity and are considered sacred symbols of Sikhism.

2. **Symbol of Sikh Values**: The kirpan symbolizes key Sikh values such as courage, justice, and the defense of truth. By wearing the kirpan, Sikhs express their commitment to upholding these values in their daily lives.

3. **Historical Significance**: The tradition of wearing the kirpan dates to the time of Sri Guru Hargobind Sahib Ji, the sixth Sikh Guru, who Amritdhari the practice as a means of self-defense and protection for the needed communities. The kirpan thus carries significant historical and cultural importance for Sikhs.

4. **Spiritual Preparedness**: Beyond its physical presence, the kirpan serves as a reminder of the Sikh's spiritual preparedness to confront challenges and defend righteousness. It symbolizes the Sikh's readiness to confront injustice and oppression, both internally and externally.

5. **Legal Recognition**: In many countries, Sikhs have fought for and secured legal exemptions, allowing them to wear the kirpan in public spaces, recognizing its religious significance, and the rights of Sikhs to practice their faith freely.

The Five Ks are five articles of faith that are an integral part of the Khalsa Panth, the community of Amritdhari Sikhs. These articles, mandated by Sri Guru

Gobind Singh Ji, the tenth Sikh Guru, symbolize the Sikh identity, values, and commitment to the Sikh faith.

*****

THE SAINT SPIRIT OF THE KHALSA

THE SAINT SPIRIT OF THE KHALSA

The word "Khalsa" was indeed coined by Guru Gobind Singh Ji himself, and its meaning goes beyond its literal translation. In Sikh tradition, "Khalsa" refers to the collective body of one or more Amritdhari Sikh(s) who have undergone the Amrit Sanskar, also known as Amrit Sanchar, and have dedicated themselves fully to the principles and teachings of Sikhism as outlined by the Guru. The word "Khalsa" itself means "pure" or "belonging to the divine," signifying a state of spiritual purity and devotion.

Sri Guru Gobind Singh Ji established the Khalsa on April 13, 1699, during the Vaisakhi, by revealing the Panj Pyare (the Five Beloved Ones) and then receiving Amrit from them, thereby symbolizing the equality and unity among all Sikhs. The Khalsa was envisioned as a community of saint soldiers who would uphold righteousness, fight against oppression and injustice, and serve humanity selflessly.

The term "Khalsa," as introduced by Guru Gobind Singh Ji, represents the highest ideals of Sikhism, including purity of heart, dedication to truth, courage in the face of adversity, and unwavering commitment to serving others. It is not just a word but a sacred identity that encapsulates the essence of Sikh spirituality and the divine mission entrusted to its followers.

Khalsa

- **Meaning**: The term "Khalsa," meaning "pure," "free," "Army of Akaal (God)," "Dedicated to

Akaal," "Sant (Saint)" or "one who belongs to the eternal," "immortal,"" protector," etc.

- **Significance**: The Khalsa is considered the ideal and purest form of Sikhism, embodying the highest spiritual and ethical principles. Initiation into the Khalsa entails a commitment to live according to the Sikh code of conduct, known as the Rehat Maryada, and to uphold the values of truth, equality, justice, and selfless service.

- **Characteristics**: Members of the Khalsa are identified by the Five Ks, or Panj Kakkar, which include Kesh (uncut hair), Kangha (a wooden comb), Kara (an iron bracelet), Kirpan (a ceremonial sword), and Kachera (cotton undergarments). These articles symbolize the Khalsa's commitment to Sikh ideals and principles.

- **Role**: The Khalsa community plays a central role in Sikh society and world communities, serving as spiritual leaders, warriors for justice, and exemplars of Sikh values. They are expected to lead lives of integrity, compassion, and service to humanity.

Sant (Saint)

- **Meaning**: The term "Sant" in Sikhism refers to an individual who has attained a high level of spiritual realization and enlightenment. Sant means "one who is established in truth" or "one who is a friend of all."

- **Significance**: Sants are revered as spiritual guides and exemplars of divine virtues. They are characterized by their deep devotion to Waheguru (God), their selflessness, humility, and their ability to impart spiritual wisdom to others.

- **Characteristics**: Sants are known for their inner purity, compassion, and detachment from worldly desires. They often lead simple lives focused on meditation, prayer, and service to humanity. Their teachings emphasize the importance of love, kindness, and inner transformation.

- **Role**: Sants play a vital role in guiding individuals on the spiritual path, helping them overcome ignorance and ego, and leading them towards union with the Divine. They inspire others through their exemplary lives and serve as beacons of light in a world filled with darkness.

Interrelation between Khalsa and Sant:

- While the Khalsa and Sant may appear distinct in their outward manifestations and roles within Sikh society, they are deeply interconnected in their underlying principles and aspirations.

- The Khalsa strives to embody the virtues and qualities of a Sant within the context of active engagement in the world. They seek to cultivate inner purity, humility, and devotion to Waheguru while also serving as warriors for truth, justice, and righteousness.

- Similarly, Sants may draw inspiration from the principles of the Khalsa in their pursuit of spiritual realization. They may emphasize the importance of selfless service, righteous action, and standing up against injustice, aligning themselves with the ethos of the Khalsa.

- Both the Khalsa and Sant ultimately aim to transcend ego and worldly attachments, surrendering themselves completely to the divine will and dedicating their lives to the service of humanity.

While the Khalsa represents the active and engaged aspect of Sikh spirituality, the Sant embodies the contemplative and inward-focused dimension. Together, they reflect the multifaceted nature of Sikhism and its emphasis on integrating spiritual ideals into everyday life.

The Concept of Sant (Saint) in Sikh Philosophy

In Sikh philosophy, the concept of saintliness, known as "Sant," in Panjabi or "Santokh" in Sikh Granths, is highly important. The idea of Sant is deeply rooted in Sikh teachings and is considered essential for spiritual growth and realization. Saintliness in Sikh philosophy encompasses inner purity, humility, compassion, detachment, spiritual wisdom, and devotion to Waheguru. Sants serve as exemplars of these virtues, guiding seekers on the path of spiritual realization and inspiring them to live a life of righteousness and love.

Inner Purity and Divine Connection

- Saintliness in Sikhism is characterized by inner purity, moral integrity, and a profound connection with the divine. It emphasizes the purification of one's mind, heart, and soul through the practice of meditation, self-discipline, and devotion to Waheguru (God).

- Santokh, or contentment, is a fundamental aspect of saintliness. It involves being satisfied with one's present circumstances, accepting the divine will with grace, and finding inner peace regardless of external conditions.

Humility and Compassion

- A true Sant in Sikhism embodies humility and compassion towards all beings. They see the divine presence in everyone and treat everyone with kindness, respect, and empathy.

- Saintliness is marked by selflessness and a willingness to serve others without any expectation of reward or recognition. Sants are known for their acts of charity, generosity, and love towards humanity.

Detachment from Ego and Worldly Desires

- Sants in Sikh philosophy transcend ego and worldly attachments, realizing the impermanence of material possessions and the fleeting nature of worldly pleasures. They remain detached from desires and cravings, focusing instead on the pursuit of spiritual enlightenment and union with the divine.

- Detachment does not mean renunciation of the world but rather a state of inner freedom from attachment to material possessions and transient pleasures. Sants engage in worldly duties and responsibilities with a sense of detachment, performing their duties with sincerity and dedication while remaining unaffected by success or failure.

Spiritual Wisdom and Guidance

- Sants are revered as spiritual guides and mentors in Sikh tradition. They possess deep spiritual wisdom and insight into the mysteries of existence, which they impart to their followers through their teachings, discourses, and exemplary lives.

- The guidance of a Sant is considered invaluable on the spiritual path, helping seekers navigate the challenges of life, overcome obstacles, and attain union with the divine.

Devotion and Love for Waheguru

- At the heart of saintliness is unwavering devotion and love for Waheguru, the Supreme Being in Sikhism. Sants cultivate a deep and intimate relationship with the divine through meditation, prayer, and contemplation, seeking to merge their consciousness with the universal consciousness.

- Love for Waheguru is the driving force behind all their thoughts, words, and actions. It inspires them to live a life of virtue, righteousness, and service to humanity.

Sohamta (Inner Purity)

Sants are characterized by their inner purity, which reflects a state of harmony and alignment with the divine. They have purified their minds and hearts of ego, selfish desires, and negative emotions, allowing the divine light to shine through them. Inner purity enables Sants to perceive the divine presence in all creation and to embody virtues such as love, compassion, and kindness towards all beings. Inner purity is the cornerstone of saintliness in Sikh tradition, enabling Sants to embody divine virtues, perceive the presence of the divine in all creation, and serve as instruments of divine grace in the world. It is through the cultivation of inner purity that Sants become conduits for the divine light, illuminating the path of spirituality for seekers and inspiring them to strive for higher levels of consciousness and realization.

1. **Harmony and Alignment with the Divine**: Inner purity reflects a state of harmony and alignment with the divine essence, known as Waheguru in Sikhism. Sants have purified their inner being to resonate with the divine frequency, allowing them to experience a profound sense of connection and oneness with the universe.

2. **Purification of Mind and Heart**: Sants undertake a rigorous process of self-purification, cleansing their minds and hearts of all impurities. This involves overcoming ego, selfish desires, and negative emotions such as anger, greed, and envy. By purifying their inner being, Sants create a vessel for divine grace to flow through them unhindered, illuminating their consciousness with the radiance of spiritual enlightenment.

3. **Perception of Divine Presence**: Inner purity enables Sants to perceive the divine presence in all creation, recognizing the underlying unity and interconnectedness of all beings. They see the divine spark within every soul, regardless of outward appearances or differences. This perception of divine presence infuses Sants with a sense of reverence and awe towards all forms of life, inspiring them to treat every being with love, respect, and compassion.

4. **Embodiment of Virtues**: Sants embody virtues such as love, compassion, and kindness towards all beings as a natural expression of their inner purity. Their actions are guided by the principle of selfless service and a genuine concern for the welfare of others. Inner purity enables Sants to act as conduits for divine grace, radiating love and light wherever they go and uplifting the hearts of those around them.

5. **Source of Spiritual Power**: Inner purity serves as the source of Sant's spiritual power and authority. It enables them to perform miracles,

heal the afflicted, and transmit spiritual blessings to seekers. By maintaining a state of inner purity, Sants become channels for divine energy, empowering them to fulfill their divine mission of spreading love, wisdom, and spiritual upliftment in the world.

In the Sikh tradition, inner purity is considered the foundation of saintliness. This purity allows Sants to embody divine virtues and perceive the presence of the divine in all of creation. They then become instruments of divine grace in the world. Through cultivating inner purity, Sants become channels for divine light, illuminating the path of spirituality for seekers and inspiring them to strive for higher levels of consciousness and realization.

Nimrata (Humility)

Humility is a hallmark of saintliness in Sikh tradition. Sants are deeply humble, recognizing their own insignificance in comparison to the vastness and magnificence of Waheguru (God). Despite their spiritual attainment, Sants remain humble and unassuming, treating everyone with respect and dignity. They do not seek recognition or praise for their spiritual achievements but instead attribute everything to the grace of the divine.

1. **Recognition of Insignificance**: Sants deeply acknowledge their own insignificance in comparison to the vastness and magnificence of Waheguru, the Supreme Being in Sikhism. They realize that their individual existence is but a small part of the divine creation, and any

spiritual attainment they may have achieved pales in comparison to the infinite expanse of divine grace. This recognition of their own limitedness fosters a sense of humility and reverence towards the divine, prompting Sants to approach their spiritual journey with awe and gratitude for the blessings bestowed upon them.

2. **Unassuming Nature**: Despite their spiritual attainment and elevated status within the Sikh community, Sants remain humble and unassuming in their demeanor. They do not flaunt their spiritual achievements or seek recognition for their piety, preferring instead to lead a life of simplicity and humility. Sants interact with others on equal terms, treating everyone with respect and dignity regardless of social status, wealth, or background. They do not consider themselves superior to others but rather as servants of the divine, humbly striving to fulfill their divine mission.

3. **Absence of Ego**: Humility among Sants is characterized by the absence of ego or self-importance. They do not harbor feelings of pride or arrogance, nor do they seek to assert their authority or dominance over others. Instead, Sants embody a sense of selflessness and self-effacement, prioritizing the welfare of others above their own interests and desires. They are willing to sacrifice personal comfort and recognition for the greater good of humanity.

4. **Attribution to Divine Grace**: Sants attribute all their spiritual achievements and blessings to the

grace of the divine rather than to their own efforts or merits. They recognize that any progress they have made on the spiritual path is solely due to the benevolence and mercy of Waheguru. By acknowledging their dependence on divine grace, Sants cultivate a profound sense of humility and gratitude, remaining ever mindful of their own limitations and shortcomings.

5. **Role Model for Others**: The humility displayed by Sants serves as a powerful example for others to emulate. It inspires seekers on the spiritual path to cultivate humility in their own lives, recognizing the importance of humility in spiritual growth and self-realization. By embodying humility, Sants create an atmosphere of inclusivity, acceptance, and compassion, inviting others to join them on the journey towards divine realization and liberation from the cycle of birth and death.

Humility is a virtue that is highly respected and associated with saintliness. It involves acknowledging one's own insignificance compared to the divine, possessing an unassuming nature, absence of ego, and attributing all accomplishments to divine grace. Sants are the epitome of humility, and they demonstrate it through their words, actions, and interactions. They inspire others to follow their example and walk the path of humility and devotion to Waheguru.

Daya (Compassion)

Sants are known for their boundless compassion towards all beings. They see the suffering of others as their own and are moved to alleviate it through acts of kindness, service, and selflessness. Compassion is not just a feeling but a guiding principle in the lives of Sants, motivating them to engage in charitable deeds, uplift the oppressed, and provide solace to the afflicted.

1. **Empathetic Understanding**: Sants possesses a deep empathetic understanding of the suffering and struggles of all beings. They see the pain and hardships faced by others as their own, and their hearts are moved with compassion and empathy. This empathetic understanding enables Sants to connect with the pain and suffering of others on a profound level, inspiring them to take compassionate action to alleviate the suffering and bring comfort to those in need.

2. **Selfless Service**: Compassion is not just a passive feeling but a guiding principle that motivates Sants to engage in selfless service and charitable deeds. They are driven by a genuine desire to help alleviate the suffering of others and to uplift the oppressed and marginalized. Sants willingly extend a helping hand to those in need, regardless of their background, religion, or social status. They view service to humanity as a sacred duty and an expression of their love and devotion to Waheguru.

3. **Uplifting the Afflicted**: Sants actively work towards uplifting the afflicted and alleviating their suffering through various means. They may provide material assistance such as food, clothing, and shelter to the needy, as well as emotional support and spiritual guidance to those going through difficult times. Sants advocate for social justice and equality, speaking out against oppression, discrimination, and injustice wherever they may be found. They strive to create a more compassionate and inclusive society where all beings can live with dignity and respect.

4. **Providing Solace and Comfort**: Sants offer solace and comfort to the afflicted through their presence, prayers, and words of wisdom. They provide a listening ear to those in distress, offering words of encouragement, hope, and reassurance. Sants serve as beacons of light in times of darkness, offering spiritual guidance and support to those facing challenges and difficulties. Their compassionate presence brings healing and upliftment to those who are suffering.

5. **Leading by Example**: The compassionate actions of Sants serve as powerful examples for others to emulate. They inspire seekers on the spiritual path to cultivate compassion in their own lives and to make a positive difference in the world. By embodying compassion in their words and deeds, Sants create a ripple effect of kindness and goodness, transforming the lives

of those they touch and spreading love and compassion throughout the world.

Compassion is a fundamental principle in Sikhism, guiding the lives of Sants and inspiring them to practice acts of kindness, service, and selflessness towards all living beings. Their boundless compassion is a source of comfort for the afflicted, provides relief to the suffering, and encourages others to develop compassion in their own lives.

Vairag (Detachment)

Sants practice detachment from worldly possessions, desires, and attachments, recognizing the transient and illusory nature of material existence. Detachment enables Sants to remain unaffected by the ups and downs of life, maintaining inner equilibrium and peace amidst the fluctuations of the external world. It allows them to focus single-mindedly on their spiritual quest and the attainment of union with the divine.

1. **Recognition of Transience**: Sants recognize the transient and impermanent nature of material possessions, desires, and attachments. They understand that worldly pursuits are temporary and ultimately illusory, leading to temporary satisfaction but not lasting fulfillment. By acknowledging the fleeting nature of material existence, Sants cultivate a sense of detachment towards worldly possessions and desires, freeing themselves from the chains of materialism and consumerism.

2. **Inner Equilibrium and Peace**: Detachment enables Sants to remain unaffected by the ups

and downs of life, maintaining inner equilibrium and peace amidst the fluctuations of the external world. They do not allow external circumstances or worldly events to disturb their inner tranquility. This inner peace allows Sants to navigate life's challenges with grace and equanimity, responding to situations with clarity of mind and serenity of heart. They remain centered in their spiritual consciousness, unaffected by the changing tides of fortune.

3. **Single-minded Focus on Spiritual Quest**: Detachment from worldly distractions allows Sants to focus single-mindedly on their spiritual quest and the attainment of union with the divine. They prioritize their spiritual growth and realization above all else, dedicating themselves wholeheartedly to the pursuit of higher consciousness. Freed from the entanglements of worldly attachments, Sants devote themselves to meditation, prayer, and contemplation, seeking to deepen their connection with Waheguru and attain spiritual enlightenment.

4. **Freedom from Cravings and Attachments**: Detachment liberates Sants from the bondage of cravings and attachments, allowing them to experience true freedom and inner contentment. They no longer seek fulfillment in external possessions or worldly achievements but find true joy and satisfaction in the pursuit of spiritual realization. This freedom from cravings and attachments leads to a state of contentment and

fulfillment that transcends the fleeting pleasures of the material world. Sants experience a profound sense of inner richness and abundance, regardless of their external circumstances.

5. **Role Model for Spiritual Seekers**: The practice of detachment by Sants serves as a powerful example for spiritual seekers, inspiring them to cultivate detachment in their own lives and prioritize their spiritual growth above worldly pursuits. By embodying the principles of detachment, Sants demonstrates that true happiness and fulfillment lie not in the accumulation of wealth or possessions but in the realization of one's true self and union with the divine.

Detachment is a cornerstone of saintliness in Sikh tradition, enabling Sants to maintain inner peace, focus on their spiritual quest, and experience true freedom and contentment. Their practice of detachment serves as a guiding light for spiritual seekers, inspiring them to cultivate detachment in their own lives and embark on the journey towards self-realization and union with the divine.

Bhakti (Devotion)

Devotion to Waheguru is the essence of saintliness in Sikh tradition. Sants cultivate an intense and unwavering love for the divine, seeking union with Waheguru through meditation, prayer, and selfless service. Their entire being is infused with devotion, and every action is imbued with the spirit of love and surrender to the divine will. Devotion sustains them on their spiritual journey and serves as a source of inspiration for others.

1. **Essence of Saintliness**: Devotion to Waheguru, the Supreme Being in Sikhism, is indeed the essence of saintliness. Sants cultivate an intense and unwavering love for the divine, recognizing Waheguru as the source and sustainer of all existence. Their devotion is not merely a superficial sentiment but a deep and profound expression of their soul's longing for union with the divine. It permeates every aspect of their being, infusing their thoughts, words, and actions with the spirit of love and surrender to Waheguru.

2. **Seeking Union with Waheguru**: Sants are driven by a burning desire to attain union with Waheguru, to merge their individual consciousness with the universal consciousness. They view this union as the ultimate goal of human existence and the culmination of their spiritual journey. Through practices such as meditation, prayer, and contemplation, Sants seek to deepen their connection with Waheguru and dissolve the illusion of separation between themselves and the divine. Their devotion serves as a powerful catalyst for this process of spiritual transformation.

3. **Infusion of Every Action with Devotion**: For Sants, devotion is not confined to specific religious rituals or practices but permeates

every aspect of their lives. Every action they undertake is imbued with the spirit of love and surrender to the divine will. Whether engaged in meditation, selfless service, or daily chores, Sants perform their duties with utmost devotion and dedication, seeing them as opportunities to express their love and gratitude towards Waheguru.

4. **Sustaining Spiritual Journey**: Devotion serves as the fuel that sustains Sants on their spiritual journey, providing them with the strength, inspiration, and resilience to overcome obstacles and challenges along the way. Even in the face of adversity or setbacks, Sants remain steadfast in their devotion, trusting in the divine guidance and grace of Waheguru to lead them on the path of righteousness and truth.

5. **Source of Inspiration for Others**: The unwavering devotion displayed by Sants serves as a source of inspiration for others, inspiring them to deepen their own connection with the divine and cultivate devotion in their own lives. Through their exemplary devotion, Sants demonstrate the transformative power of love and surrender to Waheguru, inspiring others to embark on the journey of spiritual awakening and self-realization.

Devotion is considered the core essence of saintliness in the Sikh tradition. It permeates every aspect of Sant's life with the spirit of love and surrender to Waheguru, the Almighty. The unwavering and intense devotion of the Sant sustains them on their spiritual journey, and their devotion serves as an inspiration for seekers who are on the path of spiritual awakening and self-realization.

Gyan (Wisdom)

Sants possess deep spiritual wisdom and insight into the nature of reality, gained through direct experience of the divine. Their teachings are characterized by profound truths and practical guidance for living a righteous and fulfilling life. Wisdom enables Sants to guide seekers on the spiritual path, dispelling ignorance and leading them towards self-realization and liberation from the cycle of birth and death.

1. **Deep Spiritual Insight**: Sants possess deep spiritual insight into the nature of reality, gained through direct experience of the divine. Their wisdom transcends mere intellectual knowledge, arising from a profound realization of the ultimate truth. This insight enables Sants to perceive the underlying unity and interconnectedness of all existence, recognizing the divine presence in every aspect of creation. Their wisdom illuminates the path of spiritual seekers, guiding them towards self-realization and liberation from the cycle of birth and death.

2. **Teachings of Profound Truths**: The teachings of Sants are characterized by profound truths and practical guidance for living a righteous and fulfilling life. Rooted in their own direct experience of the divine, their wisdom addresses the fundamental questions of

existence and provides solutions to the challenges of human life. Sants impart timeless wisdom that transcends cultural, religious, and philosophical boundaries, offering universal truths that resonate with seekers from all walks of life. Their teachings inspire individuals to live with integrity, compassion, and spiritual awareness.

3. **Dispelling Ignorance**: Wisdom enables Sants to dispel ignorance and illusion, leading seekers out of the darkness of ignorance and into the light of truth. Through their teachings and spiritual guidance, Sants illuminate the path of self-realization, helping seekers overcome the obstacles of ego, attachment, and delusion. By shining the light of wisdom on the illusions of the mind, Sants empower seekers to see through the transient nature of worldly phenomena and to recognize the eternal reality of the divine presence within themselves and all creation.

4. **Guiding Seekers on the Spiritual Path**: Sants play a vital role in guiding seekers on the spiritual path, offering them practical guidance, encouragement, and support in their quest for self-realization. They serve as mentors and spiritual guides, helping seekers navigate the complexities of the inner journey. Through their words and actions, Sants exemplify the principles of righteousness, compassion, and selflessness, inspiring seekers to embody these virtues in their own lives. Their guidance leads seekers towards spiritual growth, inner

transformation, and ultimately, liberation from the cycle of birth and death.

5. **Source of Inspiration and Liberation**: The wisdom of Sants serves as a source of inspiration and liberation for seekers on the spiritual path. Their teachings awaken individuals to their true nature as divine beings, empowering them to break free from the shackles of ignorance and illusion and to realize their innate potential for spiritual awakening and self-realization. By following the guidance of Sants and assimilating their wisdom into their lives, seekers can attain liberation from the cycle of birth and death and experience the eternal bliss of union with the divine.

Wisdom is considered a defining characteristic of saintliness. Sants, , possess a deep understanding of spirituality and use it to guide seekers on their journey towards self-realization and liberation. Through their teachings of profound truths, they inspire individuals to live with integrity, compassion, and spiritual awareness, ultimately leading them towards the ultimate goal of union with the divine.

How Khalsa Embodies Saintly Virtues and Principles

The Khalsa, as envisioned by Guru Gobind Singh Ji, embodies saintly virtues and principles while also fulfilling the role of warrior for justice and righteousness.

1. **Pavitar (Purity)**: Just as Sants strive for inner purity, members of the Khalsa maintain physical

and spiritual purity through the observance of the Sikh code of conduct, known as the Rehat Maryada. The Khalsa's commitment to maintaining Kesh (uncut hair), wearing the Five Ks (articles of faith), and adhering to moral and ethical principles reflects their dedication to purity in thought, word, and deed.

2. **Nimrata (Humility)** Humility is a core value within the Khalsa. Despite their martial prowess and spiritual commitment, Khalsa members are expected to remain humble, recognizing their own insignificance in comparison to the magnificence of Waheguru. The wearing of the Kara (steel bracelet) symbolizes the unbroken and humble bond of the Khalsa with the divine, reminding them of the importance of humility in their lives.

3. **Daya (Compassion)**: While the Khalsa is associated with the warrior spirit, compassion lies at the heart of their actions. The Kirpan (ceremonial sword) represents the Khalsa's duty to protect the oppressed and defend the weak against injustice. Khalsa members are taught to embody compassion in their interactions with others, treating everyone with kindness, respect, and empathy.

4. **Vairag (Detachment)**: The Khalsa practices detachment from worldly desires and attachments while remaining actively engaged in the world. They are taught to view material possessions and worldly pursuits as transient and illusory. The Khalsa's readiness to sacrifice

their own comforts and safety for the welfare of others reflects their detachment from personal desires and ego.

5. **Bhakti (Devotion)**: Devotion to Waheguru is the driving force behind the Khalsa's actions. Their commitment to the Sikh faith, exemplified through the initiation ceremony of Amrit Sanskar, signifies their unwavering devotion to the Guru and the Sikh principles. The Khalsa's daily practice of Nitnem (daily prayers) and participation in community service reflect their dedication to spiritual growth and service to humanity.

6. **Gyan (Wisdom)**: The Khalsa is expected to embody wisdom in their decision-making and actions. They are guided by the teachings of the Guru Granth Sahib and the principles of Sikh philosophy, which emphasize righteousness, truth, and compassion. Through the study of Gurbani and the guidance of spiritual mentors, Khalsa members cultivate wisdom and discernment in navigating the complexities of life.

Seva, Simran, and Santokh

Seva, Simran, and Santokh play integral roles within the Khalsa, shaping its collective identity and guiding its members on the path of spiritual growth and self-realization. Through the practice of seva, Khalsa members express their devotion to Waheguru and serve humanity with humility and compassion. Simran deepens their connection with the divine, fostering spiritual awareness and inner transformation. Santokh cultivates contentment and inner peace, enabling Khalsa members to find joy and fulfillment in the present moment, regardless of external circumstances. Together, these principles form the foundation of the Khalsa, embodying the timeless values of Sikhism and inspiring its members to lead lives of purpose, integrity, and service.

Seva (Selfless Service)

- Seva is at the heart of the Khalsa, reflecting the Sikh principle of selfless service to humanity. Khalsa members engage in seva as a way of expressing their devotion to Waheguru and serving the community with humility and compassion.

- Seva takes many forms within the Khalsa, including langar (community kitchen), where free meals are provided to all regardless of caste, creed, or social status; serving in gurdwaras (Sikh places of worship) and participating in community outreach programs; and volunteering in humanitarian efforts such as disaster relief and healthcare initiatives.

- Through seva, Khalsa members embody the spirit of equality, social justice, and solidarity, working towards the upliftment of the marginalized and the empowerment of the oppressed. Seva fosters a sense of unity and belonging within the Khalsa, strengthening bonds of brotherhood and sisterhood among its members.

Simran (Remembrance of the Divine)

- Simran, or remembrance of the divine, is a central practice within the Khalsa, serving as a means of cultivating spiritual awareness, devotion, and connection with Waheguru.

- Khalsa members engage in Simran through the repetition of Waheguru's name or the recitation of Gurbani, such as the Japji Sahib or the Mool Mantar. This practice helps to still the mind, purify the heart, and align one's consciousness with the divine presence.

- Simran is not limited to formal meditation but extends to all aspects of life, as Khalsa members strive to live in constant remembrance of Waheguru and to see the divine presence in all beings and experiences. Simran brings a sense of peace, joy, and fulfillment, enriching the spiritual lives of Khalsa members and deepening their connection with the Guru.

Santokh (Contentment)

- Santokh, or contentment, is a virtue cherished within the Khalsa, encouraging its members to be satisfied with what they have and to accept the divine will with grace and equanimity.

- Khalsa members cultivate Santokh by practicing gratitude for the blessings bestowed upon them by Waheguru and by refraining from excessive desires and cravings for material wealth or worldly success.

- Santokh does not imply complacency or indifference towards improving one's circumstances but rather a sense of inner peace and fulfillment that transcends external conditions. It fosters a state of inner equilibrium and joy, allowing Khalsa to navigate life's challenges with resilience and optimism.

Saintly Practice of Khalsa

Cultivating saintliness among the Khalsa involves a combination of rituals, practices, and daily routines that foster spiritual growth, moral development, and selfless service.

Amrit Sanskar (Initiation Ceremony):

Amrit Sanskar, also known as Amrit Sanchar and as the Khalsa initiation ceremony, is a sacred rite through which individuals become initiated into the Khalsa brotherhood. This ceremony involves the preparation and consumption of Amrit (sacred nectar), signifying the commitment to living according to the Sikh code of conduct and principles. Amrit Sanskar instills a sense of spiritual identity and belonging among Khalsa members, marking their formal initiation into the Sikh faith and their dedication to the path of righteousness and service.

1. **Preparation**: Before the ceremony, there is typically a period of preparation during which the individual undergoes spiritual and physical purification. This involves abstaining from certain foods, engaging in meditation and prayer, and reflecting on the commitment to the Sikh faith.

2. **Gathering**: The ceremony usually takes place in the presence of the Sahib Sri Guru Granth Sahib Ji (the living Guru of Sikhism)) and members of the Sikh community, including Panj Pyare (the Five Beloved Ones), who play a central role in administering the Amrit.

3. **Recitation of Prayers**: The ceremony begins with the recitation of specific prayers and hymns from the Sri Guru Granth Sahib Ji and Sri Dasam Grand Sahib Ji, invoking the blessings of Waheguru and seeking divine guidance and protection for the initiates.

4. **Preparation of Amrit**: The Amrit, or sacred nectar, is prepared in an iron vessel known as an Amritsar. It consists of water (and required and determined amount of Patasa) and stirred with a double-edged sword (Khanda). The Panj Pyare continuously does Jaap (read) the five Banis (Jap Ji Sahib, Jap Sahib, Tav Prasad Savaiye, Chaupai Sahib, and Anand Sahib Ji) during the preparation of Amrit.

5. **Ceremony**: The Sikhs, known as Khalsa candidates, stand in a line and are taken Amrit one by one from the Panj Pyare. Each Sikh bows before the Panj Pyare and receives a symbolic sip of Amrit while the Panj Pyare recites specific prayers and instructions.

6. **Five Ks and Rehat Maryada**: Following the Amrit Sanchar, Sikhs are required to wear the Five Ks, which include Kesh, Kara, Kanga, Kachera, and Kirpan. They also commit to

following the Sikh code of conduct, known as the Rehat Maryada, which includes guidelines for personal conduct, daily prayers, and adherence to Sikh principles.

7. **Declaration of Brotherhood**: After receiving the Amrit and donning the Five Ks, the initiates are welcomed into the Khalsa brotherhood. They declare their commitment to living according to the Sikh faith and principles, dedicating themselves to the service of humanity and the pursuit of spiritual growth.

The Amrit Sanskar serves as a pivotal moment in the life of a Sikh, marking their formal initiation into the Khalsa brotherhood and their dedication to living according to the principles of Sikhism. It instills a sense of spiritual identity, belonging, and purpose, empowering individuals to lead lives of righteousness, service, and devotion to Waheguru.

Nitnem (Daily Prayer)

Nitnem holds immense significance within the daily spiritual practice of Khalsa. Nitnem provides a framework for regular prayer and meditation and fosters a deeper connection with Waheguru and the Sikh Gurus. Through the recitation of Nitnem prayers, Khalsa cultivate spiritual discipline, seek spiritual guidance and protection, and experience profound spiritual upliftment and connection with the divine.

1. **Recitation of Specific Prayers:** Nitnem consists of reciting specific prayers and hymns from the Sri Guru Granth Sahib Ji and Sri Dasam Granth Sahib Ji. These prayers include

Japji Sahib, Jaap Sahib, Tav-Prasad Savaiye, Chaupai Sahib, Anand Sahib, Rehras Sahib, and Kirtan Sohila, among others. Each prayer has its own unique significance and is recited at specific times throughout the day, such as morning (Amrit Vela), evening (Rehras), and night (Kirtan Sohila). The recitation of these prayers helps Khalsa connect with the divine and seek spiritual guidance and protection.

2. **Establishing a Regular Routine**: Nitnem serves as a spiritual discipline, helping Khalsa establish a regular routine of prayer and meditation. By committing to the daily recitation of Nitnem prayers, Khalsa dedicates time each day to connect with Waheguru and deepen their spiritual practice. The practice of Nitnem instills a sense of consistency and commitment in one's spiritual life, providing a framework for daily devotion and spiritual growth.

3. **Fostering a Deeper Connection with Waheguru**: Through the recitation of Nitnem prayers, Khalsa members cultivate a deeper connection with Waheguru and the Sikh Gurus. The sacred words and hymns contained within Nitnem serve as a means of communion with the divine, guiding individuals on the path of righteousness and spiritual awakening. Nitnem helps Khalsa attune their minds and hearts to the divine presence, fostering a sense of inner peace, clarity, and devotion. The practice of reciting Nitnem prayers regularly strengthens

one's spiritual connection and deepens their relationship with Waheguru.

4. **Spiritual Upliftment and Protection**: Nitnem prayers are believed to have transformative power, bringing spiritual upliftment and protection to those who recite them with sincerity and devotion. The sacred words and vibrations of these prayers purify the mind, uplift the soul, and provide solace and strength in times of difficulty and adversity. By immersing themselves in the recitation of Nitnem prayers, Khalsa members invoke the blessings of Waheguru and the Sikh Gurus, seeking spiritual guidance, protection, and grace in their lives.

Simran (Remembrance of the Divine)

Simran holds profound significance within the spiritual practice of Khalsa. Simran is a central practice among Khalsa, serving as a means of cultivating spiritual awareness, devotion, and connection with Waheguru. Through the repetition of Waheguru's name and the recitation of Gurbani, individuals deepen their understanding of Sikh teachings, purify their hearts, and experience the divine presence in their lives. Simran helps Khalsa members align their consciousness with the eternal truth and realize their inherent unity with Waheguru, the ultimate source of all creation.

1. **Repetition of Waheguru's Name**: Simran involves the repetition of Waheguru's name, which is considered to be the divine mantra in Sikhism. The word "Waheguru" is derived from

two Panjabi words: "Wahe" meaning "wondrous" or "great" and "Guru" meaning "enlightener" or "dispeller of darkness." Khalsa engages in the continuous repetition of "Waheguru" as a means of invoking the divine presence, cultivating spiritual awareness, and expressing devotion to Waheguru.

2. **Recitation of Gurbani**: In addition to repeating Waheguru's name, Simran also involves the recitation of Gurbani, which consists of hymns and verses from the Sri Guru Granth Sahib Ji, the current and eternal Guru of Sikhs. Gurbani is imbued with spiritual wisdom, divine love, and transformative power. Khalsa recite Gurbani as a means of connecting with the divine teachings of the Sikh Gurus, seeking spiritual guidance, and deepening their understanding of Waheguru's divine attributes and qualities.

3. **Individual and Collective Practice**: Simran can be practiced both individually and collectively by Khalsa. Individuals may engage in private meditation and contemplation, repeating Waheguru's name or reciting Gurbani verses in solitude. Additionally, Simran is often practiced collectively in Sangat (congregational gatherings) and Kirtan (devotional singing sessions), where Khalsa come together to chant Waheguru's name and sing hymns from the Sri Guru Granth Sahib Ji.

4. **Cultivating Spiritual Awareness and Devotion**: Simran serves as a powerful tool for cultivating spiritual awareness and devotion

among Khalsa. Through the repetition of Waheguru's name and the recitation of Gurbani, individuals deepen their connection with the divine presence and align their consciousness with the eternal truth. Simran helps to still the mind, quieten the restless thoughts, and purify the heart of ego and worldly attachments. It fosters a sense of inner peace, clarity, and serenity, allowing Khalsa to experience the divine presence within themselves and all creation.

5. **Deepening Connection with Waheguru**: The practice of Simran is aimed at deepening one's connection with Waheguru and experiencing union with the divine. Through regular and sincere Simran, Khalsa cultivates a profound sense of love, reverence, and surrender to Waheguru, transcending the limitations of the ego and merging with the infinite consciousness.

Seva (Selfless Service)

Seva is a cornerstone of Khalsa's saintliness, embodying the Sikh values of humility, compassion, and selflessness. Through various forms of Seva, Khalsa members express their devotion to Waheguru, contribute to the welfare of the community, and cultivate a deeper understanding of Sikh teachings and principles. Seva serves as a spiritual practice that fosters unity, empathy, and social solidarity among Khalsa members, empowering them to live lives of service and righteousness in accordance with Sikh values and ideals.

1. **Various Forms of Seva**: Khalsa engage in various forms of Seva, including:

    - **Langar:** The community kitchen where free meals are served to all, regardless of caste, creed, or social status. Langar embodies the principle of equality and serves as a symbol of the Sikh commitment to serving humanity.

    - **Serving in Gurdwaras:** Khalsa volunteers their time and effort to perform various tasks in Gurdwaras, such as cleaning, cooking, serving food, and assisting with religious ceremonies and events.

    - **Community Outreach Programs:** Khalsa members actively participate in community outreach programs, such as organizing blood donation drives, providing humanitarian aid to those in need, and supporting local initiatives for social welfare and development.

2. **Spiritual Practice**: Seva is not merely an act of charity or social service but a spiritual practice that cultivates humility, compassion, and selflessness among Khalsa. By serving others selflessly, Khalsa express their devotion to Waheguru and embody the Sikh principle of seva. Through the practice of Seva, Khalsa transcends their ego and worldly attachments, recognizing the divine presence in all beings and serving humanity with love and compassion. Seva helps Khalsa cultivate a sense of interconnectedness and unity with all

creation, fostering a deeper understanding of the Sikh concept of "Sarbat da Bhala" (welfare of all).

3. **Expressing Devotion to Waheguru**: Seva is considered a sacred duty and a means of expressing devotion to Waheguru in Sikhism. Khalsa views Seva as an opportunity to serve Waheguru in the form of humanity and to fulfill their spiritual obligation to serve and uplift others. By engaging in Seva with humility and selflessness, Khalsa seeks to emulate the example set by the Sikh Gurus, who devoted their lives to serving humanity and fighting for social justice and equality.

4. **Contributing to Community Welfare**: Seva plays a vital role in contributing to the welfare of the community and promoting social cohesion and solidarity among Khalsa. Through acts of Seva, Khalsa address the needs of the marginalized, empower the oppressed, and foster a sense of unity and belonging within the community. Seva also serves as a vehicle for building bridges across diverse communities and promoting interfaith dialogue and cooperation. By working together to address shared challenges and serve the common good, Khalsa contributes to building a more compassionate, just, and inclusive society.

Sangat and Pangat (Community and Equality)

Sangat and Pangat hold profound significance within the spiritual and social practices of Khalsa, embodying the principles of community, equality, and inclusivity in Sikhism. Sangat and Pangat are integral aspects of Khalsa spirituality and community life, providing opportunities for collective worship, fellowship, and service. Through Sangat, Khalsa members deepen their spiritual practice and draw inspiration from one another, while Pangat reinforces the principle of equality and inclusivity within the community. Together, Sangat and Pangat embody the spirit of Sikhism, fostering unity, compassion, and solidarity among Khalsa members and promoting a more just and compassionate society.

1. **Sangat (Congregational Gatherings)**: Sangat refers to congregational gatherings where Khalsa members come together to engage in collective worship, spiritual discourse, and fellowship. Sangat provides an opportunity for individuals to connect with fellow Sikhs, seek spiritual guidance, and deepen their understanding of Sikh teachings. In Sangat, Khalsa participates in prayers, kirtan (devotional singing), and katha (spiritual discourse), led by knowledgeable individuals or spiritual leaders. Sangat fosters a sense of community and solidarity among Khalsa, reinforcing their shared commitment to living according to Sikh principles and values. Through Sangat, Khalsa members draw inspiration and support from one another, sharing their spiritual experiences, challenges, and aspirations. Sangat serves as a source of spiritual nourishment and encouragement, empowering individuals to

persevere on the path of righteousness and self-realization.

2. **Pangat (Equality in Langar)**: Pangat refers to the practice of sitting together in equality and partaking in langar, the community kitchen where free meals are served to all, regardless of social status, caste, or creed. Pangat emphasizes the principle of equality and inclusivity within the Khalsa community, transcending barriers of caste, class, and ethnicity. In Pangat, Khalsa members sit side by side as equals, sharing meals prepared with love and devotion. This practice symbolizes the Sikh belief in the inherent dignity and equality of all human beings, irrespective of their background or socio-economic status. Through Pangat, Khalsa members experience firsthand the spirit of brotherhood and sisterhood that defines the Khalsa community. Pangat promotes unity, compassion, and solidarity, fostering a sense of belonging and acceptance among all members of the community.

3. **Spiritual and Social Benefits**: Both Sangat and Pangat offer numerous spiritual and social benefits to Khalsa members. Sangat provides a supportive environment for individuals to deepen their spiritual practice, seek guidance from spiritual mentors, and experience the collective power of prayer and devotion. Pangat promotes social cohesion and harmony within the Khalsa, breaking down barriers of discrimination and fostering a culture of mutual

respect and understanding. By sitting together in equality and sharing meals in the langar, Khalsa cultivate empathy, compassion, and solidarity, strengthening the bonds of brotherhood and sisterhood. Together, Sangat and Pangat serve as pillars of the Khalsa community, nurturing spiritual growth, fostering social unity, and embodying the timeless values of Sikhism. Through collective worship, fellowship, and service, Khalsa members uphold the principles of community, equality, and inclusivity, enriching their spiritual journey and contributing to the welfare of society as a whole.

Rehat Maryada (Code of Conduct)

The Rehat Maryada serves as a foundational guide for Khalsa, offering a set of principles and guidelines for living a righteous and fulfilling life according to Sikh values and teachings. The Rehat Maryada plays a vital role in guiding Khalsa in their daily lives, providing a framework for moral and ethical conduct, dietary practices, and personal discipline. By following the principles and guidelines of the Rehat Maryada, Khalsa cultivates saintly virtues and strives to live in accordance with Sikh teachings and values, embodying the highest ideals of righteousness, humility, and compassion in their lives.

1. **Moral and Ethical Precepts**: The Rehat Maryada outlines moral and ethical precepts that govern the conduct of Khalsa in their daily lives. These precepts include principles such as honesty, integrity, compassion, humility, and

respect for all beings. By adhering to the moral and ethical guidelines of the Rehat Maryada, Khalsa cultivates saintly virtues and uphold the highest standards of personal conduct and integrity. The Rehat Maryada serves as a moral compass, guiding individuals in making ethical decisions and living with integrity and righteousness.

2. **Dietary Guidelines**: The Rehat Maryada includes dietary guidelines that prescribe certain dietary restrictions and practices for Khalsa. These guidelines emphasize the importance of maintaining a pure and wholesome diet that nourishes the body, mind, and spirit. Khalsa is encouraged to abstain from consuming intoxicants such as alcohol, tobacco, and drugs, as these substances are believed to cloud the mind and inhibit spiritual growth. Additionally, there are guidelines regarding the preparation and consumption of food, emphasizing the importance of cleanliness, moderation, and mindfulness in eating habits.

3. **Rules for Personal Conduct**: The Rehat Maryada includes rules for personal conduct that govern various aspects of Khalsa's lives, including dress code, honest practices, and social interactions. These rules are aimed at fostering a sense of discipline, self-respect, and adherence to Sikh principles. Khalsa are expected to maintain a distinct appearance by wearing the Five Ks (Kesh, Kara, Kanga, Kachera, and Kirpan) as symbols of their

commitment to Sikhism. They are also encouraged to practice humility, compassion, and respect towards others in their interactions and relationships.

4. **Cultivating Saintly Virtues**: Following the Rehat Maryada helps Khalsa cultivate saintly virtues such as purity, humility, compassion, and self-discipline in their lives. By adhering to the principles and guidelines outlined in the Rehat Maryada, Khalsa strives to embody the highest ideals of Sikhism and live with integrity, righteousness, and devotion to Waheguru. The Rehat Maryada serves as a practical guide for Khalsa members on their spiritual journey, providing a framework for personal growth, moral development, and adherence to Sikh principles. Through adherence to the Rehat Maryada, Khalsa deepens their commitment to living a life of service, righteousness, and devotion to Waheguru.

Some Saintly Nature Leaders of the Khalsa

The Saintly essence of the Khalsa is enriched and molded by the exemplary lives and teachings of various individuals, both men and women, who have devoted themselves to the path of righteousness, devotion, and service. These individuals, commonly known as Sikh leaders or saints, play a pivotal role in embodying and promoting the core principles of Sikhism and the Khalsa tradition. Through their exemplary lives, teachings, and sacrifices, these figures, along with many others, have contributed to shaping the virtuous nature of the Khalsa. Their unwavering dedication to Waheguru, unwavering commitment to Sikh principles, and selfless service to humanity serve as timeless models for Sikhs to follow in their spiritual journey. Some notable personalities who have contributed to shaping the Saintly nature of the Khalsa include:

1. Baba Budha Ji
2. Bibi Nanaki Ji
3. Mata Khivi Ji
4. Mata Ganga Ji
5. Bhai Gurdas Ji
6. Mata Sahib Kaur Ji
7. Bahi Mani Singh Ji
8. Baba Deep Singh
9. Bhai Mati Das Ji
10. Bhai Kanhaiya Ji
11. Bhai Taru Singh Ji

Baba Budha Ji

Baba Budha Ji, also known as Bhai Budha Ji, occupies a revered position in Sikh history and spirituality. He was a prominent figure during the time of the first three Sikh Gurus and played a pivotal role in the establishment and growth of the Sikh community. Baba Budha Ji epitomizes the saintly spirit of Khalsa through his unwavering devotion, selfless service, and profound spiritual wisdom.

Early Life and Association with the Sikh Gurus

Baba Budha Ji was born in 1506 in the village of Katthu Nangal, located in the present-day Amritsar district of Panjab. His birth name was Bura, and from a young age, he exhibited a deep longing for spiritual knowledge and enlightenment. As a devout follower of Guru Nanak Dev Ji, Baba Budha Ji was drawn to the teachings of the Sikh Gurus and became a dedicated disciple of Guru Nanak.

His association with the Sikh Gurus began with Guru Nanak Dev Ji, the founder of Sikhism, under whose guidance he learned the principles of humility, compassion, and devotion to Waheguru. Baba Budha Ji's spiritual journey continued as he served as a trusted companion and disciple of Guru Angad Dev Ji, Guru Amar Das Ji, Guru Ramdas Ji, Guru Arjun Dev Ji and Guru Hargobind Sahib Ji.

Role as the First Granthi of Harmandir Sahib

One of Baba Budha Ji's most significant contributions to Sikhism was his role as the first Granthi of the Sri Harmandir Sahib, also known as the Sri Darbar Sahib or Golden Temple, in Amritsar, Panjab. Guru Arjan Dev Ji, the fifth Sikh Guru, appointed him to this esteemed position and entrusted him with the responsibility of managing the daily affairs of the Harmandir Sahib and conducting religious ceremonies.

As the Granthi of Sri Harmandir Sahib Ji, Baba Budha Ji played a central role in disseminating Sikh teachings and preserving Sikh writings. He recited Gurbani from memory and imparted spiritual guidance to the growing Sikh community. Baba Budha Ji's unwavering dedication and spiritual insight earned him the respect and admiration of Sikhs and non-Sikhs alike.

Spiritual Wisdom and Guidance

Baba Budha Ji's life exemplified the saintly virtues of humility, compassion, and devotion to Waheguru. He possessed profound spiritual wisdom and insight into the teachings of Sikhism, which he shared with disciples and seekers who came to him seeking guidance on their spiritual journey.

His association with the Sikh Gurus and his deep immersion in Gurbani enriched Baba Budha Ji's spiritual understanding and enabled him to guide others on the path of righteousness and devotion. He emphasized the importance of Naam Simran (remembrance of the divine), selfless service, and adherence to Sikh principles as the means to attain spiritual liberation and union with Waheguru.

Legacy and Influence on the Khalsa

Baba Budha Ji's legacy continues to inspire generations of Sikhs and embodies the saintly spirit of Khalsa. His life of devotion, selflessness, and spiritual wisdom exemplifies the ideals of Sikhism and serves as a guiding light for Sikhs seeking to deepen their connection with Waheguru and live according to Sikh principles.

Baba Budha Ji's association with the Sri Harmandir Sahib and his role as the first Granthi symbolize the centrality of Gurbani and the Sikh scripture in the life of the Khalsa. His dedication to preserving and disseminating Sikh teachings laid the foundation for the Sikh community's spiritual and cultural identity.

Baba Budha Ji's life reflects the essence of the saintly spirit of Khalsa, characterized by unwavering devotion to Waheguru, selfless service to humanity, and profound spiritual wisdom. He remains an iconic figure in Sikh history and spirituality, revered for his contributions to Sikhism and his embodiment of the highest ideals of righteousness, humility, and compassion.

Bibi Nanaki Ji

Bibi Nanaki Ji played a significant role in Sikh history as she was the elder sister of Sri Guru Nanak Dev Ji, the founder of Sikhism. Her life is a shining example of the saintly spirit of Khalsa as she had an unyielding faith, unwavering devotion to Waheguru, and steadfast support for her brother's spiritual mission. Bibi Nanaki Ji's own spiritual achievements serve as a testament to her profound influence on Sikhism and the Khalsa tradition.

Early Life and Spiritual Journey

Bibi Nanaki Ji was born in 1464 in the village of Chahal, near Lahore, in present-day east Panjab. From a young age, she exhibited a deep reverence for spirituality and a keen interest in religious matters. She was deeply devoted to her younger brother, Nanak, whom she affectionately called "Nanak."

Support of Guru Nanak Dev Ji

Bibi Nanaki Ji played a pivotal role in nurturing and supporting Guru Nanak Dev Ji's spiritual journey. She recognized his divine mission from an early age and provided unwavering encouragement and guidance to him as he embarked on his spiritual quest. Despite societal norms and expectations, she stood by Guru Nanak Dev Ji's side and supported him in spreading his message of universal love and spiritual enlightenment.

Spiritual Accomplishments

Bibi Nanaki Ji's own spiritual accomplishments are often overshadowed by her role as Guru Nanak Dev Ji's sister. However, she was revered for her piety, wisdom, and devotion to Waheguru. She lived a life of humility, compassion, and service to others, embodying the core principles of Sikhism.

Concept of Seva and Sarbat Da Bhala

Bibi Nanaki Ji exemplified the principles of seva (selfless service) and Sarbat Da Bhala (welfare of all) throughout her life. She was known for her generosity and compassion towards those in need, regardless of their social or economic status. Her acts of kindness and service to humanity reflected the ethos of the Khalsa tradition, emphasizing the importance of serving others and working towards the welfare of all.

Legacy and Influence on the Khalsa

Bibi Nanaki Ji's legacy as a saintly figure in the Khalsa tradition continues to inspire Sikhs worldwide. Her unwavering faith, devotion to Waheguru, and steadfast support of Guru Nanak Dev Ji serve as a beacon of inspiration for Sikhs on their spiritual journey.

Bibi Nanaki Ji epitomizes the saintly spirit of Khalsa through her unwavering faith, devotion to Waheguru, and steadfast support of Guru Nanak Dev Ji's spiritual mission. Her life and teachings continue to serve as a source of inspiration for Sikhs worldwide, reminding them of the timeless principles of Sikhism and the importance of living a life of humility, compassion, and service to others.

Mata Khivi Ji

Mata Khivi Ji is widely known as a symbol of selfless service and compassion in Sikh history. She was the wife of Guru Angad Dev Ji, the second Sikh Guru, and her life represents the saintly spirit of Khalsa. Mata Khivi Ji was deeply committed to seva (selfless service), and she strongly believed in equality and spiritual insight. Her contributions to Sikhism and her role in forming the Khalsa tradition serve as a great example of the core principles of Sikh teachings.

Early Life and Marriage to Guru Angad Dev Ji

Mata Khivi Ji was born in 1506 in the village of Sanghar in present-day East Panjab. She was known for her piety, humility, and compassion. Mata Khivi Ji married Guru Angad Dev Ji at a young age and became his devoted companion and partner in spreading the message of Sikhism.

Role in the Sikh Community

Mata Khivi Ji played a crucial role in nurturing and supporting the Sikh community during Sri Guru

Angad Dev Ji's tenure as the second Sikh Guru. She was instrumental in organizing langar (community kitchen) and ensuring that all members of the Sikh Sangat (congregation) were provided with food, regardless of their caste, creed, or social status.

Promotion of Equality and Inclusivity

Mata Khivi Ji was a staunch advocate for equality and inclusivity within the Sikh community. She challenged social norms and traditions by establishing langar as an institution of equality, where all individuals, regardless of their background, were treated with dignity and respect. Mata Khivi Ji's commitment to equality and inclusivity laid the foundation for the egalitarian principles of Sikhism and the Khalsa tradition.

Spiritual Insight and Devotion

Mata Khivi Ji's spiritual insight and devotion to Waheguru were evident in her selfless service and compassionate nature. She viewed seva as a means of attaining spiritual enlightenment and believed in the importance of serving others with humility and compassion. Mata Khivi Ji's devotion to Waheguru and her commitment to seva exemplify the core principles of Sikhism and the saintly spirit of Khalsa.

Legacy and Influence on the Khalsa

Mata Khivi Ji's legacy as a saintly figure in the Khalsa tradition continues to inspire Sikhs worldwide. Her selfless service, compassion, and commitment to equality serve as a beacon of inspiration for Sikhs on their spiritual journey. Mata Khivi Ji's contributions to

Sikhism and her role in shaping the Khalsa tradition highlight the importance of seva, equality, and devotion to Waheguru in Sikh teachings.

Mata Khivi Ji epitomizes the saintly spirit of Khalsa through her dedication to seva, her commitment to equality, and her profound spiritual insight. Her life and teachings continue to inspire and guide Sikhs on their spiritual journey, reminding them of the timeless principles of Sikhism and the importance of living a life of humility, compassion, and service to others.

Mata Ganga Ji

Mata Ganga Ji, also known as Mata Ganga Sahib Kaur, holds a revered place in Sikh history as the wife of Guru Arjan Dev Ji, the fifth Sikh Guru, and the mother of Guru Hargobind Sahib Ji, the sixth Sikh Guru. Her life exemplifies the saintly spirit of Khalsa through her unwavering devotion to Waheguru, her dedication to seva (selfless service), and her role in nurturing and supporting the Sikh community during challenging times.

Early Life and Marriage to Sri Guru Arjan Dev Ji

Mata Ganga Ji was born in 1562 in the village of Mau in present-day Uttar Pradesh, India. She was known for her piety, humility, and devotion to Waheguru. Mata Ganga Ji married Sri Guru Arjan Dev Ji, the fifth Sikh Guru, and became his devoted companion and partner in spreading the message of Sikhism.

Support of Guru Arjan Dev Ji

Mata Ganga Ji played a crucial role in supporting Sri Guru Arjan Dev Ji during his tenure as the fifth Sikh Guru. She provided unwavering encouragement and support by devoting herself completely to him as he stood against the persecution and oppression by the Mughal authorities. Mata Ganga Ji stood by Guru Arjan Dev Ji's side and supported him in spreading the message of Sikhism and promoting the principles of peace, equality, and compassion.

Promotion of Seva and Equality

Mata Ganga Ji was a staunch advocate for seva and equality within the Sikh community. She played a pivotal role in organizing langar (community kitchen) and ensuring that all members of the Sikh Sangat (congregation) were provided with food, regardless of their caste, creed, or social status. Mata Ganga Ji's commitment to seva and equality reflected the core principles of Sikhism and the saintly spirit of Khalsa.

Nurturing the Sikh Community

Mata Ganga Ji played a vital role in nurturing and supporting the Sikh community during challenging times. She provided spiritual guidance and moral support to Sikh women and children, ensuring that they remained steadfast in their faith and committed to Sikh principles. Her compassionate nature and nurturing spirit endeared her to the Sikh community and earned her respect and admiration.

Legacy and Influence on the Khalsa

Mata Ganga Ji's legacy as a saintly figure in the Khalsa tradition continues to inspire Sikhs worldwide. Her unwavering devotion to Waheguru, her dedication to seva, and her commitment to promoting equality serve as a beacon of inspiration for Sikhs on their spiritual journey. Mata Ganga Ji's contributions to Sikhism and her role in nurturing and supporting the Sikh community highlight the importance of seva, equality, and devotion to Waheguru in Sikh teachings.

Mata Ganga Ji epitomizes the saintly spirit of Khalsa through her unwavering devotion to Waheguru, her dedication to seva, and her role in nurturing and supporting the Sikh community. Her life and teachings continue to inspire and guide Sikhs on their spiritual journey, reminding them of the timeless principles of Sikhism and the importance of living a life of humility, compassion, and service to others.

Bhai Gurdas Ji

Bhai Gurdas Ji is a significant figure in Sikh history who played a prominent role in Sikh literature, philosophy, and spirituality. Due to his deep insights into Sikh scripture and teachings, he is often referred to as the "key" to understanding Sikhism. Bhai Gurdas Ji's life and works demonstrate the saintly spirit of Khalsa through his devotion to Waheguru, his scholarly pursuits, and his contributions to preserving and disseminating Sikh wisdom.

Early Life and Association with the Sikh Gurus

Bhai Gurdas Ji was born in 1551 in Goindval, Panjab, into a devout Sikh family. He was the nephew of Sri Guru Amar Das Ji, the third Sikh Guru, and the cousin of Sri Guru Ram Das Ji, the fourth Sikh Guru. From a young age, Bhai Gurdas Ji showed a keen interest in spirituality and education, and he received his early education under the guidance of Guru Amar Das Ji.

His association with the Sikh Gurus deepened as he became a close companion and disciple of Sri Guru Arjan Dev Ji, the fifth Sikh Guru. Bhai Gurdas Ji spent much of his life in the company of Sri Guru Arjan Dev Ji, absorbing the teachings of Sikhism and contributing to the compilation of the Sri Guru Granth Sahib Ji.

Role as a Scholar and Writer

Bhai Gurdas Ji is best known for his Vaars (ballads) and Kabits (couplets), which provide valuable insights into Sikh philosophy, history, and spirituality. His writings serve as a bridge between the teachings of the Sikh Gurus and the Sikh community, elucidating complex concepts and providing commentary on Sikh scripture.

One of Bhai Gurdas Ji's most significant contributions is his Vaars, a collection of poetic compositions that offer a comprehensive overview of Sikhism. In his Vaars, he explores themes such as the nature of Waheguru, the concept of Hukam (divine will), the importance of humility and devotion, and the role of the Guru in guiding seekers on the spiritual path.

Spiritual Insight and Guidance

Bhai Gurdas Ji's writings reflect his deep spiritual insight and understanding of Sikh philosophy. He elucidates the core principles of Sikhism, emphasizing the importance of Naam Simran (remembrance of the divine), Seva (selfless service), and living in accordance with the teachings of the Guru.

His Kabits, in particular, are filled with practical wisdom and guidance for leading a righteous and virtuous life. Bhai Gurdas Ji's teachings emphasize the importance of humility, compassion, and devotion to Waheguru as the means to attain spiritual liberation and union with the divine.

Legacy and Influence on the Khalsa

Bhai Gurdas Ji's legacy continues to inspire and guide the Sikh community, embodying the saintly spirit of Khalsa. His writings serve as a source of spiritual nourishment and guidance for Sikhs seeking to deepen their understanding of Sikhism and live according to its principles. Bhai Gurdas Ji's role as a scholar and writer played a crucial role in preserving and disseminating Sikh wisdom and tradition. His Vaars and Kabits provide a timeless repository of Sikh philosophy and spirituality, serving as a beacon of light for generations of Sikhs.

Bhai Gurdas Ji exemplifies the saintly spirit of Khalsa through his devotion to Waheguru, his scholarly pursuits, and his role in preserving and disseminating Sikh wisdom. His life and works continue to inspire and guide Sikhs on their spiritual journey, reminding them of the timeless principles of righteousness, humility, and devotion that lie at the heart of Sikhism.

Mata Sahib Kaur Ji

Mata Sahib Kaur Ji, also known as Mata Sahib Devan Ji, holds a revered place in Sikh history as the spiritual mother of the Khalsa and the consort of Sri Guru Gobind Singh Ji, the tenth Sikh Guru. Her life exemplifies the saintly spirit of Khalsa through her unwavering devotion to Waheguru, her leadership in nurturing the Khalsa Panth, and her embodiment of Sikh values such as courage, compassion, and selflessness.

Early Life and Marriage to Guru Gobind Singh Ji

Mata Sahib Kaur Ji was born in 1681 in Rohtas, Panjab, in present-day East Panjab. She was known for her piety, humility, and devotion to Waheguru. Mata Sahib Kaur Ji married Sir Guru Gobind Singh Ji in 1700, becoming his devoted companion and partner in spreading the message of Sikhism.

Support of Sri Guru Gobind Singh Ji

Mata Sahib Kaur Ji played a crucial role in supporting Sri Guru Gobind Singh Ji during his tenure as the tenth Sikh Guru. She was completely devoted to him in difficult times. Mata Sahib Kaur Ji stood by Sri Guru Gobind Singh Ji's side and supported him in his mission to establish the Khalsa Panth and uphold the principles of righteousness, justice, and equality.

Leadership in Nurturing the Khalsa Panth

Mata Sahib Kaur Ji played a pivotal role in nurturing and supporting the Khalsa Panth during challenging times. She provided spiritual guidance and moral support to Sikh men, women, and children, ensuring that they remained steadfast in their faith and committed to Sikh principles. Mata Sahib Kaur Ji's compassionate nature and nurturing spirit endeared her to the Sikh community and earned her respect and admiration.

Promotion of Sikh Values

Mata Sahib Kaur Ji promoted Sikh values such as courage, compassion, and selflessness through her actions and teachings. She encouraged Sikhs to live according to the principles of Sikhism and to uphold the ideals of equality, justice, and service to humanity. Mata Sahib Kaur Ji's devotion to Waheguru and her commitment to Sikh values serve as a shining example for Sikhs worldwide, inspiring them to lead lives of righteousness and virtue.

Legacy and Influence on the Khalsa

Mata Sahib Kaur Ji's legacy as a saintly figure in the Khalsa tradition continues to inspire Sikhs worldwide. Her unwavering devotion to Waheguru, her leadership in nurturing the Khalsa Panth, and her embodiment of Sikh values serve as a beacon of inspiration for Sikhs on their spiritual journey. Mata Sahib Kaur Ji's contributions to Sikhism and her role in shaping the Khalsa tradition highlight the importance of devotion, leadership, and service in Sikh teachings.

Mata Sahib Kaur Ji epitomizes the saintly spirit of Khalsa through her unwavering devotion to Waheguru, her leadership in nurturing the Khalsa Panth, and her embodiment of Sikh values such as courage, compassion, and selflessness. Her life and teachings continue to inspire and guide Sikhs on their spiritual journey, reminding them of the timeless principles of Sikhism and the importance of living a life of humility, compassion, and service to others.

Bhai Mani Singh Ji

Bhai Mani Singh Ji is a highly respected figure in Sikh history, celebrated for his scholarship, martyrdom, and his custodianship of Sikhism. His life is an embodiment of the saintly spirit of Khalsa, demonstrated through his unwavering devotion to Waheguru, his commitment to Sikh principles, and his ultimate sacrifice for the Sikh faith. Bhai Mani Singh Ji's contributions to Sikhism, especially his role in preserving Sikh scripture and heritage, highlight his profound dedication to the Khalsa ideals of righteousness, courage, and selflessness.

Early Life and Education

Bhai Mani Singh Ji was born in 1644 in the village of Alipur in the present-day Tarn Taran district of Panjab. From a young age, he displayed a keen interest in learning and spirituality. He received his early education in Sikh scripture and philosophy under the guidance of Sikh scholars and gurus.

Association with the Sikh Gurus

Bhai Mani Singh Ji had the privilege of serving under the patronage of Guru Gobind Singh Ji, the tenth Sikh Guru. He was known for his exceptional scholarship and piety, and he played a significant role in transcribing and preserving Sikh scripture during the time of Sri Guru Gobind Singh Ji.

Role as a Custodian of Harmandir Sahib

Bhai Mani Singh Ji played a crucial role as the Granthi of the Sri Harmandir Sahib Ji, the most sacred Sikh Gurdwara in Amritsar. He was entrusted with the responsibility of managing the Gurdwara's affairs and overseeing the recitation of Gurbani, the foundation of Sikhism. His remarkable contributions in this role have left a lasting impact on the Sikh community and continue to inspire millions around the world.

Compilation of Sri Guru Granth Sahib Ji

Bhai Mani Singh Ji played a crucial role in compiling the Sri Guru Granth Sahib Ji, the Sikh scripture. He meticulously transcribed the hymns of the Sikh Gurus and saints, ensuring the accuracy and authenticity of the Gurbani. His efforts helped preserve the teachings of the Sikh Gurus for future generations.

Martyrdom for Sikh Faith

Bhai Mani Singh Ji's unwavering commitment to Sikh principles and his refusal to compromise his faith led to his martyrdom. In 1737, during the reign of the Mughal Emperor Zakaria Khan. As punishment, Zakaria Khan ordered Bhai Mani Singh Ji's execution in a gruesome manner. Despite the option of saving his life by converting to Islam, Bhai Mani Singh Ji chose to embrace martyrdom, upholding the dignity and integrity of Sikhism.

Legacy and Influence on the Khalsa

Bhai Mani Singh Ji's martyrdom epitomizes the saintly spirit of Khalsa, characterized by unwavering devotion to Waheguru and the willingness to sacrifice one's life for the principles of righteousness and truth. His steadfastness in the face of persecution continues to inspire and galvanize the Sikh community, reinforcing the values of courage, resilience, and spiritual fortitude.

Bhai Mani Singh Ji's life and martyrdom exemplify the essence of the Khalsa spirit, embodying the virtues of courage, devotion, and selflessness. His contributions to Sikhism, particularly in preserving Sikh scripture and heritage, serve as a testament to his profound dedication to the Sikh faith and his enduring legacy as a saintly figure in Sikh history.

Baba Deep Singh Ji

Baba Deep Singh Ji, also known as Baba Deep Singh Shaheed, is celebrated as one of the most revered figures in Sikh history. His life exemplifies the saintly spirit of Khalsa through his unwavering devotion to Waheguru, his courage in defending Sikh principles, and his ultimate sacrifice for the Sikh faith. Baba Deep Singh Ji's legacy continues to inspire generations of Sikhs, embodying the highest ideals of righteousness, courage, and selflessness.

Early Life and Spiritual Journey

Baba Deep Singh Ji was born in 1682 in the village of Pahuwind in the present-day Amritsar district of Panjab. From a young age, he displayed a profound interest in spirituality and Sikh teachings. He was deeply influenced by Sri Guru Gobind Singh Ji, the tenth Sikh Guru, and dedicated his life to serving the Sikh community.

Association with the Khalsa

Baba Deep Singh Ji became a devout follower of Sri Guru Gobind Singh Ji and was initiated into the Khalsa order, adopting the title of "Singh" as a symbol of his commitment to Sikh principles. He was known for his exceptional courage, piety, and selflessness, earning the respect and admiration of Sikhs and non-Sikhs alike.

Defender of Sikhism

Baba Deep Singh Ji played a pivotal role in defending Sikhism during times of persecution and oppression. He was instrumental in organizing Sikh resistance against the tyrannical rule of the Mughal Empire and other adversaries who sought to suppress Sikh faith and identity.

One of the most significant events in Baba Deep Singh Ji's life was his leadership in the Battle of Amritsar in 1757. When the Sri Harmandir Sahib came under attack by Afghan forces, Baba Deep Singh Ji led a contingent of Sikh warriors to defend the sanctity of the shrine. Despite being critically wounded in the battle, he continued fighting with his severed head in one hand and his sword in the other, displaying unparalleled courage and determination.

Martyrdom for Sikh Faith

Baba Deep Singh Ji's ultimate sacrifice occurred during the Battle of Amritsar when he vowed to reach Sri Harmandir Sahib and lay down his life to defend it from desecration. Despite sustaining grievous injuries, he fulfilled his oath by fighting bravely until he reached the vicinity of the Gurdwara, where he breathed his last.

Baba Deep Singh Ji's martyrdom symbolizes the indomitable spirit of Khalsa, characterized by unwavering devotion to Waheguru and the readiness to lay down one's life for the principles of righteousness and truth. His selfless sacrifice continues to inspire Sikhs worldwide, reinforcing the values of courage, resilience, and spiritual fortitude.

Legacy and Influence on the Khalsa

Baba Deep Singh Ji's legacy remains an integral part of Sikh tradition and heritage. His exemplary life and martyrdom inspire Sikhs seeking to uphold Sikhism's principles and defend the rights and freedoms of all humanity.

Baba Deep Singh Ji epitomizes the saintly spirit of Khalsa through his unwavering devotion to Waheguru, his courage in defending Sikh principles, and his ultimate sacrifice for the Sikh faith. His life and legacy continue to inspire and guide Sikhs on their spiritual journey, reminding them of the timeless principles of righteousness, courage, and selflessness that lie at the heart of Sikhism.

Bhai Mati Das Ji

Bhai Mati Das Ji is a highly respected figure in Sikh history. He is known for his unshakeable devotion to Waheguru and for making the ultimate sacrifice for the Sikh faith. His life is a shining example of the Khalsa spirit, as he exhibited immense courage, resilience, and unwavering commitment to Sikh principles despite facing brutal persecution and martyrdom.

Early Life and Spiritual Journey

Bhai Mati Das Ji was born in the village of Karyala in the present-day Hoshiarpur district of Panjab, in the early 17th century. From a young age, he displayed a deep reverence for spirituality and Sikh teachings, and he was profoundly influenced by the teachings of Sri Guru Tegh Bahadur Ji, the ninth Sikh Guru.

Association with the Khalsa

Bhai Mati Das Ji became a devout follower of Guru Tegh Bahadur Ji and embraced the Khalsa way of life, adopting the title of "Das" as a symbol of his devotion to Waheguru and his commitment to Sikh principles. He was known for his piety, humility, and selflessness, earning the respect and admiration of Sikhs and non-Sikhs alike.

Defender of Sikhism

Bhai Mati Das Ji played a significant role in defending Sikhism during times of persecution and oppression. He was one of the Sikhs who accompanied Sri Guru Tegh Bahadur Ji on his mission to protect the rights and freedoms of Hindus who were being forcibly converted to Islam by the Mughal Emperor Aurangzeb.

Martyrdom for Sikh Faith

Bhai Mati Das Ji's ultimate sacrifice occurred during the brutal persecution of Sikhs under the reign of Aurangzeb. In 1675, when Sri Guru Tegh Bahadur Ji was martyred in Delhi for defending the rights of the common people, Bhai Mati Das Ji stood steadfast in his faith and embraced martyrdom alongside his Guru.

One of the most poignant moments in Bhai Mati Das Ji's life was his execution by being sawn alive. Despite facing excruciating pain and suffering, he remained unwavering in his devotion to Waheguru and remained steadfast in his commitment to Sikh principles until his last breath.

Legacy and Influence on the Khalsa

Bhai Mati Das Ji's martyrdom remains a symbol of courage, resilience, and unwavering faith for Sikhs worldwide. His selfless sacrifice serves as a testament to the enduring spirit of Khalsa, characterized by unwavering devotion to Waheguru and the readiness to lay down one's life for the principles of righteousness and truth.

Bhai Mati Das Ji epitomizes the saintly spirit of Khalsa through his courage, resilience, and unwavering commitment to Sikh principles. His life and martyrdom continue to inspire and guide Sikhs on their spiritual journey, reminding them of the timeless principles of righteousness, courage, and selflessness that lie at the heart of Sikhism.

Bhai Kanhaiya Ji

Bhai Kanhaiya Ji, also known as Bhai Kanhaiya Singh, is a highly respected figure in Sikh history. He is admired for his compassion, selflessness, and devotion to Waheguru. Bhai Kanhaiya Ji's life serves as an example of the Khalsa spirit, which is rooted in Sikh principles of compassion, equality, and service to humanity.

Early Life and Spiritual Journey

Bhai Kanhaiya Ji was born in 1648 in the town of Sodhra, near Wazirabad, in present-day East Panjab. From a young age, he displayed a deep reverence for spirituality and Sikh teachings, and he was profoundly influenced by the teachings of Sri Guru Tegh Bahadur Ji and Sri Guru Gobind Singh Ji, the ninth and tenth Sikh Gurus, respectively.

Association with the Khalsa

Bhai Kanhaiya Ji became a devout follower of Sri Guru Tegh Bahadur Ji and Sri Guru Gobind Singh Ji, embracing the Khalsa way of life and adopting the title of "Singh" as a symbol of his commitment to Sikh principles. He was known for his humility, kindness, and selflessness, earning the respect and admiration of Sikhs and non-Sikhs alike.

Compassionate Service

One of the most remarkable aspects of Bhai Kanhaiya Ji's life was his unwavering commitment to seva, or selfless service, regardless of caste, creed, or religion. He dedicated his life to serving the needy and the marginalized, providing food, shelter, and medical care to those in need without discrimination.

Bhai Kanhaiya Ji's compassion knew no bounds, and he often risked his own safety to help others in times of hardship and adversity. His selfless acts of kindness and generosity earned him the affectionate title of "Sevapanthi" or "the one who serves all."

Concept of Sarbat Da Bhala

Bhai Kanhaiya Ji embodied the Sikh principle of "Sarbat Da Bhala," which translates to "the welfare of all." He believed in the inherent dignity and worth of every human being, regardless of their social or economic status, and dedicated his life to serving the welfare of all humanity.

Spiritual Teachings

Bhai Kanhaiya Ji's teachings emphasized the importance of love, compassion, and selflessness in the pursuit of spiritual enlightenment. He encouraged others to cultivate a spirit of humility and service, recognizing the divine presence in all beings and treating everyone with kindness and respect.

Legacy and Influence on the Khalsa

Bhai Kanhaiya Ji's legacy remains an integral part of Sikh tradition and heritage. His exemplary life and teachings continue to inspire generations of Sikhs and reinforce the values of compassion, equality, and service to humanity.

Bhai Kanhaiya Ji epitomizes the saintly spirit of Khalsa through his compassion, selflessness, and devotion to Waheguru. His life and teachings serve as a timeless reminder of the fundamental principles of Sikhism, emphasizing the importance of love, compassion, and service to humanity in the pursuit of spiritual enlightenment.

Bhai Taru Singh Ji

Bhai Taru Singh Ji is celebrated as a revered saint and martyr in Sikh history, and he is known for his unwavering faith, courage, and dedication to Sikh principles. His life exemplifies the saintly spirit of Khalsa through his steadfast commitment to Waheguru, his resilience in the face of adversity, and his ultimate sacrifice for the Sikh faith.

Early Life and Spiritual Journey

Bhai Taru Singh Ji was born in 1720 in the village of Poohla in present-day Panjab. From a young age, he displayed a deep reverence for spirituality and Sikh teachings, and he was profoundly influenced by the teachings of Sri Guru Granth Sahib Ji.

Association with the Khalsa

Bhai Taru Singh Ji became a devout follower of Sikhism and embraced the Khalsa way of life, adopting the title of "Singh" as a symbol of his commitment to Sikh principles. He was known for his piety, humility, and devotion to Waheguru, earning the respect and admiration of Sikhs and non-Sikhs alike.

Defender of Sikhism

Bhai Taru Singh Ji played a crucial role in defending Sikhism during times of persecution and oppression. He was instrumental in organizing Sikh resistance against the tyrannical rule of the Mughal Empire and other adversaries who sought to suppress Sikh faith and identity.

One of the most significant events in Bhai Taru Singh Ji's life was his refusal to comply with the orders of the Mughal governor to cut his hair and renounce his faith. Despite facing severe torture and persecution, he remained steadfast in his devotion to Waheguru and refused to compromise his Sikh identity.

Martyrdom for Sikh Faith

Bhai Taru Singh Ji's ultimate sacrifice occurred when he was subjected to brutal torture by the Mughal authorities. In 1745, he was arrested and brought before the Mughal governor, Zakaria Khan, who ordered him to convert to Islam or face death.

Despite enduring excruciating pain and suffering, Bhai Taru Singh Ji remained resolute in his faith and refused to renounce Sikhism. As a result, he was subjected to the barbaric act of having his scalp removed from his skull with a sharp instrument (Rambi).

Even in his final moments, Bhai Taru Singh Ji remained calm and composed, reciting Gurbani and offering prayers to Waheguru. His martyrdom testifies to his unwavering commitment to Sikh principles and willingness to sacrifice his life for the Sikh faith.

Legacy and Influence on the Khalsa

Bhai Taru Singh Ji's martyrdom remains a symbol of courage, resilience, and unwavering faith for Sikhs worldwide. His selfless sacrifice serves as a reminder of the enduring spirit of Khalsa, characterized by unwavering devotion to Waheguru and the readiness to lay down one's life for the principles of righteousness and truth.

Bhai Taru Singh Ji epitomizes the saintly spirit of Khalsa through his courage, resilience, and unwavering commitment to Sikh principles. His life and martyrdom continue to inspire and guide Sikhs on their spiritual journey, reminding them of the timeless principles of righteousness, courage, and selflessness that lie at the heart of Sikhism.

Saint Spirit

The Saint Spirit of the Khalsa encapsulates the essence of Sikh spirituality and the timeless principles that define the Khalsa tradition. Throughout history, the Khalsa has been enriched and shaped by the saintly nature of various personalities, both men and women, who have dedicated themselves to the path of righteousness, devotion, and service.

From the teachings of Sri Guru Nanak Dev Ji, the founder of Sikhism, to the selfless service of individuals like Mata Khivi Ji and Bhai Kanhaiya Ji, the saintly spirit of the Khalsa is reflected in acts of compassion, humility, and devotion to Waheguru. These saintly figures have not only embodied Sikh values but also inspired generations of Sikhs to lead lives of righteousness and service to humanity.

The saintly nature of the Khalsa is not confined to any one individual or time period but is a living tradition that continues to thrive through the actions and teachings of Sikh leaders and saints. Whether through acts of selfless service, spiritual insight, or fearless courage, these individuals have exemplified the core principles of Sikhism and the Khalsa tradition, inspiring Sikhs worldwide to walk the path of righteousness and uphold the values of compassion, equality, and devotion to Waheguru.

As Sikhs strive to embody the saintly spirit of the Khalsa in their daily lives, they draw inspiration from the rich legacy of those who have gone before them, recognizing that the true essence of the Khalsa lies in selfless service, devotion to Waheguru and unwavering commitment to Sikh principles. In embracing the saintly spirit of the Khalsa, Sikhs find strength, guidance, and purpose on their spiritual journey towards union with the divine.

*****

318

THE
WARRIOR
SPIRIT OF
THE KHALSA

THE WARRIOR SPIRIT OF THE KHALSA

In 1699, Guru Gobind Singh Ji, the Tenth Sikh Guru, initiated a profound transformation within Sikhism that reverberates through history to the present day. This pivotal moment was marked by the establishment of the Khalsa, a community of saint-soldiers dedicated to defending righteousness and upholding justice. At the heart of this transformation was the Amrit Sanchar ceremony, a sacred initiation ritual that not only solidified Sikh identity but also infused the community with a resilient martial spirit.

To understand the significance of this event, it's essential to delve into the historical context of 17th-century Asia. During this time, the Mughal Empire ruled over much of the Panjab and Indian subcontinent, imposing religious intolerance and persecution upon non-Muslim communities, including Sikhs. Sikhism, a relatively young religion founded by Sri Guru Nanak Dev Ji in the 15th century, faced significant challenges as its followers endured oppression and violence.

In this tumultuous era, Sri Guru Gobind Singh Ji emerged as a visionary leader determined to defend Sikh principles and safeguard the rights of all people to practice their faith freely. As the Tenth Guru, he was not only a spiritual guide but also a warrior-poet, imbued with a deep sense of duty to protect the weak and oppressed.

The year 1699 marked a turning point in world history. Sri Guru Gobind Singh Ji gathered thousands of Sikhs from across the region to celebrate the festival of Vaisakhi at Sri Anandpur Sahib. Amidst the joyous festivities, he initiated a transformative process that forever redefined Sikhism.

It was on this sacred occasion that Sri Guru Gobind Singh Ji introduced the Amrit Sanchar ceremony, a ritual of spiritual rebirth and initiation into the Khalsa. The ceremony involved the preparation of Amrit, a sweetened mixture of water and sugar (Patasas) stirred with Khanda (a double-edged sword), symbolizing the divine authority and power of the Guru.

The Amrit Sanchar ceremony was a solemn affair steeped in tradition and symbolism. Five devout Sikhs, known as the Panj Pyare or Five Beloved Ones, were chosen by Sri Guru Gobind Singh Ji to receive the first offering of Amrit. With each sip of the sacred nectar, the initiated Sikhs underwent a profound spiritual transformation, shedding their old identities and embracing a new life dedicated to the principles of Sikhism.

The significance of the Amrit Sanchar ceremony extended far beyond the act of initiation itself. It served as a unifying force, bringing together Sikhs of diverse backgrounds and social statuses under a common banner. The Khalsa was not just a military order but a spiritual fraternity bound by principles of equality, brotherhood, and selflessness.

Central to the ethos of the Khalsa was the infusion of a robust martial spirit. Sri Guru Gobind Singh Ji emphasized the importance of courage, discipline, and readiness to defend righteousness in the face of adversity. The Khalsa was tasked with the noble mission of protecting the weak, upholding justice, and standing against tyranny wherever it may arise.

The Amrit Sanchar ceremony also formalized the distinct identity of the Khalsa through the adoption of the Five Ks, or articles of faith, which every Amritdhari Sikh was required to wear. These included Kesh, Kangha, Kara, Kirpan, and Kachera. Each of these articles carried deep symbolic meaning and served as a constant reminder of the Khalsa's commitment to Sikh principles.

The establishment of the Khalsa by Sri Guru Gobind Singh Ji was not merely a historical event but a spiritual awakening that continues to inspire millions of people worldwide. The legacy of the Khalsa endures as a testament to the resilience, courage, and unwavering devotion of the Sikh community to the principles of Sikhism.

In the centuries that followed, the Khalsa has faced numerous challenges and adversities, yet its spirit remains unbroken. Today, Sikhs proudly carry on the tradition of the Khalsa, embodying the values of righteousness, equality, and service to humanity. The Amrit Sanchar ceremony continues to be performed, symbolizing the eternal bond between the Guru and the Khalsa and reaffirming the timeless message of Sikhism: to live honestly, work hard, and always remember the Divine.

Divine Mission

Sri Guru Gobind Singh Sahib Ji, the Tenth Guru of Sikhism, assumed leadership during a tumultuous period in world history. Born to Sri Guru Tegh Bahadur Ji, the Ninth Sikh Guru, and Mata Gujri Ji in 1666, Sri Guru Gobind Singh Ji inherited a legacy of sacrifice and spiritual fortitude. From a young age, Guru Gobind Singh Ji displayed remarkable courage, wisdom, and a deep sense of devotion to the Sikh faith. Through his teachings, actions, and sacrifices, Sri Guru Gobind Singh Ji exemplified the epitome of Sikh values and principles. His mission to safeguard Sikhism, foster a community capable of defending itself against tyranny, and promote justice and equality continues to inspire millions of Sikhs worldwide. Sri Guru Gobind Singh Ji's legacy serves as a guiding light for those who seek to uphold the principles of truth, righteousness, and compassion in the face of adversity. Sri Guru Gobind Singh Ji's mission can be understood through several key dimensions:

1. **Protection of Sikh Principles:** Sri Guru Gobind Singh Ji was entrusted with the sacred duty of safeguarding the core principles of Sikhism laid down by his predecessors, particularly Sri Guru Nanak Dev Ji. These principles included the belief in one God, equality of all human beings regardless of caste, creed, or gender, and the pursuit of truth and righteousness. Sri Guru Gobind Singh Ji recognized the importance of preserving these foundational tenets amidst the turbulent socio-political landscape of his time.

2. **Fostering a Spirit of Resistance:** Sri Guru Gobind Singh Ji's mission also involved nurturing a community capable of resisting

tyranny and injustice. He understood that the small communities faced grave threats from the oppressive Mughal regime, which sought to suppress religious freedoms and impose its authority. To counter these challenges, Sri Guru Gobind Singh Ji put a spirit of resilience, courage, and self-defense among his followers.

3. **Establishment of the Khalsa:** Central to Sri Guru Gobind Singh Ji's mission was the establishment or revelation of the Khalsa, a community of saint-soldiers dedicated to upholding Sikh values and protecting the weak. Through the initiation ceremony of Amrit Sanchar, Sri Guru Gobind Singh Ji transformed his followers into disciplined warriors ready to confront oppression and injustice. The Khalsa was not merely a military force but a spiritual fraternity bound by the principles of equality, brotherhood, and selflessness.

4. **Promotion of Social Justice:** Sri Guru Gobind Singh Ji's mission extended beyond the realm of religious freedom to encompass broader principles of social justice and equality. He condemned the prevailing caste system and advocated for the upliftment of the downtrodden and marginalized sections of society. Sri Guru Gobind Singh Ji envisioned a society where all individuals were treated with dignity and respect, regardless of their social status or background.

5. **Preservation of Sikh Identity:** In addition to safeguarding Sikh principles, Sri Guru Gobind

Singh Ji was committed to preserving the distinct identity of the Sikh community. He introduced the Five Ks, or articles of faith, which every Amritdhari Sikh was required to adorn. These articles, including the Kesh, Kanga, Kara, Kirpan, and Kachhera, served as visible markers of Sikh identity and a symbol of the Khalsa's commitment to Sikh ideals.

Amrit Sanchar Ceremony

The first Amrit Sanchar ceremony, conducted by Sri Guru Gobind Singh Ji in 1699, stands as a seminal moment in Sikh history. This sacred ritual not only marked the birth of the Khalsa but also symbolized the spiritual rebirth and transformation of devout Sikhs.

1. **Administration of Amrit:** Sri Guru Gobind Singh Ji recognized the need for a unified and resilient community to withstand oppression and initiated the Amrit Sanchar ceremony. Amrit, often referred to as the nectar of initiation, was prepared using a mixture of water and sugar stirred with a Khanda (double-edged sword), symbolizing the Guru's divine authority and power. The act of administering Amrit represented a sacred covenant between the Guru and the Amritdhari Sikhs, binding them to the path of Sikhism and its principles.

2. **Ritualistic Elements:** The Amrit Sanchar ceremony was steeped in tradition and symbolism. It involved meticulous preparation, including the washing of utensils, recitation of prayers from the Sri Guru Granth Sahib Ji and

Sri Dasam Granth Sahib Ji, and the chanting of sacred hymns, such as the Mool Mantar. Each element of the ceremony served to sanctify the Amrit and imbue it with spiritual potency, preparing the Sikhs for their transformation.

3. **Symbolic Significance:** The Amrit Sanchar ceremony carried profound symbolic significance for Sikhs. It represented a spiritual rebirth wherein the Amritdhari Sikhs renounced their old identities and embraced a new life dedicated to the principles of Sikhism. By partaking in the ceremony, individuals affirmed their commitment to Sikh values, including the pursuit of truth, justice, and righteousness.

4. **Panj Pyare (The Five Beloved Ones):** Sri Guru Gobind Singh Ji chose five devout Sikhs to receive the first offering of Amrit, known as the Panj Pyare or the Five Beloved Ones. These individuals, representing diverse backgrounds and social statuses, were united by their unwavering faith and devotion to the Guru.

5. **Courage and Commitment:** The Panj Pyare exemplified the qualities of the Khalsa – courage, selflessness, and unwavering commitment to Sikh principles. Despite the risks and challenges, they willingly offered their heads to the Guru, demonstrating absolute trust and surrendering to his divine will.

6. **Standard-Bearers of the Khalsa:** The Amrit Sanchar of the Panj Pyare into the Khalsa set the standard for future generations of Sikhs.

Their selfless sacrifice and unyielding devotion inspired countless others to follow in their footsteps, embodying the spirit of the Khalsa and upholding Sikh ideals in the face of adversity.

The Amrit Sanchar ceremony, conducted by Sri Guru Gobind Singh Ji, symbolized the spiritual rebirth and transformation of Sikhs into the Khalsa. The participation of the Panj Pyare, or the Five Beloved Ones, in this sacred ritual, exemplified the courage, commitment, and selflessness required to embody the ideals of the Khalsa. Their legacy continues to inspire Sikhs worldwide to walk the path of righteousness and uphold the principles of Sikhism with unwavering dedication.

Significance of The Amrit Sanchar

The Amrit Sanchar ceremony represents a profound spiritual and communal awakening within Sikhism. It serves as a transformative rite of passage, marking the individuals into the Khalsa and imbuing them with a sense of duty, unity, and martial valor. Through this sacred ritual, Sri Guru Gobind Singh Ji laid the foundation for a community of saint soldiers devoted to defending righteousness and upholding justice – a legacy that continues to inspire Sikhs worldwide.

Spiritual Rebirth

The Amrit during the Amrit Sanchar ceremony represents a transformative and sacred moment in the life of a Sikh. It symbolizes a spiritual rebirth, reaffirms one's commitment to Sikh principles and values, and establishes a profound bond between the Guru and the Amritdhari Sikh. Through this act, individuals embrace their identity as members of the Khalsa and dedicate themselves to living a life guided by the teachings of Sikhism.

1. **Shedding Old Identities:** Consuming Amrit symbolizes the shedding of old identities and attachments. It signifies a willingness to let go of past affiliations, biases, and limitations and embrace a new life dedicated to Sikh ideals. By partaking in Amrit, individuals declare their readiness to embark on a spiritual journey guided by the teachings of the Guru.

2. **Embracing Sikh Principles:** Consuming Amrit is a declaration of one's allegiance to Sikh principles and values. It signifies a wholehearted acceptance of the core tenets of Sikhism, including belief in one God, equality of all human beings, and the pursuit of truth and righteousness. Through this act, Amritdhari Sikhs reaffirm their commitment to living a life aligned with Sikh teachings and embodying the virtues espoused by the Guru.

3. **Sacred Covenant:** The consumption of Amrit serves as a sacred covenant between the Guru and the Amritdhari Sikhs. It symbolizes a deep spiritual bond and mutual commitment to the path of Sikhism. By partaking in Amrit, individuals enter into a divine contract, pledging to uphold the principles of Sikhism and follow the Guru's guidance in all aspects of life.

4. **Spiritual Rebirth:** The act of consuming Amrit represents a profound spiritual rebirth for the Sikhs. It signifies a transformative moment where individuals experience a spiritual awakening and embark on a new chapter in their spiritual journey. Through this ritual, Sikhs are reborn into the Khalsa, a community of saint-soldiers dedicated to defending righteousness and upholding justice.

5. **Binding to Spiritual Ideals:** Consuming Amrit binds the Amritdhari Sikhs to Sikhism's spiritual ideals. It reminds them of their sacred duty to lead a life of integrity, compassion, and service to humanity. By partaking in Amrit, Sikhs commit to walking the path of righteousness and striving to embody the divine virtues encapsulated in Sikh teachings.

Unity and Brotherhood

The Amrit into the Khalsa through the Amrit Sanchar ceremony fosters a profound sense of unity and brotherhood among Sikhs. Regardless of their backgrounds or differences, Amritdhari Sikhs come together as members of a cohesive community bound by shared beliefs, values, and a commitment to the path of righteousness. This unity serves as a source of strength and resilience, enabling the Khalsa to confront challenges and adversity with solidarity and collective resolve.

1. **Inclusive Community:** The Amrit Sanchar ceremony welcomes individuals from all walks of life, regardless of their backgrounds, social

statuses, or caste affiliations. Through this initiation, all Sikhs are welcomed into the Khalsa brotherhood on an equal footing, without discrimination or prejudice. This inclusive ethos creates a sense of belonging and acceptance, ensuring that every member of the Khalsa community feels valued and respected.

2. **Shared Beliefs and Values:** Amritdhari Sikhs share a common set of beliefs and values rooted in Sikh teachings. They affirm their commitment to principles such as belief in one God, equality of all human beings, and the pursuit of truth and righteousness. This shared spiritual foundation forms the basis of unity within the Khalsa community, binding its members together in a common purpose and vision.

3. **Transcending Societal Barriers:** The Khalsa transcends societal barriers and divisions, uniting individuals from diverse backgrounds under a common identity. Regardless of their social or economic status, Amritdhari Sikhs are united by their allegiance to Sikh principles and their dedication to the path of righteousness. This sense of unity enables Sikhs to overcome external differences and forge strong bonds of brotherhood based on mutual respect and solidarity.

4. **Strength in Diversity:** The Khalsa community thrives on diversity, recognizing the unique contributions and perspectives of its members. Amritdhari Sikhs come from a variety of cultural,

linguistic, and regional backgrounds, enriching the community with their distinct experiences and insights. This diversity strengthens Khalsa and enhances its ability to confront challenges and adversity with resilience and adaptability.

5. **Collective Resolve:** Unity and brotherhood within the Khalsa Panth serve as a source of strength and resilience in the face of adversity. When confronted with challenges, Amritdhari Sikhs stand together in solidarity, drawing upon their shared values and sense of purpose to overcome obstacles and uphold Sikh ideals. This collective resolve enables the Khalsa to confront injustice and oppression with courage and determination.

Infusion of Martial Spirit

The infusion of a robust martial spirit within the Khalsa, facilitated by Sri Guru Gobind Singh Ji through the Amrit Sanchar ceremony, has been a cornerstone of Sikh identity and ethos. This martial spirit empowers Sikhs to defend themselves and others against oppression and injustice, embodying courage, discipline, and readiness for battle. Central to this martial ethos are the Five Ks, or articles of faith, which serve as visible symbols of the Khalsa's commitment to Sikh principles and its duty to protect the weak and uphold justice.

1. **The Five Ks**

    - **Kesh (Uncut Hair):** The practice of maintaining Kesh, as ordained by Guru Gobind Singh Ji, symbolizes the acceptance of God's will and the rejection of vanity. For Sikhs, their uncut hair represents their connection to the divine and serves as a reminder of their commitment to Sikh ideals.

- **Kangha (Wooden Comb):** The wooden comb is a practical tool for maintaining hair cleanliness and hygiene. Symbolically, it represents discipline and self-care, reminding Sikhs to keep themselves clean and presentable while adhering to the principles of Sikhism.

- **Kara (Iron Bracelet):** The iron bracelet is worn on the wrist as a symbol of strength and unity within the Khalsa community. It signifies the unbreakable bond between Sikhs and their commitment to Sikh principles. The circular shape of the Kara represents the eternity of God and the cyclical nature of life.

- **Kirpan (Ceremonial Sword):** The Kirpan is a ceremonial sword carried by Amritdhari Sikhs as a symbol of their readiness to defend themselves and others against injustice. It embodies the martial spirit of the Khalsa and serves as a reminder of the duty to protect the weak and uphold righteousness.

- **Kachera (Undershorts):** The Kachera is a specially designed undergarment worn by Amritdhari Sikhs, symbolizing modesty, self-discipline, and readiness for battle. It serves as a practical garment for physical activity while also carrying deep symbolic significance within Sikh tradition.

2. **Sense of Purpose and Responsibility:** The infusion of the martial spirit within the Khalsa imbues its members with a sense of purpose and responsibility. Amritdhari Sikhs understand that they are entrusted with the duty to stand firm in the face of adversity and defend the principles of Sikhism with unwavering courage. The wearing of the Five Ks serves as a constant reminder of this responsibility and inspires Sikhs to embody the virtues of bravery, compassion, and selflessness in all aspects of their lives.

3. **Upholding Justice and Protecting the Weak:** The martial spirit of the Khalsa is not just about physical combat but also about upholding justice and protecting the weak. Amritdhari Sikhs are called upon to stand up against oppression and injustice, using their strength and courage to defend those who cannot defend themselves. The Five Ks serve as symbols of this commitment, reminding Sikhs of their duty to serve humanity and uphold the values of Sikhism.

The infusion of the martial spirit within the Khalsa, facilitated by Guru Gobind Singh Ji through the Amrit Sanchar ceremony, is a central aspect of Sikh identity and ethos. The wearing of the Five Ks serves as the visible symbol of the Khalsa's commitment to courage, discipline, and readiness for battle, inspiring Sikhs to stand firm in the face of adversity and defend the principles of Sikhism with unwavering courage and determination.

Ideals and Principles of the Khalsa

The ideals and principles of the Khalsa warrior, shaped by Sikh teachings and the martial spirit infused by Sri Guru Gobind Singh Ji, encompass a blend of spiritual values, ethical conduct, and a commitment to defending righteousness. Grounded in Sikh teachings and the teachings of the Guru, the Khalsa warrior embodies courage, integrity, compassion, and a steadfast commitment to defending righteousness and upholding justice in the world.

Courage and Fearlessness

Courage and fearlessness are essential qualities that define the Khalsa warrior's character. Rooted in deep faith, belief in righteousness, and a commitment to justice, these attributes empower them to confront adversity, uphold Sikh principles, and inspire positive change in the world.

1. **Confronting Adversity:** The Khalsa warrior faces adversity with unwavering courage, meeting challenges head-on rather than shying away from them. Whether it's facing oppressive regimes, defending the rights of the marginalized, or standing up against injustice, they approach every situation with a determined spirit. Instead of succumbing to fear or doubt, they draw upon their inner strength and conviction to persevere in the face of adversity.

2. **Standing Up for Justice:** Fearlessness compels the Khalsa warrior to stand up for justice, regardless of the risks involved. They are unafraid to speak truth to power and challenge injustice, even when doing so may put them in harm's way. Their commitment to righteousness and the welfare of others outweighs any personal concerns, driving them to act with boldness and integrity in pursuit of a just cause.

3. **Deep Faith and Belief:** The courage of the Khalsa warrior is rooted in a deep faith in the divine and a firm belief in the righteousness of their cause. They draw strength from their connection to Waheguru (God) and the teachings of the Guru, trusting in divine guidance and providence to sustain them through trials and tribulations. This faith instills them with a sense of purpose and confidence, enabling them to face even the most daunting challenges with unwavering resolve.

4. **Righteousness of Their Cause:** The Khalsa warrior's courage is fueled by their belief in the righteousness of their cause. They are driven by a commitment to upholding Sikh principles, defending the rights of the oppressed, and fighting against tyranny and injustice. Their actions are guided by a moral compass rooted in Sikh teachings, ensuring that they remain steadfast in their pursuit of justice and righteousness.

5. **Inspirational Leadership:** Through their courage and fearlessness, the Khalsa warrior serves as an inspirational leader and role model for others. Their willingness to confront adversity and stand up for what is right inspires courage and conviction in those around them, galvanizing communities to unite in the fight against oppression and injustice. In times of crisis, their leadership shines as a beacon of hope and resilience, guiding others through challenging times with strength and determination.

Self-Discipline and Self Control

Self-discipline and self-control are essential virtues for the Khalsa warrior. They maintain mastery over their thoughts, words, and actions, ensuring that they act with integrity and restraint in all situations. Through disciplined practice and adherence to Sikh principles, they cultivate inner strength and resilience.

1. **Mastery Over Thoughts:** The Khalsa warrior exercises self-discipline by mastering their thoughts and emotions. They cultivate a calm and focused mind, free from distractions and negative influences, allowing them to make clear and rational decisions even in challenging circumstances. Through practices such as meditation and prayer, they develop inner peace and clarity, enabling them to navigate life's complexities with wisdom and discernment.

2. **Integrity in Actions:** Self-discipline compels the Khalsa warrior to act with integrity and

honesty in all their dealings. They adhere to the principles of Sikhism with unwavering commitment, ensuring that their actions align with their values and beliefs. Whether in times of ease or difficulty, they remain steadfast in their adherence to truthfulness, transparency, and ethical conduct, earning the trust and respect of others through their consistent behavior.

3. **Restraint in Speech:** The Khalsa warrior exercises self-control in their speech, using words wisely and responsibly to uplift and inspire others. They refrain from engaging in gossip, slander, or harmful speech, recognizing the power of words to either heal or harm. Instead, they communicate with clarity, kindness, and compassion, fostering harmony and understanding within their communities.

4. **Discipline in Practices:** Self-discipline is reflected in the Khalsa warrior's commitment to disciplined practices and routines. They adhere to a strict regimen of spiritual disciplines, including Nitnem (daily prayers), meditation, and reading of Sikh scriptures. Through consistent practice and devotion, they deepen their connection to the divine and strengthen their resolve to live according to Sikh principles.

5. **Cultivation of Inner Strength:** Self-discipline enables the Khalsa warrior to cultivate inner strength and resilience, enabling them to withstand challenges and adversity with grace and fortitude. By exercising restraint and self-

control, they develop a strong sense of self-mastery and self-reliance, empowering them to overcome obstacles and persevere in the pursuit of their goals.

6. **Role Model for Others:** Through their exemplary behavior and disciplined lifestyle, the Khalsa warrior serves as a role model for others within their community. They inspire others to cultivate self-discipline and self-control in their own lives, recognizing that these virtues are essential for personal growth, spiritual development, and moral integrity.

Integrity and Honesty

The Khalsa warrior upholds the highest standards of integrity and honesty in all their dealings. They adhere unwaveringly to truthfulness, transparency, and ethical conduct, earning the trust and respect of others through their actions. Integrity is the cornerstone of their character, guiding them in all their endeavors.

1. **Unwavering Commitment to Truthfulness:** The Khalsa warrior is unwaveringly committed to truthfulness in all aspects of their life. They speak truthfully and honestly, even when faced with difficult circumstances or temptations to deceive. Their commitment to truth is rooted in Sikh teachings, which emphasize the importance of honesty as a fundamental virtue. By adhering to the truth, they establish credibility and reliability, fostering trust in their words and actions.

2. **Transparency and Accountability:** Transparency is a hallmark of the Khalsa warrior's character. They conduct themselves with openness and honesty, avoiding deception or concealment in their interactions. Whether in personal relationships, professional endeavors, or community affairs, they strive to maintain transparency and accountability, ensuring that their actions align with their values and principles. Transparency builds trust and confidence, enabling meaningful connections and collaborations with others.

3. **Ethical Conduct in All Situations:** Ethical conduct is central to the Khalsa warrior's way of life. They adhere to a code of ethics that guides their behavior and decision-making, ensuring that they act with integrity and fairness in all situations. Whether faced with moral dilemmas, temptations, or pressures to compromise their principles, they remain steadfast in upholding the highest standards of ethical conduct. Their commitment to integrity inspires others and sets a positive example for the community.

4. **Cornerstone of Character:** Integrity serves as the cornerstone of the Khalsa warrior's character. It is the guiding principle that shapes their thoughts, words, and actions, influencing every aspect of their life. By embodying integrity in their interactions and relationships, they build a reputation for honesty, reliability, and trustworthiness. Integrity is not just a virtue but a way of being for the Khalsa warrior, reflecting

their unwavering commitment to Sikh principles and values.

5. **Trust and Respect of Others:** Through their adherence to integrity and honesty, the Khalsa warrior earns the trust and respect of others. Their consistent behavior and moral integrity inspire confidence and admiration, fostering positive relationships and collaborations within their community. By upholding the highest standards of ethical conduct, they create an environment of trust and mutual respect, enabling meaningful connections and collective endeavors.

Compassion and Service

Compassion and service are integral to the ethos of the Khalsa warrior. They extend a helping hand to those in need, practicing selfless service (seva) as a manifestation of their devotion to humanity. Whether through acts of charity, humanitarian aid, or community service, they embody the Sikh principle of "Sarbat da Bhala" (blessings for all).

1. **Selfless Service (Seva):** Selfless service, known as seva, is a central tenet of Sikhism and a guiding principle for the Khalsa warrior. They view seva not as a duty but as a privilege and a sacred obligation to serve others without expectation of reward or recognition. Whether it's feeding the hungry, caring for the sick, or providing assistance to the marginalized, the Khalsa warrior actively seeks out opportunities

to serve those in need, embodying the spirit of compassion and selflessness.

2. **Empathy and Understanding:** Compassion is rooted in empathy and understanding for the suffering of others. The Khalsa warrior seeks to alleviate the pain and hardships faced by individuals and communities, offering support, comfort, and assistance with genuine empathy and compassion. They recognize the interconnectedness of all beings and strive to cultivate a sense of kinship and solidarity with those they serve, regardless of differences or barriers.

3. **Humanitarian Aid and Relief Work:** The Khalsa warrior engages in humanitarian aid and relief work to address urgent needs and alleviate suffering in times of crisis or disaster. Whether responding to natural disasters, conflicts, or humanitarian emergencies, they mobilize resources and volunteers to provide essential aid, including food, shelter, medical care, and emotional support. Their swift and compassionate response reflects their commitment to serving humanity in times of need.

4. **Community Building and Empowerment:** Service extends beyond individual acts of charity to encompass community building and empowerment initiatives. The Khalsa warrior works to strengthen communities, promote social cohesion, and empower individuals to lead dignified and fulfilling lives. They invest in

education, skill development, and capacity-building programs that uplift marginalized populations and foster self-reliance and resilience.

5. **Advocacy and Social Justice:** Compassion compels the Khalsa warrior to advocate for social justice and human rights, speaking out against injustice, discrimination, and oppression. They use their voice and influence to champion the rights of the marginalized, challenge systemic inequalities, and work towards creating a more just and equitable society. Their advocacy efforts are grounded in a deep sense of compassion and a commitment to upholding the dignity and rights of all individuals.

Justice and Equality

The Khalsa warrior is a champion of justice and equality, committed to upholding the rights and dignity of all individuals. They fight against oppression, discrimination, and injustice in all its forms, striving to create a more just and equitable society. Equality is not just a principle but a lived reality for the Khalsa warrior, who treats all beings with respect and compassion.

1. **Championing Justice:** The Khalsa warrior is unwavering in their commitment to justice, standing up against oppression, discrimination, and injustice wherever they encounter it. They advocate for the rights of the marginalized, oppressed, and disenfranchised, working tirelessly to ensure that all individuals are

treated with fairness, dignity, and respect. Whether confronting systemic injustices or addressing individual grievances, they use their voice and influence to champion the cause of justice and uphold the principles of righteousness.

2. **Upholding Equality:** Equality is not just a principle but a lived reality for the Khalsa warrior, who treats all beings with respect, dignity, and compassion. They reject discrimination based on race, gender, caste, or social status, recognizing the inherent worth and equality of all individuals in the eyes of the divine. The Khalsa warrior works to dismantle barriers to equality and create opportunities for all individuals to thrive and fulfill their potential.

3. **Fighting Against Oppression:** The Khalsa warrior is a staunch opponent of oppression in all its forms, whether it manifests as political tyranny, social injustice, or economic exploitation. They use their courage, determination, and moral authority to challenge oppressive systems and institutions, striving to create a world where every person enjoys freedom, dignity, and human rights. Through their actions and advocacy, they seek to empower the oppressed and bring about meaningful change.

4. **Creating a Just and Equitable Society:** Justice and equality are central to the vision of the Khalsa warrior for society. They work towards creating a world where every individual

has access to basic necessities, opportunities for advancement, and a voice in decision-making processes. By addressing the root causes of inequality and advocating for systemic change, they seek to build a society that is founded on principles of fairness, inclusivity, and social justice.

5. **Compassionate Action:** Justice and equality are infused with compassion in the actions of the Khalsa warrior. They approach their advocacy work with empathy, understanding, and a deep sense of care for those who are marginalized or oppressed. Their commitment to justice is grounded in a desire to alleviate suffering and create a world where all individuals can live with dignity, freedom, and equality.

Resilience and Perseverance

Resilience and perseverance are defining traits of the Khalsa warriors. They stay unwavering in their dedication to the principles of Sikhism, even when confronted with adversity and hardships. By being resilient, they overcome obstacles and setbacks and emerge stronger and more determined to pursue righteousness.

1. **Steadfast Commitment to Sikh Principles:** Resilience and perseverance enable the Khalsa warrior to remain steadfast in their commitment to Sikh principles, even in the face of adversity and hardship. Regardless of the challenges they encounter, they draw strength from their faith

and convictions, remaining true to the teachings of the Guru and the values of Sikhism. Their unwavering dedication to righteousness serves as a guiding light, sustaining them through difficult times and inspiring others to stay the course.

2. **Courage in the Face of Adversity:** Resilience empowers the Khalsa warrior to confront adversity with courage and determination. They do not waver in the face of challenges but instead meet them head-on, armed with fortitude and resilience. Whether facing personal trials, societal pressures, or external threats, they stand firm in their resolve, refusing to be swayed from their path by fear or doubt. Their courage serves as a beacon of hope and inspiration, encouraging others to persevere in the face of adversity.

3. **Overcoming Obstacles and Setbacks:** Perseverance enables the Khalsa warrior to overcome obstacles and setbacks on their journey. They do not let failures or setbacks deter them from their goals but instead view them as opportunities for growth and learning. With resilience and determination, they rise above challenges, finding creative solutions and alternative pathways to success. Each setback only fuels their determination to succeed, driving them to redouble their efforts and press forward with renewed vigor.

4. **Emerging Stronger and More Determined:** Through resilience and perseverance, the

Khalsa warrior emerges from adversity stronger and more determined than ever. They transform setbacks into stepping stones, using their experiences to build resilience, deepen their understanding, and strengthen their character. Every trial they face serves to sharpen their resolve and fortify their commitment to righteousness, empowering them to face future challenges with confidence and resilience.

5. **Inspiring Others through Example:** The resilience and perseverance of the Khalsa warrior serve as a source of inspiration and encouragement for others. Their ability to overcome adversity with grace and determination inspires admiration and respect, motivating others to persevere in their own struggles. By leading by example, they demonstrate the power of resilience and perseverance in overcoming obstacles and achieving success, inspiring others to cultivate these qualities in their own lives.

Humility and Humbleness

Despite their martial prowess and spiritual strength, the Khalsa warrior remains humble and grounded. They eschew arrogance and ego, recognizing that true greatness lies in humility and service to others. Humbleness is a virtue that fosters unity, cooperation, and mutual respect within the Khalsa community.

1. **Acknowledgment of Limitations:** Despite their martial prowess and spiritual strength, the

Khalsa warrior humbly acknowledges their limitations and imperfections. They recognize that true greatness does not stem from arrogance or self-aggrandizement but from a humble recognition of one's own strengths and weaknesses. By embracing humility, they cultivate a sense of authenticity and self-awareness, allowing them to approach life with a sense of openness and humility.

2. **Eschewing Arrogance and Ego:** Humility prompts the Khalsa warrior to eschew arrogance and ego, refraining from boasting or seeking validation from external sources. They remain grounded in their identity and purpose, unaffected by the trappings of fame or power. Instead of seeking personal glory, they prioritize the well-being of others and the greater good, embodying the selfless spirit of service and sacrifice.

3. **Service to Others:** Humility is closely intertwined with the Khalsa warrior's commitment to service to others. They recognize that true greatness lies not in the accumulation of wealth or status but in the selfless act of serving others with humility and compassion. Whether through acts of seva (selfless service), charitable giving, or community outreach, they prioritize the needs of others above their own, seeking to uplift and empower those who are marginalized or in need.

4. **Fostering Unity and Respect:** Humbleness fosters unity, cooperation, and mutual respect within the Khalsa community. By eschewing arrogance and ego, the Khalsa warrior creates an environment of inclusivity and equality, where all individuals are valued and respected regardless of their background or status. Humility promotes a sense of camaraderie and solidarity, strengthening the bonds of fellowship and mutual support within the Khalsa community.

5. **Cultivating a Teachable Spirit:** Humility allows the Khalsa warrior to cultivate a teachable spirit, remaining open to learning and growth. They approach life with a sense of curiosity and humility, recognizing that there is always more to learn and discover. By embracing a mindset of continuous improvement, they seek wisdom and guidance from others, humbly acknowledging that they do not have all the answers.

Duty to Protect the Oppressed and Uphold Justice

The duty to protect the oppressed and uphold justice is a sacred responsibility that lies at the heart of the Khalsa warrior's mission. Grounded in Sikh teachings of compassion, equality, and righteousness, they stand as guardians of human dignity and champions of social justice, striving to create a world where all individuals can live with dignity, freedom, and respect.

1. **Guardian of the Vulnerable:** The Khalsa warrior sees it as their duty to protect those who are vulnerable and oppressed, standing as a shield against injustice and tyranny. They advocate for the rights and dignity of all individuals, particularly those who are marginalized or disenfranchised. Whether it's defending religious freedoms, championing the rights of minorities, or advocating for gender equality, they are unwavering in their commitment to safeguarding the rights of the oppressed.

2. **Upholding the Principles of Justice:** Upholding justice is at the core of the Khalsa warrior's mission. They strive to ensure that all individuals are treated with fairness, equality, and respect under the law. This includes holding accountable those who abuse their power or exploit others for personal gain. The Khalsa warrior serves as a beacon of righteousness, challenging corruption, discrimination, and oppression wherever they may be found.

3. **Speaking Truth to Power:** The Khalsa warrior fearlessly speaks truth to power, confronting authority figures and institutions that perpetuate injustice or violate human rights. They refuse to remain silent in the face of oppression, using their voice and influence to advocate for positive change. Whether it's through peaceful protest, civil disobedience, or legal advocacy, they strive to hold accountable those who abuse their power and privilege.

4. **Defending Human Dignity:** Central to the duty of the Khalsa warrior is the defense of human dignity in all its forms. They recognize the inherent worth and value of every individual, regardless of their background, beliefs, or social status. This includes defending the rights of the marginalized, protecting the vulnerable, and advocating for the humane treatment of all beings. The Khalsa warrior is committed to creating a world where every person can live with dignity, freedom, and respect.

5. **Embodying Compassionate Justice:** While upholding justice, the Khalsa warrior does so with compassion and empathy. They recognize that true justice is not merely punitive but restorative, seeking to address root causes of injustice and promote healing and reconciliation. Their approach to justice is grounded in Sikh teachings of compassion, forgiveness, and redemption, aiming to create a society where all individuals can thrive and flourish.

6. **Sacrifice for the Greater Good:** The duty to protect the oppressed and uphold justice often requires sacrifice on the part of the Khalsa warrior. They willingly put themselves in harm's way, risking their safety and well-being for the greater good. Whether it's standing up against oppressive regimes, defending the rights of the marginalized, or advocating for social change, they are prepared to make personal sacrifices in service to their principles and values.

The Connection Between Spirituality and Warriorhood

The link between spirituality and warrior ethos in Sikhism is deeply interwoven, forming the bedrock of the Khalsa warrior's identity. In Sikh philosophy, spiritual growth, and martial valor are seen as complementary facets of a complete life.

1. **Spiritual Foundation:** Sikhism places great emphasis on spiritual development as the core of righteous living. The Sikh scripture, Sri Guru Granth Sahib, serves as a guide, offering teachings on truth-seeking, devotion, and service to humanity. The Khalsa warrior draws guidance and strength from these spiritual teachings, anchoring their actions in a profound connection to Waheguru (God) and a commitment to Sikh values.

2. **Inner Strength and Resilience:** Spiritual practices like meditation and prayer foster inner strength and resilience in the Khalsa warrior. Through spiritual introspection, they deepen their bond with the divine and draw upon spiritual wisdom to navigate life's challenges. This inner fortitude empowers them to face adversity with unwavering resolve.

3. **Moral Code:** Sikhism provides a comprehensive moral code, the Rehat Maryada, which governs the conduct of the Khalsa warrior. This code underscores virtues such as honesty, humility, and justice. Even in times of conflict, the Khalsa warrior upholds these

principles, ensuring that their actions are guided by righteousness.

4. **Warrior Ethos:** While Sikhism advocates peace, it recognizes the need for self-defense and protection against injustice. The Khalsa warrior embodies this ethos, defending the oppressed and upholding justice with courage. However, their martial spirit is tempered by spiritual values, ensuring that their actions are grounded in compassion and ethical conduct.

5. **Service to Humanity:** Spirituality and warrior ethos converge in the concept of seva, or selfless service. The Khalsa warrior views their martial skills not as tools of aggression, but as instruments for serving humanity and protecting the vulnerable. Whether through charity or community service, they embody the spirit of seva, understanding that true greatness lies in serving others.

6. **Transcendence of Ego:** Central to this connection is the transcendence of ego, a core Sikh teaching. The Khalsa warrior cultivates humility, overcoming arrogance and pride. By shedding ego, they embrace virtues like compassion and unity, fostering a sense of kinship with all beings.

The relationship between spirituality and warrior ethos in Sikhism represents a harmonious fusion of martial prowess with spiritual values. The Khalsa warrior draws strength from spiritual practice, adheres to a moral code, and serves humanity with courage and compassion, embodying Sikh ideals in both spiritual and martial pursuits.

Chardi Kala (Eternal Optimism)

Chardi Kala embodies the Sikh ethos of eternal optimism and resilience. It encourages individuals to maintain a positive outlook and unwavering spirit, even in the most challenging circumstances. This mindset fosters inner strength, courage, and hope, empowering individuals to navigate life's complexities with grace and dignity.

Chardi Kala, derived from the Panjabi words "Chardi" meaning rising or ascending, and "Kala" meaning state or spirit, embodies the idea of maintaining a mindset of eternal optimism and resilience. It reflects a deep-seated belief in the inherent goodness of life and the ability to remain hopeful and positive, even in the midst of challenges and hardships.

At its core, Chardi Kala is deeply rooted in Sikh teachings and values. It is derived from the Sikh worldview that emphasizes the transient nature of worldly affairs and the eternal nature of the soul. Sikhism teaches that life is inherently filled with challenges, trials, and tribulations, but maintaining a positive mindset is essential to navigate through these obstacles with grace and strength.

Chardi Kala encourages individuals to cultivate an indomitable spirit, fortitude, and resilience in the face of life's ups and downs. It does not imply denying or ignoring the existence of difficulties but rather approaching them with courage, optimism, and determination. This resilience enables individuals to bounce back from setbacks, overcome obstacles, and emerge stronger than before.

One of the fundamental aspects of Chardi Kala is its emphasis on hope. Regardless of the severity of the circumstances, Chardi Kala instills a sense of hopefulness and confidence in the ultimate goodness of life. It teaches individuals to find silver linings, opportunities for growth, and reasons to be grateful even amidst challenges.

Moreover, Chardi Kala is not limited to individual well-being but extends to the collective spirit of the Sikh community. It fosters a culture of solidarity, mutual support, and collective empowerment, wherein individuals uplift and inspire one another through their optimistic outlook and resilient attitude.

In practice, Chardi Kala is manifested through various aspects of Sikh life, including prayer, meditation, community engagement, and selfless service (seva). Sikh teachings emphasize the importance of maintaining a positive mindset during both joyful and difficult times, trusting in the divine will, and striving to live with courage, compassion, and integrity.

Chardi Kala serves as a guiding principle for Sikhs, encouraging them to embody optimism, resilience, and hopefulness in every aspect of life. It underscores the belief that maintaining a positive attitude is not only conducive to personal well-being but also essential for navigating life's challenges and contributing positively to the world around us.

Facing Adversity with Courage

Chardi Kala encourages individuals to confront adversity with courage and fortitude, viewing challenges as opportunities for growth and learning rather than insurmountable obstacles. It teaches that setbacks and failures are temporary and that one can emerge stronger and more resilient through perseverance and determination.

1. **Confronting Challenges Head-On:** Chardi Kala teaches individuals to confront challenges head-on without succumbing to fear or despair. Instead of avoiding difficulties or seeking shortcuts, individuals are encouraged to tackle obstacles with courage and determination. By facing adversity directly, individuals are better equipped to overcome obstacles and emerge stronger on the other side.

2. **Opportunities for Growth and Learning:** Rather than viewing adversity as a setback, Chardi Kala encourages individuals to see it as an opportunity for growth and learning. Adversity provides valuable lessons and insights that can help individuals develop new skills, strengths, and perspectives. By embracing challenges as opportunities for personal growth, individuals can transform setbacks into stepping stones toward success.

3. **Temporary Nature of Setbacks:** Chardi Kala instills the belief that setbacks and failures are temporary and transient. While challenges may seem insurmountable at the moment, they are

not permanent obstacles. By maintaining a positive outlook and persevering through difficult times, individuals can overcome adversity and emerge stronger and more resilient than before.

4. **Building Resilience Through Perseverance:** Perseverance is a key component of Chardi Kala, as it enables individuals to weather the storms of life with resilience and determination. Rather than giving up in the face of adversity, individuals are encouraged to keep pushing forward with unwavering resolve. Through perseverance, individuals build resilience and develop the inner strength needed to overcome even the most daunting challenges.

5. **Strength in Unity:** Chardi Kala fosters a sense of unity and solidarity within the Sikh community, where individuals support and uplift one another in times of adversity. By coming together as a community, individuals can draw strength from one another and face challenges with courage and determination. The collective spirit of unity and support reinforces individual resilience and empowers individuals to overcome adversity together.

Embracing Acceptance and Equanimity

Central to the concept of Chardi Kala is the idea of embracing acceptance and equanimity in the face of life's ups and downs. It encourages individuals to maintain a sense of inner peace and tranquility, regardless of external circumstances, recognizing that true happiness comes from within and is not dependent on external factors.

1. **Inner Peace Amidst Turbulence:** Chardi Kala teaches individuals to cultivate a sense of inner peace and tranquility, irrespective of external circumstances. Rather than being swayed by the highs and lows of life, individuals are encouraged to anchor themselves in a state of inner calmness and serenity. This inner peace serves as a source of strength and resilience, enabling individuals to navigate through life's challenges with grace and fortitude.

2. **Recognition of Impermanence:** Central to Chardi Kala is the recognition of the impermanent nature of worldly affairs. Sikh teachings emphasize the transient nature of material possessions, relationships, and experiences. By acknowledging the impermanence of external factors, individuals can cultivate a deeper sense of equanimity and detachment, realizing that true happiness lies beyond the fluctuations of the external world.

3. **Freedom from Attachment:** Chardi Kala encourages individuals to free themselves from attachment to external outcomes and circumstances. Rather than seeking happiness and fulfillment in external achievements or possessions, individuals are urged to find contentment and satisfaction within themselves. By releasing attachment to outcomes, individuals can maintain a sense of inner peace

and equanimity, regardless of whether situations unfold as expected or not.

4. **Embracing the Present Moment:** Embracing acceptance and equanimity involves fully embracing the present moment without dwelling on the past or worrying about the future. Chardi Kala teaches individuals to live mindfully and fully engage with each moment as it unfolds. By staying grounded in the present moment, individuals can cultivate a deeper sense of peace and tranquility, irrespective of external circumstances.

5. **Source of True Happiness:** Chardi Kala emphasizes that true happiness comes from within and is not dependent on external factors. Rather than seeking happiness in external achievements or circumstances, individuals are encouraged to cultivate inner joy and contentment. By nurturing a positive mindset and embracing acceptance and equanimity, individuals can tap into a lasting source of happiness that transcends the ups and downs of life.

Cultivating Resilience and Positivity

Chardi Kala emphasizes the importance of cultivating resilience and positivity in all aspects of life. It encourages individuals to focus on their strengths and capabilities rather than dwelling on their weaknesses or limitations. By maintaining a positive mindset, one can overcome adversity more effectively and bounce back from setbacks with renewed vigor and determination.

1. **Focus on Strengths and Capabilities:** Chardi Kala encourages individuals to focus on their strengths and capabilities rather than fixating on their weaknesses or limitations. By recognizing and leveraging their inherent strengths, individuals can approach challenges with confidence and determination. This shift in focus empowers individuals to tap into their potential and find creative solutions to overcome obstacles.

2. **Optimistic Mindset:** Central to Chardi Kala is the cultivation of an optimistic mindset. Rather than dwelling on negative thoughts or outcomes, individuals are encouraged to adopt a positive outlook and maintain faith in their ability to overcome challenges. An optimistic mindset not only enhances resilience but also fosters a sense of hopefulness and confidence in the face of adversity.

3. **Effective Coping Strategies:** Chardi Kala promotes the use of effective coping strategies to navigate through difficult times. Individuals are encouraged to develop healthy coping mechanisms, such as seeking social support, practicing mindfulness, and engaging in self-care activities. By proactively managing stress and adversity, individuals can build resilience and maintain a positive mindset even in the midst of challenges.

4. **Learning from Setbacks:** Chardi Kala emphasizes the importance of viewing setbacks as learning opportunities rather than failures. Instead of being discouraged by setbacks, individuals are encouraged to reflect on their experiences, identify lessons learned, and use them as stepping stones for personal growth and development. This mindset shift enables individuals to bounce back from setbacks with renewed determination and resilience.

5. **Renewed Vigor and Determination:** By maintaining a positive outlook and focusing on their strengths, individuals can bounce back from setbacks with renewed vigor and determination. Chardi Kala teaches individuals to persevere in the face of adversity, harnessing their inner strength and resilience to overcome obstacles and pursue their goals with unwavering resolve.

6. **Creating Positive Momentum:** Cultivating resilience and positivity creates a positive momentum that propels individuals forward in their journey. By maintaining a constructive mindset and actively seeking opportunities for growth and development, individuals can build on their successes and continue to thrive even in challenging circumstances.

Spreading Hope and Optimism

Sikhism teaches that individuals who embody Chardi Kala have the power to inspire and uplift others through their optimism and positivity. By radiating hope and optimism, they can create a ripple effect of positivity that uplifts those around them and fosters a sense of unity and solidarity within the community.

1. **Radiating Hope and Positivity:** Individuals who embody Chardi Kala are characterized by their optimistic outlook and positive demeanor. They radiate hope and positivity in their interactions with others, regardless of the challenges they may be facing personally. Their uplifting presence serves as a beacon of light, illuminating the lives of those around them and infusing hope into even the darkest of circumstances.

2. **Creating a Ripple Effect:** The optimism and positivity of individuals who embody Chardi Kala have the power to create a ripple effect within their communities. By spreading hope and optimism, they inspire others to adopt a similar mindset and approach to life's challenges. This ripple effect cascades through the community, uplifting spirits and fostering a sense of unity and solidarity among its members.

3. **Inspiring Resilience and Determination:** The presence of individuals who embody Chardi Kala inspires resilience and determination in others. Their unwavering optimism in the face of adversity serves as a source of strength and motivation for those around them. By witnessing the resilience and determination of others, individuals are encouraged to persevere through their own challenges with renewed vigor and determination.

4. **Fostering a Sense of Unity and Solidarity:** The optimism and positivity of individuals who embody Chardi Kala foster a sense of unity and solidarity within the community. Their uplifting presence brings people together, creating a supportive environment where individuals can lean on one another for strength and encouragement. This sense of unity and solidarity strengthens the bonds within the community and empowers its members to face challenges collectively.

5. **Cultivating a Culture of Hopefulness:** Over time, the presence of individuals who embody Chardi Kala cultivates a culture of hopefulness within the community. Their consistent demonstration of optimism and positivity sets a positive example for others to follow, encouraging a shift towards a more hopeful and optimistic mindset among community members. This culture of hopefulness permeates through all aspects of community life, fostering resilience and empowerment among its members.

Connection to Sikh Faith and Values

Chardi Kala is deeply rooted in Sikh faith and values, reflecting the teachings of the Sikh Gurus who exemplified resilience, courage, and optimism in the face of adversity. It is seen as a spiritual virtue that aligns with the core principles of Sikhism, including devotion to Waheguru (God), selfless service, and acceptance of the divine will.

1. **Teachings of the Sikh Gurus:** Chardi Kala finds its foundation in the teachings and example set by the Sikh Gurus, who demonstrated unwavering resilience, courage, and optimism in the face of adversity. From Sri Guru Nanak Dev Ji, the founder of Sikhism, to Sri Guru Gobind Singh Ji, the tenth Sikh Guru, each Guru exemplified the spirit of Chardi Kala, inspiring their followers to adopt a similar mindset.

2. **Resilience in the Face of Persecution:** Throughout Sikh history, the Sikh community has faced persecution and adversity, yet it has always persevered with resilience and determination. The Sikh Gurus and their followers endured countless hardships, including martyrdom, in their struggle to uphold principles of justice, equality, and righteousness. Their steadfast commitment to their faith, even in the most challenging of circumstances, exemplifies the spirit of Chardi Kala.

3. **Devotion to Waheguru (God):** At the heart of Sikhism is the concept of devotion to Waheguru, the Supreme Being. Chardi Kala encourages individuals to maintain a positive outlook and unwavering faith in Waheguru, trusting in the divine will and accepting whatever circumstances may arise as part of God's plan. This deep-seated faith provides strength and solace, enabling individuals to navigate through life's challenges with grace and resilience.

4. **Selfless Service (Seva):** Another core principle of Sikhism is the practice of selfless service or seva. Chardi Kala inspires individuals to engage in acts of kindness, compassion, and service to others, even in the face of adversity. By extending a helping hand to those in need, individuals embody the spirit of Chardi Kala and contribute to the well-being of their community.

5. **Acceptance of Divine Will:** Chardi Kala emphasizes the acceptance of the divine will, recognizing that all circumstances are part of Waheguru's plan. Even in times of difficulty or hardship, individuals are encouraged to maintain an optimistic outlook and trust in the greater purpose behind life's trials and tribulations. This acceptance fosters inner peace and resilience, enabling individuals to face challenges with courage and equanimity.

Training and Preparation of Warrior Spirit

Training and preparation are essential components of embodying the warrior spirit of the Khalsa in Sikhism. Through physical, martial, tactical, spiritual, and communal training, Khalsa warriors equip themselves with the skills, discipline, and resilience needed to uphold Sikh principles, defend righteousness, and serve humanity with unwavering dedication and courage.

Physical Training

Physical fitness is essential for Khalsa warriors, as it enables them to endure the rigors of battle and perform their duties effectively. Training in physical strength, agility, and endurance is often emphasized to prepare individuals for the demands of combat. This training may include activities such as martial arts, wrestling, running, and strength training.

1. **Endurance Training:** Endurance is crucial for Khalsa warriors, as battles can be prolonged and physically demanding. Training often includes cardiovascular exercises such as running, swimming, and cycling to build stamina and improve cardiovascular health. Endurance training helps warriors sustain their energy levels and performance throughout extended engagements.

2. **Strength Training:** Strength is essential for Khalsa warriors to wield weapons effectively, engage in hand-to-hand combat, and carry heavy gear. Strength training focuses on developing muscle strength and power through exercises like weightlifting, bodyweight exercises, and resistance training. Building strength enhances warriors' ability to execute combat maneuvers and withstand physical challenges on the battlefield.

3. **Agility and Speed Training:** Agility and speed are critical for Khalsa warriors to maneuver swiftly and evade enemy attacks. Training drills focus on improving agility, reflexes, and coordination through activities such as agility ladder drills, plyometric exercises, and speed training. Enhanced agility enables warriors to react quickly to changing battlefield conditions and outmaneuver opponents with precision.

4. **Martial Arts and Combat Training:** Khalsa warriors undergo training in martial arts and combat techniques to effectively engage adversaries in hand-to-hand combat. Training may include learning techniques from traditional Sikh martial arts, such as Gatka, as well as other combat disciplines like boxing, wrestling, and judo. Martial arts training hones warriors' striking, grappling, and defensive skills, equipping them to confront threats with confidence and proficiency.

5. **Flexibility and Mobility Exercises:** Flexibility and mobility are essential for Khalsa warriors to maintain agility and prevent injuries during combat. Stretching exercises and mobility drills help improve flexibility, range of motion, and joint mobility, reducing the risk of strains and sprains. Enhanced flexibility enables warriors to move fluidly and execute combat techniques with precision and efficiency.

6. **Recovery and Injury Prevention:** Proper recovery and injury prevention strategies are integral to physical training for Khalsa warriors. Adequate rest, hydration, and nutrition are emphasized to support muscle recovery and optimize performance. Additionally, injury prevention techniques such as proper warm-up, cool-down, and stretching routines are incorporated into training to minimize the risk of injuries during rigorous physical activities.

Gatka and Weaponry

Khalsa warriors are trained in various forms of martial arts and weaponry to defend themselves and others against oppression and injustice. Training in traditional Sikh martial arts, such as Gatka, helps individuals develop skills in hand-to-hand combat, swordsmanship, and other forms of armed and unarmed combat. Additionally, proficiency in wielding traditional Sikh weapons, such as the kirpan (ceremonial sword), is often imparted through rigorous training and practice.

1. **Traditional Sikh Martial Arts:** Khalsa warriors receive training in traditional Sikh martial arts, with Gatka being one of the prominent disciplines. Gatka is a centuries-old martial art that originated in Panjab and is characterized by its emphasis on both armed and unarmed combat techniques. Training in Gatka includes drills, forms, and sparring sessions aimed at developing proficiency in various aspects of combat, including striking, blocking, grappling, and footwork.

2. **Hand-to-Hand Combat Skills:** Martial arts training equips Khalsa warriors with effective hand-to-hand combat skills, enabling them to engage adversaries in close-quarters combat. Techniques such as punches, kicks, joint locks, and throws are taught to warriors to incapacitate opponents and defend themselves in unarmed combat situations. Training in hand-to-hand combat enhances warriors' confidence and

ability to confront threats without relying solely on weapons.

3. **Swordsmanship and Weapons Training:** Proficiency in wielding traditional Sikh weapons, such as the kirpan (ceremonial sword), is a cornerstone of Khalsa warrior training. Warriors undergo rigorous training and practice to master the art of swordsmanship, learning techniques for both offensive and defensive maneuvers. Training with weapons also extends to other traditional Sikh arms, including the talwar (sword), khanda (double-edged sword), and Chaker (throwing disc).

4. **Ranged Weapons Training:** In addition to melee weapons, Khalsa warriors receive training in the use of ranged weapons such as bows and arrows. Archery training focuses on developing accuracy, precision, and timing in shooting arrows at targets. Mastery of ranged weapons adds versatility to warriors' combat skills, allowing them to engage adversaries from a distance and complementing their proficiency in close-quarters combat.

5. **Combat Drills and Sparring:** Training in martial arts and weaponry involves regular practice of combat drills and sparring sessions. Combat drills help warriors refine their techniques, improve their timing, and develop muscle memory for effective combat execution. Sparring sessions provide warriors with practical experience in applying their skills against live opponents, simulating real-life

combat scenarios and enhancing their readiness for battle.

6. **Ethical and Spiritual Dimension:** Martial arts and weaponry training in Sikhism are not solely focused on combat skills but also emphasize ethical conduct and spiritual development. Warriors are taught to use their skills responsibly and uphold Sikh principles of righteousness, compassion, and justice. The discipline and dedication required in martial training also contribute to spiritual growth, fostering qualities such as discipline, resilience, and self-mastery.

Tactical Training

Tactical training is essential for Khalsa warriors to effectively strategize and respond to different combat scenarios. This training involves learning tactics, maneuvers, and formations tailored to specific battlefield situations. Khalsa warriors are trained to think critically, adapt quickly, and make sound decisions under pressure to outmaneuver their adversaries and achieve their objectives.

1. **Understanding Battlefield Dynamics:** Tactical training begins with a comprehensive understanding of battlefield dynamics. Khalsa warriors learn to assess terrain, identify strategic advantages, and anticipate enemy movements. By understanding the geographical and environmental factors at play, warriors can formulate effective tactical plans and make informed decisions in the heat of battle.

2. **Learning Tactical Maneuvers:** Khalsa warriors are trained in a range of tactical maneuvers designed to outmaneuver adversaries and gain the upper hand in combat. This includes tactics such as flanking, encirclement, ambush, and diversionary tactics. By mastering these maneuvers, warriors can exploit weaknesses in the enemy's defenses and create opportunities for success on the battlefield.

3. **Adapting to Changing Situations:** Tactical training emphasizes the importance of adaptability and flexibility in response to evolving combat scenarios. Khalsa warriors are taught to think critically and make rapid decisions under pressure, adjusting their tactics and strategies as the situation demands. This ability to adapt to changing circumstances is essential for maintaining the initiative and overcoming unexpected challenges.

4. **Formations and Coordination:** Tactical training includes instruction in various formations and formations designed to optimize combat effectiveness and coordination among warriors. Formations such as wedges, echelons, and skirmish lines are tailored to specific objectives and battlefield conditions. Khalsa warriors practice coordinating their movements and actions within these formations to maximize their collective strength and effectiveness.

5. **Communications and Command Structure:** Effective communication is essential for

coordinating tactical maneuvers and maintaining cohesion among Khalsa warriors. Tactical training includes instruction in communication protocols, signaling methods, and command structures to facilitate clear and efficient communication on the battlefield. This ensures that warriors can relay orders, convey situational awareness, and coordinate actions effectively, even in chaotic environments.

6. **Scenario-based Training Exercises:** Tactical training is reinforced through scenario-based exercises that simulate realistic combat situations. Khalsa warriors participate in simulated battles, ambushes, and rescue missions to apply their tactical knowledge and skills in a controlled environment. These exercises provide valuable hands-on experience and help warriors develop confidence in their ability to execute tactical maneuvers under pressure.

Discipline and Self-Control

Discipline and self-control are foundational principles in Khalsa training. Khalsa warriors undergo rigorous discipline to cultivate self-mastery and restraint in all aspects of their lives. This includes adherence to a code of conduct that upholds Sikh values of honesty, integrity, and compassion. Through disciplined practice and adherence to Sikh principles, individuals develop the inner strength and resilience needed to face challenges with courage and conviction.

1. **Adherence to a Code of Conduct:** Khalsa warriors adhere to a strict code of conduct rooted in Sikh values, including honesty, integrity, and compassion. This code governs their thoughts, words, and actions, guiding them to uphold ethical standards in all aspects of life. Through unwavering commitment to this code, warriors cultivate a sense of moral clarity and integrity that strengthens their resolve in the face of adversity.

2. **Rigorous Training Regimen:** Discipline is ingrained into every aspect of Khalsa training, from physical conditioning to spiritual practice. Warriors adhere to a rigorous training regimen that demands dedication, focus, and perseverance. Whether engaging in physical exercises, martial arts drills, or spiritual rituals, warriors approach their training with a disciplined mindset, striving for continuous improvement and mastery.

3. **Self-Mastery and Emotional Regulation:** Self-control is paramount for Khalsa warriors, enabling them to maintain composure and clarity of mind in challenging situations. Through disciplined practice, warriors learn to regulate their emotions, impulses, and reactions, preventing impulsive behavior and maintaining a calm, centered demeanor even amidst chaos. This inner discipline empowers warriors to make rational decisions and act with purpose rather than succumbing to fear or anger.

4. **Respect for Authority and Tradition:** Discipline in Khalsa training involves respecting authority and adhering to established traditions and protocols. Warriors honor their leaders, mentors, and elders, recognizing their wisdom and guidance. They also uphold the traditions and rituals passed down through generations, understanding their significance in preserving the cultural and spiritual heritage of the Khalsa community.

5. **Commitment to Continuous Learning:** Discipline in Khalsa training extends to a commitment to lifelong learning and growth. Warriors approach their training with humility and a willingness to learn from experiences, mistakes, and feedback. They continuously seek to refine their skills, deepen their knowledge, and broaden their perspective, recognizing that self-discipline is essential for personal and professional development.

6. **Integration of Spiritual Discipline:** Spiritual discipline is integral to Khalsa training, fostering a deep connection with Waheguru (God) and aligning actions with Sikh principles. Warriors engage in daily spiritual practices, including prayer, meditation, and recitation of sacred texts, to nurture their spiritual well-being and cultivate inner strength. This spiritual discipline strengthens warriors' resolve, fortifies their faith, and imbues their actions with purpose and meaning.

Spiritual Training

In Sikhism, spiritual training is inseparable from physical and martial training. Khalsa warriors undergo spiritual discipline to cultivate a deep connection with Waheguru (God) and align their actions with Sikh principles. This training involves daily prayers, meditation, and recitation of hymns from the Sri Guru Granth Sahib, the living Sikh Guru. Spiritual training strengthens Khalsa warriors' resolve, instills a sense of purpose, and provides guidance in upholding righteousness on and off the battlefield.

1. **Daily Prayer and Meditation:** Khalsa warriors engage in daily prayer and meditation practices to nurture their spiritual connection with Waheguru (God) and cultivate inner peace and tranquility. Through prayer, warriors express gratitude, seek guidance, and reaffirm their devotion to Waheguru. Meditation helps warriors quiet the mind, deepen their spiritual awareness, and develop a profound sense of presence and mindfulness.

2. **Recitation of Sacred Hymns:** Recitation of hymns from the Sri Guru Granth Sahib Ji is a cornerstone of spiritual training for Khalsa warriors. Warriors immerse themselves in the divine wisdom and teachings contained within the Sri Guru Granth Sahib Ji, drawing inspiration, solace, and guidance from its sacred verses. Reciting hymns fosters a deep connection with Sikh spirituality and reinforces warriors' commitment to Sikh principles.

3. **Study of Granths:** Khalsa warriors devote time to studying all religious Granths to deepen their understanding of Sikh philosophy, history, and ethics. Studying scripture provides warriors with spiritual insights, moral guidance, and practical wisdom that informs their actions and decision-making on and off the battlefield. It fosters intellectual curiosity and a thirst for spiritual knowledge among warriors.

4. **Participation in Religious Ceremonies:** Warriors actively participate in religious ceremonies and rituals within the Sikh tradition to cultivate a sense of community, reverence, and spiritual connection. This may include attending Gurdwara (Sikh place of worship) services, participating in Kirtan (devotional singing), and observing important Sikh festivals and commemorations. Engaging in religious practices strengthens warriors' bonds with their faith community and reinforces their spiritual identity as Khalsa warriors.

5. **Seeking Spiritual Guidance:** Khalsa warriors seek spiritual guidance from experienced mentors, spiritual leaders, and elders within the Sikh community to deepen their understanding of Sikh principles and navigate spiritual challenges. Mentors offer wisdom, counsel, and encouragement, guiding warriors on their spiritual journey and helping them integrate spiritual teachings into their daily lives. This mentorship fosters a sense of accountability, support, and growth among warriors.

6. **Integration into Daily Life:** Spiritual training is seamlessly integrated into the daily lives of Khalsa warriors, infusing every aspect of their existence with spiritual consciousness and mindfulness. Whether in combat or in times of peace, warriors strive to uphold Sikh values and principles, guided by their spiritual convictions and commitment to righteousness. Spiritual training serves as a moral compass, guiding warriors to act with compassion, integrity, and humility in all circumstances.

Community Support and Mentorship

Khalsa warriors often receive support and mentorship from experienced veterans and members of their community. Elders and seasoned warriors pass down knowledge, skills, and wisdom to the next generation, ensuring continuity in the training and preparation of Khalsa warriors. This sense of community support fosters camaraderie, accountability, and collective responsibility among Khalsa warriors as they strive to fulfill their duty to protect and serve.

1. **Passing Down Knowledge and Wisdom:** Experienced veterans and elders within the Sikh community serve as mentors, passing down their knowledge, skills, and wisdom to the next generation of Khalsa warriors. Through oral tradition, storytelling, and personal guidance, mentors impart valuable lessons learned from their own experiences on the battlefield and in life. This transfer of knowledge ensures continuity in the training and preparation of

Khalsa warriors, preserving traditional practices and teachings for future generations.

2. **Guidance and Advice:** Mentors provide guidance, advice, and mentorship to young warriors, offering support and encouragement as they navigate their training and service. Mentors draw upon their own experiences and expertise to offer insights into combat tactics, strategic thinking, and ethical conduct. They serve as trusted advisors and role models, inspiring warriors to uphold Sikh principles and strive for excellence in all endeavors.

3. **Fostering Camaraderie and Brotherhood:** Community support and mentorship foster a sense of camaraderie and brotherhood among Khalsa warriors, creating a tight-knit bond based on shared values and experiences. Warriors support and uplift one another, forming deep connections forged in the crucible of training and service. This sense of camaraderie strengthens morale, builds trust, and instills a sense of belonging within the Khalsa community.

4. **Accountability and Discipline:** Mentors hold warriors accountable for upholding the principles of Sikhism and maintaining discipline in their training and conduct. They provide constructive feedback, correction, and guidance to help warriors stay on the path of righteousness and personal growth. This accountability fosters a culture of excellence and integrity within the Khalsa community,

ensuring that warriors uphold the highest standards of conduct and service.

5. **Empowerment and Encouragement:** Mentors empower and encourage young warriors to fulfill their potential and embrace their roles as defenders of righteousness. They instill confidence, resilience, and determination in warriors, helping them overcome challenges and adversity with courage and conviction. Mentors celebrate achievements, milestones, and successes, providing unwavering support and encouragement along the journey of training and service.

6. **Building a Legacy of Service:** Community support and mentorship contribute to building a legacy of service and sacrifice within the Khalsa community. Through the guidance and mentorship of experienced veterans and elders, young warriors are inspired to carry forward the traditions and values of Sikhism, dedicating themselves to the noble cause of protecting and serving humanity. This legacy of service endures across generations, ensuring that the spirit of the Khalsa remains vibrant and resilient in the face of adversity.

Some Legendary Khalsa Warriors

The history of Sikhism is replete with stories of legendary Khalsa warriors whose valor, skill, and unwavering devotion to Sikh principles have left an indelible mark on Sikh lore. While specific details of their training regimens may vary, these warriors exemplified the spirit of the Khalsa through their exceptional courage, martial prowess, and commitment to righteousness. Some renowned Khalsa warriors and their training journeys:

1. Baba Bidhi chand Chhina
2. Bhai Bachittar Singh
3. Mai Bhago
4. Baba Deep Singh
5. Bana Banda singh Bahadur
6. Maharaja Ranjit Singh
7. Hari Singh Nalwa
8. Akali Fula Singh
9. Sardar Sham Singh Attari
10. Sant Jarnail Singh

Baba Bidhi Chand Chhina

Baba Bidhi Chand Chhina is a cherished figure in Sikh history who exemplifies the virtues of bravery, tenacity, and altruism. Hailing from the Chhina clan of Panjab, his life story is defined by his unyielding commitment to Sikh values and extraordinary feats on the front lines.

Baba Bidhi Chand's early life was steeped in his community's martial traditions. He received training in combat skills, horse riding, and weaponry, laying the foundation for his future exploits as a warrior. However, it was his encounter with Sri Guru Hargobind Sahib Ji, the sixth Sikh Guru, that transformed his life and set him on a path of spiritual and martial enlightenment.

Inspired by Sri Guru Hargobind Sahib Ji's teachings, Baba Bidhi Chand embraced the Sikh faith wholeheartedly and dedicated himself to serving the Guru's mission. He joined the Guru's retinue and became a devoted disciple, immersing himself in the study of Sikh scriptures and participating in the Guru's military campaigns against tyranny and oppression.

Baba Bidhi Chand's most famous exploit revolves around the recovery of Sri Guru Hargobind Sahib Ji's horses. When the Guru's prized steeds were seized by the Mughal governor of Lahore, Baba Bidhi Chand undertook a daring mission to retrieve them. Disguised as a Muslim faqir, he infiltrated the governor's stronghold and skillfully orchestrated the horses' rescue, leading them back to the Guru's camp with bravery.

This audacious act earned Baba Bidhi Chand widespread acclaim and cemented his reputation as a fearless warrior and master strategist. His ingenuity, resourcefulness, and unwavering commitment to the Guru's cause became legendary, inspiring awe and admiration among his fellow Sikhs.

Throughout his life, Baba Bidhi Chand remained steadfast in his devotion to Sikhism and continued to serve the community with humility and dedication. He played a pivotal role in safeguarding Sikh principles and upholding justice, earning him a revered place in Sikh folklore and history.

Baba Bidhi Chand's legacy endures as a shining example of Sikh valor, righteousness, and selfless service. His life story serves as a timeless reminder of the transformative power of faith, courage, and unwavering devotion to truth and justice. Today, Sikhs honor Baba Bidhi Chand's memory as a beloved saint-soldier whose indomitable spirit continues to inspire generations.

Bhai Bachittar Singh Ji

Bhai Bachittar Singh Ji is a revered figure in Sikh history, known for his exceptional bravery and selflessness. He has inspired generations with his unwavering commitment to Sikh principles and his valor on the battlefield. Singh Ji was trained in the ancient martial arts of Gatka and Shastar Vidiya, and he exhibited unparalleled skill with traditional Sikh weapons such as the kirpan and chakra. His training regimen was rigorous and comprehensive, emphasizing mastery of combat techniques, agility, reflexes, and mental resilience.

From a young age, Bhai Bachittar Singh Ji would have undergone intensive training under experienced mentors, learning the intricacies of Gatka and Shastar Vidiya—the traditional martial arts of the Sikhs. These disciplines encompassed a wide array of combat techniques, including swordsmanship, stick fighting, and unarmed combat. Bhai Bachittar Singh Ji would have dedicated countless hours to perfecting his skills, honing his ability to wield weapons with precision and efficiency.

Central to his training would have been the cultivation of agility and reflexes—essential attributes for success on the battlefield. Through rigorous physical conditioning and repetitive practice drills, Bhai Bachittar Singh Ji would have developed lightning-fast reactions and the ability to maneuver swiftly in combat situations. His training would have instilled in him a keen awareness of his surroundings and the capacity to anticipate and respond to enemy movements with precision.

Mental resilience was another cornerstone of Bhai Bachittar Singh Ji's training regimen. He would have undergone mental conditioning exercises designed to fortify his resolve and steel his mind against the challenges of warfare. Meditation, visualization techniques, and exposure to simulated combat scenarios would have prepared him to maintain composure and focus under the stress and chaos of battle.

Bhai Bachittar Singh Ji's valorous deeds on the battlefield against the formidable forces of the Mughals and Afghans are legendary. His unwavering courage, unwavering dedication to Sikh principles, and selflessness in the face of danger continue to inspire Sikh warriors to this day. His legacy serves as a testament to the enduring spirit of the Khalsa—a spirit characterized by courage, discipline, and an unwavering commitment to righteousness.

Mai Bhago Ji

Mai Bhago celebrated as a fearless warrior and inspirational leader in Sikh history, remains an iconic figure whose valor and dedication continue to inspire generations. Trained in the art of warfare, she demonstrated exceptional courage and determination on the battlefield, embodying the martial spirit of the Khalsa. Mai Bhago's training regimen would have encompassed various aspects essential for combat readiness, including physical conditioning, weapons proficiency, and tactical strategy. Physical conditioning would have included endurance training, strength exercises, and agility drills to ensure she was in optimal shape for battle. Additionally, Mai Bhago would have been proficient in the use of traditional Sikh weapons such as the kirpan (sword), talwar (sword), and chakar (throwing disc), honing her skills in weapon handling, swordsmanship, and marksmanship. Her leadership during the Battle of Khidrana (Muktsar) demonstrates her strategic acumen and tactical prowess, organizing a small Jatha of Sikh soldiers to return and fight alongside her against overwhelming odds. Above all, Mai Bhago exemplified unwavering courage and determination in the face of adversity, reflecting her deep commitment to the Khalsa cause and her willingness to sacrifice everything for it. Mai Bhago's legacy serves as a testament to the indomitable spirit of Sikh women and their vital role in defending Sikh principles and upholding justice, inspiring Sikhs around the world as a symbol of courage, resilience, and unwavering devotion to the Sikh faith.

Baba Deep Singh Ji

Baba Deep Singh Ji stands as an indomitable figure in Sikh history, revered for his unwavering commitment to Sikh principles and his legendary valor on the battlefield. Born in 1682, his life journey is marked by a profound dedication to Sikhism and a relentless pursuit of martial excellence. Through his exemplary deeds and unwavering devotion, Baba Deep Singh Ji has left an enduring legacy that continues to inspire generations of Sikhs around the world.

From a young age, Baba Deep Singh Ji displayed a remarkable aptitude for martial pursuits. Under the guidance of experienced mentors, he underwent rigorous training in martial arts and weaponry, honing his skills to perfection. His training regimen likely included proficiency in traditional Sikh weapons such as the kirpan (sword) and shastar (spear), as well as mastery of hand-to-hand combat techniques. Through disciplined practice and unwavering dedication, Baba Deep Singh Ji emerged as a formidable warrior, ready to defend Sikh principles and uphold justice on the battlefield.

Central to Baba Deep Singh Ji's life was his unwavering commitment to Sikhism and its values. He embodied the spirit of the Khalsa—a community of saint-soldiers devoted to righteousness and the protection of the oppressed. Baba Deep Singh Ji's faith in Sikhism was unshakeable, guiding him in all aspects of his life and shaping his actions on and off the battlefield. His deep spiritual connection to Sikh teachings served as a source of strength and inspiration, fueling his courage and determination in the face of adversity.

Baba Deep Singh Ji's legendary valor and martial prowess were put to the test during tumultuous times in Sikh history. He played a pivotal role in various battles and conflicts, defending Sikh principles against oppressive forces and safeguarding the Sikh community from persecution. One of the most iconic moments in Baba Deep Singh Ji's life came during the Battle of Amritsar in 1757. At the age of 75, he led a contingent of Sikh warriors in a courageous defense of the Sri Harmandir Sahib against Afghan invaders. Despite sustaining a mortal wound to his neck, Baba Deep Singh Ji continued to fight valiantly, fulfilling his vow to reach the sanctum of the Sri Harmandir Sahib with his severed head on his hand—a testament to his unwavering resolve and devotion to Sikhism.

The legacy of Baba Deep Singh Ji continues to resonate deeply within the Sikh community and beyond. His life exemplifies the timeless ideals of courage, selflessness, and unwavering devotion to Sikh principles. Through his legendary deeds and acts of valor, Baba Deep Singh Ji inspires Sikhs to uphold the values of justice, righteousness, and compassion in all aspects of their lives.

Baba Deep Singh Ji's legacy extends beyond the battlefield to encompass his role as a spiritual leader and a beacon of guidance for the Sikh community. His deep understanding of Sikh philosophy and his unwavering faith in Sikh teachings serve as a source of inspiration for Sikhs seeking spiritual enlightenment and guidance. Baba Deep Singh Ji's life journey exemplifies the inseparable connection between martial prowess and spiritual devotion within Sikhism—a tradition that emphasizes the importance of leading a life of courage, righteousness, and service to humanity.

The memory of Baba Deep Singh Ji continues to be honored and revered by Sikhs worldwide. His legacy lives on in the hearts and minds of millions who draw inspiration from his exemplary life and unwavering commitment to Sikh values. Through commemorations, prayers, and acts of service, Sikhs pay tribute to Baba Deep Singh Ji's enduring legacy, reaffirming their commitment to upholding the ideals of courage, devotion, and selflessness that he epitomized.

Baba Deep Singh Ji's life journey serves as a powerful testament to the enduring spirit of Sikhism— a tradition rooted in the principles of courage, righteousness, and unwavering devotion to Sikh teachings. His legendary valor on the battlefield and his unwavering commitment to Sikh principles continue to inspire generations of Sikhs to uphold the values of justice, compassion, and service to humanity. As a beacon of courage and devotion, Baba Deep Singh Ji's legacy will continue to shine brightly, illuminating the path for all those who seek to live a life of righteousness and service to others.

Baba Banda Singh Bahadur

Baba Banda Singh Bahadur, a towering figure in Sikh history, rose to prominence as a formidable Khalsa warrior during the early 18th century. Prior to embracing Sikhism, Baba Banda Singh Bahadur received training in the martial traditions prevalent at the time, including horsemanship and swordsmanship.

His upbringing likely instilled in him a foundation of physical prowess and combat skills that would prove invaluable in his later endeavors.

Upon embracing Sikhism and undergoing Amrit into the Khalsa, Baba Banda Singh Bahadur's life took on a new trajectory marked by an unwavering devotion to Sikh principles and the liberation of the oppressed. His transformation into a Khalsa warrior imbued him with a sense of purpose and duty to confront tyranny and injustice.

Baba Banda Singh Bahadur's military campaigns against the oppressive Mughal regime stand as a testament to his courage, leadership, and strategic acumen. He led the Khalsa forces in a series of audacious raids and battles, liberating numerous towns and cities in Panjab from Mughal control. His ability to inspire and mobilize his followers played a crucial role in the success of these campaigns, rallying Sikhs and other oppressed communities to join the cause of liberation.

Central to Baba Banda Singh Bahadur's success was the Kirpa of Sri Guru Gobind Singh Ji and his comprehensive training regimen, which would have encompassed a wide range of skills essential for military leadership and combat. Mastery of various weapons, including the kirpan (sword), talwar (sword), and spear, would have been fundamental to his training, enabling him to wield these weapons with precision and effectiveness on the battlefield.

Baba Banda Singh Bahadur would have honed his tactical prowess through rigorous study and practice of military strategy and warfare tactics. His ability to outmaneuver and outwit the numerically superior Mughal forces speaks to his strategic brilliance and adaptability in the face of adversity.

In addition to his martial skills, Baba Banda Singh Bahadur would have developed leadership qualities vital for inspiring and uniting his followers in the pursuit of a common goal. His charisma, determination, and unwavering commitment to the Khalsa cause earned him the respect and loyalty of his troops, solidifying his position as a revered leader within the Sikh community.

Baba Banda Singh Bahadur's legacy endures as a symbol of resistance against oppression and a champion of justice. His courageous stand against the tyrannical Mughal regime continues to inspire generations of Sikhs to uphold the values of courage, righteousness, and selfless service. Through his exemplary life and indomitable spirit, Baba Banda Singh Bahadur remains a beacon of hope and inspiration for all those who strive for freedom and equality.

Maharaja Ranjit Singh

Maharaja Ranjit Singh, often referred to as the Lion of Panjab, was a towering figure in Sikh history and a legendary ruler who unified the Sikh Empire in the early 19th century. Born on November 13, 1780, in Gujranwala, Ranjit Singh ascended to the throne at the young age of 11 following the demise of his father, Sardar Maha Singh. Despite facing numerous challenges and threats from neighboring powers,

Maharaja Ranjit Singh's leadership and vision propelled the Sikh Empire to unprecedented heights of prosperity and power.

One of Maharaja Ranjit Singh's most remarkable achievements was the consolidation of power and the establishment of a unified Sikh state and Khalsa Raj. Through shrewd diplomacy, strategic alliances, and military prowess, he succeeded in uniting the various Sikh Misls (confederacies) under his rule, thus laying the foundation for the Sikh Empire. Maharaja Ranjit Singh's keen political acumen enabled him to navigate the complex landscape of 19th-century Panjab, forging alliances with local chieftains and extending his influence across the region.

Military expansion was a central aspect of Maharaja Ranjit Singh's reign, and under his leadership, the Sikh Empire emerged as a formidable force in the Asian continent. Known for his bravery and tactical brilliance, Ranjit Singh led his armies to victory in numerous battles against rival powers, including the Afghan and British forces. His military campaigns resulted in the annexation of vast territories, including parts of present-day Panjab, Kashmir, and Peshawar, expanding the boundaries of the Sikh Empire to their greatest extent.

Beyond military conquests, Maharaja Ranjit Singh's reign was characterized by a commitment to justice, religious tolerance, and cultural flourishing. He implemented a system of impartial justice and administrative reforms that ensured the welfare of his subjects, regardless of their religious or ethnic background. Ranjit Singh's patronage of the arts and culture led to a renaissance in Sikh literature, music, and architecture, with notable landmarks such as the Sri Harmandir Sahib Ji in Amritsar undergoing significant renovation and embellishment during his reign.

Maharaja Ranjit Singh's legacy also extends to his efforts to promote religious harmony and pluralism within his realm. Despite being a devout Sikh himself, he respected the beliefs and practices of other faiths, earning the loyalty and support of Hindus, Muslims, and Christians alike. Under his rule, religious freedom flourished, and people of all backgrounds were able to practice their faith without fear of persecution.

Maharaja Ranjit Singh's death on June 27, 1839, marked the end of an era in history, but his legacy continues to endure as a symbol of Sikh pride and resilience. His vision, leadership, and indomitable spirit transformed Panjab into a prosperous and powerful kingdom, leaving an indelible mark on the history of the Asian continent. Today, Maharaja Ranjit Singh is remembered as one of the greatest rulers of Panjab, whose legacy continues to inspire generations with its message of courage, unity, and cultural richness.

Sardar Hari Singh Nalwa

Hari Singh Nalwa, a towering figure in Sikh history, is celebrated for his exceptional military acumen and unwavering dedication to the Sikh cause. From a young age, Hari Singh Nalwa received training in the rich tradition of Sikh martial arts and weaponry, laying the foundation for his future exploits on the battlefield. His training regimen would have encompassed a wide array of skills, including proficiency in traditional Sikh weapons such as the kirpan (sword), chakar (throwing disc), and talwar (sword).

Physical fitness would have been a cornerstone of Hari Singh Nalwa's training, ensuring he was in peak condition to endure the rigors of battle and lead his troops with vitality and resilience. Combat skills, including hand-to-hand combat techniques and mastery of weapons, would have been honed through disciplined practice and rigorous training sessions.

Beyond physical prowess, Hari Singh Nalwa's training regimen would have emphasized strategic thinking and tactical planning. As a leader on the battlefield, he needed to possess the foresight and cunning to outmaneuver his adversaries and secure victories for the Sikh Empire. His ability to devise innovative military strategies and adapt to changing circumstances played a crucial role in expanding the Sikh Empire's territories and defending its borders against external threats.

Hari Singh Nalwa's leadership qualities were equally integral to his success as a military commander. Charismatic and decisive, he inspired unwavering loyalty and devotion among his troops, fostering a sense of camaraderie and unity on the battlefield. His exemplary leadership and steadfast commitment to the Sikh cause galvanized the Sikh forces, enabling them to achieve remarkable victories against formidable opponents.

Throughout his illustrious military career, Hari Singh Nalwa's unwavering loyalty to the Sikh cause remained steadfast. He dedicated his life to serving the Sikh Empire and defending its principles of justice, equality, and sovereignty. His valor and sacrifice continue to inspire reverence and admiration among Sikhs worldwide, serving as a timeless reminder of the indomitable spirit of the Khalsa.

Hari Singh Nalwa's military genius and unwavering commitment to the Sikh cause have left an indelible mark on Sikh history. His exemplary leadership, tactical brilliance, and unwavering loyalty continue to serve as a source of inspiration for generations of Sikhs, epitomizing the timeless values of courage, resilience, and selfless service that define the Khalsa tradition.

Akali Phula Singh Ji

Akali Phula Singh Ji stands as an eminent figure in Sikh history, renowned for his unwavering commitment to Sikh principles and his valor on the battlefield. Born into a devout Sikh family in the late 18th century, Akali Phula Singh Ji dedicated his life to serving the Sikh faith and defending its values against external threats.

From a young age, Akali Phula Singh Ji received training in the martial traditions of the Sikhs, including proficiency in the use of traditional Sikh weapons such as the kirpan (sword), talwar (sword), and chakar (throwing disc). His training regimen would have emphasized physical fitness, combat skills, and spiritual discipline, laying the foundation for his future exploits as a Khalsa warrior.

Akali Phula Singh Ji's unwavering commitment to Sikhism was exemplified by his participation in various military campaigns and battles aimed at protecting Sikh interests and upholding Sikh sovereignty. He played a prominent role in defending Sikh shrines and gurdwaras against desecration and attack, earning him the respect and admiration of the Sikh community.

One of Akali Phula Singh Ji's most significant achievements was his leadership during the Battle of Amritsar. When the holy city of Amritsar came under threat from external forces, including the Afghan Durrani Empire, Akali Phula Singh Ji rallied a contingent of Sikh warriors to defend the sanctity of the Sri Amritsar Sahib Ji and repel the invaders. Despite being outnumbered and outgunned, Akali Phula Singh Ji's strategic brilliance and unwavering courage led to a decisive victory for the Sikh forces, securing the safety of the Sri Harmander Sahib Ji and ensuring the continued freedom of worship for Sikhs.

Beyond his military exploits, Akali Phula Singh Ji was revered for his piety, humility, and devotion to Sikhism. He lived a life of selfless service, dedicating himself to the welfare of the Sikh community and the propagation of Sikh values. His exemplary conduct and steadfast adherence to Sikh principles earned him the title of "Akali," meaning timeless or immortal, a testament to his enduring legacy within Sikhism.

Akali Phula Singh Ji's legacy continues to inspire reverence and admiration among Sikhs worldwide. His unwavering commitment to Sikh principles, his valor on the battlefield, and his selfless service to the Sikh community serve as timeless reminders of the ideals of courage, righteousness, and devotion that define the Khalsa tradition. Today, Akali Phula Singh Ji is remembered as a symbol of Sikh pride and resilience, whose legacy continues to inspire future generations to uphold the values of justice, equality, and compassion.

Sardar Sham Singh Attari

Sardar Sham Singh Attari, also known as Sham Singh Atariwala, was a revered Sikh warrior and military commander who played a significant role in the defense of Sikh territories during the 19th century. Born in the early 19th century in the Attari village of Panjab, Sham Singh was raised in a family with a strong martial tradition, instilling in him a deep sense of duty and honor towards Sikh principles.

From a young age, Sardar Sham Singh displayed exceptional bravery and leadership qualities, which earned him recognition among his peers and elders. He received training in traditional Sikh martial arts and warfare tactics, honing his skills in swordsmanship, horse riding, and military strategy. This rigorous training prepared him for the challenges he would face as a defender of Sikh sovereignty.

Sardar Sham Singh rose to prominence as a military leader during a tumultuous period in Sikh history when the Sikh Empire faced threats from multiple fronts, including the British East India Company and the expanding British Raj. In 1845, during the First Anglo-Sikh War, Sham Singh distinguished himself as a fearless commander and strategist, leading Sikh forces in several battles against the British army.

One of the most memorable moments in Sham Singh's military career came during the Battle of Sobraon in February 1846. Despite being heavily outnumbered and outgunned, Sardar Sham Singh and his troops displayed remarkable courage and resilience on the battlefield. However, in a turn of events, the Sikh forces were eventually overwhelmed, and Sardar Sham Singh, unwilling to surrender, fought bravely until the very end. His refusal to retreat or surrender earned him admiration and respect, even from his adversaries.

Though the Battle of Sobraon resulted in defeat for the Sikh forces and marked the end of the First Anglo-Sikh War, Sham Singh's valiant stand became the stuff of legend, immortalizing him as a hero in Sikh folklore. His unwavering commitment to the Sikh cause and his willingness to sacrifice his life for the defense of Sikh sovereignty cemented his legacy as one of the greatest warriors in Sikh history.

Beyond his military exploits, Sham Singh was revered for his humility, integrity, and devotion to Sikhism. He exemplified the virtues of courage, selflessness, and sacrifice, serving as a role model for future generations of Sikhs. His legacy continues to inspire reverence and admiration among Sikhs worldwide, reminding them of the indomitable spirit and resilience of the Khalsa.

Sardar Sham Singh Attari's life story serves as a testament to the enduring values of Sikhism—courage in the face of adversity, loyalty to one's principles, and selfless service to others. His unwavering commitment to these principles, even in the face of overwhelming odds, ensures that his memory will live on as an inspiration for generations to come.

Sant Jarnail Singh Ji

Sant Jarnail Singh, also known as Sant Jarnail Singh Bhindranwale or Bhindranwale, was a prominent Sikh leader, preacher, and political figure in the late 20th century, known for his role in the Sikh separatist movement and his influence in shaping Sikh politics in Panjab. Born on February 12, 1947, in the Rode village of Faridkot district in Panjab, Sant Jarnail Singh Bhindranwale rose to prominence as the leader of the Damdami Taksal, a Sikh religious institution known for its mainstream interpretation of Sikhism.

From a young age, Jarnail Singh demonstrated a deep devotion to Sikhism and a passion for religious studies. Under the guidance of Sant Kartar Singh Ji, the head of the Damdami Taksal at the time, he received religious education and training in Sikh Granths and traditions. As he matured, Sant Jarnail Singh began to assert himself as a charismatic preacher, captivating audiences with his powerful oratory and uncompromising stance on Sikh issues.

In the late 1970s and early 1980s, Panjab was gripped by political unrest and tensions between the Sikh community and the Indian government. Sant Jarnail Singh emerged as a central figure in this tumultuous period, advocating for the rights and interests of the Sikh community and challenging what he perceived as injustices perpetrated by the Indian state.

Sant Jarnail Singh's fiery speeches and charismatic leadership galvanized a generation of Sikh youth, inspiring them to take up the cause of Sikh sovereignty and self-determination. His staunch defense of Sikh religious institutions, such as the Sri Harmandir Sahib in Amritsar, and his calls for greater autonomy for Panjab resonated deeply with many Sikhs who felt marginalized and oppressed by the Indian government.

Sant Jarnail Singh's rise to prominence also sparked controversy and violence as tensions between Sikh warriors and Indian forces escalated. The situation reached a boiling point in June 1984 when the Indian government launched an attack on various Gurdwaras under Operation Blue Star, a military operation aimed to kill innocent and unarmed Sikhs. The operation resulted in a bloody standoff between Sikh warriors and Indian forces. The events of Operation Blue Star shocked the Sikh community and left a deep scar on the collective psyche of Panjab, igniting widespread protests and unrest across the region.

Sant Jarnail Singh Ji remains a polarizing figure in world history, revered as a martyr and champion of

398

Sikh rights. His legacy continues to shape Sikh politics and identity in Panjab and beyond, serving as a potent symbol of resistance against oppression and a reminder of the complexities of religious and political strife in India.

Acts of Valor and Sacrifice

Acts of valor and sacrifice are integral to the Sikh tradition, embodying the core principles of courage, selflessness, and devotion to duty. Throughout history, Sikhs have demonstrated remarkable bravery and willingness to lay down their lives in defense of their faith, their community, and their principles.

An act of valor and sacrifice that holds a special place in Sikh lore is the Battle of Chamkaur in December 1704. Sri Guru Gobind Singh Ji and a small Jatha of his followers found themselves surrounded by a vastly superior Mughal force in the village of Chamkaur (Chamkaur di Garhi). In Sri Muktsar Sahib Ji, Despite being vastly outnumbered, Sri Guru Gobind Singh Ji and his devoted followers, the Chali Mukte (Forty Liberated Ones), fought valiantly against the Mughal army, sacrificing their lives to uphold the principles of righteousness and justice. Their heroic stand against overwhelming odds serves as a timeless example of courage, sacrifice, and devotion to duty for Sikhs and people of all faiths.

One of the most renowned acts of valor and sacrifice in Sikh history is the defense of Sri Harmandir Sahib Ji during Operation Blue Star in June 1984. As Indian forces launched a military operation to kill innocent Sikhs, including Sant Jarnail Singh Ji, from the holiest Sikh Gurdwara, a small Jatha of Sikh defenders, including Sant Jarnail Singh Ji himself, chose to stay and defend the sanctity of the Sri Harmandir Sahib Ji. Despite being vastly outnumbered and outgunned, they fought bravely to the end, refusing to surrender and laying down their lives in defense of their faith and their sacred place of worship. Their sacrifice remains etched in the collective memory of the Sikh community, inspiring reverence and admiration for their unwavering commitment to Sikh principles.

In addition to these well-known examples, countless Sikhs throughout history have demonstrated acts of valor and sacrifice in various contexts, from defending their communities against external threats to standing up against injustice and oppression. Whether on the battlefield or in everyday life, Sikhs have consistently shown a willingness to put their lives on the line for the greater good, embodying the spirit of selflessness and service that lies at the heart of Sikhism.

The legacy of these acts of valor and sacrifice continues to inspire and motivate Sikhs and others around the world to uphold the values of courage, selflessness, and devotion to duty in their own lives. They serve as a reminder of the rich tradition of heroism and sacrifice that defines Sikh history and reinforces the importance of standing up for what is right, even in the face of adversity and danger.

Leadership Qualities Exemplified by Khalsa Warriors

Khalsa warriors, throughout Sikh history, have exemplified a range of leadership qualities that have guided them in times of peace and conflict. These qualities are not only essential for effective leadership on the battlefield but also for inspiring and uniting communities in times of adversity. Some of the key leadership qualities demonstrated by Khalsa warriors include:

1. **Courage:** Perhaps the most defining characteristic of Khalsa warriors is their unwavering courage in the face of danger and adversity. They fearlessly confront formidable opponents and daunting challenges, inspiring those around them to persevere in the face of adversity.

2. **Determination:** Khalsa warriors possess a strong sense of determination and resolve, refusing to back down in the face of obstacles or setbacks. Their steadfast commitment to their cause enables them to overcome adversity and achieve their objectives, no matter the odds.

3. **Integrity:** Integrity is a fundamental trait among Khalsa warriors, who adhere unwaveringly to principles of honesty, honor, and moral uprightness. Their integrity earns them the trust and respect of their peers and followers, establishing a strong foundation for effective leadership.

4. **Selflessness:** Khalsa warriors embody the spirit of selflessness, placing the needs of their community and the welfare of others above their own interests. They willingly make sacrifices for the greater good, demonstrating a commitment to serving others that inspires loyalty and devotion among their followers.

5. **Vision:** Effective Khalsa leaders possess a clear vision of their objectives and a strategic plan for achieving them. They inspire others with their vision, rallying support and mobilizing resources to accomplish their goals.

6. **Adaptability:** Khalsa warriors demonstrate adaptability and flexibility in the face of changing circumstances and unexpected challenges. They are quick to adjust their strategies and tactics to meet evolving threats, ensuring their continued effectiveness on the battlefield.

7. **Empathy:** Empathy is a crucial leadership quality among Khalsa warriors, who understand the needs and concerns of those under their command. They listen attentively to the concerns of their followers and demonstrate compassion and understanding in their interactions.

8. **Resilience:** Khalsa warriors exhibit resilience in the face of adversity, bouncing back from setbacks and setbacks with renewed determination and resolve. Their resilience enables them to endure hardships and persevere in the pursuit of their objectives.

9. **Inspiring Leadership:** Khalsa warriors lead by example, inspiring those around them with their actions and words. They motivate their followers with their bravery, dedication, and unwavering commitment to their cause, instilling a sense of pride and loyalty in their ranks.

10. **Strategic Thinking:** Khalsa leaders demonstrate strategic thinking and sound judgment in their decision-making, carefully weighing risks and opportunities to maximize their chances of success. Their ability to think critically and strategically enables them to outmaneuver their adversaries and achieve their objectives.

These leadership qualities have been central to the success and effectiveness of Khalsa warriors throughout Sikh history, guiding them in their efforts to defend their faith, protect their communities, and uphold the principles of justice, equality, and righteousness.

The Warrior Spirit of the Khalsa illuminates the rich tapestry of courage, sacrifice, and resilience that defines the ethos of Sikhism. Through the ages, Khalsa warriors have embodied the noble ideals of their faith, fearlessly defending righteousness and upholding justice in the face of adversity. From the valorous deeds of Sri Guru Gobind Singh Ji and the Five Beloved Ones to the heroic sacrifices of modern-day Sikh warriors, the spirit of the Khalsa has remained indomitable, inspiring generations to stand firm in the face of oppression and injustice.

The profound legacy of the Khalsa reminds the enduring relevance of its principles in today's world. The virtues of courage, integrity, and selflessness embodied by Khalsa warriors serve as a timeless beacon of hope and inspiration for all humanity, transcending the boundaries of race, religion, and culture. In a world beset by division and conflict, the example set by the Khalsa offers a powerful testament to the transformative power of faith, unity, and unwavering commitment to truth and righteousness.

*****

SIKHISM'S UNIVERSAL MESSAGE

SIKHISM'S UNIVERSAL MESSAGE

Sikhism, founded by Guru Nanak in the 15th century, is a monotheistic religion that emphasizes the belief in one God, known as Ik Onkar. At its core, Sikhism promotes the idea of the equality of all humans, regardless of caste, creed, gender, or social status. Central to Sikh spirituality is the Sri Guru Granth Sahib, the living Guru considered the eternal Guru by Sikhs. It contains the teachings of the Sikh Gurus as well as compositions from other saints and scholars. Sikhs practice various rituals and ceremonies, such as the recitation of hymns (kirtan), congregational worship (sangat), and the community kitchen (langar), where free meals are served to all, irrespective of background. The principles of Seva (selfless service) and Simran (meditation on God's name) are integral to the Sikh lifestyle, promoting humility, compassion, and devotion. Sikhism also emphasizes the importance of living a moral and righteous life guided by the principles of honesty, integrity, and self-discipline. The faith is symbolized by the Five Ks, which are articles of faith worn by initiated Sikhs, including uncut Kesh (hair), Kara (Iron bracelet, Kanga (a wooden comb), Kachera (cotton undergarments), and a Kirpan (ceremonial sword). These symbols serve as constant reminders of Sikh identity and commitment to the faith's principles. Sikh beliefs and practices revolve around the pursuit of spiritual growth, selfless service to humanity, and living in harmony with the divine will.

Importance of Sri Guru Granth Sahib Ji

The Sri Guru Granth Sahib Ji holds profound significance as the living Guru of Sikhism, embodying the spiritual essence and guiding principles of the faith. Compiled under the direction of Sri Guru Arjan Dev Ji and subsequently revered by Sikhs as the eternal Guru, it serves as a timeless beacon of divine wisdom and enlightenment. Within its sacred verses lie the teachings of Sikh Gurus, enlightened saints, and poets, offering profound insights into morality, spirituality, and the nature of existence. As the focal point of Sikh worship, the Sri Guru Granth Sahib Ji is venerated with utmost reverence in gurdwaras worldwide, where Sikhs gather to seek spiritual guidance, solace, and inspiration. Its universal appeal transcends cultural and religious boundaries, resonating with seekers of truth across diverse backgrounds. Through its teachings, the Sri Guru Granth Sahib Ji continues to guide Sikhs on their spiritual journey, fostering unity, compassion, and a deep reverence for the divine in all aspects of life.

Eternal Guru

Sikhs hold a profound belief in the eternal nature of the Sri Guru Granth Sahib Ji, a living embodiment of divine wisdom. Unlike previous religious scriptures of other religions, which were compiled after the passing of their founders, the Sri Guru Granth Sahib Ji was compiled by Sri Guru Arjan Dev Ji himself, the fifth Sikh Guru. Sri Guru Arjan Dev Ji made a thoughtful decision to include the writings not only of the Sikh Gurus but also those of enlightened saints and poets from diverse backgrounds. This compilation was done with the intention of creating a spiritual guide that would endure beyond the physical lifetimes of the Gurus. Thus, Sikhs regard the Guru Granth Sahib as the eternal Guru, perpetually guiding them on their spiritual journey regardless of temporal constraints. This belief instills a deep sense of reverence and devotion among Sikhs, who turn to the Sri Guru Granth Sahib Ji for spiritual solace, guidance, and inspiration in every aspect of their lives.

Direct Guidance from Gurus

One of the fundamental tenets of Sikhism is the belief in the direct connection between the Sikh community and the Sikh Gurus through the Sri Guru Granth Sahib Ji. Sikhs perceive the Sri Guru Granth Sahib as a conduit for receiving direct guidance from the Sikh Gurus themselves. The hymns and compositions contained within the Sri Guru Granth Sahib are considered the words of the Gurus, offering timeless insights into the nature of reality, the human condition, and the path to spiritual liberation. Sikhs believe that through sincere study, contemplation, and adherence to the teachings of the Sri Guru Granth Sahib Ji, they can establish a personal connection with the enlightened consciousness of the Gurus. This connection provides comfort, guidance, and strength, enabling Sikhs to navigate life's challenges and strive for spiritual growth. The Sri Guru Granth Sahib Ji serves as a direct link between the Sikh community and the divine wisdom of the Sikh Gurus, fostering a deep sense of spiritual communion and devotion among followers.

Teachings and Wisdom

The Sri Guru Granth Sahib Ji, revered as the living Guru of Sikhism, encapsulates a rich tapestry of teachings and wisdom that addresses various aspects of human existence. Within its sacred verses, one finds profound insights into morality, spirituality, social justice, and devotion. The Sri Guru Granth Sahib Ji offers timeless guidance on leading a righteous and virtuous life, emphasizing principles such as honesty, compassion, humility, and selfless service (Seva). It delves into the nature of the divine, ordering seekers to cultivate a deep and intimate connection with the Creator through meditation, prayer, and devotion. Sri Guru Granth Sahib Ji advocates for social equality and justice, condemning discrimination based on caste, creed, or social status. It champions the cause of the oppressed and marginalized, calling upon individuals to stand up against injustice and uphold the dignity and rights of all human beings. Through its teachings, the Sri Guru Granth Sahib Ji serves as a moral compass, guiding Sikhs on the path of righteousness and inspiring them to lead a life of purpose, integrity, and spiritual fulfillment.

Universal Order

Despite being rooted in the Sikh tradition; the teachings of the Sri Guru Granth Sahib Ji possess a universal order that transcends cultural and religious boundaries. Its message of love, compassion, and unity resonates with seekers of truth and wisdom across the globe, irrespective of their faith or background. The Sri Guru Granth Sahib Ji espouses universal values that are relevant to all humanity,

410

promoting virtues such as tolerance, forgiveness, empathy, and solidarity. Its teachings emphasize the inherent dignity and worth of every individual, fostering a sense of shared humanity and interconnectedness among all beings. Moreover, the Sri Guru Granth Sahib Ji's emphasis on spiritual liberation and the pursuit of divine truth speaks to the innate longing for transcendence and enlightenment present in every human heart. As such, the Guru Granth Sahib Ji serves as a source of inspiration and guidance for people of diverse cultures and faiths, offering profound insights into the nature of existence and the quest for spiritual fulfillment.

Kirtan

Kirtan, the devotional singing of hymns from the Sri Guru Granth Sahib Ji, holds a central place in Sikh worship and congregational gatherings. This practice, deeply rooted in Sikh tradition, involves the melodious recitation of Shabads (holy hymns) from the Sri Guru Granth Sahib Ji, accompanied by musical instruments such as the harmonium and tabla. Kirtan serves multiple purposes within Sikh worship. Firstly, it fosters a sense of spiritual communion and devotion among the congregation as participants collectively immerse themselves in the divine vibrations of the Shabads. Through the melodic rendition of sacred verses, Kirtan creates an atmosphere conducive to meditation, facilitating the union of the individual soul with the divine. Additionally, Kirtan serves as a means of propagating the teachings of the Sri Guru Granth Sahib Ji, as the lyrics of the hymns convey profound spiritual truths and ethical principles. Furthermore, Kirtan is believed to have transformative power, purifying the mind and uplifting the spirit of the participants. Kirtan is not merely a musical performance but a sacred act of worship that enables Sikhs to connect with the divine presence manifested in the Sri Guru Granth Sahib Ji.

Nitnem and Daily Routines

Nitnem, which translates to "daily routine," encompasses a set of prayers and readings from the Sri Guru Granth Sahib Ji and Sri Dasam Granth Sahib Ji that Sikhs are encouraged to recite daily. These prayers, prescribed by Sikh tradition, are integral to the spiritual discipline and daily routine of devout Sikhs. The Nitnem includes specific prayers to be recited in the morning (Amrit Vela: Five bani (Japji Sahib, Jap Sahib, Tav Prasad Savaiye, Chaupai Sahib, and Anand Sahib), evening (Rehras Sahib), and before sleeping (Kirtan Sohila), along with additional prayers such as Asa Di Vaar, Arti and Ardas. Each prayer holds profound significance, addressing various aspects of spiritual life, including gratitude, humility, and devotion to the divine. Through the practice of Nitnem, Sikhs cultivate a deeper connection with the Sri Guru Granth Sahib Ji, internalizing its teachings and integrating them into their daily lives. The recitation of Nitnem serves to purify the mind, uplift the spirit, and instill a sense of spiritual discipline and mindfulness. It fosters a sense of continuity and solidarity within the Sikh community, as Sikhs around the world unite in the daily recitation of these sacred prayers. Nitnem plays a pivotal role in Sikh worship, enabling devotees to nurture their spiritual growth and maintain a constant remembrance of the divine presence permeating all aspects of existence.

Personal Guidance

Sikhs turn to the Sri Guru Granth Sahib Ji for personal guidance and solace during all phases of life, be it moments of joy, sorrow, or confusion. In times of joy, Sikhs express gratitude to the divine by reciting hymns of praise and thanksgiving from the Sri Guru Granth Sahib Ji. These sacred verses serve as a reminder of the interconnectedness of all beings and the divine source of all blessings. Conversely, during times of sorrow or difficulty, Sikhs seek solace and strength from the comforting words of the Sri Guru Granth Sahib Ji. Sri Guru Granth Sahib Ji offers solace by providing reassurance that the divine presence is ever-present and that trials and tribulations are temporary aspects of the human experience. In moments of confusion or indecision, Sikhs turn to the Sri Guru Granth Sahib Ji for guidance and clarity. Through prayer, meditation, and contemplation of the Guru's teachings, individuals are able to discern the path forward and align their actions with divine will. The Sri Guru Granth Sahib Ji serves as a trusted confidant and guide, offering spiritual counsel and support to Sikhs in every aspect of their lives.

Healing and Comfort

The teachings of the Sri Guru Granth Sahib Ji have a profound healing and comforting effect on individuals facing physical, emotional, or spiritual challenges. Countless anecdotes and examples exist of individuals finding solace, healing, and comfort through the Guru's teachings. The Sri Guru Granth Sahib Ji offers words of wisdom and encouragement that provide hope and strength to those grappling with illness, loss, or adversity. Through the practice of reciting hymns and meditating on the Guru's teachings, individuals experience a deep sense of inner peace and resilience. The Guru Granth Sahib Ji teaches the importance of acceptance and surrender to the divine will, helping individuals find peace amidst life's uncertainties. The healing power of the Guru extends beyond individual suffering to collective healing and reconciliation. The teachings of the Sri Guru Granth Sahib Ji promote forgiveness, compassion, and unity, fostering reconciliation and healing in communities torn apart by conflict or division. The Guru's teachings serve as a source of healing, comfort, and hope for individuals and communities alike, offering a guiding light in times of darkness and despair.

Sangat and Pangat (Langar)

The presence of the Sri Guru Granth Sahib Ji plays a pivotal role in fostering community cohesion and unity during Sikh gatherings, particularly through the practices of Sangat and Pangat (Langar). Sangat refers to the congregation of Sikhs who gather to worship and commune with the divine presence embodied in Sri the Guru Granth Sahib Ji. In the presence of the Guru, individuals from diverse backgrounds come together as equals, transcending barriers of caste, creed, and social status. The Sangat experience spiritual upliftment and unity through the collective recitation of hymns (kirtan) and meditation on the Guru's teachings. Additionally, Pangat, the community kitchen where free meals are served to all attendees, further strengthens bonds of fellowship and solidarity among Sikhs. The act of partaking in Pangat symbolizes equality and humility, as individuals from all walks of life sit together and share a meal as equals. The Sri Guru Granth Sahib Ji serves as the spiritual focal point of these gatherings, anchoring the community in shared devotion and service to humanity.

Common Spiritual Identity

Reverence for the Sri Guru Granth Sahib Ji serves as a unifying force that transcends geographical and cultural differences, forging a common spiritual identity among Sikhs worldwide. Wherever Sikhs gather for worship, whether in a gurdwara in Punjab or a Sikh community center in a distant land, the presence of the Sri Guru Granth Sahib Ji instills a sense of reverence and unity. Sikhs across the globe share a deep reverence for the Guru Sahib as the living Guru of Sikhism, regardless of their linguistic, cultural, or regional affiliations. The teachings of the Sri Guru Granth Sahib Ji provide a common spiritual foundation that binds Sikhs together in a shared commitment to ethical living, compassion, and devotion to the divine. Through the universal message of the Guru Sahib, Sikhs find solidarity and strength in their collective identity as followers of the Sikh faith. This common spiritual identity transcends the boundaries of nationality and ethnicity, fostering a sense of belonging and kinship among Sikhs worldwide. The reverence for the Sri Guru Granth Sahib Ji serves as a powerful catalyst for unity and cohesion within the Sikh community, reinforcing the bonds of brotherhood and sisterhood among all who seek refuge in its divine wisdom.

Final Authority

The Sri Guru Granth Sahib Ji holds a preeminent position as the final authority on Sikh doctrine and practice, serving as the ultimate guide for Sikhs in matters of faith and morality. As the living Guru of Sikhism, the Guru Sahib embodies the collective wisdom and spiritual insights of the Sikh Gurus and enlightened saints. Sikhs regard the teachings contained within the Sri Guru Granth Sahib Ji as timeless and immutable, providing authoritative guidance on all aspects of life. From matters of personal conduct to questions of theology and philosophy, Sikhs turn to the Sri Guru Granth Sahib Ji for clarity and direction. Its teachings serve as a moral compass, guiding Sikhs to live virtuous lives characterized by compassion, humility, and selfless service. The Sri Guru Granth Sahib Ji's status as the final authority ensures continuity and unity within the Sikh community, safeguarding the integrity of Sikh doctrine and practice across generations.

Katha (Interpreting Gurbani)

The tradition of interpreting Gurbani (Shabads) from the Sri Guru Granth Sahib Ji is deeply rooted in Sikh scholarship and spiritual practice. Given the poetic and metaphorical nature of Gurbani, interpreting its Shabads requires careful study, reflection, and guidance. Sikh scholars and leaders play a vital role in elucidating the meanings and nuances of Gurbani, drawing upon their knowledge of Sikh Gurus, history, and tradition. These interpreters, known as Gurbani Vicharaks or Kathakars, offer insights into the spiritual, ethical, and philosophical dimensions of Gurbani, helping Sikhs deepen their understanding of the Guru's teachings. Sikh congregations often gather for Katha (discourses) and discussions on Gurbani, where scholars share their interpretations and insights with the community. Through this tradition of interpretation, Sikhs gain a deeper appreciation for the profound truths embedded within Gurbani and apply its teachings to their daily lives. However, it's essential to note that while interpretations may vary, the Guru Granth Sahib Ji remains the ultimate authority, guiding Sikhs to discern the divine message within its sacred verses.

Adapting to Modern Challenges

The teachings of the Sri Guru Granth Sahib Ji exhibit remarkable adaptability, offering timeless guidance and relevance in addressing contemporary challenges. Despite being compiled centuries ago, the Guru's teachings transcend temporal boundaries, providing profound insights into the human condition and offering solutions to modern dilemmas. In an age marked by rapid technological advancements, globalization, and societal upheavals, the Sri Guru Granth Sahib Ji serves as a beacon of moral and spiritual clarity, guiding individuals and communities through turbulent times. Its emphasis on principles such as compassion, equality, and selfless service remains as pertinent today as it was during the time of its origin. The Guru's teachings on inner peace, resilience, and mindfulness offer practical strategies for coping with stress, anxiety, and uncertainty in the modern world. By drawing upon the timeless wisdom of the Sri Guru Granth Sahib Ji, Sikhs find strength, resilience, and moral clarity in navigating the complexities of contemporary life.

Applicability to Diverse Contexts

Sikhs apply the teachings of the Sri Guru Granth Sahib Ji to navigate various aspects of modern life, encompassing personal, social, and political realms. In their personal lives, Sikhs draw inspiration from the Guru's teachings to cultivate virtues such as humility, integrity, and gratitude, fostering inner peace and spiritual fulfillment. The Sri Guru Granth Sahib Ji's emphasis on selfless service (Seva) motivates Sikhs to actively contribute to the welfare of society, addressing issues such as poverty, hunger, and inequality through humanitarian initiatives and community outreach programs. Sikhs apply the Guru's teachings to advocate for social justice, human rights, and environmental sustainability in the political arena. By upholding principles of equality, justice, and compassion, Sikhs strive to create a more just and equitable society, informed by the moral imperatives outlined in the Guru Granth Sahib Ji. Thus, the Guru's teachings resonate across diverse contexts, inspiring Sikhs to lead lives of purpose, integrity, and service in pursuit of a more harmonious and compassionate world.

Enduring Influence

The Sri Guru Granth Sahib Ji stands as a timeless beacon of spiritual wisdom and moral guidance, exerting an enduring influence on the spiritual and moral landscape of Sikh communities worldwide. As the living Guru of Sikhism, the Guru embodies the collective consciousness and divine wisdom of the Sikh Gurus and enlightened saints. Its teachings, encapsulated in poetic hymns and verses, transcend temporal and cultural boundaries, offering timeless insights into the nature of reality, the human condition, and the path to spiritual liberation. Throughout history, the Guru Granth Sahib Ji has served as a source of inspiration, solace, and guidance for Sikhs facing adversity, oppression, and persecution. Its teachings have empowered individuals and communities to uphold principles of justice, equality, and compassion, fostering resilience and unity in the face of adversity.

The Guru Granth Sahib Ji continues to shape the moral and spiritual fabric of Sikh communities worldwide, serving as a source of ethical guidance and spiritual nourishment for individuals seeking meaning and purpose in their lives. Its teachings promote virtues such as humility, integrity, and selfless service, inspiring Sikhs to lead lives of moral integrity and social responsibility. Through the practice of reciting hymns, meditation on divine virtues, and engagement in community service (Seva), Sikhs cultivate a deep and intimate connection with the divine presence manifested in the Sri Guru Granth Sahib Ji.

The enduring influence of the Sri Guru Granth Sahib Ji extends beyond the confines of Sikhism, exerting a profound impact on humanity at large. Its universal message of love, compassion, and unity resonates with seekers of truth and wisdom from diverse cultural and religious backgrounds, fostering interfaith dialogue, understanding, and cooperation. As a living legacy of spiritual enlightenment and moral guidance, the Sri Guru Granth Sahib Ji continues to inspire individuals and communities worldwide to strive for higher ideals, embrace diversity, and work towards the realization of a more just, compassionate, and harmonious world.

Ek Onkar (the concept of one God)

At the heart of Sikhism lies the profound belief in the oneness of God, encapsulated in the sacred phrase "Ek Onkar," which translates to "One Creator." This concept serves as the cornerstone of Sikh spirituality, embodying the monotheistic nature of the Sikh faith and guiding the entire framework of Sikh philosophy and practice.

Monotheistic Foundation

"Ek Onkar," the foundational principle of Sikhism, embodies a staunch belief in the singularity and unity of the divine. This sacred phrase asserts the existence of a sole, eternal, formless, and omnipresent Creator who serves as the source of all existence. In emphasizing this monotheistic foundation, Sikhism sets itself apart from polytheistic beliefs prevalent in various other religious traditions. The concept underscores the absolute oneness and indivisibility of God, rejecting the notion of multiple deities or manifestations. In Sikh theology, there exists no division or hierarchy within the divine realm but rather a unified, singular presence that permeates all of creation. This understanding of God as the sole Creator and sustainer of the universe forms the core of Sikh spirituality, guiding adherents towards a profound reverence and devotion to the singular divine essence.

Transcendent and Immanent Nature of God

The concept of "Ek Onkar" in Sikhism encapsulates the understanding of God as both transcendent and immanent, embodying His omnipotence, omniscience, and omnipresence. Sikhism acknowledges that God transcends human comprehension and all limitations. "Ek Onkar" emphasizes that God exists beyond the confines of human understanding and is not bound by the constraints of time, space, or form. Simultaneously, Sikhism teaches that God is immanent, permeating every aspect of creation. God's divine presence is not distant or removed but is intimately intertwined with the fabric of existence, manifesting within all beings and phenomena. This dual aspect of God's nature underscores His transcendence and immanence. While God remains beyond human grasp, His presence is palpable and pervasive, infusing every corner of the universe with His divine essence. In Sikh theology, the concept of "Ek Onkar" harmonizes the transcendence and immanence of God, emphasizing the inseparable unity of these seemingly opposing attributes. God's transcendence does not diminish His immanence, nor does His immanence detract from His transcendence. Understanding God as both transcendent and immanent has practical implications for Sikh spirituality. It fosters a deep sense of reverence and awe for the unfathomable nature of God while also nurturing a profound intimacy and connection with the divine in every aspect of life.

Universal and Inclusive Nature

The phrase "Ek Onkar" encapsulates the universal and inclusive essence of Sikhism, affirming the oneness of God and His creation. It acknowledges God as the Creator of all humanity, transcending divisions of race, nationality, caste, or creed. Sikhism emphasizes the inherent equality of all individuals in the eyes of God, recognizing each person's worth and potential for spiritual growth. Regardless of background or beliefs, Sikhism asserts that every individual has the opportunity to attain spiritual liberation through devotion and righteous living. "Ik Onkar" rejects exclusivity and elitism, welcoming seekers from all walks of life to embrace the universal message of love, compassion, and service. Moreover, Sikhism celebrates diversity as a reflection of God's creative expression, encouraging Sikhs to embrace the richness of human diversity and cultivate respect, tolerance, and understanding towards all individuals. "Ik Onkar" inspires humanity to unite in the pursuit of spiritual truth and harmony, fostering a world where all beings are valued, respected, and included in the divine embrace of universal love.

Spiritual Unity

The concept of "Ek Onkar" serves as a catalyst for fostering a profound sense of spiritual unity and interconnectedness among all beings within Sikhism. It acts as a reminder of the intrinsic connection that Sikhs share with the divine and with one another, inspiring virtues such as compassion, empathy, and altruism.

1. **Intrinsic Connection to the Divine:** "Ek Onkar" reminds Sikhs of their inherent connection to the divine. It emphasizes that all beings are manifestations of the same divine essence, transcending individual differences and divisions.

2. **Interconnectedness among Beings:** Sikhism teaches that all beings are interconnected and interdependent. "Ek Onkar" underscores the interconnectedness of all life forms, emphasizing the unity of the cosmic order.

3. **Cultivation of Virtues:** The recognition of the divine presence within oneself and others encourages Sikhs to cultivate virtues such as compassion, empathy, and altruism. "Ik Onkar" inspires individuals to treat others with kindness, respect, and understanding.

4. **Harmonious Relationship with God:** Through the acknowledgment of the divine presence within themselves, Sikhs strive to cultivate a harmonious relationship with God. "Ek Onkar" encourages individuals to deepen their connection to the divine through prayer, meditation, and righteous living.

5. **Loving Relationship with Creation:** In addition to fostering a relationship with God, "Ek Onkar" inspires Sikhs to cultivate a loving relationship with all of creation. Sikhs are encouraged to respect and protect the

environment, recognizing the sacredness of all living beings.

6. **Unity in Diversity:** Despite the diversity of human experiences and expressions, "Ek Onkar" teaches that all beings are ultimately united in the divine. It encourages Sikhs to embrace diversity as a reflection of God's creative expression and to celebrate the richness of human existence.

"Ek Onkar" is a guiding principle for Sikhs, inspiring them to recognize the divine presence within themselves and others and cultivate a sense of spiritual unity and interconnectedness that transcends individual differences and divisions. Through the practice of virtues such as compassion, empathy, and altruism, Sikhs strive to build a harmonious relationship with God and with all of creation, contributing to the realization of a more loving, compassionate, and unified world.

Direct Relationship with God

Sikhism advocates for a direct and personal relationship with the one Creator. It emphasizes God's accessibility to all individuals without the need for intermediaries or rituals. This principle fosters a profound sense of intimacy and devotion in Sikh spirituality.

1. **Accessibility of God:** Sikhism teaches that God is accessible to all individuals, regardless of their background, social status, or religious affiliation. There are no barriers separating

individuals from establishing a direct connection with the divine.

2. **Absence of Intermediaries:** Unlike some other religious traditions that rely on priests or intermediaries to facilitate communication with the divine, Sikhism emphasizes direct access to God. Sikhs believe that every individual has the inherent ability to commune with God without the need for intermediaries.

3. **Personal Experience of Divine Presence:** Sikhs seek to cultivate a personal and experiential relationship with God through prayer, meditation, and righteous living. They believe that one can experience the presence of the divine directly through inner contemplation and spiritual practice.

4. **Individual Responsibility and Accountability:** The emphasis on a direct relationship with God underscores each Sikh's individual responsibility and accountability in their spiritual journey. Sikhs are encouraged to cultivate their personal connection with the divine and take ownership of their spiritual growth and development.

5. **Sense of Intimacy and Devotion:** The direct relationship with God fosters a deep sense of intimacy and devotion in Sikh spirituality. Sikhs view God as a loving and compassionate presence in their lives, whom they can turn to for guidance, solace, and inspiration.

6. **Freedom from Religious Dogma:** Sikhism promotes freedom from religious dogma and encourages individuals to explore and experience their spirituality authentically. Sikhs are not bound by rigid rituals or hierarchical structures but, instead, are encouraged to cultivate a personal and meaningful relationship with the divine.

The principle of a direct relationship with God lies at the heart of Sikh spirituality, empowering individuals to connect with the divine in a personal and authentic manner. This principle underscores the accessibility of God to all individuals and fosters a sense of intimacy, devotion, and spiritual fulfillment in Sikh life.

Concept of God

Sikhism's concept of God differs from that of many other religions in several key aspects, reflecting its unique theological perspective and spiritual ethos.

1. **Monotheism versus Polytheism:** Sikhism staunchly adheres to monotheism, affirming the belief in one supreme, formless, and omnipresent Creator. This contrasts with polytheistic religions, which worship multiple gods and goddesses with distinct attributes and functions.

2. **Formless Nature of God:** In Sikhism, God is described as Nirankar or formless. Unlike some religions that attribute human-like qualities or physical forms to their deities, Sikhism emphasizes the transcendence and ineffability

of God, who exists beyond all material manifestations.

3. **Rejection of Idol Worship:** Sikhism rejects the practice of idol worship, viewing it as a hindrance to the realization of the true nature of God. While many religions venerate idols or icons as representations of divine beings, Sikhism emphasizes direct communion with the formless Creator without the need for intermediary objects.

4. **Emphasis on Oneness and Unity:** Sikhism places a strong emphasis on the oneness and unity of the divine. The concept of "Ik Onkar" encapsulates this belief, affirming that there is only one eternal, all-encompassing Creator who permeates the entire universe. This contrasts with religions that may attribute divinity to multiple distinct entities or forces.

5. **Universal Accessibility of God:** Sikhism teaches that God is accessible to all individuals, irrespective of their background, social status, or religious affiliation. This contrasts with certain religious traditions that may restrict access to the divine based on criteria such as lineage, caste, or exclusive religious practices.

6. **Emphasis on Direct Relationship:** Sikhism advocates for a direct and personal relationship with God, emphasizing the accessibility of the divine without the need for intermediaries or rituals. This stands in contrast to religious traditions that rely heavily on priests, clergy, or

religious rituals to facilitate communication with the divine.

Sikhism's concept of God differs from that of many other religions in its emphasis on monotheism, the formless nature of God, rejection of idol worship, emphasis oneness and unity, universal accessibility of God, and advocacy for a direct relationship with the divine. These distinctions reflect the unique theological perspective and spiritual ethos of Sikhism as a distinct religious tradition.

Equality and Justice

Equality and social justice lie at the heart of Sikhism, serving as fundamental principles that guide the faith and practice of Sikhs worldwide. Sikhism staunchly advocates for the inherent worth and dignity of all human beings, regardless of their social status or background. This belief is deeply rooted in the concept of "Ek Onkar," which emphasizes the oneness of humanity and affirms that all individuals are created equal in the eyes of the divine. Sikh teachings vehemently reject all forms of discrimination, including caste-based discrimination, and instead emphasize the importance of merit, virtue, and service to humanity. The Sikh Gurus led by example, standing against injustice and oppression and advocating for the rights and dignity of the marginalized. Sikhism institutionalizes the principle of equality through practices like the Pangat (langar), where individuals from all walks of life come together to share a meal as equals. Gender equality is also promoted within Sikhism, with scripture containing the writings of female saints and emphasizing the equal status and rights of women. Sikhs have a long history of advocating for human rights and standing up against oppression, embodying the principles of freedom, justice, and equality in their actions and teachings. Sikhism serves as a beacon of equality and social justice, inspiring individuals to work towards building a more just, compassionate, and inclusive society for all.

Emphasis on Equality of All Humans

Sikhism unequivocally asserts the equality of all individuals, transcending distinctions of caste, creed, gender, or ethnicity. At the core of Sikh philosophy lies the concept of "Ek Onkar," which serves as a profound affirmation of the oneness of humanity. This principle underscores the belief that all beings are created equal in the eyes of the divine, regardless of their social background or outward appearance.

1. **Rejection of Caste-Based Discrimination:** Sikhism vehemently opposes the discriminatory caste system prevalent in societies. The teachings of Sikh Gurus emphasize the futility of caste distinctions and advocate for a society where merit and virtue supersede birth-based hierarchies.

2. **Equality of Gender:** Sikhism promotes gender equality, challenging patriarchal norms and advocating for the equal status and rights of women. Sikh scripture contains the writings of female saints and emphasizes the importance of treating women with respect and dignity.

3. **Inclusivity of All:** The principle of equality extends to all aspects of human diversity,

including creed, gender identity, and ethnicity. Sikhism embraces individuals from all walks of life, welcoming them into the Sikh community as equal members regardless of their background.

4. **Universal Brotherhood:** Sikh teachings emphasize the interconnectedness and interdependence of all beings, fostering a sense of universal brotherhood and solidarity among humanity. The concept of "Ik Onkar" underscores the belief in the essential unity of all human beings, transcending superficial differences.

5. **Social Justice and Empowerment:** Equality in Sikhism is not merely a philosophical concept but a call to action. Sikhs are encouraged to actively work towards dismantling barriers to equality and promoting justice and empowerment for all individuals, especially the marginalized and oppressed.

Rejection of Caste-Based Discrimination and Advocacy for Social Justice

Sikhism stands as a steadfast opponent of caste-based discrimination, a deeply entrenched social issue that has plagued societies for centuries. From its inception, Sikhism has been at the forefront of challenging the rigid caste system and advocating for the equality of all individuals.

1. **Sri Guru Nanak Dev Ji's Opposition:** Sri Guru Nanak Dev Ji, the founder of Sikhism, vocally opposed the caste system and the social hierarchy it perpetuated. He denounced the

notion of social status being determined by birth, emphasizing the equality of all humans in the eyes of the divine.

2. **Challenging Social Hierarchy:** Sikh teachings reject the idea of high or low castes, advocating instead for a society based on merit and virtue rather than social status. Sikhs are taught to judge individuals based on their actions and character, rather than their caste or social background.

3. **Emphasis on Merit and Virtue:** Sikhism emphasizes the importance of merit and virtue over birth-based distinctions. The Sikh Gurus stressed the value of qualities such as honesty, compassion, and selflessness, considering these traits as the true measures of a person's worth.

4. **Equality in Practice:** Sikhism institutionalizes the rejection of caste-based discrimination through its practices and institutions. The langar, or community kitchen, exemplifies this principle by serving meals to all individuals, regardless of their caste or social status, fostering a sense of equality and inclusivity.

5. **Advocacy for Social Justice:** Sikh teachings advocate for social justice and equality in all spheres of life. Sikhs are encouraged to actively combat discrimination and injustice, standing up for the rights and dignity of all individuals, particularly the marginalized and oppressed.

6. **Active Engagement in Social Issues:** Sikhism encourages active engagement in social issues and the pursuit of justice. Sikhs are urged to be proactive in addressing societal problems, advocating for reforms, and working towards the betterment of society as a whole.

7. **Championing the Oppressed:** Sikhism places a profound emphasis on standing up for the rights and dignity of the oppressed and marginalized. The Sikh Gurus fearlessly confronted social injustices, speaking out against discrimination, oppression, and exploitation wherever they encountered it.

8. **Legacy of Social Activism:** Throughout Sikh history, Sikhs have played pivotal roles in advocating for social justice and equality. Whether through peaceful protests, charitable initiatives, or community organizing, Sikhs continue to uphold the legacy of their Gurus by actively working towards creating a more just and equitable society.

Seva and Service

Service, known as Seva, occupies a central place in Sikhism, reflecting the core values and beliefs of the faith. Here's an exploration of the importance of selfless service, examples of community service and humanitarian efforts by Sikhs, and how Seva reflects Sikh values and beliefs.

Importance of Seva (Selfless Service) in Sikhism

Seva holds immense significance in Sikhism, serving as a cornerstone of Sikh spirituality and ethics. It embodies the principles of selflessness, compassion, and unity and plays a vital role in promoting the welfare of all beings and fostering a deeper connection with the divine.

1. **Symbol of Selflessness:** Seva embodies the essence of selflessness, as it involves serving others without any expectation of reward or recognition. Sikhs engage in Seva purely out of a sense of duty and compassion, seeking to alleviate others' suffering and contribute to society's welfare.

2. **Integral to Sikh Spirituality:** Seva is deeply ingrained in Sikh spirituality, serving as a tangible expression of devotion and humility. It is regarded not only as a moral obligation but also as a means of spiritual growth and enlightenment. By selflessly serving others, Sikhs seek to cultivate virtues such as compassion, empathy, and humility, thereby deepening their connection with the divine.

3. **Principle of Sarbat da Bhala:** Sikhism emphasizes the principle of sarbat da bhala, which translates to the welfare of all. Seva is a manifestation of this principle, as Sikhs believe in serving all individuals, regardless of their background, caste, creed, or social status. Through acts of Seva, Sikhs strive to promote

the well-being and happiness of all beings, contributing to the greater good of humanity.

4. **Service as Worship:** In Sikhism, Seva is considered a form of worship and devotion. Just as prayers and meditation are integral to Sikh religious practice, so too is the act of serving others. Sikhs view Seva as a sacred duty and an opportunity to serve the divine present in all beings, thereby sanctifying their actions and elevating their spiritual consciousness.

5. **Community Building and Unity:** Seva plays a crucial role in fostering community building and unity within the Sikh community. Through collective acts of service such as preparing and serving langar (community meal), Sikhs come together to work towards a common goal, strengthening bonds of solidarity and cooperation.

6. **Legacy of the Sikh Gurus:** The Sikh Gurus exemplified the importance of Seva through their actions and teachings. They lead by example, engaging in selfless service and advocating for the welfare of all beings. Sikhs draw inspiration from their Gurus' exemplary lives and strive to emulate their commitment to Seva.

Examples of Community Service and Humanitarian Efforts by Sikhs

Sikhs demonstrate their commitment to Seva through a wide range of community service and humanitarian efforts, reflecting their deep-rooted values of compassion, equality, and service to humanity. These examples serve as testaments to Seva's enduring legacy within the Sikh community and its profound impact on the lives of countless individuals worldwide.

1. **Operation Blue Star:** During Operation Blue Star in 1984, when the Indian military carried out an operation in the Sri Harmandir Sahib complex in Amritsar and many other Gurdwaras complexes in India to kill innocent Sikhs, Sikhs rose to provide aid and assistance to those affected. Sikh volunteers worked tirelessly to provide medical aid, shelter, and support to the wounded and displaced individuals, embodying the spirit of Seva in the face of adversity.

2. **Disaster Relief Efforts:** Sikh organizations are frequently at the forefront of disaster relief efforts, mobilizing resources and volunteers to respond to natural disasters around the world. Whether it's earthquakes, floods, hurricanes, or other calamities, Sikhs are quick to provide assistance in the form of food, shelter, medical aid, and other essential supplies to affected communities, regardless of their background or beliefs.

3. **Pangat (Community Kitchen):** The langar, or community kitchen, is a hallmark of Sikh Seva and serves as a shining example of compassion and service. In Gurudwaras around the world, volunteers come together to prepare and serve free meals to all visitors, irrespective of their social status, caste, creed, or economic

background. The langar embodies the principles of equality, compassion, and service, fostering a sense of unity and solidarity among all who partake in it.

4. **Healthcare Initiatives:** Sikhs are actively involved in providing healthcare services to underserved communities through various initiatives. Sikh-run clinics and medical camps offer free or low-cost medical care, including check-ups, vaccinations, and treatment, to those who lack access to adequate healthcare facilities.

5. **Education and Welfare Programs:** Sikh organizations are engaged in numerous educational and welfare programs aimed at uplifting marginalized communities and empowering individuals through education, skill development, and vocational training. These initiatives help break the cycle of poverty and enable individuals to lead more dignified and fulfilling lives.

6. **Humanitarian Aid and Refugee Support:** Sikhs are known for their generosity in providing humanitarian aid and support to refugees and displaced populations around the world. Sikh organizations often collaborate with international relief agencies to provide essential supplies, shelter, and assistance to those fleeing conflict or persecution, embodying the Sikh values of compassion and solidarity with the vulnerable.

How Seva Reflects Sikh Values and Beliefs

Seva serves as a powerful manifestation of Sikh values and beliefs, embodying principles of equality, compassion, humility, and community. Through acts of selfless service, Sikhs strive to live out the teachings of their faith and make a positive impact in the world, exemplifying the timeless values of Sikhism and inspiring others to do the same.

1. **Equality:** Seva promotes the principle of equality by serving all individuals without discrimination based on social status, caste, or creed. It underscores the inherent worth and dignity of every human being, regardless of their background, and embodies the Sikh belief in the oneness of humanity. Through Seva, Sikhs actively work towards breaking down barriers and promoting inclusivity, fostering a society where all individuals are treated with respect and dignity.

2. **Compassion:** Rooted in compassion and empathy, Seva compels Sikhs to alleviate the suffering of others and address the needs of the less fortunate. It reflects the Sikh value of Daya (compassion), encouraging individuals to empathize with the struggles of others and take action to alleviate their pain and hardship. Through acts of Seva, Sikhs demonstrate their commitment to embodying the compassionate teachings of their faith and making a positive difference in the lives of those in need.

3. **Humility:** Engaging in Seva requires humility, as individuals set aside their own ego and self-interest to serve others with sincerity and humility. It reflects the Sikh principle of Nimrata (humility), reminding individuals to approach service with a sense of humility and modesty, recognizing the interconnectedness of all beings and their shared humanity. By practicing humility in Seva, Sikhs cultivate a spirit of selflessness and devotion, deepening their connection with the divine and serving as humble instruments of service in the world.

4. **Community:** Seva strengthens community bonds and fosters a sense of belonging and solidarity among Sikhs. It encourages cooperation, collaboration, and collective action for the greater good, emphasizing the importance of working together as a community to address shared challenges and uplift one another. Through Seva, Sikhs come together to create a supportive and compassionate community where individuals can find solace, support, and encouragement in times of need.

Sikhism's Teachings on Environmental Stewardship

Sikhism's teachings on environmental stewardship underscore the sacredness of nature, the interconnectedness of all beings, and the responsibility of humans to protect and preserve the Earth. By embracing principles of conservation, sustainability, and compassion, Sikhs strive to be conscientious stewards of the environment, working towards a more harmonious and sustainable relationship with the natural world.

Respect for Creation

Sikhism teaches reverence for all forms of creation, recognizing the divine presence in nature. Sikhs view the Earth as a sacred gift from the Creator, deserving of utmost respect and care. Sri Guru Nanak Dev Ji, the founder of Sikhism, emphasized the importance of treating the environment with reverence and gratitude, urging individuals to recognize nature's beauty and sanctity.

1. **Divine Presence in Nature:** Sikhism teaches that the Earth and all of its inhabitants are manifestations of the divine. Sikhs view nature as a sacred gift from the Creator, infused with divine energy and deserving of utmost reverence and care. This belief underscores the interconnectedness of all beings and the inherent sanctity of the natural world.

2. **Earth as a Sacred Gift:** Sri Guru Nanak Dev Ji, the founder of Sikhism, emphasized the significance of treating the environment with reverence and gratitude. He urged individuals to recognize the Earth as a precious gift bestowed upon humanity by the Creator, deserving of protection and preservation. Guru Nanak's teachings highlight the importance of cultivating a deep sense of appreciation for the beauty and abundance of nature.

3. **Environmental Responsibility:** Sikhs are called to be responsible stewards of the Earth,

recognizing their duty to safeguard the environment for future generations. Sikh teachings emphasize the importance of mindful consumption, sustainable living practices, and conservation efforts aimed at protecting the Earth's natural resources and biodiversity.

4. **Recognition of Beauty and Sanctity:** Sikhism encourages individuals to pause and contemplate the beauty and sanctity of nature. Sikhs are encouraged to immerse themselves in the natural world, whether through meditation in serene natural settings or through the celebration of seasonal festivals that honor the Earth's cycles and rhythms.

5. **Gratitude and Reverence:** Central to Sikh teachings is the practice of expressing gratitude and reverence for the gifts of creation. Sikhs offer prayers of thanksgiving for the abundance provided by the Earth, acknowledging their interconnectedness with the natural world and their dependence on its resources for sustenance and livelihood.

Interconnectedness of All Beings

Sikhism teaches the principle of oneness, emphasizing the interconnectedness of all beings and the intricate web of relationships that bind creation together. Sikhs believe that harming the environment ultimately harms oneself and future generations, underscoring the need for responsible stewardship of the Earth and its resources.

1. **Principle of Oneness:** Sikhism teaches that all beings are interconnected and inseparable, bound together by the divine presence that permeates the universe. Sikhs believe in the concept of Ik Onkar, the affirmation of the one Creator who manifests in all forms of existence. This principle underscores the inherent unity and interconnectedness of all beings, transcending barriers of nationality, race, religion, and species.

2. **Recognition of Interdependence:** Sikhs recognize the interdependence of all living beings and the delicate balance that sustains life on Earth. Every action, whether positive or negative, has ripple effects that reverberate throughout the interconnected web of existence. Sikhs believe that harming any part of creation ultimately harms oneself and future generations, emphasizing the importance of living in harmony with all beings.

3. **Environmental Responsibility:** Sikhism places a strong emphasis on environmental stewardship and responsible caretaking of the Earth. Sikhs believe that humans have a sacred duty to protect and preserve the environment for the well-being of all beings, present and future. By recognizing the interconnectedness of all life forms, Sikhs are motivated to adopt sustainable living practices, conserve natural resources, and minimize harm to the environment.

4. **Ethical Implications:** The principle of interconnectedness in Sikhism has ethical

implications for how individuals interact with the environment and other beings. Sikhs are called to cultivate compassion, empathy, and respect for all life forms, treating every creature with kindness and dignity. This reverence for life extends to animals, plants, and ecosystems, fostering a deep sense of responsibility towards the Earth and its inhabitants.

5. **Collective Responsibility:** Sikhism teaches that all beings share a collective responsibility for the well-being of the Earth and its inhabitants. Sikhs are encouraged to work together as stewards of the environment, collaborating with others to address environmental challenges and promote sustainable solutions. By fostering a sense of unity and solidarity, Sikhs strive to create a world where all beings can thrive in harmony with each other and the natural world.

Conservation and Preservation

Sikh teachings advocate for the conservation and preservation of natural resources, promoting sustainable practices that ensure the well-being of both present and future generations. Sikhs are encouraged to adopt a lifestyle of simplicity and moderation, minimizing waste and consumption to reduce their ecological footprint.

1. **Sustainable Practices:** Sikh teachings promote sustainable practices that prioritize the long-term health and well-being of the environment. Sikhs are encouraged to adopt

lifestyles of simplicity and moderation, minimizing waste and consumption to reduce their ecological footprint. This includes practices such as reducing energy consumption, conserving water, recycling, and using renewable resources whenever possible.

2. **Respect for Nature's Gifts:** Sikhs are taught to have deep reverence for the Earth and its resources, recognizing them as precious gifts from the Creator. By valuing and respecting nature's abundance, Sikhs are inspired to protect and preserve the environment for future generations. This respect extends to all forms of life, fostering a sense of interconnectedness and responsibility towards the natural world.

3. **Minimization of Waste:** Sikh teachings emphasize the importance of minimizing waste and avoiding unnecessary consumption. Sikhs are encouraged to be mindful of their use of resources, reducing waste through practices such as composting, reusing items, and avoiding single-use plastics. By adopting a mindset of conservation, Sikhs aim to minimize their environmental impact and promote sustainable living.

4. **Promotion of Moderation:** Sikhism promotes the value of moderation in all aspects of life, including consumption and material possessions. Sikhs are encouraged to live simply and avoid excessive consumption, recognizing that material wealth does not bring lasting happiness or fulfillment. By prioritizing

spiritual wealth over material possessions, Sikhs cultivate a deeper appreciation for life's essentials and reduce their ecological footprint.

5. **Environmental Awareness and Education:** Sikh organizations often engage in environmental awareness and education initiatives to promote conservation and sustainability within their communities. Through workshops, seminars, and outreach programs, Sikhs raise awareness about environmental issues and empower individuals to take action towards positive change. By fostering environmental literacy and consciousness, Sikhs contribute to building a more environmentally conscious society.

Daya (Compassion) for All Creatures

Sikhism teaches compassion for all living beings, including animals and plants. Sikhs are called to be mindful of their actions' impact on the well-being of other creatures and to strive to minimize harm and suffering in all aspects of life. The Sikh principle of Daya (compassion) extends to the protection and care of animals and the environment.

1. **Mindfulness of Impact:** Sikhs are encouraged to be mindful of the impact of their actions on the well-being of all creatures. This includes being aware of the consequences of their dietary choices, lifestyle practices, and consumption habits on animals, plants, and ecosystems. By cultivating mindfulness, Sikhs strive to minimize harm and suffering in all aspects of life.

444

2. **Minimization of Harm:** Sikh teachings emphasize the importance of minimizing harm and suffering inflicted upon other creatures. Sikhs are encouraged to adopt practices that reduce cruelty and exploitation towards animals, such as following a vegetarian or plant-based diet, avoiding products derived from animal exploitation, and treating animals with kindness and respect.

3. **Protection and Care:** The Sikh principle of Daya (compassion) extends to protecting and caring for animals and the environment. Sikhs are called to show compassion toward all living beings, recognizing their intrinsic value and right to live free from harm and exploitation. This includes advocating for the welfare of animals, supporting initiatives that promote animal rights and conservation, and taking practical steps to ensure their well-being.

4. **Respect for Life:** Sikhism teaches reverence for all forms of life, recognizing the divine presence in every living being. Sikhs view animals and plants as sentient beings deserving of respect and dignity, not merely as resources for human consumption or exploitation. This respect for life extends to ecosystems and the environment, fostering a sense of interconnectedness and responsibility towards the natural world.

5. **Ethical Living Practices:** Sikhs are encouraged to live ethically and compassionately, aligning their actions with the

principles of Daya (compassion) and Hukam (divine order). This includes making conscious choices that minimize harm to animals and the environment, supporting ethical and sustainable practices, and advocating for justice and compassion in all spheres of life.

Environmental Activism and Advocacy

Sikhs are increasingly engaged in environmental activism and advocacy, working to address pressing environmental issues such as pollution, deforestation, climate change, and habitat destruction. Sikh organizations worldwide collaborate with environmental groups and participate in initiatives aimed at promoting conservation, sustainability, and eco-friendly practices.

1. **Addressing Pressing Issues:** Sikhs are actively involved in addressing a wide range of environmental issues, including pollution, deforestation, climate change, habitat destruction, and water scarcity. Recognizing the severity of these challenges, Sikh organizations and individuals are working to raise awareness, mobilize resources, and implement solutions to mitigate environmental degradation.

2. **Collaboration with Environmental Groups:** Sikh organizations collaborate with environmental groups, non-profit organizations, and government agencies to amplify their impact and address environmental issues at local, national, and global levels. By forging partnerships and sharing resources, Sikhs

leverage collective expertise and resources to achieve common environmental goals.

3. **Participation in Initiatives:** Sikh organizations participate in a wide range of environmental initiatives and campaigns aimed at promoting conservation, sustainability, and eco-friendly practices. This includes tree-planting drives, clean-up campaigns, recycling programs, and advocacy efforts to protect natural habitats and endangered species.

4. **Advocating for Policy Change:** Sikhs advocate for policy change and government action to address environmental challenges through legislative reform, advocacy campaigns, and lobbying efforts. Sikh organizations engage with policymakers and decision-makers to promote environmentally responsible policies and support initiatives that prioritize conservation and sustainability.

5. **Educational Outreach:** Sikh organizations conduct educational outreach programs to raise awareness about environmental issues and empower individuals to take action. These programs include workshops, seminars, conferences, and educational materials that provide information on environmental conservation, sustainable living practices, and the importance of protecting the Earth for future generations.

6. **Incorporating Environmental Values into Sikh Practices:** Sikh organizations incorporate

environmental values into Sikh practices and traditions, emphasizing the importance of living in harmony with nature and respecting the Earth's resources. This includes promoting eco-friendly practices in Gurudwaras, such as minimizing waste, conserving energy, and using sustainable materials.

Pangat (Langar) and Food Sustainability

The langar, or community kitchen, exemplifies Sikh principles of sustainability and community sharing. Sikhs emphasize the importance of serving simple, vegetarian meals in langar to minimize the environmental impact of food production and promote food sustainability. By adopting a plant-based diet, Sikhs contribute to reducing greenhouse gas emissions and mitigating environmental degradation.

1. **Serving Simple, Vegetarian Meals:** Sikhs emphasize the importance of serving simple, vegetarian meals in the langar to minimize the environmental impact of food production. Vegetarian meals require fewer resources, such as land, water, and energy, compared to meat-based diets. By serving vegetarian meals in the langar, Sikhs reduce their ecological footprint and promote food sustainability.

2. **Minimizing Environmental Impact:** The langar promotes sustainability by minimizing waste and conserving resources. Meals are prepared using locally sourced, seasonal ingredients to reduce carbon emissions associated with transportation and support local farmers.

Additionally, langar practices emphasize the importance of conserving water, energy, and other resources during food preparation and serving.

3. **Contribution to Climate Change Mitigation:** Adopting a plant-based diet in the langar contributes to reducing greenhouse gas emissions and mitigating climate change. Livestock agriculture, particularly meat production, is a major contributor to greenhouse gas emissions, deforestation, and habitat destruction. By serving vegetarian meals, Sikhs help combat climate change and preserve natural ecosystems.

4. **Promoting Health and Well-being:** Vegetarian diets are associated with numerous health benefits, including reduced risk of chronic diseases such as heart disease, diabetes, and certain types of cancer. By promoting vegetarianism through the langar, Sikhs prioritize the health and well-being of individuals while also promoting environmental sustainability.

5. **Fostering Community Sharing and Equality:** The langar fosters a spirit of community sharing and equality, where all individuals, regardless of their background or social status, come together to share a meal as equals. This inclusive practice promotes social cohesion and solidarity while also reducing food waste and promoting sustainable consumption patterns.

6. **Educational Outreach:** Sikh organizations conduct educational outreach programs to raise awareness about the environmental and health benefits of vegetarianism. By providing information and resources on plant-based diets, Sikhs empower individuals to make informed choices that align with their values and promote sustainability.

Interfaith Dialogue and Pluralism

Interfaith dialogue and pluralism are integral to Sikhism, promoting understanding, respect, and cooperation among people of diverse religious and cultural backgrounds. Through dialogue, collaboration, and advocacy, Sikhs strive to build bridges of understanding and promote peace, harmony, and mutual respect in an increasingly diverse and interconnected world.

1. **Embracing Diversity:** Sikhism embraces the diversity of religious beliefs and practices, recognizing the inherent dignity and value of all faith traditions. Sikhs believe in the principle of Ik Onkar, affirming the oneness of the divine and the interconnectedness of all beings, irrespective of religious affiliation. This inclusive worldview encourages Sikhs to engage in dialogue with people of different faiths, fostering mutual understanding and respect.

2. **Promoting Unity in Diversity:** Sikhs advocate for unity in diversity, recognizing that differences in religious beliefs and practices are a natural part of the human experience. Rather than

seeking to convert others to their own faith, Sikhs strive to build bridges of understanding and cooperation across religious boundaries. Through dialogue and collaboration, Sikhs seek to promote peace, harmony, and mutual respect among people of diverse backgrounds.

3. **Interfaith Dialogue Initiatives:** Sikh organizations actively participate in interfaith dialogue initiatives and forums, where representatives from different religious communities come together to discuss common values, shared concerns, and opportunities for collaboration. These dialogue sessions provide opportunities for Sikhs to learn from others, share their own perspectives, and build meaningful relationships based on mutual respect and understanding.

4. **Engaging in Social Justice Issues:** Sikhs engage in interfaith dialogue not only on spiritual matters but also on social justice issues that affect communities worldwide. By working together with people of different faiths, Sikhs advocate for peace, human rights, environmental sustainability, and other social justice causes, addressing shared concerns and promoting positive change in society.

5. **Celebrating Religious Diversity:** Sikhs celebrate religious diversity through festivals, events, and interfaith gatherings that bring together people from different faith backgrounds. These occasions provide opportunities for dialogue, cultural exchange,

and mutual enrichment, fostering a sense of belonging and unity among diverse communities.

6. **Advocating for Religious Freedom:** Sikhism upholds the principle of religious freedom and advocates for the rights of individuals to practice their faith freely and without fear of discrimination or persecution. Sikhs work alongside people of other faiths to defend religious freedom and promote tolerance and acceptance of religious diversity in society.

Sikhism's Respect for All Religions and Faith Traditions

Sikhism holds deep reverence for all religions and faith traditions, recognizing the inherent wisdom and spiritual truths present in each. Sikhs believe in the equality of all religions and uphold the principle of Ik Onkar, affirming the oneness of the divine manifested in different forms. Sri Guru Nanak Dev Ji, the founder of Sikhism, emphasized the importance of respecting and learning from people of diverse religious backgrounds.

1. **Recognition of Inherent Wisdom:** Sikhism recognizes that every religion and faith tradition contains valuable insights, teachings, and spiritual practices that contribute to the well-being and spiritual growth of humanity. Sikhs believe that all paths ultimately lead to the same divine truth, and thus, they hold deep respect for the diversity of religious expressions and beliefs.

2. **Equality of All Religions:** Sikhs uphold the principle of Ik Onkar, affirming the oneness of the divine manifested in different forms. This principle underscores the equality of all religions and faith traditions, emphasizing that each has its unique contribution to the spiritual tapestry of humanity. Sikhism teaches that no single religion holds a monopoly on truth and that all are worthy of respect and reverence.

3. **Teaching of Sri Guru Nanak Dev Ji:** Sri Guru Nanak Dev Ji, the founder of Sikhism, emphasized the importance of respecting and learning from people of diverse religious backgrounds. He famously proclaimed, "There is no Hindu, there is no Muslim," emphasizing the universality of spiritual truths beyond religious labels. Guru Nanak advocated for interfaith dialogue, mutual understanding, and cooperation as essential components of spiritual growth and societal harmony.

4. **Embrace of Pluralism:** Sikhism embraces religious pluralism, recognizing that diversity is a fundamental aspect of the divine plan. Sikhs celebrate the richness of religious diversity and believe that different faith traditions offer distinct paths to spiritual enlightenment and union with the divine. This pluralistic outlook fosters a spirit of openness, tolerance, and inclusivity within Sikh communities and beyond.

5. **Promotion of Universal Values:** While respecting the diversity of religious beliefs and practices, Sikhism promotes universal values

such as compassion, love, humility, and service to humanity. Sikhs strive to embody these values in their interactions with people of all faiths, fostering understanding, harmony, and cooperation in an increasingly diverse and interconnected world.

Sikh Contributions to Religious Harmony and Understanding

Sikhs have made significant contributions to religious harmony and understanding through their commitment to interfaith dialogue and cooperation. Sikh organizations actively participate in interfaith initiatives, dialogues, and conferences, where representatives from different religious communities come together to discuss common values, shared concerns, and opportunities for collaboration. Sikhs advocate for peace, tolerance, and respect for diversity, working alongside people of other faiths to address social justice issues, promote human rights, and build a more inclusive society.

1. **Active Participation in Interfaith Initiatives:** Sikh organizations actively engage in interfaith initiatives, dialogues, and conferences, where representatives from different religious communities gather to discuss common values, shared concerns, and opportunities for collaboration. By participating in these forums, Sikhs contribute their perspectives and insights, fostering mutual understanding and respect among diverse religious groups.

2. **Advocacy for Peace and Tolerance:** Sikhs advocate for peace, tolerance, and respect for diversity as essential principles for building harmonious and inclusive societies. Through their involvement in interfaith dialogues and collaborations, Sikhs promote a culture of dialogue, reconciliation, and cooperation, challenging prejudice, discrimination, and intolerance wherever they exist.

3. **Addressing Social Justice Issues:** Sikhs actively work alongside people of other faiths to address social justice issues and promote human rights. Whether it's advocating for the rights of marginalized communities, combating poverty and inequality, or promoting environmental sustainability, Sikhs stand in solidarity with individuals and groups from diverse religious backgrounds to address shared concerns and work towards positive social change.

4. **Promoting Humanitarian Initiatives:** Sikh organizations are known for their humanitarian initiatives that transcend religious boundaries. Through langar (community kitchen) programs, disaster relief efforts, and community service projects, Sikhs demonstrate their commitment to serving humanity and alleviating suffering, regardless of religious affiliation. These acts of service exemplify the Sikh principle of seva (selfless service) and contribute to building bridges of

understanding and compassion among diverse communities.

5. **Building Inclusive Communities:** Sikhs strive to build inclusive communities where people of all faiths and backgrounds feel welcomed, respected, and valued. Gurudwaras (Sikh temples) often serve as spaces for interfaith dialogue, cultural exchange, and community engagement, hosting events and activities that bring together people from diverse religious and cultural backgrounds to celebrate shared values and foster mutual understanding.

6. **Embracing Religious Diversity:** Sikhism embraces religious diversity and pluralism, recognizing the inherent dignity and value of all faith traditions. Sikhs celebrate the richness of religious diversity and actively promote dialogue and cooperation among different religious communities, contributing to the creation of a more harmonious and inclusive society.

Challenges and Opportunities in Modern Society

Sikh teachings provide valuable insights and guidance for addressing contemporary challenges and seizing opportunities in modern society. By living according to Sikh principles of compassion, equality, service, and spiritual growth, Sikhs can contribute to creating a more just, sustainable, and compassionate world for present and future generations.

Addressing Contemporary Issues through Sikh Teachings

Sikh teachings provide a timeless framework for addressing contemporary issues such as inequality, social injustice, environmental degradation, and interfaith conflict. By emphasizing values such as compassion, equality, and service to humanity, Sikhs are inspired to actively promote social justice, environmental sustainability, and interfaith harmony.

Navigating Challenges like Materialism, Consumerism, and Globalization

Sikhism encourages individuals to adopt a balanced approach to material wealth and worldly possessions. While acknowledging the importance of meeting one's basic needs and providing for one's family, Sikh teachings caution against excessive attachment to material wealth and consumerism. By cultivating Santokh (contentment) and Vairag (detachment), Sikhs are able to resist the allure of materialism and live a more spiritually fulfilling life in harmony with nature and the universe.

1. **Cultivating Contentment and Detachment:** Sikhism emphasizes the importance of cultivating Santokh and Vairag in one's approach to material wealth and worldly possessions. While acknowledging the necessity of meeting basic needs and providing for one's family, Sikhs are encouraged to avoid excessive attachment to material possessions and the pursuit of wealth for its own sake. By practicing contentment and detachment, Sikhs

are able to find true fulfillment and inner peace beyond the transient pleasures of material wealth.

2. **Fostering Spiritual Values over Material Gain:** Sikh teachings prioritize spiritual values such as compassion, humility, and service to humanity over the pursuit of material gain and worldly success. Sikhs are encouraged to focus on developing virtues of character and contributing to the well-being of others rather than solely seeking personal wealth and accumulation of possessions. By prioritizing spiritual growth and moral integrity, Sikhs navigate the challenges of materialism and consumerism with a deeper sense of purpose and fulfillment.

3. **Embracing Simplicity and Moderation:** Sikhism advocates for simplicity and moderation in lifestyle choices, encouraging individuals to live within their means and avoid excessive consumption. Sikhs are encouraged to adopt a lifestyle that is mindful of environmental sustainability and respects the finite resources of the Earth. By embracing simplicity and moderation, Sikhs reduce their ecological footprint and contribute to a more sustainable and equitable global society.

4. **Promoting Social Responsibility and Justice:** Sikh teachings emphasize the importance of social responsibility and justice in addressing the inequities and injustices perpetuated by materialism, consumerism, and

globalization. Sikhs are called to advocate for the rights and dignity of all individuals, especially those marginalized or exploited by economic systems driven by profit and greed. By promoting social justice and equity, Sikhs work towards creating a more just and compassionate society for all.

5. **Nurturing Spiritual Fulfillment:** Ultimately, Sikhism teaches that true fulfillment and happiness are found not in the accumulation of material possessions but in spiritual growth and inner peace. Sikhs are encouraged to cultivate a deep connection with the divine through meditation, prayer, and selfless service (seva), recognizing that spiritual wealth far surpasses material wealth in value and significance. By nurturing their spiritual well-being, Sikhs find lasting fulfillment and resilience in the face of the challenges posed by materialism, consumerism, and globalization.

Conflict Resolution and Peacebuilding

Sikh teachings emphasize the importance of resolving conflicts through dialogue, negotiation, and nonviolent means. Sikhs are encouraged to promote reconciliation, forgiveness, and understanding in situations of interpersonal, community, or societal conflict. By upholding principles of compassion, empathy, and forgiveness, Sikhs contribute to building bridges of peace and reconciliation in conflict-affected regions and communities.

1. **Dialogue and Negotiation:** Sikhism promotes dialogue and negotiation as essential tools for resolving conflicts peacefully. Sikhs are encouraged to engage in open and constructive communication with conflicting parties, seeking to understand each other's perspectives and interests in order to find mutually acceptable solutions to their differences.

2. **Reconciliation and Forgiveness:** Sikhs are taught to promote reconciliation and forgiveness as pathways to healing and peace. Rather than harboring resentment or seeking revenge, Sikhs are encouraged to extend forgiveness and compassion towards those who have wronged them, fostering a spirit of reconciliation and harmony in their relationships and communities.

3. **Compassion and Empathy:** Sikh teachings emphasize the importance of compassion and empathy in conflict resolution. By cultivating a deep sense of empathy for the suffering and grievances of others, Sikhs are able to respond to conflicts with understanding and empathy, seeking to address underlying issues and restore relationships based on mutual respect and dignity.

4. **Nonviolent Resistance and Advocacy:** Sikhism upholds the principle of nonviolent resistance as a means of confronting injustice and oppression. Sikhs are encouraged to stand up for truth, justice, and human rights through peaceful means, advocating for positive change

while respecting the dignity and humanity of all individuals involved in the conflict.

5. **Building Bridges of Peace and Reconciliation:** Sikhs actively work to build bridges of peace and reconciliation in conflict-affected regions and communities. By promoting interfaith dialogue, cultural exchange, and collaborative initiatives, Sikhs foster understanding, trust, and cooperation among diverse groups, contributing to the resolution of conflicts and the building of sustainable peace.

Opportunities for Applying Sikh Principles in Personal and Societal Contexts

Sikh principles offer practical guidance for addressing personal and societal challenges in today's world. Through practices such as Simran (meditation), Seva (selfless service), and community engagement, Sikhs can cultivate inner peace, resilience, and social responsibility. By living according to the principles of Sat (honesty), Sach (integrity), and Nimrata (humility), Sikhs contribute to building a more just, compassionate, and sustainable society.

Promoting Ethical Leadership and Governance

Sikhism emphasizes the importance of ethical leadership and governance based on principles of justice, integrity, and accountability. Sikh leaders are called to serve with humility and compassion, prioritizing the well-being of the community over personal gain or power. By promoting transparency, accountability, and inclusivity in governance, Sikhs can contribute to creating a more equitable and just society for all.

Cultivating Spiritual Resilience and Well-being

In the face of life's challenges and uncertainties, Sikh teachings offer tools for cultivating spiritual resilience and well-being. Through practices such as Ardas (prayer), Simran (meditation), and Vichar (self-reflection), Sikhs develop inner strength, clarity, and peace of mind. By nurturing their spiritual and mental health, Sikhs are better equipped to navigate the complexities of modern life and contribute positively to their communities and society as a whole.

The Universal Message of Sikhism

Sikhism's core message revolves around the belief in the oneness of the divine (Ek Onkar) and the equality of all humanity. It emphasizes the importance of living a life of compassion, service, and moral integrity while cultivating a deep connection with the divine through meditation and selfless devotion. Sikh teachings promote values of love, justice, humility, and social responsibility, guiding individuals toward spiritual growth and inner peace.

Despite the passage of time and changes in society, Sikh teachings remain profoundly relevant in today's world. In an era marked by increasing division, inequality, and environmental degradation, Sikhism's emphasis on unity, equality, and reverence for nature offers a timeless antidote to the challenges we face. Sikh principles of social justice, compassion, and ethical conduct provide a moral compass for navigating complex ethical dilemmas and promoting a more just, harmonious, and sustainable society.

Sikhism's universal message of love, equality, and service offers profound insights and guidance for individuals seeking meaning, purpose, and spiritual fulfillment in today's world. By embracing Sikh teachings and applying them in our lives, we can contribute to building a more compassionate, just, and sustainable society for future generations.

*****

CONTRIBUTIONS TO SOCIETY AND GLOBAL CULTURE

CONTRIBUTIONS TO SOCIETY AND GLOBAL CULTURE

Sikhism is a rich and all-embracing faith that was established over five centuries ago in the Panjab area of South Asia. Its influence on society and global culture is unmistakable, encompassing far more than just its religious importance. Sikhs have made significant impacts in various fields, embodying the principles of compassion, equality, and service that are at the heart of their faith. The contributions of Sikhs to society and global culture are a testament to the enduring legacy of their values and faith. By adhering to the principles of service, equality, and compassion, Sikhs continue to have a profound impact on the world, improving lives and fostering a more harmonious and fair society for generations to come.

1. **Philanthropy and Humanitarian Efforts:** At the heart of Sikhism lies the principle of seva, or selfless service, which manifests in the community's philanthropic endeavors. Sikh gurdwaras worldwide operate a langar and community kitchens that offer free meals to all, irrespective of background. Moreover, Sikh charitable organizations like Khalsa Aid and United Sikhs are at the forefront of humanitarian relief efforts during crises, providing aid and support to those in need globally.

2. **Education and Healthcare Initiatives:** Sikhs have played a pivotal role in advancing education and healthcare, establishing

institutions that benefit both their communities and society at large. These institutions provide quality education and medical care, contributing to societal development and well-being. Additionally, Sikh-led initiatives extend educational and healthcare support to underserved regions, empowering individuals and enhancing societal outcomes.

3. **Advocacy for Social Justice:** Driven by a commitment to equality and human rights, Sikhs have been vocal advocates for social justice. They actively participate in movements against discrimination, oppression, and injustice, working to raise awareness and effect legislative change. Through interfaith dialogue and community outreach, Sikh activists strive to foster understanding and promote harmony in diverse societies.

4. **Cultural Preservation and Promotion:** Sikhs take pride in their rich cultural heritage and actively work to preserve and promote it. Festivals like Vaisakhi and Sri Guru Nanak Sahib Ji Gurpurab celebrate Sikh traditions and values, while artists, musicians, writers, and filmmakers contribute to cultural diversity by sharing Sikh narratives with a global audience. Through their creative endeavors, Sikhs enrich global culture and promote cross-cultural understanding.

5. **Economic and Entrepreneurial Endeavors:** Sikhs have made significant contributions to economic growth and entrepreneurship across

various sectors. They excel in industries ranging from agriculture to technology, embodying values of honesty, integrity, and hard work. Sikh entrepreneurs not only drive innovation and create jobs but also reinvest in their communities through philanthropy and social investment.

6. **Global Citizenship and Leadership:** Sikhs are active participants in global affairs, serving as leaders, diplomats, and advocates for positive change. Their engagement in civic life and commitment to ethical governance contribute to creating a more just, peaceful, and inclusive world. Through their leadership and actions, Sikhs inspire others to uphold universal values and work towards a better future for all.

Contribution During the Period of Baba Banda Singh Bahadur

Baba Banda Singh Bahadur's contributions as a military leader and visionary statesman were instrumental in shaping Sikh history during the early Khalsa period. His legacy as a champion of justice, equality, and freedom remains an enduring source of inspiration for Sikhs and all those who value human dignity and rights.

1. **Military Leadership and Resistance Against Mughal Oppression:** Baba Banda Singh Bahadur emerged as a fearless leader who led the Khalsa forces in multiple battles against the oppressive Mughal regime. He organized and trained a disciplined army of Sikh warriors,

instilling in them a spirit of courage, resilience, and determination to fight for their rights and freedom.

2. **Establishment of Khalsa Raj:** Baba Banda Singh Bahadur's most notable achievement was the establishment of the first Sikh state, known as Khalsa Raj, in the early 18th century. After a series of successful military campaigns, he captured several key Mughal territories, including Sirhind and Lohgarh, and proclaimed sovereignty over the region.

3. **Implementation of Progressive Policies:** Under Baba Banda Singh Bahadur's leadership, the Khalsa Raj implemented progressive policies aimed at promoting justice, equality, and social welfare. He abolished oppressive taxes and discriminatory practices imposed by the Mughals, ensuring fair treatment and opportunities for all citizens regardless of their background.

4. **Support for Farmers and Common People:** Baba Banda Singh Bahadur was known for his empathy and compassion towards the common people, particularly farmers who had long suffered under the exploitative Mughal regime. He implemented agrarian reforms to alleviate the burden on farmers and improve agricultural productivity, thereby enhancing the livelihoods of rural communities.

5. **Advocacy for Religious Freedom:** As a devout Sikh, Baba Banda Singh Bahadur

advocated for religious freedom and tolerance, ensuring that people of all faiths could practice their beliefs without fear of persecution or discrimination. He respected the diversity of religious traditions within his domain and fostered a spirit of coexistence and mutual respect among different communities.

6. **Inspiration for Future Generations:** Baba Banda Singh Bahadur's legacy continues to inspire Sikhs and people worldwide as a symbol of courage, resilience, and unwavering commitment to justice and righteousness. His valiant efforts laid the foundation for the Khalsa's struggle against tyranny and oppression, inspiring future generations to uphold the principles of Sikhism and fight for justice and freedom.

Facilities Provided to Common People Under Baba Banda Singh Bahadur's Leadership

Under the guidance of Baba Banda Singh Bahadur, a range of initiatives were implemented to enhance the lives of the general populace and promote justice and equality. His administration prioritized the establishment of administrative structures and the implementation of policies that catered to the welfare of the people. Baba Banda Singh Bahadur's leadership was marked by a dedication to providing opportunities and resources to the masses, while working towards the advancement of justice, equality, and socio-economic growth. His initiatives, which included governance improvement, land redistribution, justice administration, economic development, education, and social welfare, set the stage for a more just and prosperous society during the Khalsa Raj.

Administrative Reforms

Baba Banda Singh Bahadur's tenure marked a significant shift in governance, emphasizing effective administration to enhance the well-being of the common people. His administrative reforms aimed to address grievances, promote transparency, and ensure efficient service delivery. His administrative reforms were characterized by decentralization, delegation of authority, responsiveness, transparency, accountability, and efficient service delivery. These reforms aimed to empower local communities, promote public trust, and enhance the overall well-being of common people under the Khalsa Raj.

1. **Decentralization of Power:** Baba Banda Singh Bahadur recognized the limitations of centralized authority and the need to empower local communities. To this end, he decentralized power by establishing administrative structures at the grassroots level. Local administrators were entrusted with decision-making authority, allowing them to address issues promptly and effectively. This decentralization fostered a sense of ownership and accountability among administrators, ensuring responsiveness to the people's needs.

2. **Delegation of Authority:** In addition to decentralization, Baba Banda Singh Bahadur delegated authority to competent individuals capable of governing effectively. He appointed

administrators based on merit and integrity rather than hereditary privileges or political affiliations. This approach ensured that qualified individuals were entrusted with the responsibility of serving the public interest and promoting transparency and accountability in governance.

3. **Responsive Governance:** Baba Banda Singh Bahadur's administration prioritized responsiveness to the populace's needs and concerns. Local administrators were encouraged to maintain open lines of communication with the people they served, actively seeking feedback and addressing grievances. This approach facilitated swift resolution of issues, promoted public trust in the government, and strengthened the bond between rulers and subjects.

4. **Promotion of Transparency and Accountability:** Transparency and accountability were central tenets of Baba Banda Singh Bahadur's governance philosophy. He implemented measures to ensure transparency in decision-making processes, including public consultations and disclosure of administrative actions. Furthermore, he held administrators accountable for their actions, instituting mechanisms for oversight and review to prevent abuse of power and corruption.

5. **Efficient Service Delivery:** Efficient service delivery was a key focus of Baba Banda Singh Bahadur's administrative reforms. He streamlined bureaucratic processes, eliminated

unnecessary red tape, and optimized resource allocation to enhance the delivery of essential services such as justice, security, and infrastructure development. By prioritizing efficiency, his administration sought to meet the needs of the people in a timely and effective manner.

6. **Promotion of Good Governance Principles:** Baba Banda Singh Bahadur's governance model was guided by principles of good governance, including participation, transparency, accountability, rule of law, and responsiveness. These principles served as the foundation for his administrative reforms, guiding decision-making and ensuring that governance practices were aligned with the interests of the people.

Land Reforms and Redistribution

Baba Banda Singh Bahadur recognized the critical role of landownership in shaping economic and social disparities within society. To address these inequalities and promote agricultural productivity, he implemented bold land reforms aimed at redistributing land to landless peasants and small-scale farmers. These reforms played a crucial role in alleviating poverty and promoting social equity within the Khalsa Raj. Some land reforms and redistribution initiatives undertaken during his leadership are:

1. **Addressing Inequalities in Landownership:** Under the Mughal rule, landownership was concentrated in the hands of a privileged few,

leading to widespread disparities and socio-economic imbalances. Baba Banda Singh Bahadur sought to rectify this injustice by implementing policies to redistribute land more equitably among the rural population. By addressing inequalities in landownership, he aimed to create a more just and inclusive society where all individuals had access to productive resources.

2. **Redistribution of Land to Landless Peasants:** One of the key objectives of Baba Banda Singh Bahadur's land reforms was to provide landless peasants with access to agricultural land, enabling them to cultivate and improve their livelihoods. He initiated programs to identify and reclaim land that was lying fallow or underutilized, redistributing it to landless families who were willing to cultivate it. This initiative empowered landless peasants economically and socially, giving them a stake in the prosperity of the Khalsa Raj.

3. **Empowering Small-Scale Farmers:** In addition to addressing the plight of landless peasants, Baba Banda Singh Bahadur's land reforms also aimed to support small-scale farmers who were struggling to make ends meet under oppressive Mughal taxation policies. By redistributing land to small-scale farmers, he provided them with the means to sustain themselves and their families through agricultural production. This initiative fostered

economic self-sufficiency and resilience among rural communities.

4. **Alleviating Poverty and Promoting Social Equity:** Baba Banda Singh Bahadur's land reforms had a transformative impact on the socio-economic landscape of the Khalsa Raj. By redistributing land to those who needed it most, he helped alleviate poverty and reduce socio-economic disparities within society. Access to land provided marginalized communities with a source of income and food security, improving their standard of living and promoting social equity.

5. **Stimulating Agricultural Productivity:** Redistributing land to landless peasants and small-scale farmers not only promoted social equity but also stimulated agricultural productivity within the Khalsa Raj. Newly empowered landowners were motivated to invest in land improvements, adopt modern farming techniques, and increase crop yields. This led to an overall increase in agricultural output, contributing to food security and economic growth in the region.

6. **Legacy of Social Justice and Economic Empowerment:** Baba Banda Singh Bahadur's land reforms left a lasting legacy of social justice and economic empowerment within the Khalsa Raj. By prioritizing the needs of the landless and marginalized, he demonstrated a commitment to inclusive development and equitable distribution of resources. His efforts to

476

redistribute land laid the foundation for a more prosperous and equitable society where all individuals had the opportunity to thrive.

Baba Banda Singh Bahadur's land reforms and redistribution initiatives were instrumental in addressing inequalities, empowering the rural population, alleviating poverty, and promoting social equity within the Khalsa Raj. These reforms underscored his commitment to social justice and economic empowerment, leaving a profound impact on the socio-economic landscape of the region.

Justice and Equality

Baba Banda Singh Bahadur's commitment to justice and equality was central to his governance philosophy. Under his leadership, the Khalsa Raj witnessed the establishment of impartial judicial systems that ensured fair and equitable access to justice for all citizens, irrespective of their social status or background. Some examples of justice and equality that were promoted under his rule were:

1. **Impartial Judicial Systems:** Baba Banda Singh Bahadur recognized the importance of impartiality in dispensing justice. He established judicial systems free from bias and corruption, ensuring that all individuals received a fair trial and due process under the law. Judges were appointed based on their integrity and competence, and they were entrusted with upholding the rule of law and safeguarding the people's rights.

2. **Fair and Equitable Access to Justice:** Under Baba Banda Singh Bahadur's rule, every citizen, regardless of their social status or background, had access to the judicial system. Legal procedures were transparent and accessible, enabling individuals to seek redress for grievances and resolve disputes through legal channels. This ensured that justice was not reserved for the privileged few but was available to all members of society.

3. **Uniform Enforcement of Laws:** Baba Banda Singh Bahadur's administration prioritized uniform law enforcement to uphold order and ensure public safety. Laws were applied consistently and impartially, without discrimination or favoritism. Perpetrators of injustice, whether government officials, nobles, or common citizens, were held accountable for their actions and subjected to legal consequences as prescribed by law.

4. **Protection of Rights and Freedoms:** Baba Banda Singh Bahadur was committed to protecting the rights and freedoms of his subjects. He upheld principles of individual liberty, freedom of expression, and religious tolerance, ensuring that citizens could exercise their rights without fear of persecution or discrimination. His administration respected the diversity of religious beliefs and cultural practices within the Khalsa Raj, promoting a climate of inclusivity and mutual respect.

5. **Accountability and Transparency:** Transparency and accountability were fundamental principles of governance under Baba Banda Singh Bahadur's rule. Government officials and law enforcement agencies were held accountable for their actions, and mechanisms were put in place to prevent abuse of power and corruption. Public institutions operated with integrity and openness, fostering trust and confidence among the populace.

6. **Legacy of Justice and Equality:** Baba Banda Singh Bahadur's commitment to justice and equality left a lasting legacy within the Khalsa Raj. His administration set a precedent for upholding the rule of law, protecting individual rights, and promoting social justice. By ensuring fair and equitable access to justice for all citizens, regardless of their background, he laid the foundation for a more just and inclusive society.

Baba Banda Singh Bahadur's administration was characterized by its unwavering commitment to justice and equality. Through the establishment of impartial judicial systems, uniform enforcement of laws, protection of rights and freedoms, and promotion of accountability and transparency, he fostered a climate of fairness and equity within the Khalsa Raj, leaving a profound impact on its socio-political landscape.

Economic Development and Infrastructure

Baba Banda Singh Bahadur understood the pivotal role that economic development and infrastructure play in fostering prosperity and improving the lives of the populace. Under his leadership, the Khalsa Raj witnessed significant investments in infrastructure projects aimed at enhancing connectivity, facilitating trade and commerce, and stimulating economic growth. The economic development and infrastructure initiatives undertaken during his rule were:

1. **Improvement of Connectivity:** Baba Banda Singh Bahadur prioritized the development of transportation infrastructure to improve connectivity within the Khalsa Raj and beyond. He oversaw the construction of roads and highways, linking remote villages and urban centers and facilitating the movement of goods and people. Improved connectivity not only boosted trade and commerce but also enhanced access to essential services and opportunities for economic advancement.

2. **Construction of Bridges and Waterways:** Recognizing the importance of waterways in facilitating trade and transportation, Baba Banda Singh Bahadur's administration invested in the construction of bridges and canals. These infrastructure projects provided vital links between different regions and facilitated the movement of goods by water, further stimulating economic activity and promoting regional integration.

3. **Development of Markets and Trade Hubs:** Baba Banda Singh Bahadur promoted the development of markets and trade hubs as centers of economic activity and exchange. He established vibrant marketplaces where merchants from diverse backgrounds could buy, sell, and trade goods. These markets served as hubs for commercial activity, attracting traders from neighboring regions and fostering economic growth and prosperity.

4. **Diversification of Economic Activities:** To promote economic resilience and sustainability, Baba Banda Singh Bahadur encouraged the diversification of economic activities within the Khalsa Raj. He supported the development of industries such as agriculture, handicrafts, textiles, and metallurgy, creating opportunities for entrepreneurship and innovation. By diversifying the economy, he reduced dependence on a single sector and laid the foundation for long-term economic growth.

5. **Support for Entrepreneurship and Innovation:** Baba Banda Singh Bahadur's administration fostered a conducive environment for entrepreneurship and innovation, encouraging individuals to pursue new ventures and ideas. He provided support and incentives for aspiring entrepreneurs, including access to capital, training, and market opportunities. This support for entrepreneurship and innovation fueled economic dynamism and contributed to the prosperity of the Khalsa Raj.

6. **Legacy of Economic Growth and Prosperity:** Baba Banda Singh Bahadur's focus on economic development and infrastructure left a lasting legacy of growth and prosperity within the Khalsa Raj. His investments in transportation, markets, and trade infrastructure laid the foundation for a vibrant economy that thrived long after his rule. The economic progress achieved under his leadership contributed to the overall well-being and prosperity of the populace, enhancing their quality of life and fostering a sense of pride and optimism for the future.

Baba Banda Singh Bahadur's administration's emphasis on economic development and infrastructure played a crucial role in stimulating economic growth, facilitating trade and commerce, and improving the overall well-being of the populace within the Khalsa Raj. His vision and leadership paved the way for a prosperous and resilient economy that benefited generations to come.

Promotion of Education and Culture

Baba Banda Singh Bahadur understood the pivotal role of education and cultural preservation in nation-building and community development. His administration placed significant emphasis on promoting literacy, knowledge dissemination, and the preservation of Sikh culture and heritage. Initiatives undertaken to promote education and culture during his rule are:

1. **Establishment of Schools and Educational Institutions:** Recognizing that education is the cornerstone of progress and empowerment, Baba Banda Singh Bahadur supported the establishment of schools and educational institutions across the Khalsa Raj. These institutions provided formal education to children and adults, promoting literacy and fostering intellectual growth. By investing in education, his administration aimed to empower individuals with knowledge and skills essential for personal and societal advancement.

2. **Promotion of Literacy and Knowledge Dissemination:** Baba Banda Singh Bahadur prioritized the promotion of literacy and knowledge dissemination among the masses. He encouraged the widespread adoption of written language and supported initiatives to make educational resources accessible to all. Libraries, scriptoria, and learning centers were established to facilitate the dissemination of knowledge, fostering a culture of learning and intellectual curiosity within the Khalsa Raj.

3. **Preservation and Promotion of Sikh Culture and Heritage:** As a devout Sikh, Baba Banda Singh Bahadur recognized the importance of preserving and promoting Sikh culture and heritage. He encouraged the celebration of Sikh festivals, such as Vaisakhi and Sri Guru Nanak Sahib Gurpurab, which served as occasions for communal worship, reflection, and cultural expression. Furthermore, he supported

initiatives to document and preserve heritage, traditions, and historical narratives, ensuring that future generations could connect with their rich cultural heritage.

4. **Fostering Pride and Identity:** Baba Banda Singh Bahadur's administration played a crucial role in fostering a sense of pride and identity among common people. By promoting Sikh culture, language, and traditions, he instilled a sense of belonging and unity within the community. Educational initiatives and cultural events served as platforms for individuals to connect with their roots, affirm their identity, and strengthen their commitment to Sikh values and principles.

5. **Integration of Cultural Education:** In addition to formal education, Baba Banda Singh Bahadur emphasized the importance of cultural education as a means of instilling values, ethics, and moral principles. Schools and educational institutions integrated cultural education into their curriculum, teaching students about Sikh history, philosophy, and traditions. This holistic approach to education aimed to nurture well-rounded individuals who were not only academically proficient but also morally upright and culturally aware.

6. **Legacy of Cultural Enrichment:** Baba Banda Singh Bahadur's promotion of education and culture left a lasting legacy of cultural enrichment within the Khalsa Raj. His initiatives to promote literacy, preserve Sikh heritage, and

foster cultural pride contributed to the vitality and resilience of Sikh identity. The educational and cultural institutions established during his rule served as pillars of community development and empowerment, nurturing generations of individuals who were proud of their heritage and committed to upholding Sikh values.

Baba Banda Singh Bahadur's administration's promotion of education and culture played a crucial role in nurturing a vibrant and resilient society within the Khalsa Raj. His commitment to literacy, knowledge dissemination, and cultural preservation laid the foundation for a flourishing community that cherished its heritage and embraced its identity with pride and confidence.

Social Welfare Initiatives

A strong commitment to social welfare and compassion for the vulnerable and marginalized segments of society characterized Baba Banda Singh Bahadur's administration. Recognizing the importance of solidarity and empathy, he initiated various social welfare programs and established charitable institutions to provide assistance to those in need within the Khalsa Raj. Social welfare initiatives undertaken during his rule are:

1. **Support for the Elderly:** Baba Banda Singh Bahadur's administration prioritized support for the elderly, recognizing their vulnerability and the need for care and assistance in their later years. Charitable institutions and programs were established to provide shelter, food, and

medical care for elderly individuals who lacked familial support or resources. These initiatives aimed to ensure that elderly citizens could live with dignity and security during their twilight years.

2. **Assistance for Widows:** In traditional societies, widows often face social and economic challenges, including stigma, poverty, and isolation. Baba Banda Singh Bahadur's administration sought to alleviate their plight by providing them with support and assistance. Charitable programs were established to offer financial aid, vocational training, and social support to widows, empowering them to rebuild their lives and regain independence.

3. **Care for Orphans:** Orphans were among society's most vulnerable members, lacking the support and protection of family networks. Baba Banda Singh Bahadur's administration implemented initiatives to provide care and support for orphaned children, including orphanages, educational scholarships, and mentorship programs. These initiatives aimed to ensure that orphaned children received the love, care, and opportunities they needed to thrive and reach their full potential.

4. **Assistance for Disadvantaged Groups:** Baba Banda Singh Bahadur's administration extended support to various disadvantaged groups within society, including the disabled, the destitute, and those affected by natural disasters or conflicts. Charitable institutions and

welfare programs were established to provide assistance, including food aid, shelter, medical care, and rehabilitation support. These initiatives demonstrated a commitment to social justice and solidarity with society's most vulnerable members.

5. **Empowerment through Education and Training:** In addition to providing immediate assistance, Baba Banda Singh Bahadur's administration prioritized long-term empowerment through education and training. Charitable institutions offer educational opportunities, vocational training, and skills development programs to help disadvantaged individuals acquire the knowledge and skills needed to improve their livelihoods and achieve self-sufficiency. By investing in education and training, his administration aimed to break the cycle of poverty and dependency, empowering individuals to lead independent and fulfilling lives.

6. **Legacy of Compassion and Solidarity:** Baba Banda Singh Bahadur's social welfare initiatives left a lasting legacy of compassion and solidarity within the Khalsa Raj. His administration's commitment to supporting the vulnerable and marginalized segments of society reflected the core values of Sikhism, including compassion (daya) and service (seva). The charitable institutions and welfare programs established during his rule served as symbols of hope and compassion, embodying the spirit of solidarity

and collective responsibility towards those in need.

A deep commitment to compassion, solidarity, and social justice characterized Baba Banda Singh Bahadur's administration's social welfare initiatives. By providing assistance to the elderly, widows, orphans, and other disadvantaged groups, his administration demonstrated a dedication to upholding the dignity and well-being of all members of society within the Khalsa Raj.

Sikh Misls

The Sikh Misls, meaning "confederacies" or "bands," were military units formed by Sikh chieftains in the Panjab region of South Asia during the 18th century. These misls played a significant role in shaping Sikh history, particularly during the Sikh Confederacy, which led to the formation of the Sikh Empire under Maharaja Ranjit Singh.

1. **Bhangi Misl**

   - **First Jathedar:** Hari Singh Bhangi

   - **Geographical Area:** The Bhangi Misl was primarily based around Amritsar and Lahore, but its influence extended to parts of the Majha region of Panjab.

2. **Kanhaiya Misl**

   - **First Jathedar:** Jai Singh Kanhaiya

   - **Geographical Area:** The Kanhaiya Misl's territory was situated in the areas around the

Hoshiarpur, Jalandhar, and Kapurthala districts of Panjab.

3. **Ramgarhia Misl**

  - **First Jathedar:** Jassa Singh Ramgarhia

  - **Geographical Area:** The Ramgarhia Misl was centered around the regions of Amritsar and Tarn Taran in Panjab.

4. **Ahluwalia Misl**

  - **First Jathedar:** Jassa Singh Ahluwalia

  - **Geographical Area:** The Ahluwalia Misl's influence extended across regions in present-day Panjab, Haryana, and Himachal Pradesh, with significant territories around Kapurthala, Jalandhar, and parts of Doaba.

5. **Singhpuria Misl**

  - **First Jathedar:** Nawab Kapur Singh

  - **Geographical Area:** The Singhpuria Misl operated primarily in the areas around Amritsar and Gurdaspur, but its influence extended to parts of the Majha and Doaba regions.

6. **Sukerchakia Misl**

  - **First Jathedar:** Charat Singh Sukerchakia

  - **Geographical Area:** The Sukerchakia Misl was based in the Gujranwala and Sheikhupura regions of present-day east

Panjab, and its influence extended to parts of Panjab and Kashmir.

7. **Nakai Misl**

- **First Jathedar:** Naudh Singh Nakai

- **Geographical Area:** The Nakai Misl operated in the regions of Rawalpindi and Jhelum, with influence extending to parts of Panjab and the Potohar Plateau.

8. **Kanheya Misl**

- **First Jathedar:** Jassa Singh Kanheya

- **Geographical Area:** The Kanheya Misl's territory covered areas around Sialkot and Narowal in present-day east Panjab, and its influence extended to regions along the Sutlej River.

9. **Nishanwalia Misl**

- **First Jathedar:** Tara Singh Ghaiba

- **Geographical Area:** The Nishanwalia Misl operated in the regions around Ferozepur and Moga, with influence extending to parts of Malwa and Rajasthan.

10. **Dallewalia Misl**

- **First Jathedar:** Gulab Singh Dallewalia

- **Geographical Area:** The Dallewalia Misl was primarily based in the regions around Bathinda and Mansa in Panjab, with influence extending to parts of Malwa.

11. Phulkian Misl

- **First Jathedar:** Ala Singh

- **Geographical Area:** The Phulkian Misl's territory covered areas around Patiala, Nabha, and Jind in present-day Panjab, with influence extending to parts of Malwa and the Sutlej River belt.

12. Misl Shaheeda

- **First Jathedar:** Baba Deep Singh Ji

- **Geographical Area:** The Sikh Misl of Shaheeda operated primarily in the regions around Amritsar and Tarn Taran, with a focus on protecting Sikh Gurdwaras and religious sites.

Facilities Provided to Common People Under Sikh Misl's Leadership

Under Sikh Misls' leadership, common people benefited from a range of facilities and initiatives aimed at promoting agriculture, trade, and social welfare. These efforts were instrumental in fostering economic development, improving livelihoods, and enhancing the overall well-being of the population in Panjab during the 18th century.

Agriculture

The land reforms, investment in agricultural infrastructure, and provision of subsidies and support by the Sikh Misls played a crucial role in promoting agriculture and fostering economic growth in Panjab during the 18th century. These initiatives empowered farmers, improved agricultural practices, and contributed to the overall development and prosperity of the region.

1. **Land Reforms and Redistribution:** Sikh Misls recognized the inequities in landownership prevalent during their time. To address this, they implemented land reforms aimed at redistributing land to landless peasants and small-scale farmers. By redistributing land fairly, the Misls aimed to empower farmers economically and foster a sense of ownership and stewardship over the land. This initiative also aimed to reduce social disparities and promote agricultural sustainability.

2. **Infrastructure for Agriculture:** The Misls understood the importance of reliable water sources for agriculture, especially in a region like Panjab with varying climatic conditions. They invested in the development of irrigation systems, wells, and canals to improve water availability for farming. These infrastructure projects facilitated cultivation even in arid regions and during dry seasons, ensuring a consistent water supply for crops. As a result, agricultural output increased, contributing to food security and economic stability.

3. **Subsidies and Support:** Recognizing the financial constraints faced by farmers, the Sikh Misls provided subsidies, agricultural loans, and technical assistance to support agricultural activities. Farmers were offered financial support to invest in modern farming practices,

including the purchase of high-quality seeds, fertilizers, and equipment. Technical assistance and training programs were also provided to improve farming techniques and crop management practices. This support enabled farmers to enhance crop yields and agricultural productivity, leading to increased food production and economic prosperity within the region.

Trade

The Sikh Misls' efforts in developing trade routes, establishing market infrastructure, and regulating trade practices played a crucial role in promoting trade and commerce in Panjab during the 18th century. These initiatives facilitated economic exchanges, stimulated regional growth, and contributed to the overall prosperity of the region.

1. **Development of Trade Routes:** Sikh Misls recognized the importance of trade in stimulating economic activity and promoting regional prosperity. They played a significant role in developing trade routes connecting Panjab with neighboring regions and beyond. These routes facilitated the exchange of goods and services, fostering commercial interactions and cultural exchange. The Misls ensured the safety of trade caravans and merchants, protecting them from external threats and banditry, which encouraged trade activities.

2. **Market Infrastructure:** The Misls established marketplaces and trade hubs at strategic

locations throughout Panjab. These marketplaces served as centers of economic activity, where merchants could buy, sell, and exchange goods. The establishment of market infrastructure provided opportunities for entrepreneurs to engage in trade and commerce. It also facilitated the flow of goods and capital, stimulating economic growth and creating employment opportunities within the region.

3. **Regulation and Fair-Trade Practices:** Recognizing the importance of fair-trade practices in fostering trust and confidence among traders and consumers, Sikh Misls enacted laws and regulations to regulate trade activities. These regulations ensured fair competition, prevented exploitation, and resolved disputes arising from commercial transactions. By promoting transparency and accountability in trade practices, Misls created a conducive environment for trade, encouraging investment and economic development.

Social Welfare

The social welfare initiatives undertaken by the Sikh Misls during the 18th century exemplified their commitment to compassion, solidarity, and social justice. By establishing charitable institutions, providing relief assistance, and implementing empowerment programs, the Misls sought to address the needs of the vulnerable and marginalized, ensuring their well-being and fostering inclusive growth and development within the Sikh community and beyond.

1. **Charitable Institutions:** Recognizing the needs of the vulnerable and marginalized, Sikh Misls established charitable institutions such as hospitals, orphanages, and shelters. These institutions provided essential services such as healthcare, education, and social support to those in need. Hospitals offered medical care to the sick and injured, while orphanages provided shelter and care to orphaned children. Shelters offered refuge to the homeless and destitute, providing them with food, clothing, and temporary accommodation. These charitable institutions served as safety nets for vulnerable populations, including widows, orphans, and the elderly, offering them protection and support in times of hardship.

2. **Relief Measures:** Sikh Misls demonstrated their commitment to humanitarianism by providing relief assistance during times of natural disasters, famines, or emergencies. They mobilized resources and manpower to offer timely aid to affected communities. Relief measures included the distribution of food, shelter, and medical aid to alleviate the suffering of those affected by disasters. Sikh Misls prioritized the needs of the affected populations, ensuring that relief efforts were efficient and targeted.

3. **Empowerment Programs:** Sikh Misls initiated empowerment programs aimed at uplifting marginalized sections of society and providing them with opportunities for socioeconomic

advancement. These programs included vocational training, skill development, and education initiatives designed to enhance the livelihoods and opportunities of the underprivileged. Vocational training centers offered courses in various trades and crafts, equipping individuals with practical skills for employment and self-sufficiency. Education initiatives focused on providing access to formal education for children from disadvantaged backgrounds, empowering them with knowledge and opportunities for personal growth and development.

Maharaja Ranjit Singh: The Lion of Panjab

Maharaja Ranjit Singh's contributions to the world's betterment encompassed political, social, economic, and cultural spheres. His leadership and legacy continue to be celebrated, not only in Panjab but also globally, as a testament to the rich heritage and enduring legacy of the Sikh Empire.

Maharaja Ranjit Singh, born on November 13, 1780, in Gujranwala, Panjab, belonged to the Sukerchakia Misl, one of the prominent Sikh confederacies of the time. His father, Maha Singh, was the prominent leader of the Sukerchakia Misl, and his mother was Raj Kaur. Ranjit Singh's grandfather was Charat Singh, the founder of the Sukerchakia Misl. Maharaja Ranjit Singh's eldest son and heir apparent was Kharak Singh. Other prominent children included Sher Singh, Multana Singh, and Duleep Singh. His wife Maharani Jind Kaur, also known as Rani Jindan, had a significant influence during Ranjit Singh's reign and beyond.

Contribution to the World's Betterment

Maharaja Ranjit Singh is renowned for his exceptional leadership, military prowess, and statesmanship, which led to the establishment of the Sikh Empire in the early 19th century. His contributions to world betterment are multifaceted:

1. **Consolidation of the Sikh Empire:** Maharaja Ranjit Singh unified the various Sikh Misls and territories under his rule, establishing the Sikh Empire, which extended across significant parts of present-day Pakistan and northwestern India. His astute diplomatic skills and military campaigns helped him consolidate power and maintain stability within his realm.

2. **Religious Tolerance and Pluralism:** Despite being a devout Sikh, Maharaja Ranjit Singh was known for his religious tolerance and respect for all faiths. He appointed officials from diverse religious backgrounds and granted religious freedoms to his subjects, fostering a sense of pluralism and harmony within his empire.

3. **Modernization and Infrastructure Development:** Maharaja Ranjit Singh initiated extensive modernization and infrastructure projects, including the construction of roads, bridges, forts, and irrigation systems. He encouraged trade and commerce, leading to economic prosperity and growth within his empire.

4. **Cultural Renaissance:** Under Maharaja Ranjit Singh's patronage, the Sikh Empire experienced a cultural renaissance, with significant contributions to art, architecture, literature, and music. Lahore, the capital of his empire, flourished as a center of culture and learning, attracting scholars, artists, and intellectuals from across South Asia.

5. **Strategic Alliances and Diplomacy:** Maharaja Ranjit Singh skillfully navigated diplomatic relations with neighboring powers, including the British East India Company, Afghanistan, and the Persian Empire. Through strategic alliances and treaties, he maintained a balance of power in the region, safeguarding the sovereignty of the Sikh Empire.

6. **Legacy of Governance:** Maharaja Ranjit Singh's legacy extends beyond his lifetime. His efficient administrative reforms, emphasis on meritocracy, and promotion of justice and equality laid the foundation for progressive governance in Panjab. His empire became a model of good governance and inspired future leaders in the region.

Facilities Provided to Common People Under Maharaja Ranjit Singh's Leadership

Maharaja Ranjit Singh's rule ushered in a transformative period in Panjab's and world's history, characterized by infrastructure development, religious tolerance, and cultural patronage. His administration's focus on these aspects contributed to the stability, prosperity, and cultural richness of the Sikh Empire, leaving a lasting legacy that continues to be celebrated today.

Infrastructure Development

Under the visionary leadership of Maharaja Ranjit Singh, Panjab witnessed a remarkable era of infrastructure development, reflecting his astute understanding of the vital role infrastructure plays in fostering economic prosperity and efficient governance. Maharaja Ranjit Singh's administration initiated ambitious projects aimed at modernizing Panjab's infrastructure, thereby laying the groundwork for the region's progress and advancement. Key infrastructure developments undertaken during Ranjit Singh's rule are:

1. **Road Networks:** Maharaja Ranjit Singh's administration invested significantly in the construction and maintenance of an extensive network of roads and highways throughout Panjab. These roads not only facilitated the movement of goods and people but also enhanced connectivity between different regions within the empire. Improved road infrastructure stimulated trade and commerce by facilitating the transportation of goods to various markets, thereby boosting economic activity and promoting regional integration.

2. **Canal Systems and Irrigation:** Recognizing the critical importance of agriculture in Panjab's economy, Maharaja Ranjit Singh prioritized the development of canal systems and irrigation

infrastructure. His administration undertook the construction of canals and water channels to harness water resources effectively for agricultural purposes. These irrigation projects significantly expanded cultivable land and enhanced agricultural productivity, ensuring food security and prosperity for the populace.

3. **Fortifications and Defense:** Maharaja Ranjit Singh fortified key cities and strategic locations within his empire, investing in the construction and renovation of forts and defensive structures. The strengthening of fortifications not only served as a deterrent against external threats but also bolstered internal security and stability. Forts such as the Lahore Fort were renovated and expanded under Ranjit Singh's patronage, symbolizing the strength and resilience of the Sikh Empire.

4. **Urban Development:** Ranjit Singh's administration focused on the development and beautification of urban centers, with Lahore emerging as the epitome of cultural and architectural splendor. The construction of palaces, gardens, bazaars, and public buildings transformed Lahore into a vibrant and cosmopolitan city. Architectural marvels such as the Samadhi of Ranjit Singh and the Hazuri Bagh Baradari showcased the grandeur and magnificence of Sikh architecture.

5. **Trade and Commercial Infrastructure:** Maharaja Ranjit Singh encouraged the establishment of marketplaces, trade hubs, and

commercial centers across Panjab, facilitating economic exchange and commercial activities. These marketplaces served as centers of economic activity, attracting traders and merchants from various regions. The promotion of trade and commerce contributed to the prosperity and growth of Panjab's economy under Ranjit Singh's rule.

Religious Tolerance

Maharaja Ranjit Singh's reign stands out as a period of remarkable religious tolerance and pluralism in Panjab. His administration was committed to fostering harmony and coexistence among the diverse religious communities within the Sikh Empire. Maharaja Ranjit Singh's approach to governance emphasized religious tolerance as a cornerstone of his administration, leading to a flourishing environment of mutual respect and understanding.

1. **Equal Treatment of Subjects:** Maharaja Ranjit Singh ensured that people of all faiths were treated with respect and equality under his rule. Regardless of their religious affiliations, subjects were afforded the same rights and privileges, fostering a sense of inclusivity and acceptance within the empire.

2. **Religious Freedom:** Under Maharaja Ranjit Singh's administration, individuals were granted the freedom to practice their respective faiths without fear of persecution or discrimination. Sikhs, Hindus, Muslims, and members of other religious communities were free to worship

according to their beliefs, contributing to a climate of religious harmony.

3. **Appointment of Officials:** Maharaja Ranjit Singh appointed officials and administrators from diverse religious backgrounds, reflecting his commitment to meritocracy and inclusivity. This inclusive approach to governance ensured that individuals were appointed based on their qualifications and capabilities rather than their religious affiliations.

4. **Patronage of Religious Institutions:** Maharaja Ranjit Singh patronized religious institutions across Panjab, providing support for the construction and maintenance of temples, gurdwaras, mosques, and other places of worship. This patronage demonstrated his respect for religious diversity and his commitment to preserving and promoting the cultural heritage of all communities.

5. **Interfaith Dialogues and Collaboration:** Maharaja Ranjit Singh facilitated interfaith dialogues and collaboration, bringing together religious leaders and scholars from different faith traditions to promote understanding and cooperation. These initiatives helped bridge religious divides and fostered a spirit of mutual respect and empathy among diverse communities.

6. **Religious Festivals and Celebrations:** Maharaja Ranjit Singh encouraged the celebration of religious festivals and traditions from various faiths within his empire. Festivals such as Diwali, Eid, and Vaisakhi were

celebrated with great pomp and splendor, showcasing Panjab's rich cultural tapestry and promoting intercommunity harmony.

Maharaja Ranjit Singh's administration exemplified a commitment to religious tolerance and pluralism, creating an environment where individuals of diverse religious backgrounds could coexist harmoniously. His visionary leadership and inclusive governance fostered a sense of unity and mutual respect among the religious communities of Panjab, leaving behind a legacy of religious tolerance and interfaith harmony that continues to resonate today.

Cultural Patronage

Maharaja Ranjit Singh's reign marked a golden era of cultural patronage in Panjab and world history, characterized by a flourishing of artistic expression and creativity. Under his visionary leadership, Panjab experienced a renaissance in various cultural domains, including art, architecture, literature, and music. Ranjit Singh's patronage of culture not only enriched Panjab's heritage but also contributed to the region's prestige and identity.

1. **Architecture and Art:** Maharaja Ranjit Singh's patronage of architecture and art led to the creation of magnificent monuments and structures that adorned Panjab's landscape. The architectural marvels commissioned during his reign, such as the Lahore Fort, the Samadhi of Ranjit Singh, and the Hazuri Bagh Baradari, showcased the grandeur and splendor of Sikh architecture. Artists and craftsmen flourished

under Maharaja Ranjit Singh's patronage, producing exquisite paintings, sculptures, and decorative arts that adorned palaces, gurdwaras, and public buildings. These artistic endeavors celebrated Sikh culture and heritage, contributing to Panjab's rich artistic legacy.

2. **Literature and Scholarship:** Maharaja Ranjit Singh's court was a center of intellectual and literary activity, attracting scholars, poets, and writers from across South Asia. The period witnessed a proliferation of literary works in Panjabi, Persian, and other languages, exploring themes of love, valor, and spirituality.

3. **Music and Performing Arts:** Maharaja Ranjit Singh was a patron of music and the performing arts, fostering a vibrant cultural milieu that celebrated Panjab's rich musical traditions. Court musicians and performers entertained the royal court and the public with melodious compositions and captivating performances. The patronage of music and dance flourished under Maharaja Ranjit Singh's rule, with classical forms such as kirtan, Gurbani, and bhangra gaining prominence. Musicians and dancers were esteemed members of the royal court, contributing to the cultural vibrancy of Panjab.

4. **Cultural Festivals and Celebrations:** Maharaja Ranjit Singh encouraged the celebration of cultural festivals and traditions, including religious festivals such as Diwali, Eid, and Vaisakhi, as well as secular celebrations such as Baisakhi and Lohri. These festivals

were marked by grand processions, feasts, and cultural performances that brought communities together in joyous celebration. The promotion of cultural festivals fostered a sense of community and belonging among the people of Panjab, strengthening social cohesion and cultural identity.

Maharaja Ranjit Singh's patronage of culture during his reign resulted in a vibrant cultural renaissance in Panjab, characterized by artistic innovation, intellectual inquiry, and communal celebration. His support for art, architecture, literature, and music enriched Panjab's cultural heritage and left a lasting legacy of cultural excellence that continues to inspire and resonate with generations to come.

Contributions During World War I

The contributions of Sikh soldiers during World War I were integral to the Allied victory and remain a poignant reminder of their courage, sacrifice, and resilience in the face of adversity. Their legacy continues to resonate today, serving as a testament to the enduring spirit of the Sikh community and their unwavering commitment to duty and service.

Military Service and Sacrifice

Sikh soldiers made invaluable contributions to the Allied war effort during World War I, demonstrating remarkable courage, discipline, and resilience on the battlefield. Serving in various theaters of the war, including the Western Front, the Middle East, and East Africa, Sikh soldiers played a pivotal role in shaping the course of history.

1. **Crucial Role in Allied War Effort:** Sikh soldiers formed a significant part of the British Indian Army and played a crucial role in supporting the Allied war effort. Their military expertise, combat skills, and steadfast resolve contributed to the success of Allied operations on multiple fronts.

2. **Courage and Resilience:** Despite facing unfamiliar terrain, harsh climates, and formidable adversaries, Sikh soldiers displayed unwavering courage and determination on the battlefield. Their ability to endure extreme hardships and overcome daunting challenges exemplified their resilience and commitment to duty.

3. **Distinction and Recognition:** Sikh soldiers earned widespread recognition and respect for their bravery and valor in combat. Their acts of courage and selflessness were frequently acknowledged through military honors and decorations, including the Victoria Cross, the highest award for valor in the British Empire.

4. **Ultimate Sacrifice:** Many Sikh soldiers made the ultimate sacrifice, laying down their lives in defense of freedom and justice. Their willingness to make such profound sacrifices for the greater good remains a poignant testament to their unwavering commitment to duty and service.

5. **Legacy of Sacrifice:** The sacrifices of Sikh soldiers during World War I are commemorated and honored through memorials, monuments,

and ceremonies around the world. These tributes serve as a poignant reminder of their courage, valor, and sacrifice in the service of their country and humanity.

Sikh soldiers' crucial role in the Allied war effort during World War I, their exemplary courage and resilience on the battlefield, and their ultimate sacrifice in defense of freedom and justice have left an enduring legacy that continues to inspire reverence and admiration today. Their contributions stand as a testament to the indomitable spirit and unwavering commitment of Sikh soldiers to serve their country and uphold the values of courage, honor, and sacrifice.

Role in the British Indian Army

The role of Sikh soldiers in the British Indian Army during World War I was pivotal, with their regiments forming a formidable force within the Indian Expeditionary Force. Here's a closer look at their contributions and capabilities within the British Indian Army:

1. **Significance of Sikh Regiments:** Sikh soldiers constituted a significant portion of the British Indian Army, with dedicated regiments such as the Sikh Regiment, Sikh Light Infantry, and Sikh Pioneers. These regiments were renowned for their martial traditions, discipline, and combat effectiveness, earning them a reputation as elite fighting units.

2. **Military Prowess and Martial Traditions:** Sikh soldiers brought with them a rich legacy of martial traditions and military prowess, honed

through centuries of valorous service and warfare. Their fearlessness, discipline, and battlefield skills made them formidable warriors on the battlefield, capable of facing and overcoming the most formidable adversaries.

3. **Versatility and Adaptability:** Sikh soldiers served in various capacities within the British Indian Army, showcasing their versatility and adaptability in diverse combat scenarios. Whether serving as infantrymen, cavalry troopers, artillery gunners, or engineering specialists, Sikh soldiers demonstrated their proficiency and effectiveness across different roles and functions.

4. **Combat Effectiveness:** Sikh soldiers played a crucial role in key battles and engagements on multiple fronts, including the Western Front, the Middle East, and East Africa. Their combat effectiveness and resilience under fire contributed significantly to the success of Allied operations and campaigns.

5. **Leadership and Command:** Sikh officers and non-commissioned officers (NCOs) provided strong leadership and command within their units, guiding and inspiring their fellow soldiers with their professionalism, courage, and tactical acumen. Their leadership was instrumental in maintaining unit cohesion and morale during the rigors of combat.

6. **Legacy and Recognition:** The contributions of Sikh regiments within the British Indian Army

during World War I are commemorated and honored through memorials, monuments, and ceremonies. Their valor and sacrifice continue to be celebrated as part of the rich military heritage of the Sikh community and the broader Indian Army.

Sikh soldiers played a vital role within the British Indian Army during World War I, with their regiments forming a formidable backbone of the Indian Expeditionary Force. Their military prowess, martial traditions, versatility, and leadership capabilities made them invaluable assets on the battlefield. They contributed significantly to the Allied war effort and earned admiration and respect for generations to come.

Bravery and Heroism

The bravery and heroism displayed by Sikh soldiers during World War I are legendary, with numerous individuals earning prestigious honors and decorations for their gallantry in action. Their unwavering courage and indomitable spirit on the battlefield left an indelible mark on the annals of military history. Here's an exploration of their remarkable acts of valor and bravery:

1. **Acts of Extraordinary Bravery:** Sikh soldiers distinguished themselves through acts of extraordinary bravery and selflessness in the face of danger. Their unwavering commitment to duty and their comrades inspired awe and admiration among allies and adversaries alike.

2. **Recognition and Decorations:** Many Sikh soldiers were awarded prestigious honors and decorations for their acts of valor, including the Victoria Cross, the highest award for gallantry in the British Empire. These decorations symbolized the exceptional bravery and sacrifice of Sikh soldiers on the battlefield.

3. **Valor in Iconic Battles:** Sikh soldiers exhibited unparalleled valor and courage in some of the most iconic battles of World War I. Whether in the trenches of the Western Front or the rugged landscapes of Gallipoli and Ypres, they faced the horrors of war with unwavering resolve and determination.

4. **Battle of Neuve Chapelle:** Sikh soldiers played a crucial role in the Battle of Neuve Chapelle, where their bravery and tenacity helped secure a significant victory for the Allied forces. Despite heavy casualties and intense enemy resistance, Sikh soldiers pressed forward with courage and determination, earning the admiration of their comrades.

5. **Battle of Gallipoli and Battle of Ypres:** Sikh soldiers also demonstrated exceptional courage and heroism in the grueling battles of Gallipoli and Ypres. Amidst the chaos and carnage of trench warfare, they displayed unparalleled bravery in the face of adversity, inspiring their fellow soldiers and earning the respect of their commanders.

6. **Legacy of Valor:** The bravery and heroism of Sikh soldiers during World War I continue to be celebrated and honored today. Their acts of valor serve as a poignant reminder of the sacrifices made by the brave men and women who served their country with courage and honor on the battlefield.

The bravery and heroism exhibited by Sikh soldiers during World War I are testaments to their unwavering commitment to duty, honor, and sacrifice. Their valorous actions inspire reverence and admiration, serving as a shining example of the human spirit's best qualities in the face of adversity.

Cultural Identity and Symbolism

The cultural identity and symbolism associated with Sikh soldiers' appearance played a significant role in shaping their identity and resilience on the battlefield during World War I.

1. **Turbans and Unshorn Hair:** Sikh soldiers' adherence to their religious beliefs and traditions, including the practice of wearing turbans and maintaining unshorn hair, symbolized their unwavering commitment to their faith and values, even in the midst of war. The turban, an integral part of Sikh identity, served as a symbol of pride, dignity, and courage on the battlefield. Sikh soldiers wore their turbans with honor, displaying their religious and cultural identity with pride and resilience.

2. **Emblem of Resilience and Strength:** The sight of Sikh soldiers charging into battle with their flowing beards and colorful turbans became a symbol of resilience and strength on the battlefield. Despite the hardships and dangers they faced, Sikh soldiers stood firm in their beliefs and values, drawing strength from their cultural heritage and religious convictions.

3. **Symbol of Honor and Tradition:** Sikh soldiers' adherence to their religious practices, including the maintenance of unshorn hair and wearing of turbans, symbolizing their commitment to upholding honor, tradition, and integrity in the face of adversity. Their steadfast adherence to their cultural and religious identity served as a source of inspiration and admiration among their comrades and adversaries alike, earning them respect and recognition for their unwavering principles and values.

4. **Unity and Solidarity:** The distinctive appearance of Sikh soldiers, characterized by their turbans and unshorn hair, fostered a sense of unity and solidarity within their ranks. Regardless of their diverse backgrounds and experiences, Sikh soldiers stood united in their shared identity and values, forging bonds of brotherhood and camaraderie on the battlefield.

5. **Legacy of Identity and Pride:** The cultural identity and symbolism associated with Sikh soldiers' appearance continue to be celebrated and honored as part of their rich military heritage. Their commitment to their faith and

values, as reflected in their distinctive appearance, serves as a lasting legacy of identity, pride, and resilience for future generations.

The cultural identity and symbolism embodied by Sikh soldiers' appearance, including their turbans and hair, powerfully expressed their faith, values, and resilience on the battlefield. Their unwavering commitment to their identity and traditions remains a source of inspiration and pride, symbolizing the enduring spirit of Sikhism and its values of courage, honor, and integrity.

Legacy and Remembrance

The legacy of Sikh soldiers' contributions during World War I is deeply ingrained in the annals of history, honored through memorials, monuments, and ceremonies across the globe. Their bravery, sacrifice, and service to their country and humanity are commemorated in various ways, serving as a testament to their enduring legacy.

1. **Memorials and Monuments:** Sikh soldiers are commemorated through memorials and monuments erected in their honor in countries where they served during World War I. These solemn tributes pay homage to their bravery and sacrifice, ensuring that their memory is preserved for future generations. Memorials such as the Neuve-Chapelle Indian Memorial in France and the Saragarhi Memorial in India stand as solemn reminders of the valor and sacrifice of Sikh soldiers on the battlefield.

2. **Ceremonies and Commemorative Events:** Ceremonies and commemorative events are held to honor the contributions of Sikh soldiers during World War I. These events bring together communities, veterans, and descendants to pay tribute to the courage and sacrifice of those who served. Remembrance ceremonies, memorial services, and wreath-laying ceremonies are organized annually to honor the memory of Sikh soldiers and ensure that their sacrifices are never forgotten.

3. **Educational Initiatives:** Educational initiatives are undertaken to raise awareness about the contributions of Sikh soldiers during World War I. Schools, museums, and cultural institutions often host exhibitions, lectures, and educational programs to educate the public about their service and sacrifice. These initiatives aim to ensure that future generations understand and appreciate the significant role played by Sikh soldiers in shaping the course of history during World War I.

4. **Inspirational Legacy:** The legacy of Sikh soldiers' heroism and sacrifice continues to inspire future generations, reaffirming their enduring commitment to peace, justice, and freedom. Their memory serves as a source of pride and inspiration for the Sikh community and all those who cherish the values of courage, honor, and solidarity. Their selfless service and unwavering dedication to duty exemplify the

highest ideals of humanity, leaving an indelible mark on society's collective consciousness.

The memory of Sikh soldiers' contributions during World War I is honored and preserved through various memorials, ceremonies, and educational initiatives. Their legacy serves as a poignant reminder of their bravery, sacrifice, and service, inspiring future generations to uphold the values of courage, honor, and solidarity in the pursuit of peace and justice.

Contributions During World War II

The role of Sikh soldiers during World War II was profound, shaping history and earning them recognition for their bravery and resilience on the global stage. They served with distinction in various theaters of war, showcasing courage and dedication amidst formidable challenges.

1. **Military Service and Sacrifice:** Sikh soldiers served with distinction across different fronts, including Europe, North Africa, the Middle East, and Southeast Asia, contributing significantly to the Allied forces. Their valor and dedication were evident despite facing harsh conditions, demonstrating unwavering commitment to the war effort. Many Sikh soldiers made ultimate sacrifices, laying down their lives in defense of freedom and justice, underscoring their profound dedication and bravery.

2. **Role in the British Indian Army:** Sikh soldiers formed an integral part of the British Indian Army during World War II, with regiments such as the Sikh Regiment, Sikh Light Infantry, and Sikh

Pioneers playing pivotal roles. Their versatility and martial traditions were vital assets to the Allied forces, showcasing adaptability in varied combat situations. Serving across diverse units, including infantry, cavalry, artillery, and engineering, Sikh soldiers displayed remarkable skill and effectiveness in their respective roles.

3. **Bravery and Heroism:** Sikh soldiers were distinguished by acts of exceptional bravery and heroism throughout World War II. Many individuals were honored with prestigious awards such as the Victoria Cross, reflecting their extraordinary courage in the face of danger. Notable battles like Monte Cassino, the Burma Campaign, and the North African Campaign witnessed Sikh soldiers' indomitable spirit and bravery, earning admiration from allies and adversaries alike.

4. **Cultural Identity and Symbolism:** The distinct appearance of Sikh soldiers, characterized by their turbans and unshorn hair, became symbolic of their identity and resilience. Their steadfast adherence to religious beliefs and traditions represented an unwavering commitment to their faith and values, even amid the chaos of war. The sight of Sikh soldiers with their turbans and beards served as a powerful symbol of courage and determination, earning respect and admiration from those around them.

5. **Legacy and Remembrance:** Memorials, monuments, and ceremonies worldwide honor the sacrifices and contributions of Sikh soldiers

during World War II, ensuring their memory endures. Their legacy of bravery, sacrifice, and service continues to inspire future generations and reaffirm enduring commitments to peace, justice, and freedom. The memory of Sikh soldiers serves as a source of pride and inspiration for the Sikh community and all who value courage, honor, and solidarity, underscoring their profound impact on history.

Sikh soldiers' significant contributions during World War II exemplify their courage, sacrifice, and resilience, leaving a lasting legacy that continues to inspire admiration and reverence.

Innovation and Public Welfare

Sikh history is replete with instances of innovation and a strong emphasis on public welfare. From the inception of Sikhism, the ethos of serving humanity and contributing to the betterment of society has been deeply ingrained in Sikh teachings.

1. **Innovative Agricultural Practices:** Sikh communities have historically been closely associated with agriculture, pioneering innovative farming techniques to enhance agricultural productivity and sustainability. Sikh farmers have championed techniques such as crop rotation, water conservation methods, and organic farming practices, contributing to food security and environmental stewardship.

2. **Pangat (Community Kitchens or Langar):** The institution of langar exemplifies Sikh principles of equality, compassion, and

community service. Langar refers to the community kitchen where free meals are provided to all, regardless of caste, creed, or background. This tradition, initiated by Guru Nanak Dev Ji, promotes social cohesion, eliminates hunger, and fosters a spirit of generosity and inclusivity.

3. **Humanitarian Relief Efforts:** Sikhs have been at the forefront of humanitarian relief efforts in times of natural disasters, conflicts, and crises. Sikh organizations and volunteers actively engage in providing aid, shelter, and support to those in need, both locally and globally. Their selfless service and dedication to alleviating human suffering reflect the core Sikh values of seva (selfless service) and compassion.

4. **Healthcare Initiatives:** Sikh communities have established numerous healthcare institutions and clinics to provide accessible and affordable medical care to underserved populations. These initiatives range from hospitals and dispensaries to mobile medical vans and health camps, addressing healthcare disparities and promoting well-being within communities.

5. **Education and Empowerment:** Sikhs strongly emphasize education as a means of empowerment and social upliftment. Sikh educational institutions, including schools, colleges, and universities, offer quality education to students regardless of their socioeconomic status. Additionally, scholarships and vocational training programs

are provided to promote skill development and economic empowerment.

6. **Environmental Conservation Efforts:** Sikh organizations recognize the importance of environmental stewardship and actively engage in tree planting drives, waste management initiatives, and conservation projects. These efforts aim to protect natural resources, mitigate climate change, and promote sustainability for future generations.

Sikhs have demonstrated a strong commitment to innovation and public welfare through various initiatives aimed at promoting social justice, equality, and well-being. Their endeavors exemplify Sikhism's principles, emphasizing the importance of serving humanity and contributing to the betterment of society.

Innovation and Acts

Sikh innovations and acts have had a profound impact on society at large, contributing to advancements in various fields and fostering positive change.

1. **Green Revolution in Agriculture:** Sikh farmers in Panjab played a pivotal role in the Green Revolution, a period of significant agricultural transformation in India during the 1960s and 1970s. By adopting modern farming techniques, including the use of high-yielding crop varieties, irrigation technologies, and fertilizers, Sikh farmers significantly increased crop yields and transformed India from a food-deficient nation to a self-sufficient one. This innovation in

agriculture not only addressed food shortages but also contributed to economic growth and prosperity.

2. **Langar Seva During Disasters:** Sikh organizations, such as Khalsa Aid and Ranjit Nagara USA, are renowned for their rapid response and provision of langar seva (community kitchen service) and preservation during natural disasters and humanitarian crises worldwide. For example, during the Kerala floods in 2018, Sikh volunteers set up langar stalls to provide hot meals to thousands of flood-affected individuals, offering essential sustenance and comfort during times of distress.

3. **Providing Free Healthcare Services:** The Sikh community has established numerous charitable hospitals and clinics that offer free or subsidized healthcare services to those in need. One prominent example is the Sri Guru Ram Das Institute of Medical Sciences and Research in Amritsar, Panjab, which provides high-quality healthcare to patients irrespective of their ability to pay. Such initiatives ensure access to essential medical care for underserved populations and contribute to improving public health outcomes.

4. **Educational Institutions for All:** Sikh educational institutions, such as Khalsa College in Amritsar and Guru Nanak Dev University in Panjab, have been at the forefront of providing quality education to students from diverse

backgrounds. These institutions offer scholarships and financial aid to deserving students, making education accessible and affordable. By empowering individuals through education, Sikh institutions contribute to social mobility, economic development, and nation-building.

5. **Environmental Conservation Projects:** Sikh organizations actively engage in environmental conservation projects aimed at preserving natural resources and mitigating climate change. For instance, EcoSikh, a global organization, has initiated tree plantation drives, waste management programs, and renewable energy projects to promote environmental sustainability. These initiatives not only contribute to ecological balance but also raise awareness about environmental stewardship among communities.

6. **Interfaith Dialogue and Peacebuilding:** Sikhs are actively involved in interfaith dialogue and peacebuilding efforts aimed at fostering understanding and harmony among diverse religious communities. Initiatives such as the annual Nagar Kirtan procession, where Sikhs share food and celebrate with people of different faiths, promote unity and mutual respect. Such efforts help bridge cultural divides and promote social cohesion in pluralistic societies.

7. **Science and Technology:** Sikh scientists and engineers have made important contributions to the fields of science and technology. For

example, Dr. Narinder Singh Kapany, known as the "Father of Fiber Optics," made groundbreaking discoveries in fiber optics technology, revolutionizing telecommunications and optics research.

8. **Medicine and Healthcare:** Sikh doctors and healthcare professionals have played crucial roles in advancing medical science and providing healthcare services worldwide.

9. **Business and Entrepreneurship:** Sikh entrepreneurs have established successful businesses and enterprises, contributing to economic growth and innovation. Bhai Veer Singh Ji, founder and co-founder of many businesses in Panjab, is a notable example of a Sikh business leader who has made significant contributions to the corporate world.

10. **Arts and Culture:** Sikhs have made valuable contributions to the arts and culture through literature, music, and visual arts. Renowned poets and writers like Professor Puran Singh, Bhai Veer Singh and Kavi Santokh Singh have enriched Panjabi literature with their profound works. Similarly, musicians like Bhai Mardana Ji and Bhai Bahi Gurdas Ji have made significant contributions to Sikh devotional music (Kirtan).

These real-world examples illustrate how Sikh innovations and acts have made tangible and positive contributions to society, addressing critical needs, promoting inclusivity, and fostering community harmony and cooperation. Through their commitment to seva (selfless service) and compassion, Sikhs continue to inspire positive change and make the world a better place for all.

Seva (Selfless service) and Sarbat Da Bhala (Welfare for all)

Sikh values such as seva (selfless service) and sarbat da bhala (welfare of all) play a profound role in community development, empowerment, and social cohesion within Sikh communities and beyond.

1. **Community Development:** Seva and sarbat da bhala form the cornerstone of community development initiatives within Sikh society. Through Pangat (langar or community kitchen) and other service-oriented activities, Sikhs actively engage in addressing the needs of the community, including providing food, shelter, healthcare, education, and social support. These initiatives not only meet immediate needs but also foster a sense of unity, cooperation, and shared responsibility among community members.

2. **Empowerment:** Seva empowers both the giver and the receiver, as it emphasizes the dignity and agency of every individual. By engaging in acts of selfless service, Sikhs promote a culture of empowerment that transcends social barriers and fosters inclusivity. Through education, skill development, and mentorship programs, Sikhs empower individuals to realize their full potential and contribute meaningfully to society, thus

promoting social mobility and economic empowerment.

3. **Social Cohesion:** Seva and sarbat da bhala promote social cohesion by fostering a sense of belonging, solidarity, and mutual respect within Sikh communities and beyond. The practice of langar, where people from diverse backgrounds come together to share a meal without discrimination, exemplifies this spirit of inclusivity and unity. By transcending barriers of caste, class, and creed, Sikhs create a cohesive community where everyone is valued and respected, contributing to a more harmonious and compassionate society.

4. **Moral and Ethical Foundation:** Seva and sarbat da bhala serve as a moral and ethical foundation for Sikh communities, guiding individuals to live a life of compassion, generosity, and service to others. These values instill a sense of duty and responsibility towards the welfare of others, inspiring individuals to act with integrity and empathy in their interactions with others. By upholding these values, Sikhs contribute to the creation of a more just, equitable, and compassionate society.

5. **Global Impact:** The principles of seva and sarbat da bhala extend beyond Sikh communities and have a broader impact on global humanitarian efforts. Sikh organizations and volunteers actively engage in providing aid and assistance to communities affected by natural disasters, conflicts, and humanitarian

crises worldwide. Through their selfless service and commitment to the welfare of all, Sikhs contribute to building a more compassionate and inclusive world.

Sikh values such as seva and sarbat da bhala are instrumental in promoting community development, empowerment, and social cohesion. By embodying these values in their actions and interactions, Sikhs create communities characterized by compassion, solidarity, and shared responsibility, thereby contributing to society's well-being and progress.

Contemporary contribution

Sikh individuals and organizations are at the forefront of advocating for social justice, environmental conservation, and disaster relief efforts, embodying the values of compassion, solidarity, and service to humanity. Through their dedicated efforts, they make significant contributions to building a more just, equitable, and sustainable world for all.

SGPC

The Shiromani Gurdwara Prabandhak Committee (SGPC) is a prominent religious organization that manages the historical Sikh gurdwaras (places of worship) in Panjab, India, and represents the Sikh and other communities' interests worldwide.

1. **Historical Background:** The SGPC was established in 1920 by the Sikh leaders and activists as a response to the need for a centralized body to manage and oversee the affairs of Sikh religious

institutions, including gurdwaras, educational institutions, and charitable organizations. It was formed in the aftermath of the Gurdwara Reform Movement, which aimed to end the control of mahants (clergy) over Sikh Gurdwaras.

2. Mandate and Functions: The primary mandate of the SGPC is to manage and administer Sikh religious institutions, including historical gurdwaras, takhts (thrones of authority), and educational institutions, in accordance with Sikh traditions and principles. It is responsible for organizing religious ceremonies, maintaining gurdwara premises, managing finances, and promoting Sikh religious and cultural heritage. SGPC also plays a crucial role in promoting Sikh interests and concerns at the state and national levels. It represents the Sikh community's views on various social, political, and religious issues and advocates for their rights and welfare.

3. Structure and Governance: The SGPC is governed by an elected body of members known as the "General House," which comprises representatives elected from different constituencies, including Sikh organizations, educational institutions, and Sikh scholars. The General House elects the executive committee, including the President and other office bearers, to manage the day-to-day affairs of the SGPC. The President of SGPC holds significant authority and is responsible for overseeing the organization's activities, representing it in official capacities, and making decisions on important matters related to Sikh religious affairs.

4. Religious and Educational Initiatives: SGPC is involved in various religious and educational initiatives aimed at promoting Sikh values, teachings, and heritage. It sponsors religious congregations, seminars, and educational programs to disseminate Sikh teachings and promote religious literacy among the Sikh community and beyond. SGPC also manages educational institutions, including colleges, schools, and libraries, to provide quality education and preserve Sikh cultural heritage. These institutions offer courses on Sikh theology, history, and literature, fostering a deeper understanding of Sikhism among students and scholars.

5. Social Welfare and Humanitarian Work: In addition to its religious and educational functions, SGPC is actively involved in social welfare and humanitarian work. It operates charitable hospitals, dispensaries, and old age homes to provide healthcare and support to the needy. It also offers financial assistance to economically disadvantaged individuals and families through welfare programs and grants.

Some Other organizations

1. **United Sikh**

   - **Mission:** United Sikhs is a global humanitarian relief and advocacy organization dedicated to empowering marginalized communities and promoting social justice. The organization's mission is rooted in Sikh principles of seva (selfless service) and sarbat da bhala (welfare of all).

- **Activities:** United Sikhs engages in a wide range of activities, including disaster relief efforts, human rights advocacy, and community empowerment programs. They provide assistance to communities affected by natural disasters, support victims of hate crimes and discrimination, and advocate for policy changes to address systemic injustices.

- **Impact:** Through their initiatives, United Sikhs has made significant contributions to advancing civil and human rights, combating discrimination and hate crimes, and providing relief to those in need. They work tirelessly to promote equality, justice, and dignity for all individuals, regardless of their background or beliefs.

2. **Sikh Coalition**

- **Mission:** The Sikh Coalition is a leading advocacy organization dedicated to protecting the civil rights of Sikh Americans and combating discrimination, harassment, and hate crimes. Their mission is to ensure that Sikh Americans can live freely and without fear, while also promoting a more inclusive and equitable society for all.

- **Activities:** The Sikh Coalition engages in legal advocacy, community education, and policy reform to address issues such as racial profiling, bullying, workplace discrimination, and religious freedom violations. They provide legal assistance to victims of discrimination, conduct educational workshops to raise awareness about Sikhism, and advocate for policy changes at the local, state, and national levels.

- **Impact:** The Sikh Coalition's efforts have led to landmark legal victories, increased awareness about Sikh issues, and improved protections for Sikh Americans. They have successfully advocated for policy changes, implemented anti-bullying programs in schools, and provided support to individuals facing discrimination, making a tangible difference in the lives of Sikh communities across the United States.

3. Nishkam Sewa

- **Mission:** Nishkam Sewa is a Sikh non-profit organization dedicated to promoting social justice, human rights, and equality through selfless service (seva). The organization's name reflects its commitment to serving others without seeking personal gain, embodying the Sikh principle of nishkam (selflessness).

- **Activities:** Nishkam Sewa engages in grassroots initiatives and community-based projects to address issues such as poverty, inequality, and injustice. They provide food and shelter to the homeless, organize educational programs for underprivileged children, and offer healthcare services to those in need. Additionally, they advocate for policy reform and systemic change to address the root causes of social injustice.

- **Impact:** Through their dedication to seva and social justice advocacy, Nishkam Sewa has made a positive impact on the lives of marginalized communities. They work tirelessly to uplift those in need, raise awareness about social justice issues, and advocate for meaningful change, embodying the values of Sikhism and contributing to a more just and equitable society for all.

4. **Ranjit Nagara USA**

- **Mission:** Ranjit Nagara USA is dedicated to preserving and promoting Sikh cultural heritage, including historical sites, landmarks, and artifacts. Their mission is to raise awareness about the rich legacy of Sikhism and ensure the preservation of important historical sites for future generations.

- **Activities**

  1) **Documentation and Research:** Ranjit Nagara USA conducts research and documentation efforts to identify and catalog Sikh heritage sites and landmarks. This includes compiling historical data, conducting field surveys, and documenting oral histories related to significant Sikh sites.

2) **Preservation and Conservation:** Ranjit Nagara USA works to preserve and conserve Sikh historical sites and landmarks through restoration efforts, maintenance projects, and advocacy for heritage preservation policies. They collaborate with local communities, government agencies, and conservation experts to ensure the protection of these sites.

3) **Education and Outreach:** Ranjit Nagara USA engages in educational outreach activities to raise awareness about Sikh heritage and history. This includes organizing seminars, workshops, and exhibitions to share information about Sikhism's cultural significance and the importance of preserving Sikh heritage sites.

4) **Advocacy and Networking:** Ranjit Nagara USA advocates for the protection and recognition of Sikh heritage sites at the local, national, and international levels. They work with policymakers, heritage organizations, and community stakeholders to promote heritage conservation initiatives and secure support for preserving Sikh historical landmarks.

- **Impact**

  1) **Preservation of Cultural Identity:** The efforts of Ranjit Nagara USA contribute to the preservation of Sikh cultural identity by safeguarding important historical sites and landmarks associated with Sikh history and heritage.

  2) **Education and Awareness:** Through their educational initiatives and outreach programs, Ranjit Nagara USA raises awareness about Sikhism's rich cultural heritage, promoting greater understanding and appreciation of Sikh history and traditions.

  3) **Advocacy for Heritage Conservation:** Ranjit Nagara USA's advocacy efforts help prioritize the preservation and conservation of Sikh heritage sites, ensuring that these important landmarks are protected for future generations to appreciate and enjoy.

  4) **Community Engagement:** By involving local communities in heritage preservation projects and awareness campaigns, Ranjit Nagara USA fosters a sense of ownership and pride in Sikh cultural heritage, strengthening community bonds and promoting cultural sustainability.

5. Sikh Reference Library USA

- **Mission:** The mission of the Sikh Reference Library USA is to preserve, protect, and promote Sikh heritage in the United States through the collection, digitization, and dissemination of historical and cultural resources. The library aims to provide a valuable resource for scholars, researchers, students, and the general public interested in Sikh history, literature, and culture.

- **Activities**

    1) **Collection and Preservation:** The library collects and preserves a wide range of materials related to Sikhism, including rare books, manuscripts, documents, photographs, artwork, and audiovisual recordings. These materials are carefully cataloged, archived, and stored in climate-controlled facilities to ensure their long-term preservation.

    2) **Digitization and Access:** To increase accessibility and reach, the library digitizes its collections, making them available online through a searchable database or digital repository. This allows researchers, students, and the public to access valuable resources remotely and facilitates scholarly research and educational initiatives.

    3) **Research and Scholarship:** The library supports research and scholarship on

Sikh history, religion, culture, and diaspora studies. It provides access to scholarly publications, journals, dissertations, and research papers related to Sikh studies and may offer research grants, fellowships, and residency programs to support academic inquiry and exchange.

4) **Educational Outreach:** The library engages in educational outreach activities to promote awareness and understanding of Sikhism among diverse audiences. This may include organizing seminars, lectures, workshops, and educational programs for schools, universities, libraries, and community organizations.

5) **Community Engagement:** The library serves as a community hub for Sikhs and individuals interested in Sikh culture, history, and spirituality. It hosts cultural events, exhibitions, film screenings, and discussions to celebrate Sikh festivals, commemorate historical milestones, and foster dialogue and exchange among community members.

- **Impact**

  1) **Preservation of Heritage:** The Sikh Reference Library USA contributes to the preservation of Sikh heritage by

safeguarding valuable historical and cultural materials for future generations.

2) **Scholarship and Research:** The library facilitates scholarly research and academic inquiry on Sikhism, providing access to authoritative resources and supporting the advancement of knowledge in the field of Sikh studies.

3) **Education and Awareness:** Through its educational outreach efforts, the library promotes greater awareness and understanding of Sikhism's history, teachings, and contributions to humanity, fostering intercultural dialogue and mutual respect.

4) **Community Empowerment:** By serving as a resource center and gathering place for the Sikh community, the library empowers individuals to connect with their heritage, identity, and spirituality, strengthening bonds and fostering a sense of belonging and pride.

6. Khalsa Aid

Khalsa Aid is a UK-based humanitarian relief organization founded by Ravi Singh that provides aid and assistance to communities affected by natural disasters, conflicts, and humanitarian crises worldwide. The organization operates on the principles of the Sikh faith, particularly the concept of "seva," or selfless service, to alleviate suffering and promote human dignity. Here's an overview of Khalsa Aid's mission, activities, and impact:

- **Mission:** The mission of Khalsa Aid is to provide humanitarian aid and assistance to people in need, regardless of their background, religion, or nationality. The organization is committed to upholding the values of compassion, equality, and solidarity, as espoused by the Sikh faith, and strives to make a positive impact on the lives of vulnerable communities around the world.

- **Activities**

  1) **Emergency Relief:** Khalsa Aid provides immediate assistance to communities affected by natural disasters such as earthquakes, floods, hurricanes, and tsunamis. They deploy teams of volunteers to deliver essential supplies, including food, water, shelter, and medical aid, to affected areas, prioritizing the most vulnerable individuals and families.

  2) **Conflict Zones:** In conflict-affected regions, Khalsa Aid delivers aid to displaced populations, refugees, and civilians caught in the crossfire. They work to ensure access to essential services, including healthcare, education, and psychosocial support while advocating for the protection of

human rights and humanitarian principles.

3) **Food Distribution:** Khalsa Aid operates food distribution programs to address food insecurity and hunger in impoverished communities around the world. They provide nutritious meals to children, families, and individuals facing famine, malnutrition, and food shortages, working to alleviate suffering and promote food security.

4) **Shelter and Rehabilitation:** Following disasters and emergencies, Khalsa Aid assists in rebuilding infrastructure, homes, and communities, providing shelter materials, construction support, and livelihood assistance to affected populations. They aim to restore dignity and stability to those displaced or affected by crisis situations.

5) **Medical Assistance:** Khalsa Aid offers medical assistance and healthcare services to communities lacking access to adequate healthcare facilities. They deploy medical teams, mobile clinics, and emergency medical supplies to treat injuries, illnesses, and epidemics, working to save lives and improve health outcomes.

- **Impact**

    1) **Lifesaving Assistance:** Khalsa Aid's swift response and provision of emergency relief have saved countless lives and alleviated suffering in disaster-affected communities worldwide.

    2) **Empowerment and Resilience:** Through their humanitarian interventions, Khalsa Aid empowers vulnerable communities to rebuild their lives, restore livelihoods, and develop resilience in the face of adversity.

    3) **Cross-Cultural Solidarity:** Khalsa Aid's commitment to providing aid without discrimination fosters cross-cultural solidarity and understanding, promoting unity and compassion among diverse communities globally.

    4) **Inspiration and Advocacy:** Khalsa Aid's work inspires individuals and organizations to engage in humanitarian efforts and advocacy for social justice, amplifying the voices of the marginalized and advocating for systemic change.

7. Sikh Humanitarian Corps

- **Mission:** The Sikh Humanitarian Corps is dedicated to mobilizing Sikh youth and community members to provide disaster relief and humanitarian aid during emergencies. Their mission is to embody the principles of selfless service and compassion inherent in the Sikh faith by assisting those in need, regardless of their background or beliefs.

- **Activities:** The Sikh Humanitarian Corps engages in volunteer-based efforts to deliver disaster relief and humanitarian aid during emergencies. They collaborate with local and international partners to assess needs, mobilize resources, and coordinate logistics for efficient aid distribution. Activities may include providing food, water, shelter, medical assistance, and other essential supplies to affected communities.

- **Impact:** Through their volunteer efforts and collaborative approach, the Sikh Humanitarian Corps makes a significant impact in delivering timely and effective aid to communities facing emergencies. Their swift response and dedication to service provide critical support to those affected by disasters, helping alleviate suffering, restore stability, and promote resilience in affected areas. Additionally, their work fosters a sense of unity and solidarity within the Sikh community and inspires others to engage in humanitarian efforts for the betterment of humanity.

8. EcoSikh

- **Mission:** EcoSikh is committed to promoting environmental sustainability and conservation from a Sikh perspective. Their mission is to engage the global Sikh community in initiatives that address climate change, protect the environment, and uphold the principles of reverence for nature and responsible stewardship.

- **Activities:** EcoSikh organizes tree plantation drives, waste management initiatives, and advocacy efforts for renewable energy. They collaborate with Sikh institutions, communities, and environmental organizations worldwide to raise awareness, mobilize action, and implement eco-friendly practices. Through educational programs, workshops, and campaigns, they empower individuals and communities to adopt sustainable lifestyles and contribute to environmental preservation.

- **Impact:** EcoSikh's initiatives have a tangible impact on environmental conservation and sustainability. By planting trees, promoting waste reduction, and advocating for renewable energy, they contribute to mitigating climate change, conserving natural resources, and protecting ecosystems. Their efforts inspire and mobilize the Sikh community and beyond to become proactive stewards of the environment, fostering a culture of environmental responsibility and collective action.

9. Eco Amritsar

- **Mission:** Eco Amritsar is dedicated to promoting environmental awareness and sustainable development in the local community of Amritsar, Panjab. Their mission is to create a cleaner, greener, and more sustainable city by engaging residents, businesses, and institutions in environmental initiatives and educational programs.

- **Activities:** Eco Amritsar organizes clean-up drives, tree plantations, and educational programs to foster environmental stewardship and community engagement. They work closely with local authorities, schools, and civil society organizations to implement sustainable waste management practices, improve air and water quality, and create green spaces in urban areas. Through advocacy and outreach, they raise awareness about environmental issues and mobilize grassroots action for positive change.

- **Impact:** Eco Amritsar's grassroots efforts have a significant impact on improving the local environment and quality of life in Amritsar. By organizing clean-up drives and tree plantations, they beautify public spaces, enhance biodiversity, and create opportunities for community involvement. Through educational programs and advocacy, they empower residents to take ownership of environmental issues and become active participants in building a more sustainable future for their city.

10. SEED Foundation

- **Mission:** SEED Foundation is dedicated to promoting environmental education, sustainable development, and conservation efforts within the Sikh community and beyond. Their mission is to raise awareness about environmental issues, empower individuals and communities to take action, and advocate for policies that protect the planet and its resources.

- **Activities:** SEED Foundation organizes a wide range of activities and programs aimed at promoting environmental education and conservation. They conduct workshops, seminars, and educational campaigns to raise awareness about climate change, pollution, and biodiversity loss. Additionally, they collaborate with schools, colleges, and community organizations to integrate environmental education into curricula and extracurricular activities. SEED Foundation also implements practical conservation initiatives, such as tree planting drives, waste management projects, and renewable energy initiatives. They work with local communities and stakeholders to implement sustainable development practices that minimize environmental impact and promote ecological resilience.

- **Impact:** SEED Foundation's initiatives have a significant impact on promoting environmental sustainability and conservation efforts within the Sikh community and broader society. By raising awareness, providing education, and implementing practical conservation projects, they empower individuals and communities to become stewards of the environment and advocate for policies that prioritize ecological well-being. Their efforts contribute to building a more environmentally conscious and sustainable world, aligned with Sikh values of compassion, stewardship, and respect for all creation.

Sikh diaspora communities

The Sikh diaspora communities play a crucial role in promoting cultural understanding, interfaith dialogue, and global cooperation through various initiatives, including social, educational, and philanthropic.

1. **Cultural Exchange Programs:** Sikh diaspora communities organize cultural exchange programs that showcase Sikh traditions, values, and heritage to people from diverse backgrounds. These programs help foster mutual respect, appreciation, and understanding among different communities.

2. **Celebration of Festivals:** Sikh diaspora communities celebrate religious festivals such as Vaisakhi, Diwali, and Gurpurabs in multicultural settings, inviting people from various faiths and cultures to participate. These

celebrations provide opportunities for cross-cultural interaction, dialogue, and exchange of ideas.

3. **Language and Arts:** Sikh diaspora communities promote Panjabi language and Sikh arts, such as music, literature, and poetry, through cultural events, workshops, and educational programs. By sharing their language and artistic expressions, they contribute to enriching the cultural tapestry of their host countries.

4. **Interfaith Forums:** Sikh diaspora communities actively participate in interfaith forums, dialogues, and conferences where representatives of different faiths come together to discuss common values, shared concerns, and ways to promote peace and understanding.

5. **Religious Diversity Initiatives:** Sikh diaspora communities collaborate with other religious groups to promote religious diversity, tolerance, and harmony. They organize interfaith prayer services, seminars, and community projects aimed at building bridges of understanding and respect across religious lines.

6. **Advocacy for Religious Freedom:** Sikh diaspora communities advocate for religious freedom and human rights globally, raising awareness about the challenges faced by religious minorities and marginalized communities. They work with policymakers, civil society organizations, and religious leaders to

promote laws and policies that protect religious rights and promote social justice.

7. **Philanthropic Initiatives:** Sikh diaspora communities engage in philanthropic activities, including disaster relief, humanitarian aid, and community development projects, both locally and internationally. They collaborate with NGOs, governments, and international organizations to address global challenges and alleviate human suffering.

8. **Educational and Healthcare Initiatives:** Sikh diaspora communities support educational and healthcare initiatives in underprivileged regions worldwide, providing scholarships, schools, hospitals, and medical clinics. These initiatives contribute to improving the quality of life and opportunities for disadvantaged communities.

9. **Environmental Conservation:** Sikh diaspora communities participate in environmental conservation efforts globally, advocating for sustainable development, renewable energy, and ecological stewardship. They collaborate with environmental organizations and government agencies to address climate change, protect natural resources, and promote sustainable living practices.

The Sikh diaspora communities play a multifaceted role in promoting cultural understanding, interfaith dialogue, and global cooperation. Through their efforts, they contribute to building a more inclusive, peaceful, and sustainable world, guided by the principles of Sikhism, including compassion, equality, and service to humanity.

The enduring legacy of Sikh contributions to society is a testament to the values that drive them – values of compassion, equality, and service to humanity. Through centuries of challenges and triumphs, Sikhs have exemplified resilience, generosity, and a steadfast commitment to making the world a better place for all.

From their historical struggles against oppression to their modern-day efforts in promoting social justice, environmental conservation, and global cooperation, Sikhs have consistently championed the cause of human welfare, justice, and peace. Their contributions, rooted in the teachings of their faith, have left an indelible mark on society, inspiring countless individuals and communities to follow their lead.

*****

THE
LEGACY IN
ART AND
CULTURE

THE LEGACY IN ART AND CULTURE

The legacy in Art and Culture encapsulates the profound and lasting impact of artistic expression and cultural practices within society, reflecting the collective heritage, traditions, values, and achievements that span generations. Art and culture serve as powerful vehicles for transmitting knowledge, preserving traditions, and expressing emotions across time and space. From ancient cave paintings to modern digital media, art encompasses a diverse array of creative expressions, including visual arts, literature, music, theater, dance, and architecture. Each form of artistic expression offers unique insights into the cultural values, beliefs, and aspirations of a society, providing a window into the human experience. Similarly, cultural practices such as rituals, customs, traditions, and ceremonies play a fundamental role in shaping social interactions, identities, and collective values. These practices serve as anchors of continuity, connecting individuals to their past while guiding their present and inspiring their future. Moreover, art and culture serve as bridges between generations, facilitating the transmission of knowledge, traditions, and values from one generation to the next. Through the preservation and celebration of cultural heritage, societies honor their roots, nurture their identities, and enrich their collective experiences. The legacy in art and culture thus embodies the enduring influence, significance, and resilience of human creativity and expression across time and space.

Art in Sikhism

Art in Sikhism refers to the various forms of artistic expression that are inspired by Sikh beliefs, values, history, and culture. Sikhism, a monotheistic religion founded in the 15th century by Sri Guru Nanak Dev Ji in the Punjab region of the Asian continent, encompasses rich traditions of artistic expression that reflect its spiritual teachings and cultural heritage.

In Sikhism, art serves as a means of expressing devotion, reverence, and gratitude towards the divine, as well as a way of conveying the teachings and principles of the faith to followers and the wider world. Artistic representations in Sikhism can take various forms, including:

1. **Gurmat Sangeet (Sikh Sacred Music):** Music holds a central place in Sikh worship and spirituality. Kirtan, the singing of hymns from the Sri Guru Granth Sahib Ji, Sri Dasam Granth Sahib Ji, Vaara Bhai Gurdas ji, Vaara Bhai Nanad Lal Ji, and Sri Sarbloh Granth Sahib Ji, is an integral part of Sikh religious gatherings and ceremonies. Raag Kirtan, a classical musical tradition, is used to melodiously recite the Shabads, creating a deeply meditative and devotional atmosphere.

2. **Gurudwara Architecture:** Gurudwaras, the Sikh places of worship, are often characterized by distinctive architectural features that reflect Sikh principles of equality, community, and service. The most prominent feature of a Gurudwara is the Sri Darbar Sahib, the central

prayer hall where the Sri Guru Granth Sahib Ji is placed on a raised platform. Gurudwara architecture typically emphasizes simplicity, with emphasis on open spaces and the absence of idols or religious icons.

3. **Visual Arts:** Sikhism has a rich tradition of visual arts, including paintings, illustrations, and sculptures depicting Sikh gurus, historical events, and spiritual concepts. These works may be found in Gurudwaras, Sikh homes, and public spaces, serving as a means of inspiration, education, and spiritual reflection for believers and non-believers alike.

4. **Literature:** Sikhism has a vast body of literature, including poetry, prose, and Granths, that conveys its teachings and values. Most of the Sikhism Granths itself is considered a work of art, both in terms of its spiritual content and its poetic beauty. Sikh literature encompasses a wide range of themes, from devotion and morality to social justice and human rights.

5. **Performing Arts:** Sikh culture includes various forms of performing arts, such as folk music, dance, and theater, that celebrate the community's history, traditions, and values. These art forms are often used to commemorate Sikh festivals and historical events, fostering a sense of unity and pride among Sikhs.

Art in Sikhism serves as a vibrant and dynamic expression of the faith's spiritual and cultural heritage, enriching the lives of believers and contributing to the broader cultural landscape of the world.

Gurmat Sangeet

Gurmat Sangeet, particularly the practice of Kirtan, represents a sacred union of music and spirituality in Sikhism. It serves as a powerful medium for expressing devotion, cultivating inner peace, and experiencing the divine presence in its myriad manifestations. Through the practice of Kirtan, Sikhs honor and celebrate the rich musical heritage of their faith, while also connecting with the timeless wisdom and spiritual insights contained within the sacred Granths.

Kirtan

Kirtan embodies the essence of Sikh spirituality, offering a sacred pathway for devotees to connect with the divine, experience spiritual upliftment, and cultivate a deeper sense of love, devotion, and unity. As the heartbeat of Sikh worship, Kirtan continues to inspire and uplift countless souls on their spiritual journey towards enlightenment and inner peace.

1. **Sacred Practice of Kirtan:** Kirtan involves the soulful singing or recitation of hymns, known as Shabads, sourced from various Sikh Granths. These include the Sri Guru Granth Sahib Ji, Sri Dasam Granth Sahib Ji, Vaara Bhai Gurdas Ji, Vaara Bhai Nanad Lal Ji, and Sri Sarbloh Granth Sahib Ji. The selection of Shabads is guided by their profound spiritual message and resonance with the themes of devotion, love, and spiritual awakening.

2. **Uplifting and Inspiring Devotion:** Kirtan is a powerful medium for fostering a deep sense of connection and communion with the divine presence. The melodic chanting of Shabads, accompanied by the rhythmic beats of traditional musical instruments such as the harmonium, tabla, Rudab, Saranda, and Dhad, creates a soul-stirring atmosphere that elevates participants' consciousness and transports them to a state of spiritual ecstasy.

3. **Community and Unity:** Beyond its individual spiritual benefits, Kirtan also fosters a sense of community and unity among practitioners. Whether performed in the sacred confines of a Gurudwara or in the intimate setting of a Sikh household, Kirtan brings together individuals from diverse backgrounds and walks of life, transcending barriers of language, culture, and social status. Through the collective singing of Shabads, participants experience a profound sense of belonging and interconnectedness, reinforcing the ideals of equality and oneness espoused by Sikhism.

4. **Transformative Power:** The transformative power of Kirtan lies in its ability to evoke a deep spiritual awakening and inner transformation within practitioners. Through the practice of Kirtan, individuals are invited to surrender themselves to the divine presence, letting go of ego and worldly attachments, and opening their hearts to the eternal truth and love embodied in the Shabads. In this state of surrender,

practitioners experience a profound sense of peace, joy, and fulfillment, which permeates every aspect of their lives.

The Role of Raag in Kirtan

Raag, a classical musical tradition, plays a central and indispensable role in the practice of Kirtan within Sikhism. Revered for its ability to infuse depth, emotion, and spiritual resonance into musical compositions, Raag serves as a structured framework that guides practitioners in the selection of melodies to complement the spiritual message conveyed by the Shabad. Raag serves as a vital conduit for elevating the spiritual expression of Kirtan within Sikhism, enriching the musical landscape with its emotive power and transformative potential. As practitioners immerse themselves in the melodious strains of Raag-infused Kirtan, they embark on a sacred journey of self-discovery, enlightenment, and divine communion, guided by the timeless wisdom and spiritual resonance of the Shabad.

1. **Enriching Musical Expression:** Raag encompasses a sophisticated system of melodic modes or scales, each associated with a particular mood, emotion, or time of day. Within the context of Kirtan, the choice of Raag is meticulously made to enhance the spiritual expression of the Shabad being performed. Different Raags evoke different sentiments, ranging from devotion and longing to tranquility and ecstasy, thereby enriching the musical expression of the Shabad and deepening its impact on the hearts and minds of listeners.

2. **Structured Framework for Melody:** In Kirtan, Raag serves as a structured framework that guides practitioners in the selection and improvisation of melodies. Each Raag has its own set of rules and conventions governing the ascent and descent of notes, the use of ornamentation, and the interplay between rhythm and melody. These rules provide a sense of order and coherence to the musical composition, ensuring that the melodies created resonate harmoniously with the spiritual message of the Shabad.

3. **Complementing the Spiritual Message:** The careful selection of Raag is guided by the spiritual essence and thematic content of the Shabad being performed. The Raag chosen must harmonize with the Shabad's mood, sentiment, and underlying message, enhancing its emotive power and spiritual depth. Through the judicious use of Raag, practitioners can create a deeply immersive and transformative musical experience that resonates with listeners' hearts and souls.

4. **Facilitating Spiritual Connection:** The role of Raag in Kirtan is to facilitate a profound spiritual connection between practitioners and the divine presence. By harmonizing melody with meaning, Raag elevates the musical expression of the Shabad, enabling practitioners to transcend the ordinary and commune with the sacred. In this sacred union of music and spirituality, practitioners experience a deep

sense of unity, devotion, and transcendence as they journey together toward the divine realm of eternal bliss.

Creating a Meditative Atmosphere

The harmonious blend of Shabad and Raag in Kirtan creates a deeply meditative and devotional atmosphere, inviting participants to immerse themselves fully in the spiritual experience. Through rhythmic chanting and soul-stirring melodies, Kirtan facilitates a profound connection with the divine essence.

1. **Harmonious Blend of Shabad and Raag:** At the heart of Kirtan lies the harmonious union of Shabad and Raag, each complementing and enriching the other in a symbiotic relationship. The spiritual message embedded within the Shabad finds expression through the emotive power of Raag, elevating the melodic rendition to transcendent heights. As the melodious strains of Raag resonate with the profound wisdom and timeless truths of the Shabad, a sacred synergy is forged, infusing the environment with a palpable sense of spiritual energy and tranquility.

2. **Invitation to Immerse:** Kirtan's meditative atmosphere beckons participants to shed the distractions of the external world and turn their gaze inward towards the depths of their own consciousness. Through rhythmic chanting and soul-stirring melodies, Kirtan offers a sanctuary of stillness amidst the chaos of everyday life,

inviting practitioners to embark on a journey of self-discovery and inner exploration. In this sacred space of contemplation, individuals are encouraged to surrender themselves to the divine presence and experience the transformative power of spiritual introspection.

3. **Facilitating Spiritual Connection:** As participants immerse themselves in the meditative ambiance of Kirtan, a profound connection is forged with the divine essence that permeates all creation. The rhythmic chanting of Shabads, accompanied by the soul-stirring melodies of Raag, serves as a bridge between the earthly and the divine, facilitating a communion of souls with the eternal source of love and light. In this state of deep meditation and devotion, practitioners experience a sense of oneness with the universe, transcending the limitations of the material realm and basking in the boundless radiance of divine grace.

4. **Cultivating Inner Peace:** The meditative atmosphere of Kirtan serves as a sacred sanctuary where individuals can find solace, serenity, and inner peace amidst the tumult of life's challenges and uncertainties. Through the transformative power of spiritual music and contemplation, Kirtan awakens the dormant seeds of divine consciousness within the hearts of practitioners, guiding them on a path of self-realization and spiritual fulfillment.

Active Engagement with the Divine

Kirtan is not merely a passive form of worship; it encourages active participation and engagement with the divine presence. Participants are encouraged to sing along or contemplate the meaning of the Shabad, fostering personal growth, and spiritual transformation. Kirtan represents a sacred invitation for individuals to actively engage with the divine presence and embark on a journey of self-realization and spiritual transformation. Through singing, contemplation, and communal worship, participants in Kirtan find refuge in the timeless wisdom and boundless love of the divine, experiencing moments of profound connection, inspiration, and spiritual renewal.

1. **Participatory Worship**: Kirtan is a communal expression of devotion and reverence, where participants actively contribute to the melodic rendition of Shabads, either through singing along or joining in rhythmic accompaniment. This participatory aspect of Kirtan transforms the act of worship from a passive observation into a dynamic and interactive experience, where individuals are empowered to become co-creators of sacred sound and vibration.

2. **Singing Along with Devotion:** Kirtan participants are encouraged to sing along with heartfelt devotion, allowing the melodious strains of Shabads to resonate within their hearts and souls. Through vocalization, individuals not only express their love and reverence for the divine but also deepen their connection with the spiritual essence embodied

in the Shabad. Singing along with others fosters a sense of unity and community as voices blend harmoniously in collective praise and adoration.

3. **Contemplation and Reflection:** In addition to active participation through singing, Kirtan also encourages practitioners to contemplate the meaning and significance of the Shabad being performed. Participants are invited to reflect deeply on the spiritual message conveyed by the lyrics, allowing the profound wisdom and timeless truths contained within the Shabad to illuminate their minds and hearts. Through introspection and contemplation, individuals gain insights into their own spiritual journey, fostering personal growth and inner transformation.

4. **Fostering Spiritual Growth**: Kirtan serves as a catalyst for personal growth and spiritual evolution, guiding practitioners on a transformative journey of self-discovery and enlightenment. Through active engagement with the divine presence, individuals cultivate a deeper understanding of their spiritual nature and forge a stronger connection with the eternal source of love and wisdom. By actively participating in Kirtan and contemplating the spiritual teachings embedded within the Shabad, practitioners nurture their souls and expand their consciousness, experiencing profound moments of clarity, insight, and spiritual awakening.

Celebrating Sikh Musical Heritage

Gurmat Sangeet, particularly the practice of Kirtan, is a vibrant celebration of Sikh musical heritage. It honors the rich tapestry of Sikh spirituality and culture while also providing a pathway for devotees to connect with the timeless wisdom and spiritual insights contained within the sacred Granths.

1. **Preserving Cultural Legacy:** Gurmat Sangeet serves as a custodian of Sikh musical heritage, preserving and perpetuating the rich cultural legacy passed down through generations. From the soul-stirring melodies of classical Raags to the rhythmic beats of traditional musical instruments, Gurmat Sangeet encapsulates the diversity and richness of Sikh musical traditions, ensuring that they remain vibrant and alive in the hearts and minds of practitioners.

2. **Expressing Spiritual Devotion:** Through the practice of Kirtan, devotees express their deep devotion and reverence for the divine as they melodiously recite the sacred hymns drawn from the Sri Guru Granth Sahib Ji and other revered Granths. The harmonious blend of Shabad and Raag in Kirtan creates a transcendent musical experience, inviting participants to immerse themselves fully in the spiritual journey and forge a profound connection with the divine essence.

3. **Fostering Unity and Community** Gurmat Sangeet serves as a unifying force within the Sikh community, bringing together individuals

from diverse backgrounds and walks of life in collective worship and celebration. Whether performed in the sacred confines of a Gurudwara or in the intimate setting of a Sikh household, Kirtan fosters a sense of unity, harmony, and shared purpose as voices blend harmoniously in praise and adoration of the divine.

4. **Connecting with Spiritual Wisdom** In addition to celebrating Sikh musical heritage, Gurmat Sangeet also provides devotees with a direct pathway to connect with the spiritual wisdom and insights contained within the sacred Granths. Through the melodious recitation of Shabads and contemplation of their profound teachings, practitioners gain deeper insights into the eternal truths and universal principles espoused by Sikh Gurus, guiding them on a transformative journey of self-discovery and spiritual growth.

Gurdwara Architecture

Gurudwara architecture stands as a testament to the profound principles of equality, community, and service that form the bedrock of Sikhism. Characterized by distinctive features and designs, Gurudwaras serve as sacred spaces where devotees come together to worship, reflect, and connect with the divine presence. Central to Gurudwara architecture is the Sri Darbar Sahib, the central prayer hall where the Sri Guru Granth Sahib Ji, issue orders, guide and provide right direction to the Sikhism and world. Gurudwara architecture embodies the timeless values and spiritual aspirations of Sikhism, providing devotees with sacred spaces where they can come together to worship, learn, and serve. Through its distinctive features and designs, Gurudwara architecture serves as a tangible expression of Sikh identity and heritage, fostering a deep sense of connection and belonging among believers and inspiring all who enter its hallowed halls to walk the path of truth, compassion, and selfless service.

Sri Darbar Sahib Ji

The Sri Darbar Sahib stands as the beating heart of every Gurudwara, radiating the timeless wisdom, love, and compassion of Sikhism to all who enter its sacred precincts. As devotees bow before the Sri Guru Granth Sahib Ji within the Sri Darbar Sahib Ji, they are reminded of the eternal presence of the divine in their lives and inspired to walk the path of truth, righteousness, and selfless service laid out by the Sikh Gurus.

1. **Symbolism of the Sri Darbar Sahib:** The Sri Darbar Sahib holds profound symbolic significance within Sikhism, representing the eternal presence of the divine and the spiritual authority of the Sri Guru Granth Sahib Ji. As the central prayer hall of the Gurudwara, it serves as a sacred space where devotees gather to pay homage to the Guru Granth Sahib Ji, which is enshrined on a raised platform known as the Palki Sahib. This elevated position symbolizes the reverence and respect accorded to the Sikh holy Granths as the eternal Guru and guiding light for all seekers of truth.

2. **Sanctuary of Peace and Tranquility:** Beyond its symbolic significance, the Sri Darbar Sahib serves as a sanctuary of peace and tranquility amidst the chaos of the world. Within its hallowed walls, devotees find refuge from the stresses and challenges of daily life as they immerse themselves in prayer, meditation, and contemplation. The serene ambiance of Sri Darbar Sahib Ji creates an atmosphere conducive to spiritual reflection and inner healing, allowing individuals to find solace and guidance in the divine presence.

3. **Spiritual Gathering and Communal Worship:** The Sri Darbar Sahib is not merely a physical structure but a vibrant center of spiritual gathering and communal worship. It is here that devotees come together as a community to participate in Kirtan (devotional singing), Ardas (collective prayer), and other religious ceremonies. The collective recitation of hymns and prayers within the Sri Darbar Sahib fosters a sense of unity, solidarity, and shared devotion among congregants, reinforcing the principles of equality, humility, and service that lie at the heart of Sikhism.

4. **Eternal Connection with the Divine:** The Sri Darbar Sahib serves as a conduit for devotees to connect with the eternal presence of the divine. As they bow their heads in reverence before the Sri Guru Granth Sahib Ji, seekers of truth find themselves enveloped in the divine grace and love that permeates the sacred space

of the Sri Darbar Sahib. Here, amidst the sacred vibrations of Gurbani (divine hymns), devotees experience a profound sense of spiritual upliftment and inner peace, reaffirming their eternal connection with the divine and their commitment to the path of Sikh spirituality.

Simplicity and Openness

Gurudwara architecture is characterized by its emphasis on simplicity, humility, and openness. Unlike many other religious structures, Gurudwaras eschew ornate decorations and lavish embellishments in favor of clean lines, spacious interiors, and minimalistic design elements. The absence of idols or religious icons reflects Sikh beliefs in the formless nature of the divine and underscores the principle of equality among all beings.

1. **Minimalistic Design:** Gurudwaras are characterized by their minimalist design aesthetic, which eschews unnecessary ornamentation in favor of clean and uncluttered spaces. Architectural elements are kept simple and functional, allowing for a sense of serenity and focus during worship and contemplation. This minimalist approach reflects Sikh values of humility and modesty, emphasizing the importance of inner spiritual wealth over external opulence.

2. **Spacious Interiors:** One of the hallmarks of Gurudwara architecture is the emphasis on spacious interiors, providing ample room for congregants to gather and worship without

feeling crowded or constrained. Large prayer halls and open courtyards allow for comfortable seating and movement, fostering a sense of community and inclusivity among worshippers. The spaciousness of Gurudwaras also serves as a metaphor for the vastness of the divine presence, inviting devotees to expand their hearts and minds in communion with the eternal.

3. **Absence of Idols or Icons:** In Gurudwaras, you won't find any idols or religious icons adorning the sacred spaces. The reason behind this is rooted in Sikh beliefs, which preach that the divine cannot be confined to any particular physical form or representation. Instead, Gurudwaras focus solely on the worship of the Sri Guru Granth Sahib Ji, the sacred scripture that serves as the spiritual guide and eternal Guru for Sikhs all around the world. The emphasis on Guru's worship underscores the principle of equality among all beings, as the Sri Guru Granth Sahib Ji is revered as the universal teacher whose teachings are accessible to all, regardless of caste, creed, or social status.

4. **Embracing Equality and Inclusivity:** Gurudwara architecture embodies the values of equality, inclusivity, and accessibility that lie at the heart of Sikhism. By prioritizing simplicity, openness, and the absence of religious icons, Gurudwaras create an environment where all individuals can feel welcome and valued, regardless of their background or beliefs. In this

way, Gurudwara architecture serves as a physical manifestation of Sikh teachings, inspiring devotees to cultivate humility, compassion, and spiritual insight in their lives.

Community Spaces

In addition to the Sri Darbar Sahib, Gurudwara architecture often includes communal spaces such as langar halls, where free meals are served to all visitors regardless of their background or social status. These communal spaces embody the spirit of seva or selfless service, that lies at the heart of Sikhism, fostering a sense of unity, equality, and compassion among devotees. Gurudwaras also typically feature open courtyards or verandas where congregants can gather for prayer, meditation, or community events, further emphasizing the importance of communal worship and fellowship in Sikh tradition.

1. **Langar Halls (Symbol of Equality and Hospitality):** Langar halls are integral components of Gurudwara architecture, where free meals are served to all visitors, regardless of their background, religion, or social status. This tradition of communal dining, known as langar, exemplifies the Sikh values of equality, hospitality, and compassion. By breaking bread together in a spirit of shared humanity, langar halls promote social cohesion and erase distinctions of caste, creed, or economic status, fostering a sense of unity and inclusivity within the Sikh community and beyond.

2. **Spirit of Seva (Serving Others with Selflessness):** The langar tradition also embodies the spirit of seva, or selfless service, that lies at the heart of Sikhism. Volunteers, known as sevadars, selflessly dedicate their time and effort to prepare, serve, and clean up after the langar meal without seeking any personal recognition or reward. Through their acts of seva, sevadars embody the teachings of Sikh Gurus, who emphasized the importance of serving others with love, humility, and compassion. Langar halls thus serve as living embodiments of Sikh values, inspiring devotees to practice seva in their daily lives and contribute to the welfare of society.

3. **Open Courtyards (Spaces for Community Gathering):** In addition to langar halls, Gurudwaras typically feature open courtyards or verandas where congregants can gather for prayer, meditation, or community events. These communal spaces provide opportunities for devotees to come together in fellowship and worship, reinforcing the sense of community and belonging that lies at the heart of Sikh tradition. Whether engaging in collective prayer, sharing stories and experiences, or participating in cultural festivities, congregants find unity and strength in their shared spiritual journey within the welcoming embrace of the Gurudwara courtyard.

4. **Emphasizing Communal Worship and Fellowship:** Community spaces within

Gurudwara architecture play a crucial role in fostering unity, equality, and service among devotees. By providing opportunities for congregants to come together in fellowship, share meals, and engage in collective worship, Gurudwaras create environments where individuals can experience the transformative power of community and the joy of serving others. Through langar halls, open courtyards, and other communal areas, Gurudwara architecture reinforces the timeless values of Sikhism and inspires devotees to live their lives with compassion, humility, and a commitment to serving humanity.

Symbolism and Spiritual Significance

Every aspect of Gurudwara architecture is imbued with symbolic meaning and spiritual significance. From the layout of the prayer hall to the design of the entrance gate, each architectural element reflects Sikh values and teachings, inviting devotees to contemplate the deeper truths of their faith and connect with the divine presence. Through its simplicity, openness, and emphasis on community, Gurudwara architecture serves as a physical manifestation of Sikh spirituality, inspiring devotees to live their lives in accordance with the principles of love, equality, and service embodied by Sikh Gurus.

Visual Arts

Visual arts play a vital role in human culture and society, serving as a means of creative expression, communication, and reflection on human experience. It refers to any form of art that is primarily visual in nature, meaning it is perceived through the eyes. Artists use visual elements such as line, shape, color, texture, and composition to convey ideas, emotions, and narratives to viewers. Visual art can be representational, depicting recognizable subjects from the real world, or abstract, conveying ideas and emotions through non-representational forms and patterns. This encompasses a wide range of artistic expressions, including but not limited to:

1. **Painting:** The creation of images using various painting mediums such as oil, watercolor, acrylic, or gouache.

2. **Drawing:** The creation of images using pencils, charcoal, pastels, or other drawing implements on paper or other surfaces.

3. **Sculpture:** The creation of three-dimensional artworks using materials such as clay, wood, metal, stone, or plaster.

4. **Printmaking:** The creation of images on paper or other surfaces through techniques such as etching, woodcutting, lithography, or screen printing.

5. **Photography:** The art of capturing and creating images using cameras and photographic processes.

6. **Digital Art:** The creation of images using digital tools and technologies, such as computer software, graphics tablets, and digital cameras.

Historical and Spiritual Depictions

In Sikh visual arts, a significant emphasis is placed on portraying historical events and spiritual concepts central to the Sikh faith. Artists skillfully depict scenes from the lives of Sikh Gurus, pivotal historical moments, and symbolic representations of spiritual teachings. These depictions serve multiple purposes, including preservation of Sikh history, celebration of cultural heritage, and inspiration for spiritual devotion and emulation of virtuous ideals.

1. **Scenes from the Lives of Sikh Gurus:** Artworks often depict significant moments from the lives of Sikh Gurus, such as Sri Guru Nanak Dev Ji's travels and teachings, Sri Guru Gobind Singh Ji's battles and sacrifices, and Sri Guru Tegh Bahadur Ji's martyrdom. These scenes capture key events and encounters that shaped Sikh history and spirituality, offering viewers insight into the exemplary lives and teachings of the Gurus. Through vivid imagery and narrative compositions, artists bring to life the profound impact of the Gurus' words and actions, inspiring reverence and admiration among devotees.

2. **Illustrations of Historical Events:** Sikh visual arts also encompass illustrations of historical events that hold significance in Sikh history, such as the Vaisakhi of 1699, the revelation day of the Khalsa, and the battles fought by the Khalsa army against tyranny and oppression. These illustrations serve as visual narratives that convey the struggles, triumphs, and

sacrifices of the Sikh community in its quest for justice, freedom, and spiritual sovereignty. By immortalizing these events in art, artists ensure that the legacy of Sikh resistance and resilience endures for future generations to honor and learn from.

3. **Martyrdoms of Sikh Martyrs:** The martyrdoms of Sikh martyrs, such as the Sahibzade, Bhai Mati Das, and Bhai Taru Singh, are often depicted in Sikh visual arts as symbols of courage, faith, and sacrifice. These poignant portrayals capture the bravery and steadfastness of individuals who endured persecution and torture for upholding their Sikh beliefs and principles. Through their selfless acts of martyrdom, these individuals inspire devotees to stand firm in their convictions and uphold the values of truth, righteousness, and compassion, even in the face of adversity.

4. **Preservation and Inspiration:** Historical and spiritual depictions in Sikh visual arts serve a dual purpose of preservation and inspiration. They preserve the rich tapestry of Sikh history and heritage, ensuring that future generations have access to visual representations of their cultural identity and spiritual legacy. At the same time, these depictions inspire devotees to emulate the virtues and values exemplified by their spiritual ancestors, fostering a sense of reverence, pride, and spiritual devotion within the Sikh community. Through art, the stories of Sikh Gurus, historical events, and martyrs

continue to resonate with believers, enriching their spiritual journey and deepening their connection to the Sikh tradition.

Portraits of Sikh Gurus

In Sikh visual arts, portraits and paintings of Sikh Gurus occupy a sacred space, serving as focal points of devotion and reverence for believers. These artistic representations are meticulously crafted to capture the essence and character of each Guru, imbuing their portraits with a profound sense of spiritual presence and grace. Adorning the walls of Gurudwaras and Sikh homes, these portraits remind believers of the eternal guidance and inspiration offered by the revered spiritual guides of Sikhism.

1. **Symbolism of Portraits:** Portraits of Sikh Gurus are imbued with deep symbolism and spiritual significance. Each brushstroke is infused with reverence, seeking to convey not only the physical likeness of the Guru but also the divine wisdom and compassion that emanate from within. Artists carefully select elements and details to reflect the virtues and teachings associated with each Guru, ensuring that the portrait serves as a visual representation of their spiritual essence.

2. **Focal Points of Devotion:** Within Gurudwaras, portraits of Sikh Gurus serve as focal points of devotion and worship. Believers bow their heads in reverence before these sacred images, offering prayers and seeking guidance from their spiritual guides. The presence of the

Guru's portrait creates a sacred atmosphere, inviting devotees to cultivate a deep sense of connection and communion with their spiritual lineage.

3. **Inspiration and Guidance:** Portraits of Sikh Gurus serve as sources of inspiration and guidance for believers on their spiritual journey. As devotees gaze upon the Guru's serene countenance, they are reminded of the timeless wisdom and compassion embodied by their spiritual guide. The Guru's gaze offers solace and reassurance, guiding believers through life's challenges and inspiring them to uphold the values of truth, humility, and service in their daily lives.

4. **Adornment of Gurudwaras and Homes:** In Gurudwaras and Sikh homes, portraits of Sikh Gurus adorn the walls, creating a sacred ambiance that fosters spiritual reflection and devotion. These portraits serve as constant reminders of the Guru's presence and teachings, guiding believers on their path of spiritual growth and transformation. Whether in the grandeur of a Gurudwara or the intimacy of a home altar, the Guru's portrait serves as a beacon of light, illuminating the hearts and minds of devotees with divine wisdom and love.

5. **Eternal Guidance and Inspiration:** Portraits of Sikh Gurus hold a special significance in Sikh visual arts, symbolizing the eternal guidance and inspiration offered by the revered spiritual guides of Sikhism. Through their serene

expressions and compassionate gaze, these portraits invite believers to deepen their devotion, cultivate virtues, and walk the path of righteousness laid out by their beloved Gurus. As timeless icons of devotion and reverence, the portraits of Sikh Gurus continue to inspire and uplift hearts across generations, guiding believers on their journey toward spiritual fulfillment and enlightenment.

Symbolism and Allegory

Sikh visual arts are rich in symbolism and allegory, employing visual metaphors to convey profound spiritual truths and teachings. Through symbolic imagery, artists illuminate key aspects of Sikh philosophy and theology, inviting viewers to delve deeper into the mysteries of existence and contemplate Sikhism's timeless wisdom.

1. **Symbols of Sikh Philosophy:** Central to Sikh visual arts are symbols that encapsulate fundamental principles of Sikh philosophy. The Khanda, a symbol consisting of a double-edged sword, a circle, and two crossed kirpans, represents the Sikh concept of oneness, strength, and readiness to defend righteousness. The Ik Onkar symbol, depicting the numeral one and the primal sound of creation, signifies the unity of the divine and the interconnectedness of all creation. The Sikh emblem, featuring the Khanda encircled by two swords, embodies the sovereignty and martial spirit of the Khalsa.

574

2. **Illustrating Abstract Concepts:** In addition to traditional symbols, Sikh visual arts often employ allegorical imagery to illustrate abstract concepts central to Sikh theology. Artists use metaphorical representations to depict concepts such as the cycle of birth and death (samsara), the eternal nature of the soul (atma), and the interconnectedness of all beings (bandi chhor). Through symbolic imagery, viewers are encouraged to contemplate the deeper meanings behind these concepts and explore their implications for spiritual growth and enlightenment.

3. **Inviting Contemplation:** The use of symbolism and allegory in Sikh visual arts serves to stimulate contemplation and introspection among viewers. By presenting spiritual truths in a visual form, artists create opportunities for viewers to engage with complex theological concepts in a tangible and accessible manner. Symbols become gateways to deeper understanding, inviting viewers to explore the mysteries of existence and uncover the hidden truths that lie at the heart of Sikhism.

4. **Connecting with the Divine:** Symbolism and allegory in Sikh visual arts serve as pathways for viewers to connect with the divine essence and explore the spiritual dimensions of existence. Through contemplation of symbolic imagery, viewers are invited to transcend the limitations of the material world and awaken to the deeper truths of their own spiritual nature. In

this way, Sikh visual arts become vehicles for spiritual transformation, guiding viewers on a journey of self-discovery and enlightenment.

5. **Inspiration for Devotion:** Symbolism and allegory in Sikh visual arts inspire devotion and reverence among believers, reminding them of Sikhism's eternal truths and teachings. As viewers contemplate the symbolic representations of divine principles and cosmic realities, they are inspired to deepen their spiritual practice and align their lives with the timeless wisdom of Sikh Gurus. In this way, symbolism becomes a catalyst for spiritual growth and a source of inspiration for living a life of truth, compassion, and service in accordance with Sikh teachings.

Education and Inspiration

Artworks in Sikhism serve as invaluable tools for education and inspiration, providing visual representations of complex theological concepts and historical narratives. Through paintings, illustrations, and sculptures, viewers gain a deeper understanding of Sikh beliefs, practices, and heritage, fostering a sense of cultural pride and spiritual connection. Artworks in Gurudwaras often accompany religious discourses and sermons, enhancing the learning experience and reinforcing the teachings of Sikh Gurus.

1. **Visual Representations of Theological Concepts:** Sikh artworks serve as visual aids in conveying intricate theological concepts to

viewers. Whether depicting the cycle of birth and death, the eternal nature of the soul, or the interconnectedness of all creation, these visual representations provide tangible imagery that facilitates comprehension and contemplation. By translating abstract ideas into visual form, artworks make complex concepts more accessible and relatable, empowering viewers to engage more deeply with their faith.

2. **Historical Narratives and Heritage:** Artworks in Sikhism also serve as windows into the rich tapestry of Sikh history and heritage. Through paintings and illustrations, viewers are transported back in time to pivotal moments such as the Vaisakhi of 1699 or the battles fought by the Khalsa army. These visual narratives not only preserve important historical events but also evoke a sense of pride and reverence for Sikh martyrs and heroes. By celebrating Sikh history, artworks instill a deeper appreciation for the sacrifices made by past generations and inspire viewers to uphold the values of courage, resilience, and righteousness.

3. **Cultural Pride and Spiritual Connection:** Artworks in Sikhism evoke a sense of cultural pride and spiritual connection among believers. Whether admiring a painting of Guru Nanak Dev Ji's travels or contemplating a sculpture of the Khanda, viewers are reminded of the timeless wisdom and spiritual legacy of Sikh Gurus. These visual representations serve as potent

reminders of Sikh identity and heritage, fostering a sense of belonging and solidarity within the Sikh community and beyond.

4. **Enhancing the Learning Experience:** In Gurudwaras, artworks often accompany religious discourses and sermons, enriching the learning experience for attendees. Visual aids such as paintings and illustrations help to illustrate key teachings and stories from Sikh scriptures, making religious teachings more engaging and memorable. By incorporating artworks into educational settings, Gurudwaras create immersive environments that stimulate both the intellect and the senses, deepening participants' understanding and appreciation of Sikhism.

5. **Reinforcing the Teachings of Sikh Gurus:** Ultimately, artworks in Sikhism serve to reinforce the teachings of Sikh Gurus and inspire viewers to embody these teachings in their lives. Whether through images of compassion, courage, or selfless service, artworks convey the timeless values and ideals upheld by Sikhism. By immersing themselves in the visual richness of Sikh art, believers are inspired to emulate the virtues of their spiritual guides and walk the path of righteousness and devotion. Through education and inspiration, artworks in Sikhism continue to serve as beacons of light, guiding believers on their journey towards spiritual enlightenment and self-realization.

Promoting Spiritual Reflection

Above all, Sikh visual arts serve as catalysts for spiritual reflection and contemplation. Whether depicting scenes of devotion, martyrdom, or divine revelation, artworks invite viewers to engage in introspection and soul-searching, prompting them to reflect on their own relationship with the divine and their place within the cosmic order. Through the beauty and symbolism of visual arts, individuals are transported to a realm of spiritual transcendence, where the boundaries of time and space dissolve, and the eternal truths of Sikhism are revealed in all their splendor.

1. **Invitation to Introspection:** Sikh artworks extend a heartfelt invitation to viewers to engage in introspection and soul-searching. Whether through depictions of devotion, martyrdom, or divine revelation, these artworks resonate with universal themes that speak to the human condition. Viewers are encouraged to reflect on the deeper meaning behind these scenes, contemplating their own beliefs, values, and experiences in light of the spiritual truths presented before them.

2. **Exploring Personal Connection with the Divine:** As individuals engage with Sikh visual arts, they are prompted to explore their personal connection with the divine. Scenes of devotion and divine communion inspire viewers to deepen their own spiritual practice, cultivating a closer relationship with the divine presence within and around them. Through contemplation of these artworks, individuals are reminded of

the inherent divinity that resides within their own being, awakening a sense of reverence and awe for the sacredness of life.

3. **Transcending Boundaries of Time and Space:** Sikh visual arts serve as portals to realms of spiritual transcendence, where the boundaries of time and space dissolve, and the eternal truths of Sikhism are revealed in all their splendor. As viewers immerse themselves in the beauty and symbolism of these artworks, they are transported beyond the confines of the material world, entering into a realm of spiritual insight and illumination. In this sacred space, individuals experience a profound sense of connection with the divine, transcending earthly concerns and accessing higher realms of consciousness.

4. **Revelation of Eternal Truths:** Through the beauty and symbolism of Sikh visual arts, individuals are granted glimpses into the eternal truths that lie at the heart of Sikhism. Whether through allegorical representations of cosmic realities or symbolic depictions of divine grace, these artworks illuminate the path to spiritual enlightenment and self-realization. Viewers are reminded of the timeless wisdom and universal principles embodied by Sikh Gurus, inspiring them to walk the path of truth, compassion, and selfless service.

5. **Embracing Spiritual Enlightenment:** Sikh visual arts serve as guides on the journey towards spiritual enlightenment and self-

discovery. Through contemplation and reflection, individuals are invited to awaken to the divine essence that dwells within their own hearts, recognizing their interconnectedness with all of creation. In the sacred space evoked by these artworks, individuals find solace, inspiration, and the courage to embrace their true spiritual nature, transcending the limitations of the ego and merging with the infinite ocean of divine consciousness.

Literature in Sikhism

Sikhism boasts a vast body of literature that encompasses poetry, prose, and sacred texts, each conveying the profound teachings and values of the faith. From the poetic verses of revered Gurus to the scholarly writings of theologians, Sikh literature serves as a beacon of spiritual guidance and artistic inspiration. The Granths, in particular, are revered as works of art, renowned for their spiritual depth and poetic beauty, inviting readers on a transformative journey of self-discovery and enlightenment.

The Granths (Spiritual Treasures of Sikhism)

Central to Sikh literature are the Granths, sacred texts that serve as spiritual guides and sources of divine wisdom. The Sri Guru Granth Sahib Ji, revered as the eternal Guru and ultimate authority in Sikhism, stands as the pinnacle of Sikh literary achievement. Comprising hymns and compositions from Sikh Gurus, saints, and scholars, the Sri Guru Granth Sahib Ji is celebrated for its lyrical poetry, profound philosophy, and universal message of love and unity. Likewise, other Granths, such as the Sri Dasam Granth Sahib Ji and the compositions of Bhai Gurdas Ji and Bhai Nand Lal Ji, are esteemed for their spiritual insight and literary excellence, enriching the literary landscape of Sikhism.

1. **The Sri Guru Granth Sahib Ji (Eternal and Spiritual Guru):** The Sri Guru Granth Sahib Ji holds a unique position in Sikhism as the eternal Guru, offering spiritual guidance and solace to believers across generations. Compiled by Guru Arjan Dev Ji and enshrined as the Guru by Sri Guru Gobind Singh Ji, it transcends the limitations of time and space, serving as a beacon of light in the darkness of ignorance and delusion. The Guru Granth Sahib Ji comprises hymns and compositions not only from Sikh Gurus but also from saints and poets of various religious traditions, emphasizing the universality of its message and the unity of all humanity.

2. **Lyrical Poetry and Profound Philosophy:** One of the most remarkable features of the Sri Guru Granth Sahib Ji is its exquisite poetry, characterized by its lyrical beauty, rhythmic cadence, and profound symbolism. Each hymn, known as a Shabad, is a masterpiece of poetic expression, weaving together words and melodies to evoke deep spiritual emotions and insights. The Sri Guru Granth Sahib Ji addresses a wide range of existential themes, from the nature of God and creation to the path of devotion and liberation, offering readers a

profound understanding of the human condition and the ultimate reality.

3. **Other Granths:** Sikhism boasts Granths and compositions that enrich its literary heritage. The Sri Dasam Granth Sahib Ji, Sri Sarbloh Grant Ji, contains compositions that celebrate the martial spirit and valor of the Khalsa, inspiring believers to uphold righteousness and defend the truth. The writings of Bhai Gurdas Ji and Bhai Nand Lal Ji, esteemed Sikh scholars and poets, offer invaluable insights into Sikh philosophy and theology, complementing the teachings of the Gurus and enhancing the spiritual depth of Sikh literature.

4. **Enriching the Literary Landscape of Sikhism:** Collectively, the Granths and compositions of Sikhism enrich its literary landscape, embodying the spiritual essence and cultural heritage of the Sikh tradition. Through their timeless wisdom, artistic beauty, and universal appeal, these sacred texts continue to inspire and uplift believers, guiding them on a path of spiritual awakening and self-realization. As spiritual treasures of Sikhism, the Granths illuminate the path of truth, love, and unity, inviting all humanity to embrace the divine light that shines within and without.

Poetry and Prose

Sikh literature is replete with poetry and prose that reflect the devotion, wisdom, and moral values upheld by Sikh Gurus and scholars. The poetic verses of Sri Guru Nanak Dev Ji, Guru Angad Dev Ji, and other Gurus resonate with spiritual fervor and philosophical depth, conveying timeless truths in eloquent language. Prose writings, such as the teachings of Sri Guru Tegh Bahadur Sahib Ji and the compositions of Bhai Gurdas Ji, offer practical guidance on leading a virtuous life and attaining spiritual liberation. The literary works of Bhai Vir Singh Ji, Professor Puran Singh, Giani Dit Singh Ji, Kavi Santokh Singh Ji serve as sources of inspiration and moral guidance for believers, encouraging them to embody the virtues of humility, compassion, and service in their daily lives.

1. **Poetic Verses:** The poetic verses of Sikh Gurus resonate with spiritual fervor and philosophical depth, capturing the essence of divine love and universal truths in eloquent language. Through the power of metaphor and imagery, these verses evoke a sense of awe and reverence for the divine, inviting readers to embark on a journey of self-discovery and spiritual awakening.

2. **Spiritual Fervor and Philosophical Depth:** The poetry of Sikh Scholars, set to melodic tunes and sung as hymns, encapsulates the essence of Sikh spirituality and the teachings of Ik Onkar (the One Creator). Sikh Scholars' compositions continue this tradition, offering lyrical expressions of devotion and reverence for the divine. Through their poetry, Sikh scholars convey timeless truths about the nature of existence, the importance of righteous

living, and the ultimate goal of spiritual liberation.

3. **Prose Writings:** Sikh literature includes prose writings that provide practical guidance on leading a virtuous life and attaining spiritual enlightenment. The teachings of Sikh Gurus, offer profound insights into the nature of reality and the importance of selfless service to humanity. The compositions of Bhai Gurdas Ji, a revered Sikh scholar, provide invaluable commentary on Sikh philosophy and theology, enriching the spiritual understanding of believers.

4. **Practical Guidance and Moral Values:** The prose writings of Sikh Gurus and scholars serve as practical guides for navigating life's challenges and dilemmas while upholding moral values and principles. Whether expounding on the virtues of humility, compassion, and selfless service or elucidating the importance of ethical conduct and righteous living, these writings offer timeless wisdom that resonates with believers across generations.

5. **Sources of Inspiration and Moral Guidance:** The poetry and prose of Sikh literature serve as sources of inspiration and moral guidance for believers, encouraging them to embody the virtues of humility, compassion, and service in their daily lives. Through the beauty of language and the depth of spiritual insight, these literary works inspire readers to cultivate a deeper

connection with the divine and live in harmony with the principles of Sikhism.

Themes of Devotion and Social Justice

Sikh literature explores a wide range of themes, from devotion and morality to social justice and human rights. Poetic hymns celebrate the divine qualities of the Creator and inspire devotion and love among believers. At the same time, Sikh literature is imbued with a fervent commitment to social justice and equality, advocating for the rights and dignity of all human beings. Through their writings, Sikh Gurus and scholars champion the cause of the marginalized and oppressed, calling for an end to discrimination and injustice in society.

1. **Celebration of Divine Qualities:** Poetic hymns within Sikh literature celebrate the divine qualities of the Creator, inspiring devotees to cultivate a deep sense of devotion and love towards the divine. These hymns, often sung with melodic fervor, serve as expressions of reverence and gratitude for the divine presence permeating every aspect of creation. Through the lyrical beauty of these verses, believers are encouraged to surrender themselves to the divine will and seek spiritual union with the eternal truth.

2. **Fervent Commitment to Social Justice:** Sikh literature is imbued with a fervent commitment to social justice and equality, reflecting the Sikh belief in the inherent dignity and equality of all human beings. Sikh Gurus and scholars use

their writings to champion the cause of the marginalized and oppressed, calling for an end to discrimination and injustice in society. Through their teachings, they advocate for the upliftment of the downtrodden and the empowerment of the disenfranchised, emphasizing the importance of compassion, empathy, and solidarity in creating a more just and equitable world.

3. **Advocacy for Human Rights:** In addition to promoting social justice, Sikh literature serves as a platform for advocacy for human rights and dignity. Sikh Gurus and scholars use their writings to denounce oppression and tyranny in all its forms, advocating for the rights of individuals to live with dignity, freedom, and equality. Through their teachings, they challenge societal norms and structures that perpetuate inequality and exploitation, inspiring believers to stand up against injustice and oppression wherever it may be found.

4. **Emphasis on Compassion and Empathy:** Central to Sikh literature is an emphasis on compassion and empathy towards all beings, regardless of their social status or background. Sikh Gurus and scholars exhort believers to cultivate a spirit of selfless service and altruism, embodying the principles of seva (selfless service) and sarbat da bhala (welfare of all). Through their writings, they encourage believers to extend a helping hand to those in need,

fostering a culture of empathy, solidarity, and compassion in society.

Artistic Beauty and Spiritual Depth

What distinguishes Sikh literature is not only its spiritual content but also its artistic beauty and literary craftsmanship. The Granths are renowned for their exquisite poetry, rich symbolism, and melodic rhythm, captivating readers with their aesthetic appeal and profound spiritual insights. Through the artistry of language and the power of metaphor, Sikh literature transports readers to realms of spiritual enlightenment and inner transformation, inviting them to explore the depths of their own souls and discover the divine presence within.

1. **Exquisite Poetry and Lyrical Beauty:** One of the defining features of Sikh literature is its exquisite poetry and lyrical beauty. The Granths composed in poetic verse, characterized by their rhythmic cadence, melodious tunes, and evocative imagery. Each hymn, known as a Shabad, is a masterpiece of poetic expression, weaving together words and melodies to evoke deep spiritual emotions and insights. Through their lyrical beauty, these verses captivate the hearts and minds of readers, drawing them into a profound experience of divine love and transcendence.

2. **Rich Symbolism and Allegory:** Sikh literature is replete with rich symbolism and allegory, which adds layers of meaning and depth to its teachings. The Granths are filled with

metaphorical imagery that conveys profound spiritual truths and insights, inviting readers to contemplate the deeper mysteries of existence. Symbolic motifs such as the Ik Onkar (the One Creator), the Khanda (the Sikh emblem), and the Panj Pyare (the Five Beloved Ones) are woven throughout Sikh literature, serving as potent reminders of the divine presence and the eternal principles of Sikhism.

3. **Melodic Rhythm and Aesthetic Appeal:** The Granths are known for their melodic rhythm and aesthetic appeal, which enhance the spiritual experience of readers. Many hymns within Sikh literature are set to specific musical scales, known as Ragas, which evoke specific emotions and moods. The melodic interplay of voice and instrument creates a harmonious atmosphere that elevates the soul and transports the listener to a state of spiritual ecstasy. Through their aesthetic beauty, the Granths engage the senses and immerse readers in a transcendent experience of divine communion.

4. **Invitation to Spiritual Enlightenment:** Sikh literature serves as an invitation to spiritual enlightenment and inner transformation. Through its artistic beauty and spiritual depth, Sikh literature inspires readers to embark on a journey of self-discovery and self-realization, leading them to uncover the divine presence within their own hearts. The Granths, with their timeless wisdom and universal message, guide readers toward a deeper understanding of the

nature of reality and the ultimate purpose of human existence, inviting them to embrace the path of truth, love, and unity with the divine.

Inspiration for Generations

Sikh literature stands as a testament to the spiritual richness and artistic brilliance of the Sikh tradition. From the timeless wisdom of the Granths to the poetic verses of Sikh Scholars, Sikh literature continues to inspire and uplift generations of believers, guiding them on a path of spiritual awakening and self-realization. Through its profound teachings, moral values, and artistic expression, Sikh literature remains a source of enlightenment and inspiration for all who seek truth, love, and unity in the divine embrace of Waheguru.

1. **Timeless Wisdom of the Granths:** At the heart of Sikh literature lie the Granths, revered as sacred texts that encapsulate the essence of Sikh spirituality and philosophy. The Sri Guru Granth Sahib Ji, the eternal and current Guru of Sikhism, serves as a beacon of divine wisdom, offering profound insights into the nature of reality, the purpose of human existence, and the path to spiritual liberation. Its teachings, timeless and universal, resonate with believers of all ages, providing guidance and solace in times of joy and adversity alike.

2. **Poetic Verses and Scholarly Insights:** Sikh literature comprises a wealth of poetic verses and scholarly insights that enrich the spiritual understanding of believers. The lyrical beauty of

Sikh poetry, expressed through the words of revered figures, stirs the soul and inspires devotion to the divine. The scholarly writings of Sikh theologians and philosophers offer profound interpretations of Sikh teachings, illuminating the path of spiritual growth and self-discovery.

3. **Guiding Believers on the Spiritual Path:** Through its profound teachings, moral values, and artistic expression, Sikh literature serves as a guiding force, empowering believers to navigate the complexities of life with wisdom and grace. Its emphasis on love, compassion, and service inspires individuals to cultivate virtues that foster harmony and unity within themselves and society at large. By providing a roadmap for leading a life of purpose and integrity, Sikh literature becomes a trusted companion on the journey of spiritual awakening and self-realization.

4. **Source of Enlightenment and Inspiration:** Sikh literature remains a source of enlightenment and inspiration for all who seek truth, love, and unity in the divine embrace of Waheguru. Its timeless teachings and universal message transcend the boundaries of time and space, speaking directly to the hearts of believers and igniting the flame of divine love within them. Whether through its profound philosophical insights, its stirring poetry, or its emphasis on social justice and equality, Sikh literature continues to uplift and elevate

humanity, guiding individuals toward a deeper understanding of themselves and the world around them.

Performing Art

Sikh culture boasts a rich tapestry of performing arts, encompassing diverse forms such as folk music, dance, and theater. Performing arts in Sikh culture serve as powerful expressions of identity, community, and spirituality. Through music, dance, and theater, Sikhs celebrate their history, express their values, and unite in a shared sense of cultural pride and belonging. These art forms continue to thrive and evolve, enriching the tapestry of Sikh heritage and inspiring future generations to carry forward the legacy of Sikh culture with passion and reverence.

Folk Music

Folk music holds a special place in Sikh culture, serving as a vehicle for preserving oral traditions and passing down stories from generation to generation. Folk songs, often accompanied by traditional instruments like the dhol (drum) and tumbi (single-stringed instrument), reflect the joys, sorrows, and aspirations of the Sikh community. These songs may narrate tales of valor, love, and devotion, paying homage to Sikh heroes and spiritual figures.

1. **Preserving Oral Traditions:** Folk music in Sikh culture is a living repository of oral traditions, capturing the essence of Sikh history, spirituality, and cultural identity. Passed down through generations via word of mouth, these songs serve as a bridge between the past and

the present, connecting individuals to their ancestors and the stories that define them. By preserving oral traditions, folk music ensures that the voices of the past continue to resonate in the hearts and minds of future generations.

2. **Accompanying Instruments:** Accompanied by traditional instruments such as the dhol (drum) and tumbi (single-stringed instrument), Sikh folk songs acquire a distinctive rhythm and melody that reflects the vibrant spirit of the community. The pulsating beat of the dhol and the soulful strains of the tumbi enhance the storytelling aspect of the music, infusing it with energy and emotion.

3. **Reflection of Community Life:** Sikh folk songs mirror the joys, sorrows, struggles, and triumphs of everyday life within the Sikh community. From celebrations of harvest festivals to laments for lost loved ones, these songs encapsulate the full spectrum of human experiences. Through their lyrical narratives and evocative melodies, folk music becomes a reflection of community life, fostering a sense of solidarity and kinship among listeners.

4. **Homage to Sikh Heroes and Spiritual Figures:** Many Sikh folk songs pay homage to Sikh heroes, martyrs, and spiritual figures who embody the values of courage, sacrifice, and devotion. These songs serve not only as tributes to the bravery and resilience of Sikh ancestors but also as sources of inspiration for contemporary listeners. By commemorating the

deeds and virtues of Sikh luminaries, folk music reinforces the cultural pride and spiritual heritage of the community.

Bhangra and Gidha

Dance forms an integral part of Sikh celebrations and festivities, offering a dynamic expression of joy, devotion, and cultural pride. Meanwhile, traditional Punjabi folk dances like Bhangra and Gidha are popular across the Sikh community. These dances, characterized by graceful movements and rhythmic footwork, evoke a sense of spiritual ecstasy and communion with the divine.

1. **Bhangra**: Bhangra, perhaps the most iconic of Punjabi folk dances, is renowned for its exuberance, vigor, and infectious rhythm. Originating from the agricultural heartland of Punjab, Bhangra emerged as a celebration of vitality, resilience, and the spirit of community. Characterized by energetic movements, robust footwork, and spirited gestures, Bhangra dancers exude a sense of joy and enthusiasm that is contagious to observers. Accompanied by the lively beats of the dhol (drum) and other traditional instruments, Bhangra embodies the festive spirit of Sikh celebrations and cultural gatherings, uniting participants in a shared experience of jubilation and camaraderie.

2. **Gidha**: Gidha, a traditional Punjabi folk dance performed predominantly by women, celebrates feminine grace, strength, and empowerment. Rooted in the cultural traditions of Punjab,

Gidha showcases a unique blend of elegance, athleticism, and storytelling. Dancers, adorned in vibrant attire and adorned with traditional jewelry, engage in lively footwork, graceful gestures, and spirited singing as they narrate tales of love, camaraderie, and resilience. Gidha not only serves as a form of artistic expression but also as a platform for social bonding, solidarity, and the celebration of womanhood within the Sikh community.

Theater

Theater serves as a powerful medium for retelling Sikh history, inspiring social change, and raising awareness about contemporary issues facing the Sikh community. Through dramatic performances and stage productions, Sikh playwrights and performers bring historical events and social injustices to life, prompting audiences to reflect on the lessons of the past and advocate for a more just and equitable future. Theater also provides a platform for addressing issues such as identity, discrimination, and cultural preservation within the Sikh diaspora.

1. **Retelling Sikh History:** One of the primary functions of theater within Sikh culture is the retelling of Sikh history through dramatic narratives and reenactments. Theater productions offer audiences immersive experiences that transport them back in time to pivotal moments in Sikh history, such as the lives of the Sikh Gurus, the battles of the Khalsa, and the struggles for religious freedom. By bringing historical events to life on stage, theater

allows audiences to connect with the heroes and heroines of Sikh history, fostering a deeper appreciation for their sacrifices and contributions to Sikh identity and heritage.

2. **Inspiring Social Change**: Beyond historical reenactments, the theater serves as a catalyst for inspiring social change and raising awareness about contemporary issues facing the Sikh community. Playwrights and performers use the stage to shine a spotlight on social injustices, discrimination, and cultural challenges confronting Sikhs in the modern world. Through compelling storytelling and vivid character portrayals, theater encourages audiences to confront uncomfortable truths, challenge prevailing narratives, and advocate for a more just and equitable society for all.

3. **Addressing Identity and Discrimination:** Theater provides a vital platform for Sikhs to address issues of identity, discrimination, and cultural preservation within the Sikh diaspora. By centering Sikh narratives and experiences on stage, theater empowers Sikhs to assert their voices, challenge stereotypes, and reclaim their cultural heritage. Through performances that celebrate Sikh traditions, values, and resilience, theater becomes a means of affirming Sikh identity and fostering a sense of belonging within diverse communities.

4. **Powerful Medium:** Theater emerges as a powerful medium within Sikh culture, amplifying voices, inspiring action, and fostering solidarity

within the Sikh community and beyond. Through dramatic storytelling, theater brings Sikh history to life, raises awareness about contemporary issues, and empowers Sikhs to confront challenges with courage and resilience. As a catalyst for social change and cultural preservation, theater continues to play a vital role in shaping the narrative of Sikh identity and advancing the quest for justice, equality, and dignity for all.

Commemorating Festivals and Historical Events

Performing arts play a central role in commemorating Sikh festivals and historical events, infusing these occasions with color, music, and spectacle. Whether through lively processions, musical performances, or theatrical reenactments, Sikhs come together to celebrate their cultural heritage and religious identity. These artistic expressions serve not only to entertain but also to educate and inspire, reinforcing the values of unity, equality, and service that lie at the heart of Sikhism.

1. **Vibrant Processions and Parades:** Sikh festivals, such as Vaisakhi and Gurpurabs (Guru's anniversaries), are often marked by vibrant processions and parades that showcase the diverse cultural traditions and religious fervor of the Sikh community. Processions feature colorful banners, ornate floats, and spirited music, creating a festive atmosphere that captivates participants and spectators alike. These lively displays of devotion and celebration serve as public affirmations of Sikh

identity and solidarity, inviting individuals of all backgrounds to join in the festivities and experience the warmth and hospitality of the Sikh community.

2. **Musical Performances:** Music holds a central place in Sikh celebrations, with musical performances serving as integral components of festival gatherings and religious ceremonies. Traditional Sikh instruments, such as the harmonium, tabla, and dhol, accompany soul-stirring kirtan (devotional singing), hymns, and folk songs that uplift the spirits and evoke a sense of spiritual ecstasy among participants. Musical performances not only entertain but also inspire and uplift, fostering a deep sense of connection with the divine and reinforcing the values of unity, compassion, and service embedded within Sikhism.

3. **Theatrical Reenactments:** Theatrical reenactments of historical events from Sikh history are another hallmark of Sikh festival celebrations, offering audiences immersive experiences that bring the past to life. Through dramatic storytelling and vivid character portrayals, performers transport viewers back in time to pivotal moments in Sikh history, such as the battles of the Khalsa, the martyrdoms of Sikh Gurus, and the struggles for religious freedom. These reenactments serve as poignant reminders of the sacrifices made by Sikh luminaries and inspire audiences to uphold

the principles of courage, righteousness, and selfless service in their own lives.

4. **Educational and Inspirational:** Beyond their entertainment value, performing arts in Sikh festivals and historical commemorations serve as potent tools for education and inspiration. Through artistic expressions, Sikhs convey the timeless teachings and values of Sikhism, such as equality, justice, and humanitarianism, to audiences of all ages and backgrounds. By immersing participants in the sights, sounds, and stories of Sikh heritage, performing arts ignite a sense of curiosity, empathy, and reverence for Sikhism's rich cultural tapestry and spiritual legacy.

Cultural Impact on the Globe

Sikhism's cultural impact on the globe is profound and multifaceted, encompassing spiritual, social, and creative dimensions. Sikhs' contributions to various fields reflect the richness of their cultural heritage and the enduring relevance of Sikh values in today's interconnected world. As Sikhs continue to engage with global communities and navigate complex challenges, their commitment to equality, justice, and compassion serves as a beacon of hope and inspiration for a more harmonious and inclusive future for all.

Global Spread of Sikhism

Sikhism has transcended geographical boundaries to become a global faith, with significant Sikh communities established in countries around the world. The migration of Sikhs to various regions, particularly during the colonial period and in subsequent waves of globalization, has led to the proliferation of Sikh religious institutions, cultural practices, and community networks in diverse cultural contexts. Today, Sikhism's message of equality, tolerance, and social justice resonates with people of diverse backgrounds, contributing to its continued growth and influence on the globe.

1. **Migration Patterns:** The migration of Sikhs to various regions, particularly during the colonial period and in subsequent waves of globalization, has played a pivotal role in spreading Sikhism to different parts of the world. Economic opportunities, political upheavals, and religious persecution have been key drivers of Sikh migration, leading to the establishment of vibrant Sikh communities in countries such as the United Kingdom, Canada, the United States, Australia, and many others.

2. **Diaspora Communities:** Sikh diaspora communities have played a central role in preserving and propagating Sikh religious traditions, cultural practices, and community networks in their adopted homelands. Through the establishment of Gurdwaras (Sikh temples), educational institutions, and community organizations, Sikhs have created hubs of religious and cultural activity that serve as focal points for community cohesion, identity formation, and social solidarity.

3. **Cultural Exchange:** Sikhism's message of equality, tolerance, and social justice has resonated with people of diverse backgrounds, contributing to its appeal and acceptance in multicultural societies around the world. Sikh cultural festivals, religious celebrations, and community events provide opportunities for interfaith dialogue, cultural exchange, and mutual understanding, fostering greater harmony and cooperation among different religious and ethnic groups.

4. **Global Influence:** Sikhism's global influence extends beyond diaspora communities to impact mainstream culture, politics, and academia. Sikh values such as equality, justice, and compassion resonate with universal human aspirations, inspiring individuals and organizations to advocate for social change, human rights, and environmental sustainability on local, national, and international levels.

5. **Continued Growth:** Despite facing challenges and obstacles, Sikhism continues to grow and flourish on the globe, attracting new followers and admirers from diverse backgrounds. The resilience of Sikh communities, coupled with their commitment to preserving and promoting Sikh heritage and values, ensures that Sikhism remains a vibrant and dynamic faith with a bright future ahead.

Contributions of Sikhs Across Fields

Sikhs have left an indelible mark on various fields, showcasing their talents and expertise in arts, sciences, politics, sports, and more. In the arts, Sikh musicians, artists, and writers have enriched global cultural landscapes with their creative expressions, drawing inspiration from Sikh spirituality and heritage. In the sciences, Sikh scientists and researchers have made groundbreaking discoveries and innovations, contributing to advancements in fields such as medicine, engineering, and technology. In politics, Sikh leaders have played pivotal roles in advocating for social justice, human rights, and peace on both local and international platforms. In sports, Sikh athletes have excelled in diverse disciplines, earning accolades and representing their communities with pride on the globe.

1. **Arts:** Sikh musicians, artists, and writers have played pivotal roles in shaping global cultural landscapes. Drawing inspiration from Sikh spirituality and heritage, they have created stirring compositions, captivating artworks, and thought-provoking literature that resonate with audiences worldwide. From traditional Sikh music and classical art forms to contemporary expressions of Sikh identity, their creative endeavors have fostered greater understanding and appreciation of Sikh culture on the globe.

2. **Sciences:** Sikh scientists and researchers have been at the forefront of groundbreaking discoveries and innovations in various scientific disciplines. Their contributions have advanced

fields such as medicine, engineering, and technology, leading to significant improvements in healthcare, infrastructure, and communication. Whether pioneering new medical treatments, developing sustainable energy solutions, or pushing the boundaries of space exploration, Sikh scientists have made invaluable contributions to human progress and knowledge.

3. **Politics:** Sikh leaders have emerged as influential voices in advocating for social justice, human rights, and peace on both local and international platforms. Through their activism, diplomacy, and public service, they have championed causes such as religious freedom, gender equality, and environmental sustainability, driving positive change in society. From grassroots organizers to elected officials and diplomats, Sikh leaders have demonstrated a steadfast commitment to upholding the values of equality, justice, and compassion in the political arena.

4. **Sports:** Sikh athletes have excelled in various sports disciplines, showcasing their talent, determination, and sportsmanship on the globe. From Olympic champions to professional athletes, Sikh sports personalities have achieved remarkable success, earning accolades and inspiring millions with their achievements. Whether competing in traditional Sikh sports like Kabaddi and Gatka or excelling in mainstream sports such as cricket, hockey,

and athletics, Sikh athletes have demonstrated the power of perseverance and dedication in pursuing their athletic dreams.

Resonance of Sikh Values

The core values of Sikhism, including equality, justice, and compassion, hold universal appeal and resonate with people of all backgrounds. Sikhs are known for their commitment to seva (selfless service) and sarbat da bhala (welfare of all), principles that inspire acts of kindness, generosity, and community solidarity across borders. Sikh advocacy for social justice, environmental sustainability, and human rights aligns with global movements for equality and inclusivity, fostering cross-cultural understanding and collaboration. By embodying Sikh values in their actions and endeavors, Sikhs serve as ambassadors of goodwill and agents of positive change on the globe.

1. **Equality:** Sikhism upholds the fundamental principle of equality, affirming the inherent worth and dignity of every individual regardless of caste, creed, gender, or social status. This commitment to equality is reflected in Sikh practices such as langar (community kitchen) where all are welcome to share a meal as equals, irrespective of their background. In a world marked by discrimination and inequality, Sikhism's emphasis on equality serves as a beacon of hope and solidarity, inspiring individuals and communities to strive for a more just and equitable society.

2. **Justice:** Sikhism places a strong emphasis on social justice and the pursuit of righteousness (Dharam). Sikhs are called upon to stand up for the oppressed, challenge injustice, and uphold the principles of fairness and accountability. Whether advocating for the rights of marginalized communities, fighting against discrimination, or seeking redress for victims of violence and exploitation, Sikhs are at the forefront of movements for justice and human rights worldwide.

3. **Compassion:** Central to Sikh teachings is the principle of compassion (daya) and selfless service (seva) towards all beings. Sikhs are encouraged to cultivate empathy, kindness, and compassion in their interactions with others, embodying the spirit of sarbat da bhala (welfare of all). Through acts of seva, such as volunteering in community kitchens, serving the needy, and providing humanitarian aid in times of crisis, Sikhs demonstrate their commitment to alleviating suffering and promoting the well-being of humanity as a whole.

4. **Advocacy and Activism:** Sikh advocacy for social justice, environmental sustainability, and human rights aligns with global movements for equality and inclusivity, fostering cross-cultural understanding and collaboration. Sikhs actively engage in initiatives aimed at addressing issues such as poverty, discrimination, climate change, and conflict resolution, contributing their voices, resources, and expertise to effect positive

change on a global scale. Whether through grassroots activism, political advocacy, or humanitarian work, Sikhs serve as agents of positive change, promoting the values of compassion, justice, and equality in all aspects of life.

Legacy in Art and Culture

The Legacy in Art and Culture illuminates the profound impact of Sikhism on the artistic and cultural landscape of the world. Through depictions in art, literature, music, architecture, and performing arts, Sikhism's rich heritage and timeless teachings are celebrated and preserved for generations to come.

From the soul-stirring melodies of Gurmat Sangeet to the awe-inspiring architecture of Gurudwaras, Sikh art and culture serve as vehicles for spiritual expression, community cohesion, and cross-cultural understanding. The vibrant tapestry of Sikh festivals and traditions reflects the diversity and dynamism of Sikh identity, inviting individuals of all backgrounds to partake in the celebration of shared values and beliefs.

Sikhism's global spread and resonance of its core values of equality, justice, and compassion serve as a testament to its enduring relevance and universal appeal. Sikhs, through their contributions across various fields and their advocacy for social justice and human rights, continue to inspire positive change and foster greater unity and cooperation among all humanity.

The Legacy in Art and Culture underscores Sikhism's transformative power to enrich lives, bridge divides, and cultivate a more harmonious and inclusive world. As custodians of this rich legacy, it is our collective responsibility to honor, preserve, and promote Sikh art and culture, ensuring that its beauty and wisdom continue to inspire and uplift generations to come.

*****

APPENDIX I

BIOGRAPHY OF GURUS

(Reference book: Gumat Rehat Maryada by Sant Giani Gurbachan Singh Ji Khalsa Bhindranwale)

Sri Guru Nanak Dev Ji

- **Name:** Sri Guru Nanak Dev Ji.

- **Parkash Diwas:** 1526 Bikrami Katak Sudhi Puranmasi (Wednesday, November 29, 1469).

- **Parkash Place:** Rai Bhoi Ki Talwandi (now Sri Nankana Sahib, East Panjab).

- **Parents' Names:** Mehta Kalu (Father) and Mata Tripta (Mata), Shivram (Grandfather), Mata Banarsi (Grandmother).

- **Spouse:** Mata Sulakhani Ji.

- **Siblings:** One sister, Bibi Nanaki.

- **Children:** Two sons, Baba Sri Chand Ji and Baba Sri Lakhmi Das Ji.

- **Guruship:** 69 years 10 months and 10 days, from 1469-1539.

- **Jyoti Jot:** 1569 Bikrami Asu Vadi Dasmi, Sri Kartarpur Sahib (10 October 1539).

Sri Guru Angad Dev Ji

- **Name:** Sri Guru Angad Dev Ji.

- **Parkash Diwas:** 1561 Bikrami, Vaisakh Sudhi Ekam (Saturday, 23 April, 1504).

- **Parkash Place:** Matte Di Sarae (Naghe Di Sra) Muktsar, Panjab.

- **Parents' Names:** Bhai Pheru Mall (Father) And Mata Sabhirai (Mother).

- **Spouse:** Mata Khivi Ji.

- **Children:** Two sons, Bhai Dasu Ji And Bhai Datu Ji, One daughter, Bibi Amro Ji.

- **Guruship:** 1596 Bikrami Asu Vadi Panchami (6 October 1539), 12 years 6. months and 14 days, 1539-1552.

- **Jyoti Jot:** 1609 Bikrami Chater Sudhi Chauth, Sri Khandoor Sahib (27 March 1552).

Sri Guru Amar Das Ji

- **Name:** Sri Guru Amar Das Ji.

- **Parkash Diwas:** 1526 Bikrami Vaisakh Sudhi Chaudas (Friday, May 5, 1479).

- **Parkash Place:** Basarke (Sri Sun Sahib), Amritsar, Panjab.

- **Parents' Names:** Bhai Tej Bhan Ji (Father) and Mata Lakshmi Ji (Mother).

- **Spouse Nama:** Mata Ramo Ji.

- **Children:** Two daughters, Bibi Dani and Bibi Bhani Ji, Two sons, Bhai Mohan Ji, and Bhai Mohri Ji.

- **Guruship:** 1609 Bikrami Chater Sudhi Ekam (25 March 1552), 21 years, 5 months, 14 days, 1552-1574.

- **Jyoti Jot:** 1631 Bikrami Bhadro Sudhi Puranmasi, Sri Goindwal Sahib Ji (01 October 1574).

Sri Guru Ram Das Ji

- **Name:** Sri Guru Ram Das Ji.

- **Parkash Diwas:** 1531 Bikrami Katak Vadi Duj (Thursday, 2 November 1534).

- **Parkash Place:** Chuna Mandi, Lahore (now in East Panjab).

- **Parents' Names:** Bhai Haridas Ji (Father) and Mata Daya Vati (Mother).

- **Spouse:** Bibi Bhani Ji.

- **Children:** Three sons, Bhai Prithi Chand Ji, Bhai Mahadev Ji, and Sri Guru Arjan Dev Ji.

- **Guruship:** 1631 Bikrami Bhadro Sudhi Traudashi (27 September 1574), 6 years 11 months and 20 days, 1574-1581.

- **Jyoti Jot:** 1638 Bikrami Bhadro Sudhi Teej (19 September 1581), Sri Goindwal Sahib Ji.

Sri Guru Arjan Dev Ji

- **Name:** Sri Guru Arjan Dev Ji.

- **Parkash Diwas:** 1620 Bikrami Vaisakh Vadi Saptami (14 April 1563).

- **Parkas Place:** Sri Goindval Sahib Ji Panjab.

- **Parents' Names:** Sri Guru Ram Das Ji (Father) and Mata Bhani Ji (Mother).

- **Spouse Name:** Mata Ganga Ji.

- **Children:** One son, Sri Guru Hargobind Sahib Ji.

- **Guruship:** 1638 Bikrami Bhadro Sudhi Duj (15 September 1581), 24 years 9 months 2 days, 1581-1605.

- **Jyoti Jot:** 163 Bikrami Jeth Sudhi

Chauth (25 May 1605).

Sri Guru Hargobind Sahib Ji

- **Name:** Sri Guru Hargobind Sahib Ji.

- **Parkash Diwas:** 1652 Bikrami Harrh Vadi Ekam (Sunday, 6 June 1596), Sangradi 21 Harrh.

- **Parkash Place:** Sri Wadali Sahib (6 miles form Sri Amritsar Sahib, Panjab).

- **Parents' Names:** Guru Arjan Dev Ji (Father) and Mata Ganga Ji (Mother).

- **Spouse:** Mata Damodari Ji, Mata Nanaki Ji, Mata Marwahi (Mahadevi) Ji.

- **Children:** One daughter Bibi Veero Ji, five sons, Baba Gurditta Ji, Baba Suraj Mal Ji, Baba Ani Rai Ji , Baba Atal Rai Ji, and Baba Tyag Mal Ji (Sri Guru Teg Bahadur Sahib Ji).

- **Guruship:** 1663 Bikrami Jeth Vadi Ashtami (15 May 1605), Sri Amritsar Sahib, 32 years 10 months and 12 days, 1605-1638.

- **Jyoti Jot:** 1694 Bikrami Chet Sudhi

Panchami (28 March 1638) Patalpuri, Sri Kiratpur Sahib Ji.

Sri Guru Har Rai Sahib Ji

- **Name:** Sri Guru Har Rai Sahib Ji.
- **Parkash Diwas:** 1687 Bikrami Magh Sudhi Chaudas (05 February 1630).
- **Parkash Place:** Sri Kiratpur Sahib, Panjab.
- **Parents' Names:** Baba Gurditta Ji (Father) and Mata Nihal Kaur Ji (Mother).
- **Spouse:** Mata Krishan Kaur Ji, Mata Chand Kaur Ji, Mata Ram Kaur Ji, Kot Kalyani Ji, Mata Tokhi Ji, Mata Anokhi Ji, Mata Lado Ji, Mata Prem Kaur Ji.
- **Children:** Two sons, Baba Ram Rai Ji and Sri Guru Har Krishan Sahib Ji.
- **Guruship:** 1694 Bikrami Chetar Sudhi Tarausdi (22 March 1638), Sri Kiratpur Sahib, 22 years 8 months and 20 days, 1638-1661.
- **Jyoti Jot:** 1798 Bikrami Katak Vadi Noami (06 November 1661), Sri Kiratpur Sahib Ji

Sri Guru Har Krishan Sahib Ji

- **Name:** Sri Guru Har Krishan Sahib Ji.

- **Parkash Diwas:** 1713 Bikrami Sawan Vadi Noauvi (Thursday, 14 July 1656).

- **Parkash Place:** Sri Kiratpur Sahib, Panjab.

- **Parents' Names:** Sri Guru Har Rai Sahib Ji (Father) and Mata Krishan Kaur Ji (Mother).

- **Guruship:** 1718 Bikrami Katak Vadi Naumi (8 November 1661) Sri Kiratpur Sahib, 2 years 8 months, 2 days, 1661-1664.

- **Jyoti Jot:** 1721 Bikrami Chetar Sudhi Chaudas (06 April 1664) Gurdwara Sri Bala Sahib Ji, Delhi.

Sri Guru Tegh Bahadur Sahib Ji

- **Name:** Guru Tegh Bahadur Sahib Ji.

- **Parkash Diwas:** 1678 Bikrami Vaisakh Vadi Panchami (Tuesday, 12 April 1621).

- **Parkash Place:** Sri Amritsar Sahib Ji, Gurdwara Guru Ke Mehal, Panjab.

- **Parents' Names:** Sri Guru Har Rai Sahib Ji.

(Father) and Mata Krishan Kaur Ji (Mother).

- **Spouse:** Mata Gujri Ji.

- **Children:** One son, Sahib Sri Guru Gobind Singh Ji.

- **Guruship:** 1721 Bikrami Chater Sudhi Chaudas (06 April 1664), 10 years 7 months 15 days, 1664-1675.

- **Jyoti Jot:** 1732 Bikrami Magar Sudhi Panchami (19 December 1675).

Sri Guru Gobind Singh Ji

- **Name:** Sri Guru Gobind Singh Ji.

- **Parkash Diwas:** 1723 Bikrami Poh Sudhi Saptami (Sunday, 01 January 1666), Sankranti 23 Poh.

- **Parkash Place:** Sri Patna Sahib, Bihar.

- **Parents' Names:** Sri Guru Tegh Bahadur Sahib Ji (Father) and Mata Gujri Ji (Mother).

- **Spouse:** Mata Ajit (Jito) Kaur Ji, Mata Sundar (Sundri) Kaur Ji, Mata Sahib Kaur Ji (Mata Sahib Deva Ji).

- **Children:** Four sons, Baba Ajit Singh, Baba Jujhar Singh, Baba Zorawar Singh, and

	Baba Fateh Singh, One eternal son Khalsa Panth.
• **Guruship:**	1732 Bikrami, Magar Sudhi Teej (17 December 1675), 32 years 11 months 8 days, 1675-1708.
• **Jyoti Jot:**	1765 Bikrami, Katak Sudhi Panchami (19 November 1708) Sri Hazur Sahib Ji, Nanded.

Sri Guru Granth Sahib Ji

• **Name:**	Sri Guru Granth Sahib Ji.
• **Parkash Diwas:**	1661 Bikrami, Bhadro Sudhi Ekam (01 September 1604).
• **Parkash Place:**	Sri Harmandir Sahib Ji, Amritsar Sahib.
• **Guruship:**	1775 Bikrami, Katak Sudhi Duj (20 October 1708), Sri Hazur Sahib Ji, 1708-Eternal.
• **Children:**	Whole humanity and Universe.

*****

APPENDIX II

PANJ

Panj Banis (From Sri Guru Granth Sahib Ji and Sri Dasam Granth Sahib Ji)

1. **Japji Sahib:** Sri Guru Nanak Dev Ji
2. **Jaap Sahib:** Sri Guru Gobind singh Ji
3. **Tav-Prasad Savaiye:** Sri Guru Gobind Singh Ji
4. **Chaupai Sahib:** Sri Guru Gobind Singh Ji
5. **Anand Sahib:** Sri Guru Amar Das Ji

Panj Pyare

1. **Bhai Daya Singh**

   - **Place of Birth:** Lahore.
   - **Date of Birth:** Sunday, 1725 Bikrami, Phagan di Sankrant.
   - **Parents Name:** Bhai Mayea Ram (Father), Mata Soba Devi (Mother).
   - **Contribution:** Compassion.

2. **Bhai Dharam Singh**

   - **Place of Birth:** Hastinapur
   - **Date of Birth:** Monday, 1727 Bikrami,

Vaisakh 13.

- **Parent's Name:** Bhai Param Sukh (Father) and Mata Ananti Ji (Mother)
- **Contribution:** Righteousness.

3. Bhai Himmat Singh

- **Place of Birth:** Jagannath
- **Date of Birth:** 1721 Bikrami, Jeth 15
- **Parent's Name:** Bhai Maal Deo (Father) and Mata Lal Devi (Mother)
- **Contribution:** Unwavering courage, standing for truth and justice.

4. Bhai Mohkam Singh

- **Place of Birth:** Dwarka
- **Date of Birth:** 1736 Bikrami, 5 Chater
- **Parent's Name:** Bhai Jagjiwan Rai (Father) and Mata Sambali (Mother)
- **Contribution:** Firm resolve and commitment to the Sikh cause.

5. Bhai Sahib Singh

- **Place of Birth:** Bidar
- **Date of Birth:** 1732 Bikrami, 5 Magar
- **Parent's Name:** Bhai Gur Narayan (Father) and Mata Ankampa ji (Mother)
- **Contribution:** Humility and devotion, values through service, and sacrifice.

Panj Kakar

1. Kesh (Uncut Hair)

- Kesh refers to the uncut hair on all parts of the body.
- It symbolizes acceptance of God's will and the natural state of being.
- Keeping Kesh is a reminder of the Sikh's commitment to the Guru's teachings and identity.

2. Kanga (Wooden Comb)

- The Kanga is a small wooden comb used to maintain cleanliness and untangle the hair.
- It symbolizes discipline and cleanliness.
- The Kanga reminds Sikhs to keep their thoughts pure and untangled, free from negativity and distractions.

3. **Kara (Iron Bracelet):**

- The Kara is an iron bracelet worn on the wrist.

- It symbolizes the eternal nature of God and the Sikh's connection to the Divine.

- The Kara serves as a reminder of the Sikh's commitment to righteousness and the Guru's teachings.

4. **Kirpan (Ceremonial Sword):**

- The Kirpan is a small ceremonial sword carried by all Amritdhari Sikhs.

- It symbolizes the Sikh's duty to protect the innocent, defend the weak, and uphold justice.

- The Kirpan represents the Sikh's readiness to stand up against oppression and tyranny.

5. **Kachhera**

- The Kachhera represents modesty and chastity in Sikhism. It emphasizes the importance of maintaining purity in thoughts and actions. Wearing the Kachhera serves as a constant reminder to lead a life of moral integrity and restraint.

- The Kachhera symbolizes self-discipline and control over one's desires. It reminds Sikhs to practice restraint and moderation in all aspects of life. Through wearing the

Kachhera, Sikhs strive to cultivate inner strength and spiritual maturity.

- The Kachhera signifies readiness for physical activity and service to others. It reflects the Sikh's commitment to be prepared at all times to assist those in need. Wearing the Kachhera reinforces the principle of selflessness and the duty to serve humanity.

Panj Takhat (Five Thrones)

1. Sri Akal Takht Sahib Ji

- Located in Sri Amritsar Sahib Ji, Panjab.

- The highest temporal seat of authority in Sikhism.

- Established by Sri Guru Hargobind Sahib Ji, the sixth Sikh Guru.

2. Takht Sri Keshgarh Sahib Ji

- Located in Sri Anandpur Sahib, Panjab.

- Associated with the Khalsa Panth's revelation and the Khalsa revelation ceremony.

- Established by Sri Guru Gobind Singh Ji, the tenth Sikh Guru.

3. Takht Sri Damdama Sahib Ji

- Located in Talwandi Sabo, Bathinda District, Panjab.

- Associated with Sri Guru Gobind Singh Ji and Sri Guru Granth Sahib Ji.

- It is a significant center for Sikh learning and religious discourse.

4. **Takht Sri Patna Sahib Ji**

   - Located in Patna, Bihar.

   - Commemorates the Parkash (birthplace) of Sri Guru Gobind Singh Ji.

   - It is a site of historical and religious importance for Sikhs.

5. **Takht Sri Hazur Sahib Ji**

   - Located in Nanded, Maharashtra, India.

   - Marks the site where Guru Gobind Singh Ji left his physical body.

   - It is a revered pilgrimage site for Sikhs worldwide.

Panj Sarovar

1. **Sarovar at Sri Harmandir Sahib Ji:** The Sarovar at Sri Harmandir Sahib Ji is the most famous and revered Sarovar in Amritsar. It surrounds the Sri Harmandir Sahib Ji complex and is called Amritsar, meaning "Pool of Nectar." Pilgrims from all over the world visit this sacred

site to bathe in its Pawitar Jal (holy waters), which is believed to possess healing properties. The Sri Harmandir Sahib complex, including the Sarovar, is the heart of Sikhism and a symbol of peace and equality.

2. **Sarovar at Sri Santokhsar Sahib:** Santokhsar Sahib is a historic Gurdwara located near the southeast corner of Amritsar city. It houses a Sarovar called Santokhsar Sarovar. According to Sikh tradition, Sri Guru Ram Das Ji, the fourth Sikh Guru, used to perform voluntary service (sewa) here. **Santokh (ਸੰਤੋਖ)** is a word that means contentment, satisfaction, or peace of mind. It refers to the state of being satisfied or content with one's circumstances, possessions, or experiences.

3. **Sarovar at Sri Ramsar Sahib:** Sri Ramsar Sahib is another historical Gurdwara in Amritsar, It is situated near the southeast corner of the city. Sri Ramsar Sahib features a Sarovar known as Ramsar Sarovar. Sri Guru Arjan Dev Ji spent a considerable amount of time here, and it is believed that he prepared the Sri Adi Granth Sahib at this site. **Ram (ਰਾਮ)** means the Akal (God) itself.

4. **Sarovar at Sri Bibeksar Sahib:** Sri Bibeksar Sahib is a small Gurdwara located in the northern part of Amritsar city. It houses a Sarovar called Bibeksar Sarovar. **Bibek (ਬਿਬੇਕ)** means discernment or wisdom, implying the

ability to judge wisely and make sound decisions.

5. **Sarovar at Sri Kaulsar Sahib:** Kaulsar Sarovar, nestled within the city of Amritsar alongside its revered counterparts, embodies the essence of promise and commitment in Sikh tradition. The name "Kaulsar," derived from 'Kaul,' meaning promise, signifies the sacred covenant between individuals and the divine. This Sarovar serves as a reservoir of spiritual significance, where pilgrims seek solace and reaffirmation of their faith. Surrounded by tranquility, Kaulsar inspires devotees to renew their vows of righteousness and deepen their connection with Sikh principles.

Panj Vikar (Five Thieves)

1. **Krodh (Anger):** Uncontrolled anger leads to harm, violence, and destruction. Sikhism teaches the importance of controlling one's emotions and practicing forgiveness and patience.

2. **Kam (Lust):** Excessive desire or attachment to sensual pleasures can lead to selfishness, exploitation, and moral degradation. Sikhs are encouraged to maintain purity of thought and action.

3. **Lobh (Greed):** Excessive desire for material wealth or possessions can lead to selfishness, dishonesty, and exploitation of others. Sikh

teachings emphasize contentment and the sharing of resources with those in need.

4. **Moh (Attachment):** Excessive attachment to worldly relationships, possessions, or status can lead to suffering and prevent spiritual progress. Sikhs are encouraged to cultivate detachment and focus on the pursuit of spiritual enlightenment.

5. **Ahankar (Ego):** Pride, arrogance, and self-centeredness hinder spiritual growth and disrupt harmonious relationships with others. Sikhism teaches humility and the recognition of the Divine within all beings.

Panj Bajjar Kurehata (Five Cardinal Sins).

1. **Kesh Katal Karna (Cutting Hair):** Cutting one's hair, particularly the hair on any part of the body (Kesh), is a serious transgression within Sikhism. Sikhs are required to maintain uncut hair as a symbol of their commitment to the Sikh faith and as one of the Five Ks (Panj Kakar) mandated for every Sikh.

2. **Par-nari Sang (Engaging in Extramarital Affairs):** Engaging in extramarital affairs or adultery is considered a grave violation of Sikh moral and ethical principles. Sikhism emphasizes the sanctity of marriage and fidelity within marital relationships.

3. **Eating Halal Meat:** In Sikhism, the consumption of meat prepared through the Halal method

(according to Islamic dietary laws) is considered unacceptable. Sikhs are encouraged not to eat any meat, but if the situation or circumstance takes them to a severe condition, they can consume Jhatka meat, which is meat prepared through a specific ritualistic method as per Sikh tradition.

4. **Use of Tobacco:** The use of tobacco in any form, including smoking, chewing, or any other consumption method, is strongly discouraged in Sikhism. Tobacco use is considered detrimental to one's physical, mental, and spiritual well-being, and it is incompatible with the Sikh way of life.

5. **Separation of Kakar (Removal of the Five Ks):** The Five Ks (Panj Kakar) are essential articles of faith for Amritdhari Sikhs, and removing or intentionally abandoning them is considered a serious offense. The Five Ks include Kesh, Kangha, Kara, Kirpan, and Kachera. Violating the requirement to maintain these articles of faith can lead to disciplinary action within the Sikh community.

*****

www.ingramcontent.com/pod-product-compliance
Lightning Source LLC
Chambersburg PA
CBHW051128120626
46547CB00012B/709